W9-BSM-877

Corporate and
Governmental Deviance

Corporate and Governmental Deviance

Problems of Organizational Behavior in Contemporary Society

Sixth Edition

M. David Ermann
University of Delaware

Richard J. Lundman
The Ohio State University

New York   Oxford
OXFORD UNIVERSITY PRESS
2002

Oxford University Press

Oxford   New York
Athens   Auckland   Bangkok   Bogotá   Buenos Aires   Calcutta
Cape Town   Chennai   Dar es Salaam   Delhi   Florence   Hong Kong   Istanbul
Karachi   Kuala Lumpur   Madrid   Melbourne   Mexico City   Mumbai
Nairobi   Paris   São Paulo   Shanghai   Singapore   Taipei   Tokyo   Toronto   Warsaw

and associated companies in
Berlin   Ibadan

Published by Oxford University Press, Inc.
198 Madison Avenue, New York, New York 10016
http://www.oup-usa.org

Oxford is a registered trademark of Oxford University Press

Library of Congress Cataloging-in-Publication Data

Corporate and governmental deviance : problems of organizational behavior in
contemporary society / [edited by] M. David Ermann, Richard J. Lundman.—6th ed.
       p. cm.
    Includes bibliographical references.
    ISBN 0-19-513529-6 (pbk.)
    1. White collar crimes—United States   2. Political crimes and offenses—United
States. I. Ermann, M. David.   II. Lundman, Richard J., 1944- .

HV6769.C667   2001
364.16'8'0973—dc21   2001018551

Printing number: 9 8 7 6 5 4 3

Printed in the United States of America
on acid-free paper

To
Marlene, Michael, and Natalie Ermann
and
Julie and Bob Lundman

Contents

Preface

This book is for courses on deviance, social problems, criminology, organizations, and business and society. In these courses, reading assignments frequently include a comprehensive text and supplemental readings focusing on particular topics.

Whether comprehensive or supplemental, the assigned readings usually direct nearly exclusive attention to the deviant actions of individuals. Students therefore routinely come away from their readings in these courses with little or no appreciation of the fact that organizations, not just individuals, commit deviant acts.

Our goal in this book, accordingly, is to expose students to the deviant actions of the large business and governmental organizations that are central features of contemporary society. Students who read our book will come away with an appreciation of when, how, and why organizations, and the people in them, commit deviant acts.

As with the previous five editions, we kept the student reader in mind while writing our introductory materials and making our selections. We have tried to maximize reader interest while simultaneously treating our student readers as serious scholars who deserve exposure to the very best classic and contemporary material on corporate and governmental deviance. Hence, the sixth edition returns to print earlier scholarly works, retains previous selections that have captured student attention, and complements both with new analyses of the deviance of big business and big government.

This book is grounded in our experiences teaching courses that concentrate on the deviance of organizations. For nearly 30 years, the students in our classes have listened and responded as our initial ideas took shape. They continue to help us as we work to better understand the deviant actions of business organizations and governmental agencies. We greatly appreciate the enthusiasm, interest, and frequently helpful suggestions of the student scholars in our classes.

We are proud of the fact that with this sixth edition, this book will have been in print for almost a quarter century. Oxford University Press has consistently supported our efforts and we appreciate and admire Oxford's commitment to making it possible for instructors and students to continue to learn about corporate and governmental deviance.

Every aspect of this book is the product of our joint efforts. We shared equally in its creation and are equally responsible for the result.

Newark, Delaware   M. D. E.
Columbus, Ohio   R. J. L.

Corporate and
Governmental Deviance

I
Overview

1

Corporate and Governmental Deviance
Origins, Patterns, and Reactions
M. David Ermann and Richard J. Lundman

Common images of deviance rarely include organizational actors.[1] When people think about the financial losses associated with theft, for instance, the more likely image is burglary, not illegal corporate price-fixing. When people think about being physically injured, most imagine assault, perhaps by someone high on or desperate for drugs, not a plane crash caused by a known safety defect or an injury or death caused by police officers who believe their department will cover their deviant actions.

Consider data collected by one of the coeditors of this book (Lundman) in his criminology class between 1993 and 2000. On the first day of class, students were asked to, "Please list three crimes you think are serious, troublesome, and worth trying to do something about." After being given 60 seconds to respond to the first statement, they were then given an additional 60 seconds to, "Please list three corporate crimes you think are serious, troublesome, and worth trying to do something about."

As can be seen in Table 1.1, students directed almost exclusive attention to crimes by individuals in their responses to the first question. Year after year, students said that murder and rape are two crimes they think are serious, troublesome, and worth trying to do something about. Only about 2 percent of their responses directed attention to crimes by corporations.

When asked in the second statement to focus exclusively on corporate crimes, slightly less than half provided three answers. The crime they mentioned most often, embezzlement, is not even a crime by a corporation, but is instead a crime committed by an

---

1. Allen E. Liska, *Perspectives on Deviance*, 2nd ed. (Englewood Cliffs, NJ: Prentice-Hall, 1987), p. 157; J. L. Simmons, "Public Stereotypes of Deviants," *Social Problems* 13 (1965): 223–4.

TABLE 1.1

Three Crimes and Three Corporate Crimes Identified by Students as "serious, troublesome, and worth trying to do something about," Sociology 410, Criminology, The Ohio State University, 1993–2000.

Year	Number of Students	Three Crimes				Percent of Answers Involving Corporate Crime	Three Corporate Crimes			
		Percent with Three Answers	Answer One	Answer Two	Answer Three		Percent with Three Answers	Answer One	Answer Two	Answer Three
1993	90	100%	Murder	Rape	Drugs	2.4%	46%	Embezzlement[a]	Fraud	Insider Trading
1994	49	98	Murder	Rape	Child Abuse	2.0	53	Embezzlement	Fraud	Tax Evasion
1995	45	98	Murder	Rape	Child Abuse	1.5	55	Embezzlement	Fraud	Unsafe Products
1996	40	98	Rape	Murder	Child Abuse	2.5	35	Embezzlement	Fraud	Unsafe Products
1997	82	96	Murder	Rape	Drugs	1.6	49	Embezzlement	Employment Discrimination	Fraud
1998	98	97	Murder	Rape	Child Abuse	2.4	45	Embezzlement	Fraud	Tax Evasion
1999	116	97	Murder	Rape	Child Abuse	1.7	50	Embezzlement	Fraud	Employment Discrimination
2000[b]	22	100	Murder	Rape	Child Abuse	0.0	54	Embezzlement	Employment Discrimination	Monopoly
2000	139	100	Murder	Rape	Child Abuse	0.1	54	Embezzlement	Employment Discrimination	Sexual Harassment

a. Embezzlement is not a corporate crime but is instead a crime committed by an employee against a corporation.
b. Honors class.

employee against a corporation, as when a bank teller pilfers bank funds. The remaining responses, most commonly fraud and employment discrimination, are clearly crimes by corporations. Overall, however, students, like their fellow citizens, maintain images of deviance that largely exclude the actions of large organizations.

We believe that images of deviance that exclude organizational actors are limiting and misleading. The organizational actions these images exclude are frequently more personally and socially important[2] than the individual deviance on which most people concentrate. In addition, organizational deviance is often more interesting because it takes us inside the large corporations and governmental agencies that are so powerful in contemporary society.

This book directs exclusive attention to corporate and governmental deviance. It explains how organizations—not just individuals—commit deviant acts. It probes the origins and establishes the patterns of deviant actions by large organizations. It also analyzes social reactions to organizational deviance, and explores the effectiveness of attempted controls.

Organizations as Deviant Actors

At first glance, it may appear difficult to study the deviance of businesses and government agencies while largely ignoring the individuals who make up these organizations. After all, organizations do not think or act.[3] Individuals must think and act for there to be corporate or governmental deviance. How is it possible to study

2. Bari-Ellen Roberts, with Jack E. White, *Roberts vs. Texaco: A True Story of Race and Corporate America* (New York: Avon Books, 1998); Jeff Bendict, *Public Heroes, Private Felons: Athletes and Crimes Against Women* (Boston: Northeastern University Press, 1997); Keith Schneider, "Judge Rejects $100 Million Fine for Exxon in Oil Spill as Too Low," *The New York Times*, April 25, 1991, p. 1: Marshall B. Clinard, *Corporate Corruption: The Abuse of Power* (New York: Praeger, 1990); Tim Weiner, *Blank Check: The Pentagon's Black Budget* (New York: Warner Books, 1990); Robert F. Meier and James F. Short, Jr., "The Consequences of White-Collar Crime," in Herbert Edelhertz and Thomas D. Overcast (eds.), *White-Collar Crime: An Agenda for Research* (Lexington, Mass.: Heath, 1982), pp. 23–49.

3. Katherine M. Jamieson, *The Organization of Corporate Crime: Dynamics of Antitrust Violation* (Thousand Oaks, Calif.: Sage, 1994), p. 3; James William Coleman, "Toward an Integrated Theory of White-Collar Crime," *American Journal of Sociology* 93 (1987): 409–14; Lawrence W. Sherman, *Scandal and Reform: Controlling Police Corruption* (Berkeley and Los Angeles: University of California Press, 1978), p. 6.

the deviance of big business and big government apart from particular organizational members?

Positions as Building Blocks

One answer is that a large organization can be viewed as "a collection of jobs or social positions, each with its own skills, power, rules, and rewards.[4] These organizational positions include chief executive officers or agency directors, workers, secretaries, and vice presidents or deputy administrators. Together with other positions, they are the building blocks of all large organizations.

Large organizations thus are not mere collections of people. Instead, large organizations are collections of positions that powerfully influence the work-related thoughts and actions of the replaceable people who occupy positions in them.

People Are Replaceable

A second answer is that people occupying positions within large organizations are replaceable.[5] Large organizations routinely replace their workers, managers, and top-level members, with little effect on the organization. Such turnover is not threatening because the recruitment and training of replacements is well organized.[6] New organizational members quickly learn what is expected of them, by following formal work rules and job descriptions as well as the informal understandings associated with particular positions. Except in unusual circumstances, particular people regularly come and go while the organization continues to operate in an orderly fashion.

4. Jerald Hage and Michael Aiken, *Social Change in Complex Organizations* (New York Random House, 1970), p. 11. Also see Richard H. Hall, *Organizations: Structures, Processes and Outcomes*, 4th ed. (Englewood Cliffs, N.J.: Prentice-Hall, 1987), pp. 42–43.

5. James S. Coleman, "The Rational Reconstruction of Society," *American Sociological Review* 58 (1993): 1–15; James S. Coleman, *Foundations of Social Theory* (Cambridge, Mass.: Harvard University Press, 1990), p. 427; James S. Coleman, *The Asymmetric Society* (Syracuse, N.Y.: Syracuse University Press, 1982), pp. 19–30; James S. Coleman, *Power and the Structure of Society* (New York: Norton, 1974), pp. 35–54.

6. Robert Jackall, *Moral Mazes: The World of Corporate Managers* (New York: Oxford University Press, 1988), pp. 41–46; Hall, *Organizations*, pp. 42–46; Rosabeth Moss Kanter, *Men and Women of the Corporation* (New York: Basic Books, 1977), pp. 47–68; Diane Rothbard Margolis, *The Managers: Corporate Life in America* (New York: Morrow, 1979).

Consider what happened as E. Gordon Gee made his way through three universities.[7] He served seven years as Ohio State's president and then announced he was leaving to become president of Brown University, effective January 1, 1998. Ohio State's new president became William Kirwan, who had been president at the University of Maryland and therefore had to be replaced at that institution. Two years passed and Professor Gee announced that he was leaving Brown University to become president at Vanderbilt University. Within 48 hours, Provost Sheila Blumstein was appointed interim president at Brown and in November 2000, Dr. Ruth J. Simmons, who had been president at Smith College, was appointed president at Brown. Despite these changes in the people occupying the position of university president, intellectual life at each institution went on as students attended classes and professors professed.

Students also come and go on a regular basis with little or no effect on their colleges or universities. Each spring during commencement ceremonies, universities solemnly bid farewell to about one-quarter of their undergraduate student population, and each fall a new class is warmly welcomed as its members take the places of those who graduated. So too with professors. Each year some quit and go elsewhere; a handful are fired; and others retire or die. Search committees quickly find replacements, and the universities continue to operate as if nothing had happened.

For social scientists who study large organizations, then, particular people are replaceable. Sociologist James S. Coleman observed that:

> The . . . structure exists independently of the persons occupying positions within it, like a city whose buildings exist independently of the particular persons who occupy them . . . In an organization that consists of positions in a structure of relations, the persons who occupy the positions are incidental to the structure. They take on the obligations and expectations, the goals and the resources, associated with their positions in the way they put on work clothes for their jobs. But the obligations and expectations, the goals and resources, exist apart from the individual occupants of the positions.[8]

7. www.osu.edu/newsrel; www.umd.edulpres/pressrel; www.brown.edu (and click on Presidential Search–News); and www.vanderbilt.edu/transition. Illustration based upon Murray Sperber, *College Sports Inc.: The Athletic Department vs the University* (New York: Holt, 1990). p. 159.

8. Coleman, *Foundations*, p. 427.

For workers occupying positions in large business and governmental organizations, there is a clear sense of marginality and recognition that they can easily be replaced. Indeed, if they think about it at all, workers will quickly recognize that once they leave, they will be replaced and the organization likely will not skip a beat. Life inside large organizations for individuals is therefore profoundly different than life inside other important contemporary institutions such as the family.[9] People inside families are not easily replaced because the building blocks of families are specific people, not positions. Grandparents, parents, children, and other kin are not just occupants of positions, but particular and frequently special people. When a family member dies, there is no replacement for that person. We do not tell children, for instance, "Uncle Ned is dead, this your new Uncle Ned." Although new people do enter families, including new uncles, they do so as distinct people, not as handy replacements. That is why when members of a family die or otherwise exit, families almost always skip several beats.

Organizations Influence Thoughts and Actions

A third reason for looking at organizations as acting units capable of deviance is that large organizations influence the work-related thoughts and actions of the people in them. Most people in large organizations occupy positions with circumscribed information and responsibility.[10] Their jobs require only limited knowledge, and their work makes only small contributions to the overall activity of the organization. They are told what to do and usually do as they are told.

Of course, people occupying top-level positions tell other people what to do. But even these organizational elites are influenced by their own past experiences and current positions.[11] Elites have been

9. Coleman, "The Rational Reconstruction," p. 7.

10. Jackall, *Moral Mazes*, pp. 43–44; Hall, *Organizations*, p. 43.

11. Henry Rosovsky, *The University: An Owner's Manual* (New York: Norton, 1990) pp. 40–45; Jackall, *Moral Mazes*; James Q. Wilson, *Bureaucracy: What Government Agencies Do and Why They Do It* (New York: Basic Books, 1989), pp. 113–232; David R. James and Michael Soref, "Profit Constraints on Managerial Autonomy: Managerial Theory and Unmaking of the Corporation President," *American Sociological Review* 46 (1981): 1–18; Theodore Caplow. *Managing an Organization*, 2nd ed. (New York: Holt, Rinehart and Winston, 1983), pp. 158–85; Warren Bennis, *The Unconscious Conspiracy: Why Leaders Can't Lead* (New York: American Management Association, 1976).

socialized by the powerful experiences of working for decades in the world of the large organization. In addition, they are paid to think and act for an organization that can easily replace them should they consistently fail in their efforts to advance its interests.

In sum, we believe there are three good reasons for conceiving of large organizations as acting units capable of deviance. The building blocks of all large organizations are positions. The people occupying those positions are replaceable. The positions replaceable people occupy profoundly influence their thoughts and actions. And, as we detail next, organizations provide especially fertile grounds for the origins of deviant actions.

Origins

The structure and operation of large organizations can encourage organizational deviance in at least three ways. First, limited information and responsibility can lead to deviance. Second, organizational elites can indirectly cause deviant actions by establishing norms, rewards, and punishments that encourage deviance. Third, elites can consciously initiate deviance and use hierarchically linked positions to implement it.

Deviance Traceable to Limited Information and Responsibility

Large organizations divide tasks into small component parts. Each person makes only a limited contribution, and no single person can complete any job alone. Moreover, people generally are discouraged from doing other than their assigned jobs or undertaking actions independent of their supervisors.

Thus, well-intentioned individuals in organizational settings may produce deviant actions, even though none of them have deviant knowledge, much less deviant motivations. Indeed, employees may do their jobs well and nevertheless produce deviance. This happens when no one person has the knowledge, responsibility, incentive, time, or skill to collect, analyze, and use the information needed to alter organizational actions before problems begin. Writing well in advance of the Three Mile Island (United States) nuclear accident in 1979, the Chernobyl (Russia) nuclear accident in 1986, and Tokaimura (Japan) nuclear accident in 1999, law professor Christopher Stone provided a chillingly accurate preview of how organizational positions, each with limited information and responsibility, can produce a deviant act:

> Suppose . . . the case of an electric utility company that maintains a nuclear power plant. We can readily imagine that there might be knowledge of physics, evidence of radiation leakage, information regarding temperature variations, data related to previous operation runs in this and other plants, which if gathered in the mind of one single person, would make . . . continued operation of that plant, without a shutdown, wanton and reckless—that is, if an explosion resulted, strong civil and criminal liability could and would be brought to bear. . . . But let us suppose what is more likely to be the case in modern corporate America: that the information and acts are distributed among many different employees engaged in various functional groups within the corporation. The nuclear engineer can be charged with bit of information a, the architect knows b, the night watch. . . . knows c, the research scientist task force knows d. Conceivably there will not be any single individual who has . . . such knowledge and intent as will support a charge against [that person] . . . individually.[12]

One of the coeditors (Ermann) had a similar experience with how limited information and responsibility can lead to deviance. As a recently graduated financial analyst working in Detroit for a major automobile corporation's international division, his name, for no special reason, was on the routing list for documents about a transmission developed by our British subsidiary. The transmission used a new and more efficient technology that forced gears onto shafts under great pressure. It was supposed to give the gears a fit on the shafts tight enough so that no additional steps were needed to prevent slippage. The new design passed testing with flying colors, and of course the company put it into production.

As luck would have it, though, unexpected problems appeared when tens of thousands of British automobiles gave the design what was, in effect, its final road test. A fraction of 1 percent of the gears slipped on their shafts, causing friction that in turn

---

12. Christopher D. Stone, *Where the Law Ends: Social Control of Corporate Behavior* (New York: Harper and Row. 1975), pp. 51–52.

caused transmission parts to heat, expand, and eventually jam. The cars careened off the road and killed enough people to attract public attention. The company recalled the British vehicles and modified their transmissions.

The documents explained that the responsible American executives intended to withhold knowledge of this hazard from owners of American automobiles with the same transmissions, on an untested hunch that the heavier American vehicles would have enough momentum to break and drop their locked transmissions. The cars, company engineers hoped, would then coast safely to a stop, rather than careen off the road. Fortunately a savvy Detroit reporter used trade reports about the British experience to ask publicly whether the company would recall and repair the American vehicles, a question the company quickly answered in the affirmative.

The troublesome transmission was not planned deviance. Decision-makers had incomplete knowledge when they tested and adopted a new design. But they could not wait for complete knowledge before proceeding. No amount of testing could have determined whether, in widespread use, their new transmission would be hazard-free. They could not know that their product had a design fault that produced failures at a rate so low that it would not become apparent during extensive initial testing. Perversely, only putting the transmission in use could give them sufficient data to identify its risk to users.

Later, when the transmission was placed in service, decision-makers did begin to receive failure data, but these data were deeply embedded among other bits of important and unimportant information. Furthermore, responsible employees were not in a constant state of alertness to possible gear slippage (or any other issue). They had no reason to suspect a problem. Even if they could have recognized that the slippage problem existed, they could not have known how common it was.

However, when the data flow gradually reached a point that they could know dimensions of the danger, these decision-makers chose concealment. They were more likely to conceal information at this time because they and others had committed themselves to this particular design when they were testing it and deciding to use it. Their earlier decisions encouraged them to escalate their commitment[13] to a course of action they did not envisage when they began. (Readers who have bid or bought more at an auction than they originally planned can understand this process.) As is often the case, human activity continued for reasons unrelated to why it began.

Deviance Indirectly Traceable to Organizational Elites

Other deviance is more directly associated with the preferences of organizational elites, though still incidental and unplanned. Top-level managers regularly confront opportunities and problems for which they must devise organizationally beneficial solutions. They respond to these opportunities and problems by establishing goals and then delegating to subordinates the day-to-day responsibility for attaining these goals. Occasionally delegated responsibility and routine procedures and rewards yield unintended results.

Beech-Nut's "Apple Juice" for Babies.[14]   Beech-Nut was founded in upstate New York in 1891 as a purveyor of smoked hams and bacon. By the mid-1960s, the company had diversified and offered many familiar products, including Tetley Tea, Life Savers, gum, and baby food. In late 1968 Squibb merged with Beech-Nut to form Squibb Beech-Nut. Squibb then spun off the baby foods product line and sold it in 1973 to Frank Nicholas, a Pennsylvania attorney and entrepreneur. Mr. Nicholas, who paid $16 million, sold the company three years later to Nestle, the Swiss food conglomerate, for $35 million. In late 1989, Nestle sold it for $65 million to Ralston Purina, which in turn sold it in 1998 for $68 million to The Milnot Company. In late 2000, Milnot was trying to get government permission to sell Beech-Nut to Heinz for $185 million.

---

13. Barry M. Staw and Jerry Ross, "Behavior in Escalation Situations: Antecedents, Prototypes, and Solutions," *Research in Organizational Behavior* 9 (1987): 39–78.

14. Standard and Poor's Corporation, *Standard Corporate Description* (New York: McGraw Hill, 1990), p. 2,485; "Bad Apples in the Executive Suite," *Consumer Reports*, May 1989, pp. 294–6; Robert C. Cole, "Ralston Purina to Buy Beech-Nut Baby Food," *The New York Times*, September 16, 1989, p. 37; James Traub, "Into the Mouths of Babes," *The New York Times Magazine*, July 24, 1988, pp. 18–20, 37–38, 52–53: Chris Welles, "What Led Beech-Nut Down the Road to Disgrace'?" *Business Week*, February 22, 1988, pp. 124–8: "Former Beech-Nut Execs Guilty," *Columbus Dispatch*, February 18, 1988, p. 4A; "Beech-Nut Admits It Sold Bogus Apple Juice," *Columbus Dispatch*, November 14, 1987, p. 2A: "Beech-Nut: The Case of the Ersatz Apple Juice," *Newsweek*, November 17, 1986, p. 66; Bernice Kanner, "Into the Mouths of Babes: Jar Wars," *New York*, November 14, 1986. pp. 27–31. The purchase of Beech-Nut by The Milnot Company is from "Business Briefs," *Wall Street Journal*, July 30, 1998, p. B10.

One of Beech-Nut's three plants, in Canajoharie, New York, just west of Albany, abuts the New York Thruway. Drivers can easily see the big Beech-Nut sign and the stacks of empty crates they might assume were used to deliver apples and other fruits Beech-Nut uses for its baby juices. Indeed, a factory making fruit juice would seem to require fruit, or at least fruit juice. The crates suggested the Canajoharie plant was receiving shipments of fruit.

Closer inspection, however, revealed that the crates were badly weathered and many had deteriorated. Moreover, most juices, including Beech-Nut's, are now made from concentrate:

> [By] the time apple juice reaches the store, the typical juice has been screened, filtered, blended with apples from other orchards, and perhaps dosed with a little ascorbic acid to help maintain its clarity. Then it has been concentrated, reconstituted with water, and pasteurized. . . . Apple juice . . . is best understood as a manufactured product . . . brewed in the bottler's plant.[15]

The weathered crates at the back of the Canajoharie plant were perhaps a throwback to an earlier time. In any case, the crates had not contained apples for many years.

Neither did Beech-Nut's apple juice for babies between late 1977 and the middle of 1982. Although Beech-Nut advertisements told parents: "Our nutritionists prepare fresh-tasting vegetables, meats, dinners, fruits, cereals and juices without artificial flavorings, preservatives or colorings,"[16] Beech-Nut's apple juice consisted of sugar water colored brown to look like apple juice. The product brewed at the Canajoharie plant and labeled as "100 percent apple juice"[17] contained many things, including beet sugar, cane sugar, corn syrup, and caramel for color. The one thing it did not contain was apple juice.

There was no apple juice because each time Beech-Nut was merged, spun off, or sold, the price of the company went up. New owners had invested millions of dollars in Beech-Nut and understandably insisted that the Canajoharie plant show a profit: "Beech-Nut was under great financial pressure and using cheap, phony concentrate saved millions of dollars."[18] In addition, Beech-Nut was

15. "Bad Apples," p. 295.
16. Ibid., p. 294.
17. "Beech-Nut," p. 66.
18. Welles, "What Led Beech-Nut," p. 125.

in intense competition with Gerber, the market leader with 70 percent of baby-food sales.

Also, detecting adulterated juice is surprisingly difficult. Even after Beech-Nut had been prosecuted, chemists who specialize in testing food samples estimated in late 1993 that 10 percent of fruit juice sold in the United States is adulterated with, among other things, sugar, pulp wash (watery residue from soaking squeezed oranges in water and squeezing them again), difficult-to-detect preservatives such as natamycin, and preservatives not approved as safe for use in juices or even banned outright as hazardous (e.g., diethyl pyrocarbonate). Even if the Food and Drug Administration or state agencies had adequate enforcement budgets, adulteration is difficult to detect.[19] It is not easy to find clear evidence of apples even in juice that does contain apples.

Neither Mr. Nicholas when he owned Beech-Nut, nor Nestle after it bought the company, ordered corporate officers or plant managers to make bogus juice. The new owners only made it clear that they expected a return on their investment, for which they paid a premium price. They then delegated profit making to the people in Canajoharie. Charged with showing a profit, these people cut corners. One of the corners cut was leaving apple juice out of the apple juice.

Beech-Nut has understandably worked very hard to distance itself from this distasteful episode. A visit to its Web site[20] reveals healthy looking infants and, especially, the Beech-Nut products the corporation wants parents to feed to their infants. Beech-Nut teaches that it was the first to put baby food in glass jars in 1931, a time when it says all other manufacturers put their baby food in lead-soldered metal cans. Beech-Nut emphasizes the purity of its products, offers feeding advice to new and experienced parents, and provides several stages of baby food that the company claims eases the move to solid foods. There is no mention of its purchase by The Milnot Company and certainly no mention of the fact that its apple juice once contained no apple juice. It did, though, and not too long ago. Indeed, odds are that many of the college and

19. Diana B. Henriques, "10% of Fruit Juice Sold in U.S. is Not All Juice, Regulators Say." *The New York Times*, October 31, 1993. p. 1.

20. www.beechnut.com.

university students reading this book were, as infants, fed the caramel-colored sugar water Beech-Nut passed off as apple juice.

Deviance Directly Traceable to Organizational Elites

Not all organizational actions are accidents in the sense implied by Professor Stone's hypothetical nuclear plant, or indirectly traceable to elite actions as illustrated by Beech-Nut's "apple juice." Organizational elites sometimes knowingly use the hierarchy of organizational positions to command deviant actions. The concentration of Japanese Americans during World War II is a good example of deviance directly traceable to elite decisions.

Concentration of Japanese Americans During World War II.[21] Prejudice against Japanese Americans was part of American life long before Japan attacked Pearl Harbor in December 1941. In May 1905, for instance, the San Francisco School Board put all Japanese students in a single "Oriental School" because "our children should not be placed in any position where their youthful impressions may be affected by association with pupils of the Mongolian race."[22] California's Alien Land Law of 1913 prohibited Japanese immigrants, many of whom were farmers, from owning land. In 1924 the federal government changed the immigration laws specifically to exclude Japanese. Even President Franklin Delano Roosevelt was not above such prejudice. Before his 1932 presidential election, Mr. Roosevelt had shown himself entirely capable of strong "anti-Oriental racism,"[23] and as president he showed himself to be equally capable of harsh discrimination.

In 1941, before the start of the World War II, approximately 120,000 Japanese Americans lived in Washington, Oregon, Califor-

---

21. "Japanese Wait, Trustfully, for Overdue Checks," *Columbus Dispatch*, March 27, 1990, p. 8A; John Hersey, "Behind Barbed Wire," *The New York Times Magazine*, September 11, 1988, pp. 56–59, 73–74, 76, 120–1; Peter Wright and John C. Armor, *Manzanar* (New York: Times Books, 1988) (this book contains the wonderfully insightful photographs of Manzanar and its people by Ansel Adams); Commission on Wartime Relocation and Internment of Civilians, *Personal Justice Denied* (Washington, D.C. U.S. Government Printing Office, 1982); Roger Daniels, *The Decision to Relocate the Japanese Americans* (Philadelphia: Lippincott, 1975); Roger Daniels, *Concentration Camps, U.S.A.: Japanese Americans and World War II* (New York: Holt, Rinehart and Winston, 1972).

22. Commission, *Personal Justice*, p. 3.

23. Daniels, *Concentration Camps*, p. 9.

nia, and Arizona, with three-quarters living in California. Seventy percent were American citizens because they were born in the United States; American law prohibited the 30 percent born overseas from ever becoming citizens. By any measure, "Japanese Americans were model members of society."[24]

Nonetheless, by June 1942, no Japanese Americans lived on the West Coast. All had been forced to store or quickly sell their possessions (often at a steep discount) and report to train and bus stations, bringing only what they could carry. Once there, they were taken to "assembly centers, most of which were located at fairgrounds and racetracks . . . [surrounded by] barbed wire and searchlights, and the guard of guns."[25] From these centers, the American government moved them to 10 isolated, hastily built relocation centers under armed military guard (see Box 1.1).

Joining them were 2,000 people of Japanese ancestry, many speaking neither English nor Japanese, that U.S. troops took from Peru and other Latin American countries to internment camps in Texas.[26] By contrast, American officials interned only 1,600 of the 600,000 Italian citizens living in the United States, all of them classified as "enemy aliens," and 10,900 of the millions of Americans of German ancestry.

At the time of their internment, no evidence suggested that Japanese Americans supported Japan's imperial war efforts. And no credible evidence surfaced following the attack on Pearl Harbor. As the war progressed, the Nisei (second-generation Japanese Americans) released from the camps to join the U.S. Army quickly distinguished themselves in battle and returned home the "most decorated and distinguished combat unit of World War II."[27]

Many individuals and organizations—with a wide variety of contradictory positions—had knowledge that might affect the decision to put Japanese Americans into concentration camps. Without exception, the U.S. intelligence community opposed internment because it could find no credible grounds for such a massive and

24. Ibid., p. 4.
25. Hersey, "Behind Barbed Wire," p. 59.
26. Associated Press, "Payment to Some Interned Japanese in Doubt," *Boston Globe*, February 11, 1999, p. A21; Lena H. Sun, "U.S. Apologizes for Internment: Japanese Latin Americans Taken During WWII Due Reparations," *Washington Post*, June 13, 1998, p. A4.
27. Commission, *Personal Justice*, p. 3.

BOX 1.1 THE RELOCATION CENTERS

Eleven relocation centers were built, starting with the camp at Manzanar, California, in June 1941. That camp eventually held 10,200 Japanese Americans. The other camps (along with their estimated populations) were Gila River, Arizona (13,400); Granada, Colorado (7,600); Heart Mountain, Wyoming (11,100); Jerome, Arkansas (8,600); Mindoka, California (9,990); Poston, Arizona (18,000); Rohwer, Arkansas (8,500); Topaz, Utah (8,300); and the two camps at Tule Lake, California (18,800). Following the release of the Japanese Americans from these camps at the conclusion of World War II, several were maintained on a standby basis through 1971, including those at Tule Lake, California.

Sources: John Hersey, "Behind Barbed Wire," *New York Times Magazine,* September 11, 1988, pp. 56–59, 73–74, 76, 120–21; Peter Wright and John C. Armor, *Manzanar* (New York: Times Books, 1988); Commission on Wartime Relocation and Internment of Civilians, *Personal Justice Denied* (Washington, D.C.: U.S. Government Printing Office, 1982); Roger Daniels, *The Decision to Relocate the Japanese Americans* (Philadelphia: Lippincott, 1975); Roger Daniels, *Concentration Camps, U.S.A.: Japanese Americans and World War II* (New York: Holt, Rinehart and Winston, 1972).

---

repressive action. Even the consistently conservative FBI dismissed claimed threats, unambiguously stating that it had "no evidence of planned sabotage."[28] Indeed, in a report that went directly to the president, intelligence analyst Curtis B. Munson simply stated: "There will be no armed uprising of Japanese . . . the local Japanese are loyal to the United States. . . . We do not believe that they would be . . . any more disloyal than any other racial group in the United States with whom we went to war."[29] Most cabinet members also opposed internment. Secretary of War Henry L. Stimson correctly worried that the forced relocation of Japanese Americans would "make a tremendous hole in our constitutional system."[30]

Some others, however, advocated exclusion. Army General John L. De Witt was responsible for West Coast security and a staunch supporter of concentration. In February 1942 he wrote:

28. Daniels, *Concentration Camps,* p. 48.
29. Ibid., p. 54.
30. Ibid., p. 79.

The Japanese race is an enemy race and while many second and third generation Japanese born on United States soil, possessed of United States citizenship, have become "Americanized," the racial strains are undiluted.... It ... therefore ... follows that along the vital Pacific Coast ... potential enemies, of Japanese extraction, are at large today.[31]

Los Angeles Mayor Fletcher Bowron observed in a radio address: "Right here in our city are those who may spring to action at an appointed time ... wherein each of our little Japanese friends will know his part in the event of any possible invasion or air raid."[32] There also were self-serving hate groups that used the war to further their economic interests. The Grower-Shipper Vegetable Association was one such group, and stated its position unambiguously: "If all the Japs were removed tomorrow, we'd never miss them.... [W]hite farmers can take over and produce everything the Jap grows. And we don't want them back when the war ends, either."[33]

In the end, though, only one person could make such a decision. That person was the president, and the decision was really quite simple, for he had only two viable choices. He could side with the intelligence experts and cabinet members who told him that there was no threat and that the concentration of Japanese Americans was unnecessary and undesirable. Or he could appear decisive in a season of defeat by siding with the voices of fear, hatred, and hysteria. On February 19, 1942, President Franklin Roosevelt signed Executive Order 9066 authorizing the secretary of war to relocate "any or all persons ... [at] his discretion ... [and] ... to provide ... transportation, food, shelter, and other accommodations as may be necessary."[34] The result was the internment of 120,000 Japanese Americans during World War II.

Decades passed before the U.S. government finally admitted that the concentration of Japanese Americans was wrong.[35] In 1976, Presi-

---

31. Ibid., p. 6.

32. Daniels, *Concentration Camps*, p. 41.

33. Commission, *Personal Justice*, p. 69.

34. Daniels, *Concentration Camps*, p. 113.

35. Mitchell T. Maki, *Achieving the Impossible Dream: How Japanese Americans Obtained Redress* (Urbana, Ill.: University of illinois Press, 1999): Richard Simon, "California and the West: $4.8 Million Sought for Preservation of Internment Sites," *Los Angeles Times*, February 9, 2000, p. A3.

dent Gerald Ford asked Congress to investigate the internment, and in 1980 Congress established the Commission on Wartime Relocation and Internment of Civilians. The commission reported in 1982 that the internment had been groundless. In 1988, Congress passed and President Reagan signed a bill offering a formal letter of apology and $20,000 compensation for each interned Japanese American, with final payments made in 1992. In 1998, the United States responded to a lawsuit by offering an apology and $5,000 to each surviving Japanese Latin American interned by the United States, but by 1999 had funded payment for only 181 victims. And, in 2000 Vice President Al Gore announced on behalf of the Clinton Administration a request for nearly $5 million to create a visitor's center at the Manzanar internment camp in California and to purchase the sites of internment camps in other states.

Stages of Corporate and Governmental Deviance

Long-standing episodes of organizational deviance generally go through three stages. In the first "initiating deviance" stage, one or more individuals authorize or commit deviant actions. In the second stage, "institutionalization," the behavior takes on a life of its own, often continuing for reasons unrelated to why it started. Participants typically think little about its consequences for themselves or their organization. The third stage, "reactions," is reached if the public somehow finds out about the behavior. Courageous insiders may blow the whistle and alert the rest of us, or suspicious outsiders may take a careful look and reveal what they found.

Initiating Deviance

In this first stage, individuals or groups define a new situation as organizationally problematical, and then try to devise solutions. They may establish guidelines to which subordinates must adapt, or they may mandate a specific action such as concentrating Japanese Americans.

Their initial actions may not even be deviant. Participants in a long-running price-fixing conspiracy among companies making electrical equipment (please see Selection 6) built cooperative networks and learned to trust one another when they worked together, with government encouragement, to develop standards for interchangeable parts. Their links were further strengthened when government again asked them to cooperate with one another, this time to keep prices from plummeting during the Great Depression. This early legal cooperation to solve problems established the personal contacts, experiences, and trust that encouraged later illegal cooperation to fix prices. In the words of one participant, fixing prices for these companies was as "easy as falling off a log."[36]

To illustrate how deviance is introduced, we will now describe one governmental agency's abuse of its unique investigative powers. The agency is the FBI, and the behavior in question violated basic First Amendment rights (see Box 1.2).

FBI Investigation of CISPES.[37]   In the early 1980s, many Americans were upset by the government of El Salvador's violence against its political opponents and by U.S. support of that government. They had good reasons to be upset. Right-wing "death squads" murdered innocent noncombatants accounting for the vast majority of the estimated 12,000 noncombatant deaths in 1981 alone. (With a population of less than 5 million, the El Salvador death toll is equivalent to the extralegal murder of more than one-half million Americans in a single year.) Despite these atrocities, the American government continued to provide financial aid and training to the El Salvador government.

In opposition to American policy, a group of Americans and their organizations joined in late 1980 to form the Committee in Solidarity with the People of El Salvador (CISPES). The FBI responded by launching a series of investigations of CISPES that were not productive, violated the law, and contradicted the letter and spirit of its own policies.

FBI actions began routinely enough. In January 1981, it learned from the U.S. Park Service that CISPES planned a large demon-

---

36. Richard Austin Smith, *Corporations in Crisis* (New York: Anchor, 1966), p. 121.

37. U.S. Congress, House, Subcommittee on Civil and Constitutional Rights of Committee on the Judiciary, *CISPES and FBI Counter-Terrorism Investigations* (Washington, D.C.: U.S. Government Printing Office, 1988); U.S. Congress, Senate, Select Committee on Intelligence, *The FBI and CISPES* (Washington, D.C.: U.S. Government Printing Office, 1989).

BOX 1.2 FIRST AMENDMENT RIGHTS

The First Amendment gives American citizens the right to disagree publicly with their government. While carrying out its domestic investigative responsibilities, the FBI therefore is required to avoid actions so extensive or intrusive that they violate the First Amendment rights of those who dissent. To investigate groups simply because they oppose policies of people who currently happen to control foreign policy or government agencies is to discourage free speech and the expression of political opinion:

The mere collection of publicly available information can have a significant adverse effect . . . on people's exercise of their constitutional rights. The fear of possible government surveillance can . . . [discourage] people from participating in certain activities. It is impossible to know how, or even if, the information collected may come back to haunt someone who has done absolutely nothing wrong. But experience has shown . . . that in cases involving the intelligence surveillance of political organizations, the potential for abuse tends to outweigh the benefit of the information.

Source: U.S. Congress, House, Subcommittee on Civil and Constitutional Rights of Committee on the Judiciary, *CISPES* and *FBI Counter-Terrorism Investigations* (Washington, D.C.: U.S. Government Printing Office, 1988), p. 11.

---

stration. In June, it sent Frank Varelli, an informant, to infiltrate the Dallas chapter of CISPES. It also launched an investigation to determine whether CISPES was an agent of a foreign government and thus required to register. The FBI concluded CISPES was not an agent of a foreign government. Up to this point, the FBI had violated no laws or internal policies, except for sending Mr. Varelli before it had obtained official authorization.

Beginning in March 1983, however, the FBI launched a massive investigation of CISPES that gradually involved all 59 of its field offices. Initial efforts produced 178 "spin-off" investigations, some of which lasted into 1988. Despite clear evidence that Mr. Varelli was an unreliable informant and its own conclusion that CISPES was not an agent of a foreign government, the FBI devoted 20,000 employee hours to the project, collecting information on 2,375 people and 1,330 organizations. As recounted during congressional hearings:

> The FBI undertook . . . photographs during demonstrations, surveillance of rallies on college campuses, and attendance at a mass at a local university. . . . In one case a Xavier University professor was investigated on the basis of an exam question and a speaker invited to the class. Spin-off investigations were apparently initiated solely on the basis of attendance at the showing of a CISPES-sponsored film, the appearance of names on lists of participants at CISPES conferences, and similar associations [with CISPES] having no other relevance to the purpose of the original investigation.[38]

According to the Congress and then FBI Director William Sessions,[39] the agency's actions were deviant for three reasons. First, the FBI launched its investigation on the basis of allegations that were not credible. Though it claimed to base some of its actions on assertions that the Nicaraguan government was directing CISPES actions, the FBI actually had no such evidence.

Second, the FBI's investigations were far broader than would have been justified even if the allegations had been true. Professors' exams and college students attending mass are not the stuff of terrorist investigations. So too with attention the FBI directed at owners of automobiles with bumper stickers critical of U.S. policy in El Salvador. Consider a cable sent by the Louisville field office to FBI headquarters in Washington, D.C.

> On November 7, 1983 a vehicle described as a 1976 Datsun, 4-door green, bearing the Kentucky vehicle tag KXM-498, and bumper sticker "US OUT OF EL SALVADOR" was observed in front of University of Louisville School of Law at 12:20 P.M., at which time Nicaraguan judges Mariano Barahona and Humberto Obregon were speaking on "Justice and the Legal System in Nicaragua" at a public lecture sponsored in part by CISPES.[40]

Third, the FBI continued its investigation, even though the information it gathered did not meet its own criteria for continuation. Very early in its investigation, FBI agents and administrators should have known that CISPES was a group of Americans exer-

38. U.S. Congress, House, *CISPES*, p. 11.
39. U.S. Congress, Senate, *The FBI*, p. 1.
40. Ibid., p. 243.

cising their First Amendment rights. The FBI, however, continued to investigate CISPES. Among the reasons were complaints that critics of government policy were "pressuring legislators," an entirely legal activity that most of us call "lobbying."

No single leader or decision caused the introduction of deviance into the FBI in the CISPES case. Instead, the deviance was the result of a combination of people, events, and procedures. An FBI informant and employee initially provided distorted information. Domestic protest against El Salvador attracted the FBI's attention and apparently personally offended some FBI officials.

In addition, the FBI's internal administrative procedures were flawed. The agency provided inadequate organizational control over the employee in the Terrorism Section who made such decisions. It accepted, without serious questioning, material from ideologically motivated outside groups, and converted unsubstantiated assertions to postulates for future action. Orders and actions that originally justified by the FBI's antiterrorist responsibilities lost their purpose, focusing instead on simple public disagreement with U.S. government policy.

The FBI had not committed resources needed to avoid initiating this deviance. It had no in-house expertise in Central America or international politics generally, although it was conducting investigations in these areas. Further, two busy upper-level administrators were responsible for protecting First Amendment rights, and both failed to monitor the CISPES investigation.

CISPES continues to exist[41] and it is currently concentrating on labor issues in El Salvador, including closing of sweatshops making clothing. CISPES also organizes protests in the United States focused on the elimination of Christmas firings of workers in El Salvador that deny them legally guaranteed holiday bonuses.

The FBI, meanwhile, continues to grapple with its conflicting needs to identify potential terrorists while simultaneously respecting protected free speech. In the wake of the terrorist bombings of New York's World Trade Center and the Alfred P. Murrah federal building in Oklahoma City, the FBI has sought to expand its investigative powers. On the other hand, the FBI has been sanctioned for its abuse of the powers it already enjoys. The exposure of the

41. www.blank.org/sweatgear/cispes.

blatant violations of CISPES members' constitutional rights (only
the most recent in a string of similar incidents that date from the
FBI's founding in 1908) eventually forced the FBI in 1997 to agree
to enhance First Amendment training for its agents, and to pay
$190,000 of CISPES's legal costs for the court cases it brought
against the FBI.[42]

Institutionalization

In the second stage, institutionalization, deviant solutions to organizational problems are woven into the fabric of organizational life.
Participants no longer think very much about their deviance, save
for necessary but taken-for-granted precautions. In fact, their motives can change as their involvement continues. Ethicists and others
use the vivid image of a "slippery slope" to describe this tendency.

Consider the changing motives that cause some executives to
conceal known drug hazards. The drug development process takes
5 to 10 years, and involves a wide variety of specialists in many technical and administrative areas. During this time, important relationships and commitments develop among the participating people
and departments. Hiding hazards is not planned in advance. It instead results from a process of increasing commitments, as illustrated by one pharmaceutical executive's description of how scientists' motives change:

> [C]hemist[s] who synthesize . . . a new compound . . . [are] . . . very
> possessive about it. It is . . . [their] . . . off-spring, and they defend
> . . . it like a son or daughter. Also pharmacologist[s] who show . . .
> that this new compound has certain effects of therapeutic value see
> . . . it as . . . [their] . . . baby. It is not so much that they will lie and
> cheat to defend it, but they will be biased.[43]

In all organizations, employees who initiate deviance move on
to new positions as time passes. Their replacements find that deviant behavior is an expected part of their new positions. These new
members conclude they must either comply with role expectations

42. Charles Nicodemus, "FBI Agents Get Training About Rights: Decree Ends Spying Case
Here," *Chicago Sun Times*, December 15, 1997, p. 8; David LaGesse, "Ex-Activists Decry Extra
FBI Powers: History of Abuse Has Many Wary," *The Times Picayune*, May 14, 1995, p. A23.

43. John Braithwaite, *Corporate Crime in the Pharmaceutical Industry* (London: Routledge and
Kegan Paul, 1984). pp. 93–94.

or be replaced by people more willing to do as they are told. Accordingly, once deviant actions are institutionalized, they become intertwined with legitimate ones, and both become routine. Thus, Beech-Nut passed bogus apple juice as the real thing for five years, and the U.S. government continued its internment of Japanese Americans virtually without challenge. In the following section, we analyze in detail one classic example of deviance being institutionalized—Gulf Oil's illegal political campaign contributions.

Gulf Oil's Illegal Campaign Contributions.[44]   At the start of the 1970s, the Gulf Oil Corporation had been laundering and clandestinely distributing cash to American politicians for more than 15 years. The system worked exceptionally well, and during its long history those who ran it hardly thought about what they were doing, even though their actions were clearly illegal (see Box 1.3).

Routine orders and illegal cash moved along the following path. When the head of Gulf's Government Relations Office in Washington, D.C., needed money, he called Gulf's headquarters in Pittsburgh. There, the company's comptroller authorized its treasurer to transfer money to a nearly inactive Gulf subsidiary in The Bahamas. A Gulf employee in The Bahamas then laundered the money by passing it through several Bahamian bank accounts. The laundered cash was then taken to Washington, where employees in Gulf's Government Relations Office distributed it to politicians. This system operated for nearly 15 years, distributing slightly more than $5 million to hundreds of national, state, and local politicians.

What made Gulf's system of laundering and distributing so elegant was its use of employees who did not have, need, or probably want complete information or responsibility. They simply made small contributions to the overall system by quietly doing what was defined for them as part of their jobs. Consider the role of Gulf's comptrollers. After the comptroller who helped develop the system left, three other people sequentially occupied the position. None of them had to make any difficult decisions, much less consciously involve themselves in criminal activities. They merely were

---

44. Securities and Exchange Commission, Plaintiff, v. Gulf Oil Corporation, Claude C. Wild, Jr., Defendants, *Report of the Special Review Committee of the Board of Directors of Gulf Oil Corporation*, United States District Court, District of Columbia, December 30, 1975.

BOX 1.3 CORPORATE CAMPAIGN CONTRIBUTIONS

Corporate campaign contributions have been illegal for almost ninety years. In 1907 the Congress passed what came to be known as the "Corrupt Practices Act," a law that bans corporations from providing funds to people campaigning for federal office. The states then quickly passed similar laws outlawing the contribution of corporate funds to candidates for state and local office.

The logic behind these laws is straightforward. The resources of America's largest corporations far exceed those of individuals, so corporations are in a position to make large monetary contributions to candidates and unduly influence the actions of those elected. Corrupt practices acts are intended to limit corporate influence on the electoral process.

Corporations nonetheless have considerable clout when it comes to financing political campaigns. They are allowed to use corporate funds to administer political action committees (PACs), which collect voluntary donations from employees and give this money to people running for public office. But corporations are not allowed to contribute corporate funds.

Sources: James Ring Adams, *The Big Fix: Inside the S & L Scandal* (New York: Wiley, 1990); Brooks Jackson, *Honest Graft: Big Money and the American Political Process* (New York: Knopf, 1988); Amitai Etzioni, *Capital Corruption: The New Attack on American Democracy* (San Diego: Harcourt Brace Jovanovich, 1984); Larry Sabato, *PAC Power: Inside the World of Political Action Committees* (New York: Norton, 1984).

---

told that they would receive requests for cash. All they did was write notes to treasurers asking that the money be provided. Easy to do and easy to live with.

Gulf's treasurers also did little and could choose to know very little. They were simply told that the account in The Bahamas "was highly sensitive and confidential."[45] All they did was send money to that account on receipt of a note from a comptroller. Tens of other Gulf employees engaged in similar actions, knowing or choosing to know very little and making small contributions to the over-

---

45. Securities and Exchange Commission, *Special Review Committee . . . Gulf Oil Corporation*, p. 223.

all system as part of their work. The actions and attitudes of one Gulf employee who actually gave the cash to the people being bribed nicely illustrates the limited knowledge and responsibility required of individuals in organizations such as Gulf Oil in which deviance is institutionalized:

> Most often delivery would be at an airport or at the recipient's office, but occasionally it would be at a place suggestive of a desire for secrecy . . . [H]e handed an envelope to Representative Richard L. Roudebush of Indiana . . . in the men's room of a motel in Indianapolis . . . Time and again, asked whether he knew what was in the envelope he had delivered, he replied, "I do not," or "I have no knowledge." A minor figure . . . apparently content to spin constantly above the cities, plains, and mountains of America, not knowing why, not wanting to know why.[46]

It is important to recognize that institutionalized deviance at Gulf existed alongside normal organizational activities. Some Gulf employees did spend some of their working days moving money, but even these people could rationalize that they spent most of their time on entirely legal activities.

Reactions

Institutionalized deviance typically continues until stopped from inside or outside the organization. Internally, the impetus for initiating deviance may disappear, or internal whistle blowers may step forward with accusations and evidence of wrongdoing. Externally, the media, prosecutors, or victims may challenge organizational actions.

Organizations have their own versions of events and respond to accusations of deviance with accusations and assertions of their own. In the exchange of claims and counterclaims, whether an organizational action actually comes to be seen as deviant is fundamentally a matter of definition.

---

46. John Brooks, "The Bagman," in Rosabeth Moss Kanter and Barry A. Stein, eds., *Life in Organizations: Workplaces as People Experience Them* (New York: Basic Books, 1979), p. 369.

The Organizational Deviance-defining Process[47]

Many sociologists who study marijuana use, gambling, and other actions by individuals assert that no behavior is intrinsically deviant.[48] Instead, they argue that actions are deviant only if they are defined as deviant. They suggest that the deviance-defining process happens in somewhat the following way:

> For deviance to become a social fact, somebody must perceive an act, situation, or event as a departure from social norms, must categorize that perception, must report that perception to others, must get them to accept this definition of the situation, and must obtain a response that conforms to their definition. Unless all these requirements are met, deviance as a social fact does not come into being.[49]

Accusations. We believe that a similar view of the deviance-defining process should be taken for organizational actions. When viewed through this lense, no organizational action is intrinsically deviant. Instead, organizational actions are deviant only to the extent that they are perceived, reported, defined, accepted, and treated as deviant.

This perspective emphasizes the disagreement that typically surrounds definitions of organizational deviance. Whereas some voices insist that what an organization is doing is wrong, other voices insist that nothing improper is taking place. Members of the general public hearing both voices may be confused by the contradictory assertions. Even when there does appear to be a consensus, as with a corporation that knowingly releases an unsafe product, there are still important differences in perception and definition. Agreement on broad generalities does not necessarily yield a consensus on what is to be defined as deviant.

Consider the Department of Justice's accusations of price-fixing directed against some of the nation's most visible colleges (including Williams, Bowdoin, Bates, and Colby) and universities (including Harvard, Yale, Princeton, and Stanford) at the start of the

---

47. For an earlier statement see M. David Ermann and Richard J. Lundman, *Corporate Deviance* (New York: Holt, Rinehart and Winston, 1982), pp. 16–30.

48. A classic statement of this position is by Howard S. Becker, *Outsiders: Studies in the Sociology of Deviance* (New York: Free Press, 1963).

49. Earl Rubington and Martin S. Weinberg, ed., *Deviance: The Interactionist Perspective*, 2nd ed. (New York: Macmillan, 1973), p. vii.

1990s.[50] It accused more than 50 colleges and universities of conspiring to fix tuition fees and financial aid for students, and salaries for faculty. Following the accusations, some of the accused institutions acknowledged membership in what they called the "Overlap Group," admitted agreeing on financial aid offers made to students who had been accepted for admission by more than one institution, and defended their actions. In the words of former Williams College President Francis Oakley: "Overlap . . . exchange[s] information about family and student resources of students accepted by more than one Overlap school . . . Were Overlap to disappear, colleges and universities . . . would come under increasing pressure . . . to . . . use financial aid to try to 'buy' particularly attractive applicants."[51]

Other university administrators stated that they exchanged information on not only tuition, but faculty salaries as well. Writing just before the Justice Department investigation began, Professor Henry Rosovsky, dean of the faculty of arts and sciences at Harvard University, described his next appointment of the day:

> Appointment 2: my chief financial officer. Two topics: next year's tuition and faculty salaries. This is deadly serious stuff, among the main factors determining faculty income and costs. Both have to be considered competitively; the decisions of Stanford, Berkeley, MIT, Yale, and others are crucial. We share information quite freely.[52]

Many people outside these colleges and universities agreed with the positions these institutions had taken because they saw nothing wrong with educational institutions coordinating tuition, offers

50. Herschel Grossman, "Rebirth of the Ivy Cartel," *Wall Street Journal*, January 26, 1994. p. A15; William Honan, "M. I. T. Wins Right to Share Financial Aid Data in Antitrust Accord," *The New York Times*, December 23, 1993, p. A13; Anthony DePalma, "M. I. T. Ruled Guilty in Antitrust Case," *The New York Times*, September 3, 1992, p. Al; Rohit Menezes. "The Anti-Trust Saga: Williams' Future Hangs in the Balance," *The Williams Observer*, November 14, 1990, p. 1; Robert Weisberg, "Justice Department Opens Investigation of Williams," *The Williams Record*, September 12, 1989, p. 1; "U.S. Price Fixing Probe Said to Add Hopkins and Goucher," *Evening Sun*, September 15, 1989, p. F4; Robert Weisberg, "Wesleyan Senior Files Lawsuit Against Williams, 11 Others," *The Williams Record*, September 26, 1989, p. 1; Francis Oakley, "The Antitrust Inquiry and Higher Education," *Williams Reports* (Williams College, Office of Public Information), October 1989; Mike Elliot, "Justice Department Suspects Schools of Price-Fixing, Antitrust Violations," *U:The National College Newspaper*, December 1989, p. 1.

51. Oakley, "The Antitrust," pp. 4–5. Francis Oakley is now Edward Dorr Griffin professor of the history of ideas at Williams and president emeritus of the college.

52. Rosovsky, *The University*, p. 42.

of financial aid, and faculty salaries. They believed that colleges and universities already charge outrageous fees and provide dizzying salaries to their faculty, especially the expensive and highly selective institutions that were the primary targets of Department of Justice accusations. They argued that if Overlap and similar arrangements were eliminated, the price of education and faculty salaries at schools would be even higher. They rejected efforts at labeling.

But others defined Overlap and related agreements as deviant. They asserted that colleges and universities, like businesses, should be bound by free-market forces. Without competition, all of these institutions would be free to charge artificially high tuition and make artificially low financial aid offers, denying students the benefits traceable to free-market financial competition. The money saved could then be spent in other areas, including even higher salaries for faculty and administrators.

Among those defining Overlap agreements as deviant were the attorneys working inside the Antitrust Division of the Justice Department. They pushed their definition and threatened legal action.

Organizational Responses. Most of the institutions decided not to take their chances in court or experience the negative publicity that would accompany prolonged litigation. They signed consent decrees indicating that while they had not necessarily been fixing financial aid offers, they would stop communicating with each other about such offers.

Massachusetts Institute of Technology (MIT) resisted Antitrust's definitions of its actions, went to court, and lost. MIT then appealed and the higher court instructed the lower court to reconsider the case. By then, however, Antitrust was under considerable pressure to abandon the case,[53] so it settled with MIT. The agreement stipulated that institutions must practice need-based financial aid and can talk to each other via computer only after independent auditors report "gross discrepancies" in financial aid offers.

In the wake of the agreement, MIT and Antitrust attorneys both claimed their definition of Overlap and other financial aid prac-

---

53. For examples see these editorials: "Drop the MIT Case," *Washington Post*, October 14, 1993, p. A30; "The MIT Case: Time to Back Off," *The New York Times*, December 27, 1993, p. A12.

tices had been vindicated. They were both correct because both definitions were recognized by the settlement. In this and many other situations, individuals and groups attempt to hold organizations to their own particular normative expectations. When people or groups feel that an organization has violated their norms, they may try to label the organization and its actions deviant. However, organizations do not stand passively to the side and allow their fate to be shaped by others' definitions and reactions. Instead, nearly all organizations work diligently to escape a deviant label. They build reservoirs of goodwill and provide alternative accounts of their behavior to interested audiences. Organizations also sometimes play verbal hardball as they pitch words at the heads of their accusers and audiences.

Goodwill. Organizations try to build goodwill long before anyone has accused them of specific deviant acts. Writing about business organizations, sociologist Edwin H. Sutherland (see Box 1.4) observed in 1949: "The corporation attempts not only to 'fix' particular accusations against it, but also to develop good will before accusations are made."[54]

Mobil Oil, now merged with Exxon to form ExxonMobil, is an especially good example of a corporation that has worked very hard to develop goodwill.[55] Mobil has long been a generous contributor to the Public Broadcasting Service (public television), including sponsorship of public television's *Masterpiece Theater*. Mobil's actions are an important part of its overall public relations effort and its goal is to reach the "loyal, affluent, and well-educated audience, particularly the elusive . . . 'light viewers' who prefer *Masterpiece Theater* . . ."[56] A Mobil executive responsible for public relations explained that being

associated with excellence helps present the company view. . . . A reader sees a Mobil message and associates it with Big Oil. So he may be wary. But he also associates it with the company that brings

---

54. Edwin H. Sutherland, *White Collar Crime* (New York: Dryden, 1949), p. 32.

55. M. David Ermann, "The Operative Goals of Corporate Philanthropy: Contributions to the Public Broadcasting Service, 1972–1976," *Social Problems* 25 (1978): 504–14.

56. Laura Bird, "Public TV Plugs Getting Closer to Network Ads," *Wall Street Journal*, August 10, 1992, p. B4. Also see Elizabeth Kolbert, "A New 'Good Evening' From 'Masterpiece Theater," *The New York Times*, February 24, 1993, p. C13.

BOX 1.4 EDWIN H. SUTHERLAND, 1883–1950

Edwin H. Sutherland received his Ph.D. in sociology from the University of Chicago in 1913 and spent most of his academic career at Indiana University. He made many important contributions to the sociological study of crime. To us, his most important contribution was his analysis of what he called "white-collar crime." Professor Sutherland coined the phrase and most contemporary researchers in the field trace their work to his pioneering efforts.

In 1939, Professor Sutherland presented a paper at the annual meeting of the American Sociological Society. He spoke as president of the society and entitled his address "White Collar Criminality." In his paper, he demonstrated that crime in the suites was as worthy of sociological attention as was crime in the streets.

Professor Sutherland followed his presidential address with a book, *White Collar Crime*, in 1949. This book was the culmination of nearly a quarter century of frequently single-handed research. Although not permitted to identify the corporations because his publisher feared libel suits and because his university feared a reduction in corporate funding, Professor Sutherland reported that seventy of the nation's largest corporations had been convicted of a total of 980 illegal actions and that many of the corporations had been convicted more than once. Of those with at least one conviction, the average was four, making them "habitual offenders" under then existing laws in most states and eligible for contemporary "three strikes and you are out" sentencing.

In 1983, the "uncut version" of *White Collar Crime* was published, restoring the integrity of the original book by identifying the corporations studied.

Sources: Edwin H. Sutherland, *White Collar Crime* (New York: Dryden, 1949); Edwin H. Sutherland, with an introduction by Gilbert Geis and Colin Goff, *White Collar Crime: The Uncut Version* (New Haven, CT: Yale University Press, 1983).

---

him . . . [Public Broadcasting Service programs] . . . so maybe he's a little more open-minded and a little more receptive.[57]

A middle-level Mobil executive stated that the purpose of sponsoring public television programs was "to win credibility and . . .

---

57. Quoted in Irwin Ross, "Public Relations Isn't Kid-Glove Stuff at Mobil," *Fortune* 94 (1976): p. 110.

provide access to, and rapport with, key groups and special publics—legislators and regulators; the press; intellectuals and academics."[58] The next-level Mobil executive said, "These programs, we think, build enough acceptance to allow us to get tougher on substantive issues."[59]

Today ExxonMobil says two things about its sponsorship of *Masterpiece Theater*.[60] First, it is proud of its 29-year commitment to and support of the program. Second, ExxonMobil explains that long-standing commitment by noting: "Our goal was to set a standard, to fill a void, and to stick with it. Along the way, we've enjoyed a terrific partnership with PBS, the support of a fiercely loyal audience and the satisfaction of proving that ratings aren't the only measure of success."[61] No doubt all of these things are true. Also true is the considerable goodwill ExxonMobil has purchased and deposited in its banks of corporate conformity.[62]

Mobil is not alone among corporations in building goodwill in anticipation of difficult times. Each Friday evening, *Wall Street Week* with Louis Rukeyser on public television begins and ends with acknowledgments of financial support from major corporations. Internationally based corporations seek to Americanize their image by supporting U.S. Olympic teams, with Subaru providing automobiles for the skiers. Still others, like McDonald's and its Ronald McDonald Houses, use high-visibility charitable activities to garner goodwill.

Building goodwill is not limited to the world of business. Colleges and universities make their facilities available to community organizations, and faculty members regularly leave campus to talk to community groups about their research. Police departments have community relations officers who speak to groups about crime prevention, organize neighborhood crime watches, run "safety city"

---

58. Quoted in Phillis S. McGarath, *Business Credibility: The Critical Factors* (New York: The Conference Board, 1976), p. 30.

59. Ross, "Public Relations," p. 110.

60. www.exxonmobil.com/masterpiece.

61. Ibid.

62. The idea of deposits in banks of conformity is from Paul M. Roman, "Settings for Successful Deviance: Drinking and Deviant Drinking Among Middle and Upper-Level Employees," in Clifton D. Bryant, ed., *Deviant Behavior: Occupational and Organizational Bases* (Chicago: Rand McNally, 1974), pp. 109–28.

programs for small children, and dare older children to stay clear of drugs.

Failure to build goodwill can harm an organization and its mission, as the Internal Revenue Service (IRS) recently learned.[63] The IRS had for decades seen its role as enforcement, and was not greatly concerned with gaining public affection. But Senate hearings in 1998 that highlighted instances of IRS taxpayer abuse (most of which were subsequently discredited) produced unfriendly legislation, organizational change, and widespread employee demoralization. In two years, Congressional funding for IRS staff declined, the number of audits was to be reduced by at least 30 percent from record lows, and agents reported their reluctance to penalize wayward taxpayers.

To try to rebuild goodwill with powerful constituencies, the IRS now calls taxpayers "customers" whom it "serves," assigns many more employees to customer service, and in two years reduced property seizures from about 10,000 to exactly 161.[64]

Rebuilding goodwill in the wake of being labeled deviant is not limited to the IRS. In the mid 1990s, Texaco admitted to long-standing race discrimination directed at African-American employees.[65] Texaco was embarrassed by the widespread negative publicity it received and anxious to improve its image in many communities, especially the African-American community. Toward that end, Texaco is now the underwriter for *Tony Brown's Journal* on PBS and each edition of the program begins and ends with the following statement: "We are pleased to support the intellectual, spiritual, and cultural energy of the African American Community. Texaco, a world of energy." So too with Archer Daniels Midland (ADM). Eager to have its mid-1990s conviction for price-fixing forgotten, ADM[66] supports PBS's *The NewsHour* with Jim Lehrer telling viewers ADM is "Supermarket to the world."

Alternative Accounts. When accused of deviance, organizations provide alternative accounts of their behavior. These accounts differ

63. David Cay Johnston, "Reducing Audits of the Wealthy, I.R.S. Turns Eye on Poor," *The New York Times*, December 15, 1999, p. Al.

64. Ibid.

65. Roberts, *Roberts vs. Texaco.*

66. www.usdoj.gov/atr/public/press_releases/1996/508at.htm. According to the Justice Department, the $100 million ADM paid was the "largest criminal antitrust fine ever."

very little from those offered by accused individuals.[67] Organizations attribute troublesome actions to particular individuals ("scapegoating"), assert that no one was injured ("denial of injury"), and accuse attackers of being dishonest and self-serving ("condemnation of the condemners").

Immediately following the *Valdez* oil tanker disaster, for instance, Exxon was unprepared to offer anything more than traditional accounts of what had happened,[68] and so it initially directed attention to the tanker's captain. The corporation also asserted that the environmental damage was minimal, and suggested that the Coast Guard was responsible for the delay in starting to clean up the mess.

Audiences. Observing this process of accusation and response are audiences. These audiences are large, diverse, and they can cause significant damage to successfully labeled organizations. The general public may avoid purchasing products from deviant businesses, or Congress may reduce public funding for colleges and universities. Regulatory agencies may force corporations to undertake expensive remedial actions. Consumers may sue for past injuries, and civilian review boards may be instituted to monitor police actions.

However, audiences typically have two significant weaknesses. First, audience members lack the knowledge to independently assess the accuracy of accusations and responses. According to Department of Justice Antitrust attorneys, Microsoft is a corporation that needs to be broken up to restore competition to the market. In the words of Attorney General Janet Reno: "This is the right remedy at the right time. Our proposal will stimulate competition, promote innovation, and give consumers new and better choices in the marketplace."[69]

67. See especially Gresham M. Sykes and David Matza, "Techniques of Neutralization: A Theory of Delinquency," *American Sociological Review* 22 (1957): 664–70. Also see C. Wright Mills, "Situated Actions and Vocabularies of Motive," *American Sociological Review* 5 (1940): 904–13; Lawrence Nichols, "Reconceptualizing Social Accounts: An Agenda for Theory Building and Empirical Research," *Current Perspectives in Social Theory* 10 (1990): 113–44.

68. William J. Small. "Exxon Valdez: How to Spend Billions and Still Get a Black Eye," *Public Relations Review* 17 (1991): 9–25; Allana Sullivan, "Rawl Wishes He'd Visited Valdez Sooner," *Wall Street Journal*, June 30, 1989, p. B3; John Holusha, "Exxon's Public-Relations Problem," *The New York Times*, April 21, 1989, p. Cl. Also see www.exxonmobil.com/news/valdez/index.html.

69. www.usdoj .gov/atr/public/press_releases/2000/4646.htm.

Microsoft strongly disagrees. In the words of Microsoft chair Bill Gates: "We believe there is no basis in this case for the government's unprecedented breakup proposal, and we are hopeful that the Court will dismiss this excessive demand immediately so that the case can move forward much more rapidly."[70]

Equally important, accused organizations typically are better able than their accusers to craft and disseminate compelling accounts. Accusers' voices tend to be more muted, less frequent, less well-crafted, and less appealing. Audience members hear and see much more of what accused organizations want heard and seen.

In sum, organizational deviance results from public interactions between accusers and responding organizations, with interested audiences as frequently important final arbiters (also see Box 1.5). Whether a perceived departure from social norms comes to be widely labeled and penalized as deviant depends on the power of the accusers to make their labels stick, as compared with the power of the organizations to resist labeling. Because audience members typically cannot independently assess what comes their way, and because organizations almost always are more powerful than their accusers, audiences rarely label or penalize organizations. Consider some of the accusations of deviance directed at the Central Intelligence Agency (CIA).

Deviance and the CIA.[71]   In the early 1970s, the Central Intelligence Agency was experiencing another of its periodic rounds of attack and accusation by outsiders. Foremost among the numerous accusations was the assertion that the agency gathered domestic intelligence information. Despite legislation banning domestic spying, the CIA was accused of gathering information on antiwar and other dissident groups. Some accusers asserted that as much as one-third of the officially listed CIA workforce of 18,000 was involved in domestic intelligence gathering, that CIA personnel had infiltrated more than 250 domestic political groups, and that the agency had assembled secret files on thousands of Americans.

70. www.microsoft.com/presspass/trial/default.asp.

71. Weiner, *Blank Check*, pp. 111–42; William Waegel, M. David Ermann, and Alan M. Horowitz, "Organizational Responses to Imputations of Deviance," *Sociological Quarterly* 22 (1981): 43–55.

BOX 1.5 THE FORD EXPLORER,
BRIDGESTONE/FIRESTONE EPISODE

During the second half of the year 2000, the Ford Motor Company
and Bridgestone/Firestone were at the front end of what almost
certainly will be a protracted deviance defining episode. Rocked by
bad publicity, troublesome company memos, aggressive critics, and
attacks against each other, the two corporations were trying to cope
with accusations that they concealed what they knew about Ford
Explorer and Firestone tire dangers that may have contributed to
more than 119 deaths under review by government regulators.
    As is sometimes the case, chance played a role in the emergence
of accusations of organizational deviance. The crisis began when an
investigative reporter for the Houston, Texas, CBS television affiliate, who never imagined the story would grow, did a story about
Firestone tire problems. The crisis was fed by disclosure that an obscure analyst at State Farm Insurance had noted and reported to
federal regulators that some types of Firestone tires were having an
unusual number of problems. Also important was a rollover tire-
related accident that severely injured the son and killed the baby-sitter
of a powerful Venezuelan lawyer who had represented both companies, and was now using his power and influence to go after both.
    Poor crisis management, especially at Bridgestone/Firestone
headquarters in Japan, helped feed the scandal. Management of
Bridgestone's responses was in the hands of officials, particularly
lawyers, who emphasized legal over public relations concerns, and
operated at a geographical and cultural distance that made full
appreciation of the problem difficult. The company accordingly
never got out in front of the issue, first claiming nothing was amiss,
then saying that replacement of tires would be spread over a full
year and would only be available at authorized company dealerships,
later failing to effectively handle Congressional hearings on the
scandal. Each time it acted, the company almost immediately was
forced to retreat, thereby adding confusion. Even its public relations firm quit in frustration. Ford is generally credited with having
done a better crisis management job (after an initial stumble in
selecting a company spokesperson), thanks in part to a 500-plus
person "war room" that was immediately assembled to craft, test,
and polish corporate accounts and other statements.
    But, as the scandal continued to unfold, new data emerged as
major newspapers (including the *Wall Street Journal, The New York
Times,* and *Washington Post*) commissioned their own statistical

studies which pointed a finger of blame at both companies and effectively challenged some of their responses. A California judge's ruling (under appeal as we write this) that Ford must recall millions of cars in California for long-concealed ignition problems gained greater than usual publicity. Ford itself then announced a voluntary recall 351,000 Focus subcompact cars to fix three distinct problems. And Congress passed legislation with breathtaking speed, providing stricter safety reporting standards, and jail sentences for future executives who might conceal automobile or parts safety defects from government regulators.

It is important to note that this deviance defining episode is in its very early stages. Law suits are only now beginning to be filed, additional Congressional hearings will almost certainly be held, it is likely the press will present new information, and the two corporations will advance new accounts and recast older ones. As was the case with the Ford Pinto episode (please see Selection 15), it is likely that years will pass before the negative publicity fully subsides and, far more important, audience members, scholars, and other outsiders have a relatively clear idea of what really happened.

Sources: Timothy Aeppel, Clare Ansberry, Milo Geyelin, and Robert L. Simison, "Ford and Firestone's Separate Goals, Gaps in Communication Gave Rise to Tire Fiasco," *Wall Street Journal Interactive Edition*, September 6, 2000; Dan Keating and Caroline E. Mayer, "Explorer Has Higher Rate of Tire Accidents," *The Washington Post Online*, October 9, 2000, p. A01; Jim Rutenberg, "Local TV Uncovered National Scandal," *The New York Times on the Web*, September 11, 2000. Sources cited above are a sample of the many we examined in preparing this box.

Congress and the president responded to these accusations by establishing separate investigative bodies. Both attracted an audience, although their final reports sponsored very different versions of CIA activities. A Senate Special Subcommittee on Intelligence strongly supported accusations of misconduct. In contrast, the Rockefeller Commission concluded that no widespread pattern of deviant activity existed, and that accusations of domestic intelligence gathering were largely unfounded.

The CIA did not stand idly by and permit its fate to be determined by accusers or investigative bodies. Instead, it used its considerable organizational power to turn away accusations of deviance. It scapegoated by arguing that it did not bear full responsibility for the infrequent, objectionable activities that may have occurred, noting that government agencies seldom question the orders of executive branch officials. It thus asserted that if it had done something wrong, it did so because others with more power had ordered these actions. It also promoted alternative interpretations of the extent and importance of domestic spying operations. One top-level CIA official denied that any substantial injury had taken place, observing that domestic operations may have involved "some violations of rights, but nothing earth-shattering."

Bolder tactics were used against the agency's critics. It charged that journalist Daniel Schorr (who had disseminated classified CIA material to document misconduct accusations) jeopardized the safety of agency personnel, with one former CIA official labeling him "Killer Schorr." Similar attempts were made to condemn vocal accusers in the House of Representatives, by noting their role in releasing secret testimony. How, the CIA implied, could the audience trust accusers who risked the lives of others by releasing information that was supposed to be secret?

These and other CIA responses to accusations of deviance succeeded. Congress imposed no meaningful constraints. In the wake of accusations of deviance, the CIA's structure, operational authority, and autonomy remain essentially unchanged to this day, even though the agency continues to be the target of numerous accusations of deviance.[72]

In sum, individuals and groups accused the CIA of departing from important social norms by engaging in domestic intelligence gathering. They alerted others to their perceptions and argued that something needed to be done. The CIA used its considerable power to respond to accusations and shape audience reactions. It scape-

---

72. These include accusations of secret funds hidden from the Congress at the start of the 1980s, covert sales of weapons in Afghanistan in the mid-1980s, a Soviet spy deep inside the CIA in the early 1990s, selling crack cocaine in the mid-1990s, and accusations that the CIA played a central role in the bungled bombing of the Chinese embassy in Belgrade in the late 1990s. See *Front Line*, PBS, April 21, 1991; Weiner, *Blank Check*, pp. 143–213 and p. 164; Tim Weiner, "Congress Decides to Conduct Study of Need for C.I.A.," *The New York Times*, September 28, 1994, p. A17; Tim Weiner, "Report Finds Ames's Sabotage More Vast Than C.I.A. Admitted," *The New York Times*, September 24, 1994. p. A1; Anthony Lewis. "Maurice the Waiter," *The New York Times*, December 14, 1992, p. A17; The CIA–Contra–Crack Cocaine Controversy: A Review of the Justice Department's Investigations and Prosecutions (December 1997; available at www.usdoj.gov/oig/c4rpt/c4toc.htm); and State Department Report on Accidental Bombing of Chinese Embassy (July 1999; available at www.usconsulate.org.hk/uscn/state/1999/0706.htm).

goated, denied that serious injury had occurred, and condemned those accusing the agency of misconduct. Although it did experience some very rough times, this agency (unlike the IRS) continued with business pretty much as usual.

Punishment

Punishment of organizational deviance is relatively rare. The reasons are several (see Box 1.6), but one seems most important. Organizations are wealthy and powerful actors, and they use their resources well. Consider the U.S. Sentencing Commission that Congress established in 1984.[73] The commission's goal was to produce more certain and uniform punishment for individuals and corporations convicted in federal courts. Its recommendations to Congress in 1987 for punishing individuals met little sustained resistance, so the commission turned its attention to corporate sentencing.

But the commission's draft corporate guidelines in 1990 generated a storm of self-serving corporate protest. Corporate representatives described the proposals as "extremely harsh," "critically flawed," and "overwhelmingly intrusive." Corporate lobbying was intensive, and very effective. The Department of Justice withdrew its previous support for the guidelines, and the White House instructed the commission to recall, revise, and resubmit them. In 1992, the commission's more timid guidelines went into effect.[74] Recent efforts at expansion have met the same corporate resistance.[75]

Even when guidelines and laws are in place, organizations use their resources in other ways. For example, an organization, Industrial Crisis Institute, and a journal, *Public Relations Review*, shape corporate responses in the minutes and hours following major crises. Industrial Crisis Institute president Paul Shrivastava notes that all "crises have a window of opportunity to gain control of 45 minutes to 12 hours. If you don't move in that time you might as well go back

---

73. Amitai Etzioni, "Going Soft on Corporate Crime," *Wilmington News Journal*, April 15, 1990, p. G1.

74. Joseph E. Murphy, "Protections, Incentives for Self-Policing Lacking," *The National Law Journal*, March 8, 1993, p. S12.

75. Richard B. Schmitt, "Plan for Tough Pollution Penalties Sparks Opposition from Business," *Wall Street Journal*, March 14, 1994, p. B4; David Hanson, "New Guidelines Would Dictate Corporate Fines," *Chemical and Engineering News* 72 (February 7, 1994): 18.

BOX 1.6 PUBLIC OPINION AND ORGANIZATIONAL DEVIANCE

Public indifference is *not* among the explanations for the infrequent punishment of organizational deviance. Public opinion surveys consistently reveal strong condemnation of organizationally deviant actions, especially when the behavior causes illness, injury, or death. In a survey of members of the public, participants were asked to assign penalties to forty-one offenses: "Knowingly manufacturing and selling contaminated food that results in death" was given the third highest sentence (behind "assassination of a public official" and "killing of a police officer in the course of a terrorist hijacking of a plane"). This offense was punished more severely than "killing someone during a serious argument," "forcible rape of a stranger in a park," and "armed robbery of a bank."

Other findings also reveal strong public reaction to organizational deviance. Research has consistently shown that the general public believes that white collar criminals are treated too leniently. Similarly, the public considers corporations that harm innocent people to be more reckless and morally wrong, and deserving of more serious punishment, than individuals who commit identical acts under identical circumstances.

Sources: Peter Grabosky, John Braithwaite, and P. R. Wilson, "The Myth of Community Tolerance Toward White-Collar Crime," *Australia and New Zealand Journal of Criminology* 20 (1987): 34; Valerie P. Hans, "Factors Affecting Lay Judgments of Corporate Wrongdoing." Paper presented at the Third European Conference of Law and Psychology, University of Oxford, Oxford, England, September 19, 1992; John Braithwaite, "Challenging Just Deserts: Punishing White Collar Criminals," *Journal of Criminal Law and Criminology* 73 (1982): 723–63; Valerie P. Hans and M. David Ermann, "Responses to Corporate Versus Individual Wrongdoing," *Law and Human Behavior* 13 (1989): 151–66.

---

to sleep."[76] The institute helps corporations find the high ground. It recommends sending the CEO to the scene to signal corporate interest and concern and to ensure that the corporation's position is a visible part of the news. Papers in *Public Relations Review* agree.[77]

76. Holusha, "Exxon's Public-Relations Problem," p. Cl.

77. Samuel Coad Dyer, Jr., M. Mark Miller, and Jeff Boone, "Wire Service Coverage of the Exxon Valdez Crisis," *Public Relations Review* 17 (1991): 27–36; Falguni Sen and William G. Egelhoff, "Six Years and Counting: Learning from Crisis Management at Bhopal," *Public Relations Review* 17 (1991): 69–83.

When the crisis intervention fails, Litigation Services and Metricus, Inc.,[78] may be able to help. Sociologists, psychologists, marketers, graphic artists, and technicians at both firms predict and shape jury decisions using "pretrial opinion polls . . . profiles of 'ideal' jurors . . . mock trials and shadow juries . . . and . . . courtroom graphics."[79]

Two other factors are important. Even in the best of circumstances, investigating organizational deviance is extraordinarily complex and time-consuming because organizational deviance is typically very complex and organizations generally work hard to hide their actions.[80] During the Iran-Contra episode,[81] cash came from a variety of interesting sources, including a secret Pentagon budget, a Saudi prince, and a Texas billionaire. After careful laundering, conspirators used the money to purchase antitank missiles sent to Iran via Israel. The conspirators then laundered the profit from the illegal sales and used it to illegally buy and ship weapons for the contras. Despite exhaustive investigations, only a small fraction of the overall conspiracy has been brought to light.

Equally important, punishment is difficult to assign fairly. Should attention be directed at the people who committed the deviance for the organization, or at the organization itself? Individuals claim that they should not be punished because the organization pressured or directed them to act as they did. Using this approach, student athletes who remain eligible by cheating on examinations and submitting fraudulent summer school courses, point to the extraordinary time commitments that their sports require.[82]

78. American Sociological Association, *Employment Bulletin*, February, 1995, p. 6, contained an opening for a position at Metricus, Inc.; Junda Woo, "Legal Beat," *Wall Street Journal*, April 14, 1993, p. B1; Stephen J. Adler, "Consultants Dope Out the Mysteries of Jurors for Clients Being Sued," *Wall Street Journal*, October 24, 1989, p. A1. Also see www.preview.com/solutions/litigationservices.

79. Adler, "Consultants Dope," p. A1.

80. Michael Benson, William J. Maakestad, Francis T. Cullen, and Gilbert Geis, "District Attorneys and Corporate Crime." Paper presented at the annual meeting of the American Society of Criminology, Montreal, 1987.

81. Weiner, *Blank Check*, pp. 199–213

82. Sperber, *College Sports*, pp. 302–6; Peter Golenbock, *Personal Fouls: The Broken Promises and Shattered Dreams of Big Money Basketball at Jim Valvano's North Carolina State* (New York: Carroll and Graf, 1989), pp. 167–8: Bendedict, *Public Heroes, Private Felons*, p. 216; Murray Sperber, *Onward to Victory: The Creation of Modern College Sports* (New York: H. Holt, 1998).

On the other hand, corporations, universities, and governmental agencies argue that an entire organization should not be punished for the actions of a few "bad apples" who deliberately or carelessly misunderstand what is being asked of them. Universities under NCAA investigation for improper payments to student athletes ask for leniency on the grounds that a handful of overzealous alumni boosters are responsible.[83]

In the end, though, punishment must be directed at either individuals or organizations, for there are no other choices. We therefore conclude by looking first at punishing individuals and then at punishing organizations.

Punishing Individuals.   Punishment seldom is directed at the people responsible for organizational deviance. When a tire-making machine at Bridgestone's Dayton, Ohio, factory crushed Robert Julian to death, OSHA fined the corporation for its "unjustifiable and offensive" failure to provide padlocks and warning signs ("lockout/tagout") to secure equipment before employees get in them to make repairs.[84] No corporate officials were prosecuted. And when a scrap metal compaction and cutting machine sliced Mario Barraza in half while he was working inside, OSHA took no action against managers of Acme Iron and Metal of Albuquerque, New Mexico. The company was merely fined for the absence of lockout/tagout equipment.[85]

Marshall Clinard (see Box 1.7) and Peter Yeager's data indicate that reluctance to direct attention to the individuals responsible for organizational actions has long existed. Professors Clinard and Yeager report that only 1.5 percent of all federal enforcement efforts directed at corporations in 1975 and 1976 produced a conviction of a corporate officer.[86] Jail sentences for those convicted of offenses in the course of "normal" business activity rarely exceeded 30 days, and monetary fines generally were small.

83. Frederick C. Klein, "No Bowl for Auburn," *Wall Street Journal*, November 22, 1993, p. A12.

84. Kevin G. Salwen, "Bridgestone Unit is Fined $7.5 Million by Labor Department in Worker Death," *Wall Street Journal*, April 19, 1994, p. A4.

85. Barbara Marsh, "Workers at Risk: Chance of Getting Hurt Is Generally Far Higher at Smaller Companies," *Wall Street Journal*, February 2, 1994, p. Al.

86. Marshall B. Clinard and Peter C. Yeager, *Illegal Corporate Behavior* (Washington, D.C.: U.S. Government Printing Office, 1979).

BOX 1.7 MARSHALL B. CLINARD

Marshall B. Clinard received his Ph.D. in sociology from the University of Chicago in 1941 and is now emeritus professor of sociology at the University of Wisconsin. He currently holds, as well, a distinguished research professorship in sociology at the University of New Mexico.

Professor Clinard has made four distinctive contributions to the study of white-collar and corporate crime. The first was a 1952 book entitled *The Black Market: A Study of White Collar Crime*. In this book, Professor Clinard examined corporate violations of price regulations during World War II. He reported that even during times of national emergency, corporations did not hesitate to maximize their profits illegally.

In 1980, Professor Clinard and his colleague's important book *Corporate Crime* was published. It revealed that in 1975 and 1976 the nation's 582 largest corporations had accumulated 1,553 violations of federal law. Of the 582 corporations, 350 (60.1 percent) had at least 1 violation, and of those with at least 1 violation, the average was 4.4 per corporation. Professor Clinard and his colleagues thus established that corporate crime was just as common as when it was first studied by Professor Sutherland a quarter of a century earlier.

Professor Clinard's 1983 book *Corporate Ethics and Crime* probed the origins of corporate crime by conducting lengthy interviews with 68 retired middle-management executives of Fortune 500 corporations. Not surprisingly, these middle-level managers portrayed corporate crimes as determined by top managers who pushed too hard and made demands that could be met only by breaking the law.

Professor Clinard's most recent contribution is his 1990 book entitled *Corporate Corruption,* about the many ways in which major corporations abuse their enormous power. Professor Clinard recounts familiar and important examples, along with those that are less well known, in order to reveal patterns of corporate corruption.

Sources: Marshall B. Clinard, *The Black Market: A Study of White Collar Crime* (New York: Holt, Rinehart and Winston, 1952); Marshall B. Clinard and Peter C. Yeager, with the collaboration of Ruth Blackburn Clinard, *Corporate Crime* (New York: Free Press, 1980); Marshall B. Clinard, *Corporate Ethics and Crime* (Beverly Hills, CA: Sage, 1983); Marshall B. Clinard, *Corporate Corruption: The Abuse of Power* (New York: Praeger, 1990).

Some individuals are punished, although in the instances we have isolated the punishment has been meted out by state courts rather than federal agencies. When Stefan Golab died in 1983 from inhaling cyanide gas at the now-closed Film Recovery Systems plant in Elk Grove Village, Illinois, a state court found officials guilty of homicide two years later. This "marked the first prosecution of individual corporate officials for a work-related employee death."[87] The convictions, however, were overturned and the case was finally scheduled for a second trial in 1993. Before the trial began, all three targets of the second prosecution pleaded guilty to involuntary manslaughter. Two were sentenced to prison while the third was sentenced to probation.[88]

Similarly, in the wake of the fire that killed 25 and injured 56 at the Imperial Food Products factory in Hamlet, North Carolina, in 1992 (please see Selection 14) three corporate officials were charged in state court with homicide, including the owner and his son.[89] The owner, Emmett Roe, pleaded guilty to involuntary manslaughter in exchange for the dropping of the charges against his son and the other corporate official, and was sentenced to 20 years in prison. Mr. Roe was paroled in April 1997 after serving four and one-half years of his 20-year sentence, an average of slightly more than two months for each of the 25 deaths he admitted causing.[90]

Punishing Organizations. Organizations cannot be imprisoned, and they rarely are given "death sentences"[91] forcing them to disband. The commonly imposed punishments are monetary, including regulatory fines, criminal fines, and private damage suits. For the most part, these financial penalties fail to exceed or even equal the gains from corporate violations of the law. Thus, the Sentencing Commis-

---

87. Dana Milbank and James P. Miller, "Legal Beat," *Wall Street Journal*, September 9, 1993, p. B7. Also see William Presecky, "3rd Guilty Plea in Worker's Death," *Chicago Tribune*, September 10, 1993, p. 2L; Garth L. Magnum, "Murder in the Workplace: Criminal Prosecution v. Regulatory Enforcement," *Labor Law Journal* 39 (1988): 220–31; William J. Maakestad, "States's Attorneys Stalk Corporate Murderers," *Business and Society Review* 56 (1986): 21–25.

88. Presecky, "3rd Guilty Plea."

89. "Meat-Plant Owner Pleads Guilty In a Blaze That Killed 25 People," *The New York Times*, September 15, 1992, p. A20; Laurie M. Grossman, "Owner Sentenced to Nearly 20 Years Over Plant Fire," *Wall Street Journal*, September 15, 1992, p. B2; "Chicken Plant Operators Indicted," *The New York Times*, March 10, 1992, p. A14.

90. North Carolina State Government News Service, *The Insider* V. 5 No. 74 (April 18, 1997): 6. Also available at www.ncinsider.com/insider/1997/april/insd0418.

91. For an exception see "Corporate Death Sentence," *Wall Street Journal*, May 20, 1994, p. B6.

sion found that federal courts fined only two corporations in its sample more than $500,000. The average fine was $141,000.[92]
This seems like a lot of money, and it is for most individuals. But it is insignificant for most corporations. To get a sense of the impact of an average fine for a corporation, we calculated the equivalent fine for a person earning $35,000 per year.[93] If a "small" corporation with annual sales of $600 million—about one-tenth of Apple Computer sales in 1999—were fined $141,000, it would be the equivalent of $8 for a person earning $35,000.

Some laws impose penalties that appear far greater than the ones we have examined thus far. The Sherman Antitrust Act[94] permits civil suits by victims for financial damages because of price-fixing. The experiences of the corporations convicted in the school milk price-fixing conspiracies show how a corporation can usually treat criminal penalties and civil fines as little more than minor costs of doing business for one of its many operations.[95] Consider Borden. Between 1987 and 1990, Borden paid slightly over $21 million in criminal penalties to the courts and civil fines to the school districts it victimized.[96] During those same years, however, Borden's total operating revenues were $28.9 billion,[97] making the criminal and civil fines the equivalent of $101.43 for a person earning $35,000 per year during each of those years.

Some Exceptions.   There are exceptions involving actions so unusual that they yield significant, but not necessarily lasting, financial and other consequences for large organizations. Union Carbide's experience in the wake of the deaths and injuries in Bhopal, India, is

92. Mark A. Cohen, "Corporate Crime and Punishment: A Study of Social Harm and Sentencing Practice in the Federal Courts," *American Criminal Law Review* 26 (1989): 605–60.

93. Our comparison is based on one first advanced by Professor Gilbert Geis. See Selection 6, where Professor Geis observes that for "General Electric, a half million dollar loss was no more unsettling than a $3 parking fine would be to a . . . [person] . . . earning $175,000 a year."

94. Ermann and Lundman. *Corporate Deviance*, pp. 85–86.

95. "U.S. Charges Borden Again," *The New York Times*, October 10, 1993, p. D6; "Borden Milk-Bidding Settlement," *Wall Street Journal*, March 26, 1992, p. A4; "School Milk Bid-Rigging Probe Spreads," *Washington Post*, September 6, 1991, p. A9; "Southland Corp., Borden Inc. Admit Guilt in Milk Case," *Wall Street Journal*, March 2, 1990, p. C2.

96. Ibid.

97. Standard and Poor's, *Standard and Poor's Industry Surveys* (New York: Standard and Poor's, 1993), p. F40.

one example, and the *Exxon Valdez* environmental disaster in Alaska is a second.

In December 1984, Union Carbide's Bhopal plant released a deadly cloud of liquid methyl isocyanate that quickly spread through nearby residences.[98] The Indian government initially put the official toll at 3,415 killed and 200,000 injured, 50,000 of them seriously. Others estimates ranged up to 8,000 deaths and 400,000 injuries.[99] Bhopal is easily the "world's worst industrial accident."[100]

Initially, Union Carbide was barely hanging on.[101] Following Bhopal, the firm's profit decreased and its stock took a nosedive. In 1985, GAF tried to buy Union Carbide because its stock was underpriced. To repel the GAF takeover and prevent others, Union Carbide made its stock unattractive by selling Prestone antifreeze. Eveready batteries, and Glad Bags, and by deliberately going deeply in debt by buying back its own stock. In February 1989, Union Carbide settled most claims out of court, including those by the Indian government, for $480 million, and sold its share of the Indian subsidiary to the Indian government. For Union Carbide, Bhopal was a human tragedy of unprecedented proportions and a corporate catastrophe. By the early 1990s, there was real doubt that the corporation could survive.[102]

By the mid-1990s, however, Union Carbide was in the midst of a remarkable corporate resurgence. Its stock was one of the top per-

---

98. Warren Getler, "Union Carbide Shares Are Gobbled Up by Insiders," *Wall Street Journal*, January 4, 1995, p. C1: Molly Moore: "Bhopal Gas Leak Victims Caught in Cycle of Despair," *Washington Post*, September 13, 1993, p. Al; Edward Felsenthal, "Legal Beat," *Wall Street Journal*, January 27, 1993, p. B2; Robert D. Kennedy, "Kicked Us When We're Down, but Getting Up (Letter to the Editor)," *Wall Street Journal*, March 6, 1992, p. A9 (Mr. Kennedy was CEO of Union Carbide at the time he wrote this letter and he wrote in response to the next article): Scott McMurray, "Wounded Giant: Union Carbide Offers Some Sober Lessons In Crisis Management," *Wall Street Journal*, January 28, 1992, p. Al; Clinard, *Corporate Corruption*, pp. 137–41; Alyssa A. Lappen, "Breaking Up Is Hard to Do" *Forbes*, December 10,1990, pp. 102–6; Subrata N. Chakravarty, "The Ghost Returns," *Forbes*, December 10, 1990, p. 108; Russel Mokhiber. *Corporate Crime and Violence: Business Power and the Abuse of the Public Trust* (San Francisco: Sierra Club Books, 1988), pp. 86–195; Dan Kurzman, *A Killing Wind* (New York: McGraw-Hill, 1987): David Weir, *The Bhopal Syndrome* (San Francisco: Sierra Club Books, 1987).

99. Moore, "Bhopal."

100. Clinard, *Corporate Corruption*, p. 87.

101. Standard and Poor's Corporation, *Standard NYSE Stock Reports* (New York: Standard and Poor's Corporation, 1991), p. 2,276; Lappen, "Breaking Up"; Chakravarty, "The Ghost."

102. McMurray, "Wounded Giant."

formers among the 30 corporations that make up the Dow Jones
Industrial Average (DJIA).[103] Its top-level administrators were buying Union Carbide shares in anticipation of even better corporate
profits.[104] Despite Bhopal-related financial hits, Union Carbide was
once again a financially healthy major corporation.

As the century ended, economic forces (including the rise of
an Internet economy and increased raw material costs) had caused
the company to experience lagging profits, replacement by a
high-tech firm in the DJIA, and a stockholder vote in December
1999 to merge with the much larger Dow Chemical Company.[105]
Seven Union Carbide Indian employees were on trial in Bhopal
for negligence, and the company's Web page prominently displayed its policies and successes in "employee health and safety,"
"emergency response," and other aspects of its "Responsible Care"
program.

In Bhopal,[106] meanwhile, 10,000 deaths were now attributed to
the accident, local resources still inadequately served the ill, clinics
to help victims cope with their breathing and other problems were
planned, and about one-third of the money Union Carbide paid to
settle claims still had not been dispersed.[107]

Exxon's experiences following the Valdez accident also are
mixed.[108] On March 24, 1989, the tanker *Valdez* veered off course,
hit Bligh Reef, and dumped almost 11 million gallons of crude oil
into the waters of Alaska's Prince William Sound. From day one,
Valdez was a public relations nightmare for Exxon.[109] Its CEO,
Lawrence Rawl, failed to go to the scene, and the disaster's envi-

103. Getler, "Union Carbide's Shares."

104. Ibid.

105. www.unioncarbide.com.

106. Moore, "Bhopal."

107. Ibid.

108. Caleb Solomon, "Exxon Is Told to Pay $5 Billion for Valdez Spill," *Wall Street Journal*,
September 19, 1994, p. A3; Schneider, "Judge Rejects"; Allanna Sullivan, Charles McCoy, and
Paul M. Barrett, "Judge Rejects Exxon Alaska-Spill Pact; Net Income Rose 75% in First Quarter," *Wall Street Journal*, April 25, 1991, p. A3: "Judge Rejects 'Exxon Valdez' Settlement," *Columbus Dispatch*, April 25, 1991, p. 3; Peter Nutty, "Exxon's Problem: Not What You Think,"
Fortune, April 23, 1990, pp. 202–4; Bryan Hodgson, "Alaska's Big Oil Spill: Can the Wilder-
ness Heal?" *National Geographic* 177 (1990): 4–42.

109. Dyer, "Wire Service"; Sullivan, "Rawl Wishes"; Holusha. "Exxon's Public-Relations
Problem."

ronmental consequences therefore dominated the news. Exxon went from sixth on the Fortune list of Most Admired Corporations to 110th, and industry sources described morale inside the giant corporation as very low.[110] Exxon's future was never in doubt, however. The Valdez spill held down profits and stock prices for a time, but it left operations unaffected.[111] There were no unfriendly takeover attempts, and Exxon accumulated no unusual debts. The corporation did take some financial hits. By April 1990, Exxon had paid $2 billion in penalties and cleanup costs.[112] A 1994 decision directed Exxon to pay an additional $5 billion in punitive damages. As we write this entering the second decade after the accident, the company continues its appeals and "the 40,000 people expected to share . . . punitive damages have yet to see a cent."[113] And the company had successfully completed its merger with Mobil to form ExxonMobil over objections, among others, by Valdez plaintiffs.

Summary

This essay on corporate and governmental deviance made four major points. First, large organizations can usefully be conceived of as acting units entirely capable of deviance. Second, large organizations can and do originate deviant actions. Third, episodes of corporate and governmental deviance follow some predictable patterns. Fourth, reactions to the deviant behavior of big business and big government vary but rarely involve lasting financial and other penalty impacts.

Our introductions and the readings that now follow expand and illustrate each of these points.

---

110. Nutty, "Exxon's Problem," p. 202.

111. Standard and Poor's, *Standard*, p. 846F; Nutty, "Exxon's Problem," p. 203.

112. Nutty, "Exxon's Problem."

113. Stephanie Anderson Forest, "A Gusher from Valdez Funds?" *Business Week*, no. 3,620 (March 15. 1999), p. 6. Also see Sullivan et al., "Judge Rejects 'Exxon Valdez' Settlement;" Solomon. "Exxon Is Told;" and www.exxonmobil.com/news/valdez.

II
Scholarly Foundations

Editors' Introduction

The readings in this section establish the scholarly foundations of the study of corporate and governmental deviance. Selection 2, "The Criminaloid," by Professor Edward Alsworth Ross (1866–1951) is one of the earliest statements (1907) by a sociologist on the deviant actions of powerful people and the organizations they control. Professor Ross defines criminaloids as powerful people whose actions are harmful but lack the "brimstone smell" of commonly recognized harms associated with conventional crimes. They are bribe givers and bribe takers, tax dodgers, and the crafty constructors of large organizations that prosper from a variety of deviant actions.

Selection 3, "White Collar Crime" is from the uncut version of *White Collar Crime* (first published in 1949) by Edwin H. Sutherland (1883–1950). Professor Sutherland coined the term "white-collar crime" and was one of the first sociologists to draw attention to and document corporations' frequent violations of the law. His ideas and data were so novel when first presented that they gained front-page attention in *The New York Times*. Consider why. Professor Sutherland reported that seventy of the nation's largest corporations had been convicted of a total of 980 illegal actions, and of those with at least one conviction, the average was four.

Selection 4, "Corporate Crime," written by Marshall B. Clinard and Peter C. Yeager, examines cases brought by federal agencies against the nation's 582 largest corporations in 1975 and 1976. Despite the much-shorter time period under examination when compared with Professor Sutherland, Professors Clinard and Yeager report that 60 percent of the corporations had at least one action brought against them and of those with at least one case,

the average was 4.4 cases. Their data therefore mirror Professor
Sutherland's.

   In Selection 5, "Organizational Actors and the Irrelevance of
Persons," James S. Coleman (1926–1995) begins by tracing the
growth of large organizations in contemporary society. He then
examines the great power of organizations as compared to individuals and emphasizes that corporate actors are wholly independent
of the replaceable people who occupy positions in them. Professor
Coleman thus directs our attention to the corporate and governmental actors that are the focus of the remainder of this book.

Annotated Bibliography

Barker, Thomas, and Julian Roebuck. *An Empirical Typology of Police Cor-
     ruption: A Study in Organizational Deviance.* Springfield, Ill.: Thomas,
     1973. An early examination of the concept of organizational devi-
     ance.
Bernard, Thomas J. "The Historical Development of Corporate Criminal
     Liability." *Criminology* 22 (1984): 3–17. Traces the development of
     the legal doctrine that corporations can be held liable for criminal
     actions.
Blankenship, Michael B., ed. *Understanding Corporate Criminality.* New
     York: Garland, 1993. A good collection of scholarly papers about
     corporate crime.
Coleman, James S. *Power and the Structure of Society.* New York: Norton,
     1974. Details the emergence of organizational actors and the im-
     plications for individuals.
———. *Foundations of Social Theory.* Cambridge: The Belknap Press of
     Harvard University Press, 1990. About rational choice theory, with
     a sustained examination of organizational actors (see especially
     pp. 325–577).
———. "The Rational Reconstruction of Society." *American Sociological Review*
     58 (1993): 1–15. Professor Coleman's 1992 Presidential Address to
     the annual meeting of the American Sociological Association. Of-
     fers more on corporate actors and, especially, their rational recon-
     struction to better fit the needs of the individuals in them.
Pontell, Henry N., and David Sichor, ed. *Contemporary Issues in Crime and
     Criminal Justice: Essays in Honor of Gilbert Geis.* Upper Saddle River,
     N. J.: Prentice Hall, 2001. Essays in honor of Professor Gilbert Geis,
     one the leading contemporary students of white-collar crime. Most
     of the essays focus on recent episodes of white-collar and organi-
     zational deviance.

Shover, Neal, and John Paul Wright, ed. *Crimes of Privilege: Readings in White-Collar Crime*. New York: Oxford University Press, 2000. Collection of mostly scholarly essays on white-collar crime and its control, organized from a rational-choice perspective.

Snider, Laureen. *Bad Business: Corporate Crime in Canada*. Scarborough, Ontario: Nelson Canada, 1993. Emphasizes competing explanations of corporate crime, and Canadian attempts to control it.

Tonry, Michael, and Albert J. Reiss, Jr. *Beyond the Law: Crime in Complex Organizations*. Chicago: University of Chicago Press, 1993. Case-oriented discussion of organizational crimes.

2

The Criminaloid

An Early Sociologist Examines Deviance by Powerful
People and Their Organizations

Edward Alsworth Ross

The Edda has it that during Thor's visit to the giants he is challenged to lift a certain gray cat. "Our young men think it nothing but play." Thor puts forth his whole strength, but can at most bend the creature's back and lift one foot. On leaving, however, the mortified hero is told the secret of his failure. "The cat—ah! we were terror-stricken when we saw one paw off the floor; for that is the Midgard serpent which, tail in mouth, girds and keeps up the created world."

How often today the prosecutor who tries to lay by the heels some notorious public enemy is baffled by a mysterious resistance! The thews of Justice become as water; her sword turns to lath. Though the machinery of the law is strained askew, the evildoer remains erect, smiling, unscathed. At the end, the mortified champion of the law may be given to understand that, like Thor, he was contending with the established order, that he had unwittingly laid hold on a pillar of society and was therefore pitting himself against the reigning organization in local finance and politics.

The real weakness in the moral position of Americans is not their attitude toward the plain criminal, but their attitude toward the quasicriminal. The shocking leniency of the public in judging conspicuous persons who have thriven by antisocial practices is not due, as many imagine, to sycophancy. Let a prominent man commit some offense in bad odor and the multitude flings its stones with right goodwill. The social lynching of the self-made magnate who put away his faded, toilworn wife for the sake of a soubrette proves that the props of the old morality have not rotted through. Sex righ-

Reprinted from *The Atlantic Monthly* 99 (January 1907), pp. 44–50.

teousness continues to be thus stiffly upheld simply because man has not invented *new* ways of wronging woman. So long ago were sex sins recognized and branded that the public, feeling sure of itself, lays on with promptness and emphasis. The slowness of this same public in lashing other kinds of transgression betrays, not sycophancy or unthinking admiration of success, but perplexity. The prosperous evildoers that bask undisturbed in popular favor have been careful to shun—or seem to shun—the familiar types of wickedness. Overlooked in Bible and prayer book, their obliquities lack the brimstone smell. Surpass as their misdeeds may in meanness and cruelty, there has not yet been time enough to store up strong emotion about them; and so the sight of them does not let loose the flood of wrath and abhorrence that rushes down upon the long-attainted sins.

The immunity enjoyed by the perpetrator of new sins has brought into being a class for which we may coin the term "criminaloid." (Like "asteroid," "crystalloid," "anthropoid," the term "criminaloid" is Latin–Greek, to be sure, but so is "sociology.") By this we designate those who prosper by flagitious practices which have not yet come under the effective ban of public opinion. Often, indeed, they are guilty in the eyes of the law; but since they are not culpable in the eyes of the public and in their own eyes, their spiritual attitude is not that of the criminal. The lawmaker may make their misdeeds crimes, but, so long as morality stands stock-still in the old tracks, they escape both punishment and ignominy. Unlike their low-browed cousins, they occupy the cabin rather than the steerage of society. Relentless pursuit hems in the criminals, narrows their range of success, denies them influence. The criminaloids, on the other hand, encounter but feeble opposition, and, since their practices are often more lucrative than the authentic crimes, they distance their more scrupulous rivals in business and politics and reap an uncommon worldly prosperity.

Of greater moment is the fact that the criminaloids lower the tone of the community. The criminal slinks in the shadow, menacing our purses but not our ideals; the criminaloid, however, does not belong to the half-world. Fortified by his connections with "legitimate business," "the regular party organization," perhaps with orthodoxy and the *bon ton*, he may even bestride his community like a Colossus. In his sight and in their own sight the old-style, square-dealing sort are as grasshoppers. Do we not hail him as "a man who does things," make him director of our banks and railroads, trustee of our hospitals and libraries? When Prince Henry visits us, do we not put him on the reception committee? He has far more initial weight in the community than has the arraigning clergyman, editor, or prosecutor. From his example and his excuses spreads a noxious influence that tarnishes the ideals of ingenuous youth on the threshold of active life. To put the soul of this pagan through a Bertillon system and set forth its marks of easy identification is, therefore, a sanitary measure demanded in the interest of public health.

The key to the criminaloid is not evil impulse, but moral insensibility. The director who speculates in the securities of his corporation, the banker who lends his depositors' money to himself under divers corporate aliases, the railroad official who grants a secret rebate for his private graft, the builder who hires walking delegates to harass his rivals with causeless strikes, the labor leader who instigates a strike in order to be paid for calling it off, the publisher who bribes his textbooks into the schools, these reveal in their faces nothing of the wolf or vulture. Nature has not foredoomed them to evil by a double dose of lust, cruelty, malice, greed, or jealousy. They are not degenerates tormented by monstrous cravings. They want nothing more than we all want—money, power, consideration—in a word, success; but they are in a hurry and they are not particular as to the means.

The criminaloid prefers to prey on the anonymous public. He is touchy about the individual victim and, if faced down, will even make him reparation out of the plunder gathered at longer range. Too squeamish and too prudent to practice treachery, brutality, and violence himself, he takes care to work through middlemen. Conscious of the antipodal difference between doing wrong and getting it done, he places out his dirty work. With a string of intermediaries between himself and the toughs who slug voters at the polls or the gang of navvies who break other navvies' heads with shovels on behalf of his electric line, he is able to keep his hands sweet and his boots clean. Thus he becomes a consumer of custom-made crime, a client of criminals, oftener a maker of criminals by persuading or requiring his subordinates to break the law. Of course, he must have "responsible" agents as values to check the return flow of guilt from such proceedings. He shows them the goal, provides the money, insists on "results," but vehemently declines to know the foul methods by which alone his understrappers can get these "results." Not to bribe, but to employ and finance the briber; not to lie, but to admit to your editorial columns "paying matter"; not to commit perjury, but to hire men to homestead and make over to you claims they have sworn were entered in good faith and without collusion; not to cheat, but to promise a "rake-off" to a mysterious go-between in case your just assessment is cut down; not to rob on the highway, but to make the carrier pay you a rebate on your rival's shipments; not to shed innocent blood, but to bribe inspectors to overlook your neglect to install safety appliances—such are the ways of the criminaloid. He is a buyer rather than a practitioner of sin, and his middlemen spare him unpleasant details.

Secure in his quilted armor of lawyer-spun sophistries, the criminaloid promulgates an ethics which the public hails as a disinterested contribution to the philosophy of conduct. He invokes a pseudo-Darwinism to sanction the revival of outlawed and bygone tactics of struggle. Ideals of fellowship and peace are "unscientific." To win the game with the aid of a sleeveful of aces proves one's fitness to survive. A sack of spoils is nature's patent of nobility. A fortune is a personal attribute, as truly creditable as a straight back or a symmetrical face. Poverty, like the misshapen ear of the degenerate, proves inferiority. The wholesale fleecer of trusting, workaday people is a "Napoleon," a "superman." Labor defending its daily bread must, of course, obey the law; but "business," especially the "big proposition," may free itself of such trammels in the name of a "higher law." The censurers of the criminaloid are "pinheaded disturbers" who would imitate him if they had the chance or the brains.

The criminaloid is not antisocial by nature. Nationwide is the zone of devastation of the adulterator, the rebater, the commercial freebooter, the fraud promoter, the humbug healer, the law-defying monopolist. Statewide is the burnt district of the corrupt legislator, the corporation-owned judge, the venal inspector, the bought bank examiner, the mercenary editor. But draw near the sinner and he whitens. If his fellowmen are wronged clear to his doorstep, he is criminal, not criminaloid. For the latter loses his sinister look, even takes on a benign aspect, as you come close. Within his home town, his ward, his circle, he is perhaps a good man, if judged by the simple old-time tests. Very likely he keeps his marriage vows, pays his debts, "mixes" well, stands by his friends, and has a contracted kind of public spirit. He is ready enough to rescue imperiled babies, protect maidens, or help poor widows. He is unevenly moral: oak in the family and clan virtues, but basswood in commercial and civic ethics. In some relations he is more sympathetic and generous than his critics, and he resents with genuine feeling the scorn of men who happen to have specialized in virtues other than those that appeal to him. Perhaps his point of honor is to give bribes, but not to take them; perhaps it is to "stay bought," that is, not to sell out to both sides at once.

This type is exemplified by the St. Louis boodler, who after accepting $25,000 to vote against a certain franchise was offered a larger sum to vote for it. He did so, but returned the first bribe. He was asked on the witness stand why he had returned it. "Because it wasn't mine!" he exclaimed, flushing with anger. "I hadn't earned it."

Seeing that the conventional sins are mostly close-range inflictions, whereas the long-range sins, being recent in type, have not yet been branded, the criminaloid receives from his community the credit for the close-in good he does, but not the shame of the remote evil he works.

Sometimes it is time instead of space that divides him from his victims. It is tomorrow's morrow that will suffer from the patent soothing syrup, the factory toil of infants, the grabbing of public lands, the butchery of forests, and the smuggling-in of coolies. In such a case, the short-sighted many exonerate him; only the far-sighted few mark him for what he is. Or it may be a social interval that leaves him his illusion of innocence. Like Robin Hood, the criminaloid spares his own sort and finds his quarry on another social plane. The labor grafter, the political "striker," and the blackmailing society editor prey upward; the franchise grabber, the fiduciary thief, and the frenzied financier prey downward. In either case, the sinner moves in an atmosphere of friendly approval and can still any smart of conscience with the balm of adulation.

It is above all the political criminaloid who is social. We are assured that the king of the St. Louis boodlers was "a good fellow— by nature, at first, then by profession. . . . Everywhere Big Ed went, there went a smile also and encouragement for your weakness, no matter what it was." The head of the Minneapolis ring was "a good fellow—a genial, generous reprobate . . . the best-loved man in the community . . . especially good to the poor." "Stars-and-Stripes Sam" was the nickname of a notorious looter of Philadelphia, who amassed influence by making "a practice of going to lodges, associations, brotherhoods, Sunday schools, and all sorts of public and private meetings, joining some, but making at all speeches patriotic and sentimental." The corrupt boss of another plundered city is reported to be "a charming character," possessing "goodness of heart and personal charm," and loved for his "genial, hearty kindness." He shrank from robbing anybody, but was equal, however, to robbing everybody. Of this type was Tweed, who had a "good heart," donated $50,000 to the poor of New York, and was sincerely loved by his clan.

It is now clear why hot controversy rages about the unmasked criminalold. His home town, political clan, or social class insists that he is a good man maligned, that his detractors are purblind or jealous. The criminaloid is really a borderer between the camps of good and evil, and this is why he is so interesting. To run him to earth and brand him, as long ago pirates and traitors were branded, is the crying need of our time. For this Anak among malefactors, working unchecked in the rich field of sinister opportunities opened up by latter-day conditions, is society's most dangerous foe, more redoubtable by far than the plain criminal, because he sports the livery of virtue and operates on a Titanic scale. Every year that sees him pursue in insolent triumph his nefarious career raises up a host of imitators and hurries society toward moral bankruptcy.

The criminaloid practices a protective mimicry of the good. Because so many good men are pious, the criminalold covets a high seat in the temple as a valuable private asset. Accordingly he is often to be found in the assemblies of the faithful, zealously exhorting and bearing witness. Onward thought he must leave to honest men; his line is strict orthodoxy. The upright may fall slack in devout observances, but he cannot afford to neglect his church connection. He needs it in his business. Such simulation is easier because the godly are slow to drive out the open-handed sinner who eschews the conventional sins. Many deprecate prying into the methods of any brother "having money or goods ostensibly his own or under a title not disapproved by the proper tribunals." They have, indeed, much warrant for insisting that the saving of souls rather than the salvation of society is the true mission of the church.

The old Hebrew prophets, to be sure, were intensely alive to the social effect of sin. They clamor against "making the ephah small and the shekel great," falsifying the balances, "treading upon the poor." "Sensational," almost "demagogic," is their outcry against those who "turn aside the stranger in his right," "take a bribe," "judge not the cause of the fatherless," "oppress the hireling in his wages," "take increase," "withhold the pledge," "turn aside the poor in the gate from their right," "take away the righteousness of the righteous from him." No doubt their stubborn insistence that God wants "mercy and not sacrifice," despises feast days, delights not in burnt offerings, will not hear the melody of viols, but desires judgment to "run down as waters and righteousness as a mighty stream," struck their contemporaries as extreme. Over against their antiquated outlook may be set the larger view that our concern should be for the sinner rather than the sinned against. He is in peril of hell fire whereas the latter risks nothing more serious than loss, misery, and death. After all, sin's overshadowing effect is the pollution of the sinner's soul; and so it may be more Christian not to scourge forth the traffickers from the temple, but to leave them undisturbed where good seed may perchance fall upon their souls.

Likewise, the criminaloid counterfeits the good citizen. He takes care to meet all the conventional tests—flag worship, old-soldier sentiment, observance of all the national holidays, perfervid patriotism, party regularity and support. Full well he knows that giving a fountain or a park or establishing a college chair on the Neolithic drama or the elegiac poetry of the Chaldeans will more than outweigh the dodging of taxes, the grabbing of streets, and the corrupting of city councils. Let him have his way about charters and franchises, and he will zealously support that "good government" which consists in sweeping the streets, holding down the "lid," and keeping taxes low. Nor will he fail in that scrupulous correctness of private and domestic life which confers respectability. In politics, to be sure, it is often necessary to play the "good fellow"; but in business and finance a studious conformity to the *convenances* is of the highest importance. The criminaloid must perforce seem sober and chaste, "a good husband and a kind father." If in this respect he offend, his hour of need will find him without support, and some callow reporter or district attorney will bowl him over like any vulgar criminal.

The criminaloid, therefore, puts on the whole armor of the good. He stands having his loins girt about with religiosity and wearing the breastplate of respectability. His feet are shod with ostentatious philanthropy; his head is encased in the helmet of spread-eagle patriotism. Holding in his left hand the buckler of worldly success and in his right the sword of "influence," he is "able to withstand in the evil day and, having done all, to stand."

The criminaloid plays the support of his local or special group against the larger society. The plain criminal can do himself no good by appealing to his "Mollies," "Larrikins," or "Mafiosi," for they have no social standing. The criminaloid, however, identifies himself with some legitimate group, and when arraigned he calls upon his group to protect its own. The politically influential Western land thieves stir up the slumbering local feeling against the "impertinent meddlers" of the forestry service and the land office. Safe behind the judicial dictum that "bribery is merely a conventional crime," the boodlers denounce their indicter as "blackening the fair name" of their state, and cry, "Stand up for the grand, old commonwealth of Nemaha!" The city boss harps artfully on the chord of local spirit and summons his bailiwick to rebuke the upstate reformers who would unhorse him. The law-breaking saloon keeper rallies merchants with the cry that enforcement of the liquor laws "hurts business." The labor grafter represents his exposure as a capitalist plot and calls upon all Truss Riveters to "stand pat" and "vindicate" him with a re-election. When a pious buccaneer is brought to bay, the Reverend Simon Magus thus sounds the denominational bugle: "Brother Barabbas is a loyal Newlight and a generous supporter of the Newlight Church. This vicious attack upon him is, therefore, a covert thrust at the Newlight body and ought to be resented by all the brethren." High finance, springing to the help of self-confessed thieves, meets an avenging public in this wise: "The integrity trust not only seeks with diabolical skill a reputation to blast, but, once blasted, it sinks into it wolfish fangs and gloats over the result of its fiendish act"—and adds, "This is not the true American spirit." Here twangs the ultimate chord! For in criminaloid philosophy it is "un-American" to wrench patronage from the hands of spoilsmen, un-American to deal federal justice to rascals of state importance, un-American to pry into arrangements between shipper and carrier, un-American to pry the truth out of reluctant magnates. The claims of the wider community have no foe so formidable as the scared criminaloid. He is the champion of the tribal order as opposed to the civil order. By constantly stirring up on his own behalf some sort of clannishness—local, sectional, partisan, sectarian, or professional—he rekindles dying jealousies and checks the rise of the civic spirit. It is in line with this clannishness that he wants citizens to act together on a personal basis. He does not know what it is to rally around a principle. Fellow partisans are "friends." To scratch or to bolt is to "go back on your friends." The criminaloid understands sympathy and antipathy as springs of conduct, but justice strikes him as hardly human. The law is a club to rescue your friends from and to smite your enemies with, but it has no claim of its own. He expects his victims to "come back" at him if they can, but he cannot see why everything may not be "arranged," "settled out of court." Those inflexible prosecutors who hew to the line and cannot be "squared" impress him as fanatical and unearthly, as monsters who find their pleasure in making trouble for others. For to his barbarian eyes society is all a matter of "stand in."

So long as the public conscience is torpid, the criminaloid has no sense of turpitude. In the dusk and the silence, the magic of clan opinion converts his misdeeds into something rich and strange. For the clan lexicon tells him that a bribe is a "retaining fee," a railroad pass is a "courtesy," probing is "scandal mongering," the investigator is an "officious busybody," a protest is a "howl," critics are "foul harpies of slander," public opinion is "unreasoning clamor," regulation is "meddling," any inconvenient law is a "blue" law. As rebate giver he is sustained by the assurance that "in Rome you must do as the Romans do." As disburser of corruption funds he learns that he is but "asserting the higher law which great enterprises have the right to command." Blessed phrases these! What a lint for dressing wounds to self-respect! Often the reminiscent criminaloid, upon comparing his misdeeds with what his clansmen stood ready to justify him in doing, is fain to exclaim with Lord Clive, "By God, sir, at this moment I stand amazed at my own moderation!" When the revealing flash comes and the storm breaks, his difficulty in getting the public's point of view is really pathetic. Indeed, he may persist to the end in regarding himself as a martyr to "politics" or "yellow journalism" or the "unctuous rectitude" of personal foes or "class envy" in the guise of a moral wave.

The criminaloid flourishes until the growth of morality overtakes the growth of opportunities to prey. It is of little use to bring law abreast of the time if morality lags. In a swiftly changing society the law inevitably tarries behind need, but public opinion tarries behind need even more. Where, as with us, the statute has little force of its own, the backwardness of public opinion nullifies the work of the legislator. Every added relation among men makes new chances for the sons of Belial. Wider interdependencies breed new treacheries. Fresh opportunities for illicit gain are continually appearing, and these are eagerly seized by the unscrupulous. The years between the advent of these new sins and the general recognition of their heinousness are few or many according to the alertness of the social mind. By the time they have been branded, the onward movement of society has created a fresh lot of opportunities, which are, in their turn, exploited with impunity. It is in this gap that the criminaloid disports himself. The narrowing of this gap depends chiefly on the faithfulness of the vedettes that guard the march of humanity. If the editor, writer, educator, clergyman, or public man is zealous to reconnoiter and instant to cry aloud the dangers that present themselves in our tumultuous social advance, a regulative opinion quickly forms and the new sins soon become odious.

Now, it is the concern of the criminaloids to delay this growth of conscience by silencing the alert vedettes. To intimidate the molders of opinion so as to confine the editor to the "news," the preacher to the "simple Gospel," the public man to the "party issues," the judge to his precedents, the teacher to his textbooks, and the writer to the classic themes—such are the tactics of the criminaloids. Let them but have their way, and the prophet's message, the sage's lesson, the scholar's quest, and the poet's dream would be sacrificed to the God of Things As They Were.

3
White Collar Crime
Formulating the Concept and Providing Corporate Crime Baseline Data
Edwin H. Sutherland

[The Concept]

The thesis of this [selection], stated positively, is that persons of the upper socioeconomic class engage in much criminal behavior; that this criminal behavior differs from the criminal behavior of the lower socioeconomic class principally in the administrative procedures which are used in dealing with the offenders; and that variations in administrative procedures are not significant from the point of view of causation of crime. The causes of tuberculosis were not different when it was treated by poultices and bloodletting than when treated by streptomycin.

These violations of law by persons in the upper socioeconomic class are, for convenience, called "white collar crimes." This concept is not intended to be definitive, but merely to call attention to crimes which are not ordinarily included within the scope of criminology. White collar crime may be defined approximately as a crime committed by a person of respectability and high social status in the course of his occupation. Consequently it excludes many crimes of the upper class such as most cases of murder, intoxication, or adultery, since these are not a part of the occupational procedures. Also, it excludes the confidence games of wealthy members of the underworld, since they are not persons of respectability and high social status. . . .

[Corporate Crime Baseline Data]

In order to secure more definite information regarding the crimes of persons of the upper socioeconomic class, an attempt has been made to tabulate the decisions of courts and administrative commissions against the 70 largest manufacturing, mining, and mercantile corporations.* The 70 largest corporations used in this analysis are, with two exceptions, included in each of two lists of the 200 largest nonfinancial corporations in the United States. One of these lists was prepared by Berle and Means in 1929 and the other by the Temporary National Economic Committee in 1938. From these lists were excluded the public utility corporations, including transportation and communications corporations, and also the petroleum corporations. This left 68 corporations common to both lists. To these were added two corporations which appeared in the list for 1938 but not in the list for 1929. One of these was Standard Brands, which was organized by the merger of preexisting corporations in 1929 and had grown to the dimensions of the other large corporations by 1938. The other was Gimbel Brothers, which was not far below the other corporations in 1929, and which was added to the present list in order to secure a larger representation of mercantile corporations. The list of 70 corporations is, therefore, unselected except as to size and type of specialization, with the two exceptions mentioned, and neither of these exceptions was selected with knowledge of its rank among large corporations as to violations of laws.

The present analysis covers the life careers of the 70 corporations. The average life of these corporations is approximately 45 years, but decisions as to the date of origin are arbitrary in a few cases. The analysis, also, includes the decisions against the subsidiaries of the 70 corporations, as listed in the standard manuals, for the period these subsidiaries have been under the control of the parent corporation.

The analysis is concerned with the following types of violations of laws: restraint of trade, misrepresentation in advertising; infringe-

---

*ED NOTE: In the original version of *White Collar Crime* published in 1949, Professor Sutherland's publisher (Dryden Press) would not permit identification of the corporations for fear of being sued. The version from which you are now reading was the first time the corporations studied by Professor Sutherland were publicly identified.

ment of patent, trademarks, and copyrights; "unfair labor practices" as defined by the National Labor Relations Board and a few decisions under other labor laws; rebates; financial fraud and violation of trust; violations of war regulations; and some miscellaneous offenses. All of the cases included in the tabulation are defined as violations of law, most of them may properly be defined as crimes, and the others are closely allied to criminal behavior. . . .

The sources of information regarding these violations of law are the decisions of the federal, state, and, in a few cases, municipal courts, as published in the *Federal Reporter* and the *American State Reports*; the published decisions of the Federal Trade Commission, the Interstate Commerce Commission, the Securities and Exchange Commission, the National Labor Relations Board, and, for the period 1934–37, of the Federal Pure Food and Drug Administration. These official reports have been supplemented, as to infringement, by the reports on infringement cases listed in the *Official Gazette* of the Patent Office, and as to violations of law in general by reports of decisions in newspapers. The *New York Times* has been used, especially, because its material has been indexed since 1913. The name of each of the 70 corporations and its subsidiaries was checked against the index of each of these series of reports and of the *New York Times*.

The enumeration of decisions as reported in these sources is certainly far short of the total number of decisions against these 70 corporations. First, many of the decisions of the lower courts are not published in the series of federal and state reports, and many of them are not published in the newspapers. Second, many suits are settled out of court and no outcome is reported in the series of reports or in newspapers. The number of suits initiated against the 70 corporations which dropped out of sight after preliminary motions and were presumably settled out of court is approximately 50 percent of the number included in the tabulation in this chapter. Presumably many of these involved violations of law and could have been tabulated as such if more complete information were available. Third, the Pure Food and Drug Administration has not published its decisions by names of offenders except during the years 1924–47. Fourth, many of the decisions are indexed under names such as "The John Doe Trade Association," or "John Doe et al." Consequently, many of the 70 corporations which have been defendants in those suits were not discovered because their names did not appear in the indexes, and often were not even mentioned in the published reports. Finally, many of the subsidiaries of these corporations are not listed in the financial manuals and could not be identified for the present study.

A decision against one of the 70 corporations is the unit in this tabulation. If a decision is made in one suit against 3 of the 70 corporations, that decision is counted three times, once against each of the 3 corporations. Also, if a criminal suit and an equity suit are initiated against one corporation for essentially the same overt behavior and a decision is made against the corporation in each of those suits, two decisions are counted. This, obviously, involves some duplication. On the other hand, one decision may contain scores of counts, each of which charges a specific violation of law and, also, may refer to a policy which has been in operation for a decade or longer. These are some of the reasons why these decisions are not an accurate index of the comparative amounts of illegal behavior by the several corporations.

The term "decision" is used here to include not only the formal decisions and orders of courts, but also the decisions of administrative commissions, stipulations accepted by courts and commissions, settlements ordered or approved by the court, confiscation of food as in violation of the Pure Food Law, and, in a few cases, which will be explained in the later chapters, opinion of courts that the defendant had violated the law at an earlier time even though the court then dismissed the suit.

The enumeration of the decisions which have been discovered is presented in Table 3.1. This shows that each of the 70 large corporations has 1 or more decisions against it, with a maximum of 50. The total number of decisions is 980, and the average per corporation is 14.0. Sixty corporations have decisions against them for restraint of trade, 53 for infringement, 44 for unfair labor practices, 43 for miscellaneous offenses, 28 for misrepresentation in advertising, and 26 for rebates.

Armour & Company and Swift & Company stand at the top of the list in the total number of adverse decisions, with 50 each. General Motors has third rank with 40, and Sears Roebuck ties with Montgomery Ward for fourth rank with 39 each. These five corporations are decidedly in excess of the other corporations in the

TABLE 3.1

Decisions by Courts and Commissions against 70 Large Corporations by Types of Laws Violated

Corporation	Restraint of trade	Misrepresentation in advertising	Infringement	Unfair labor practices	Rebates	Other	Total
Allied Chemical & Dye	7	1	—	5	—	—	13
Aluminum Co. of America	4	—	1	3	3	3	14
American Can	6	—	1	—	—	1	8
American Car & Foundry	1	—	6	2	—	1	10
Amer. Radiator & Stand. San.	—	—	—	2	—	—	2
American Rolling Mills	1	—	—	3	1	—	5
American Smelting & Refin.	2	—	1	4	2	5	14
American Sugar Refining	7	—	—	—	10	6	23
American Tobacco	19	—	2	—	2	2	25
American Woolen	1	1	1	—	—	—	3
Anaconda Copper	4	—	4	2	—	7	17
Armour & Company	12	6	2	11	6	13	50
Bethlehem Steel	3	—	2	5	4	—	14
Borden	7	2	1	—	1	1	12
Chrysler	1	3	1	1	1	2	9
Corn Products	3	4	1	—	1	1	10
Crane	3	—	1	1	1	—	6
Crown Zellerbach	5	—	—	—	—	—	5
Deere	—	—	2	2	—	—	4
DuPont	7	—	4	3	—	—	14
Eastman Kodak	5	—	3	—	—	—	8
Firestone	1	1	4	2	—	—	8
Ford	1	2	8	15	1	1	28
General Electric	13	2	9	—	—	1	25

TABLE 3.1 (continued)

Corporation	Restraint of trade	Misrepresentation in advertising	Infringement	Unfair labor practices	Rebates	Other	Total
General Motors	6	2	22	9	—	1	40
Gimbel	—	12	11	—	—	—	23
Glen Alden Coal	5	—	—	1	1	—	7
Goodrich	1	1	2	3	—	—	7
Goodyear	1	1	4	3	—	5	14
Great A & P	8	3	—	1	—	7	19
Inland Steel	1	—	—	3	1	3	8
International Harvester	11	—	3	2	3	—	19
International Paper	2	—	2	—	2	2	8
International Shoe	—	2	—	—	—	1	3
Jones & Laughlin	1	—	—	4	1	1	7
Kennecott Copper	2	—	1	2	—	—	5
Kresge	—	1	9	1	—	7	18
Liggett & Myers	1	—	—	—	—	1	2
Loew's	22	—	6	—	—	3	31
Macy & Company	—	5	13	—	—	—	18
Marshall Field	1	2	2	3	—	—	8
Montgomery Ward	1	12	15	5	—	6	39
National Biscuit	2	—	1	—	—	2	5
National Dairy Products	8	1	1	—	1	1	12
National Lead	3	—	3	5	—	1	12

National Steel	1	—	—	2	2	1	6
Paramount	21	—	4	—	—	—	25
Phelps Dodge	3	—	1	9	—	1	14
Philadelphia & Reading Coal	6	—	1	—	—	—	7
Pittsburgh Coal	1	—	—	—	—	—	1
Pittsburgh Plate Glass	6	—	3	3	4	1	17
Procter & Gamble	1	8	1	1	—	2	13
RCA	3	1	2	1	—	1	8
Republic Steel	3	—	—	7	1	—	11
Reynolds Tobacco	1	—	—	—	—	—	1
Sears Roebuck	—	18	20	1	—	—	39
Singer Mfg. Co.	—	—	5	2	—	—	7
Standard Brands	2	1	—	—	—	—	3
Swift & Company	12	1	1	10	5	21	50
Union Carbide & Carbon	—	—	5	—	—	2	7
United Fruit	3	—	1	—	—	1	5
United Shoe Machinery	1	—	3	—	—	2	6
U.S. Rubber	6	1	1	1	—	1	10
U.S. Steel	9	2	5	2	5	3	26
Warner Bros.	21	—	3	—	—	1	25
Westinghouse Electric	10	1	5	2	—	1	19
Wheeling Steel	2	—	1	1	2	—	6
Wilson & Company	4	—	1	9	3	2	19
Woolworth	—	—	10	1	—	4	15
Youngstown	2	—	—	3	2	1	8
Total	307	97	222	158	66	130	980

number of decisions, for Loew's in sixth rank has only 31. These totals, however, are not a precise measure of the comparative amounts of illegal behavior by these corporations. Armour and Swift, for instance, are subject to the Pure Food and Drug Law, which does not apply to many other corporations. If the laws explicitly declared that any defects in shoes, electrical equipment, tobacco, films, or automobiles were misdemeanors, as they do in regard to foods, the number of decisions against the other corporations might be as high as the number against Swift and Armour. Table 3.1 shows, however, that Armour and Swift would be in the highest ranks even if decisions under the Pure Food Law were disregarded. General Motors, which stands in third rank, has more than half of the decisions against it on charges of infringements, while Sears Roebuck and Montgomery Ward have de cisions concentrated in "misrepresentation in advertising" and "infringements."

The corporations in one industry frequently cluster in one part of the distribution and have ranks which are not far apart, considering the possible spread of 70 ranks. Three meat-packing corporations in the list of 70 corporations have ranks of 1, 2, and 17. The two mail order corporations tie for fourth rank. The two dairy corporations tie for 33rd rank. The ranks of the three motion picture corporations are: Loew's 6th, and Paramount and Warner tied for 10th position. On the other hand, the corporations in one industry are sometimes scattered more widely. The four rubber manufacturers have ranks as follows: Goodyear 25th, U.S. Rubber 35th, Firestone 43rd, and Goodrich 48th. The nine steel corporations range between ninth and 58th positions.

Table 3.2 presents an analysis of the 980 decisions by types of jurisdictions of the courts and commissions which rendered the decisions. This shows that 158 decisions were made against 41 of the 70 corporations by criminal courts, 296 decisions against 57 of the corporations by civil courts, and 129 decisions against 44 corporations by courts under equity jurisdiction.This gives a total of 583 decisions which were made by courts. The administrative commissions made 361 decisions, and approximately one-fourth of these were referred to courts and were sustained by the courts. The commissions, also, confiscated goods in 25 cases as in violation of the Pure Food law. Eleven cases are tabulated as "settlements," and all

TABLE 3.2
Decisions by Courts and Commissions against 70 Large Corporations for Violations of Specified Laws, by Jurisdictions and Procedures

Corporation	Court			Commission			Total
	Criminal	Civil	Equity	Order	Confiscation	Settlement	
Allied Chemical & Dye	3	—	1	9	—	—	13
Aluminum Co. of America	3	3	3	4	—	1	14
American Can	2	3	2	2	—	—	8
American Car & Foundry	—	6	1	3	—	—	10
Amer. Radiator & Stand. San.	—	—	—	2	—	—	2
Amer. Rolling Mills	1	—	—	4	—	—	5
American Smelting	3	1	4	6	—	—	14
American Sugar	12	3	7	1	—	1	23
American Tobacco	10	10	2	1	—	2	25
American Woolen	—	1	1	1	—	—	3
Anaconda	6	4	4	3	—	—	17
Armour	18	4	4	17	7	—	50
Bethlehem	3	2	4	8	—	—	14
Borden	6	1	—	5	—	—	12
Chrysler	2	2	—	5	—	—	9
Corn Products	2	1	3	4	—	—	10
Crane	1	1	1	3	—	—	6
Crown Zellerbach	3	—	1	1	—	—	5
Deere	—	2	—	2	—	—	4
DuPont	4	4	1	5	—	—	14
Eastman	—	4	2	2	—	—	8
Firestone	—	4	—	4	—	—	8
Ford	2	8	—	18	—	—	28

TABLE 3.2 (continued)

Corporation	Court			Commission		Settlement	Total
	Criminal	Civil	Equity	Order	Confiscation		
General Electric	4	9	5	6	—	1	25
General Motors	1	23	4	12	—	—	40
Gimbel	—	12	—	11	—	—	23
Glen Alden Coal	1	—	4	2	—	—	7
Goodrich	—	2	—	5	—	—	7
Goodyear	2	5	—	5	—	2	14
Great A & P	7	4	—	6	2	—	19
Inland Steel	—	—	2	6	—	—	8
Intern. Harvester	10	3	1	5	—	—	19
Intern. Paper	3	4	1	—	—	—	8
Intern. Shoe	—	1	—	2	—	—	3
Jones & Laughlin	—	—	1	6	—	—	7
Kennecott	1	1	—	3	—	—	5
Kresge	2	9	5	2	—	—	18
Liggett & Myers	2	—	—	—	—	—	2
Loew's	—	15	13	3	—	—	31
Macy	—	13	—	5	—	—	18
Marshall Field	—	2	—	6	—	—	8
Montgomery Ward	—	18	2	19	—	—	39
National Biscuit	—	2	—	2	1	—	5
National Dairy Products	6	1	1	3	1	—	12
National Lead	1	5	1	5	—	—	12

National Steel	1	—	—	5	—	—	6
Paramount	—	11	10	4	—	—	25
Phelps Dodge	1	1	1	11	—	—	14
Phil. & Reading Coal	1	1	5	—	—	—	7
Pittsburgh Coal	—	—	—	1	—	—	1
Pittsburgh Plate	2	5	1	9	—	—	17
Procter & Gamble	1	1	1	9	—	1	13
RCA	—	3	1	3	—	1	8
Republic Steel	1	—	—	10	—	—	11
Reynolds Tobacco	1	—	—	—	—	—	1
Sears Roebuck	—	20	—	19	—	—	39
Singer	—	5	—	2	—	—	7
Standard Brands	—	—	—	3	—	—	3
Swift	18	3	6	10	13	—	50
Union Carbide & Carbon	—	6	—	1	—	—	7
United Fruit	—	3	1	—	1	—	5
United Shoe Mach.	—	5	1	—	—	—	6
U.S. Rubber	—	3	1	6	—	—	10
U.S. Steel	4	6	3	13	—	—	26
Warner Bros.	—	10	10	4	—	1	25
Westinghouse	3	6	3	6	—	1	19
Wheeling	—	1	1	4	—	—	6
Wilson	3	2	4	10	—	—	19
Woolworth	2	10	2	1	—	—	15
Youngstown	—	1	—	7	—	—	8
Total	158	296	129	361	23	11	980

of these were civil suits in which the settlements were approved or ordered by the courts. In hundreds of other cases, settlements were reached outside of courts but these have not been included in the tabulation in this chapter.

This analysis shows that approximately 16 percent of the decisions were made by criminal courts. . . . Even if the present analysis were limited to these decisions by criminal courts, it would show that 60 percent of the 70 large corporations have been convicted in criminal courts and have an average of approximately four convictions each. In many states persons with four convictions are defined by statute to be "habitual criminals." The frequency of these convictions of large corporations might be sufficient to demonstrate the fallacy in the conventional theories that crime is due to poverty or to the personal and social pathologies connected with poverty.

One of the interesting aspects of these decisions is that they have been concentrated in the last decade. The distribution of the decisions in time is presented by types of offenses in Table 3.3. In this analysis the date of the first adverse decision in a particular suit was used. The case was not counted, of course, unless the final decision was against the corporation. Relatively few cases initiated after 1944 have been included in this study. Consequently, it is approximately correct to conclude that 60 percent of the adverse decisions were rendered in the 10-year period 1935–44, while only 40 percent were rendered in the 35-year period 1900–34.

One possible explanation of this concentration is that violations of laws by large corporations have increased and are much more prevalent in recent years than in earlier years. Since several possible explanations may be equally significant, they are considered first.

First, the number of corporations has not remained constant during the period under consideration. Although the 70 corporations have had an average life of 45 years, only 63 of these corporations were in existence in 1920 and only 53 in 1910. This factor, however, seems to be relatively unimportant. A separate tabulation of the 53 corporations which originated prior to 1910 shows that 57.4 percent of the decisions were rendered in the period 1935–44, as contrasted with 59.7 percent for the entire list of 70 corporations.

Second, some of the laws which have been violated by these corporations were enacted during the last decade. The National Labor

TABLE 3.3
Decisions against 70 Large Corporations by Five-Year Periods and by Types of Laws Violated

Dates	Restraint of trade	Misrepresentation in advertising	Infringement	Unfair labor practices	Rebates	Other	Total	Percentages
1940–date	102	34	52	102	7	43	340	34.7
1935–39	59	42	59	50	15	20	245	25.0
1930–34	27	8	36	4	7	10	92	9.4
1925–29	28	1	26	—	—	23	78	8.0
1920–24	18	3	12	—	—	9	42	4.3
1915–19	20	7	5	—	6	7	45	4.6
1910–14	29	1	13	—	14	7	64	6.5
1905–09	17	—	9	1	14	5	46	4.7
1900–04	5	1	6	1	3	1	17	1.7
1890–99	2	—	1	—	—	3	6	0.6
Prior to 1890	—	—	3	—	—	2	5	0.5
Totals	307	97	222	158	66	130	980	100.0

Relations Law was enacted in 1935, with a similar law under the National Industrial Recovery Act of 1934, and decisions under this law are necessarily concentrated almost entirely in the period 1935–44. If this law is disregarded, 52.5 percent of the decisions under the other laws were made in the ten-year period 1935–44. The enactment and amendment of other laws applying to corporations provide some explanation of this concentration in the last decade. Although this influence cannot be measured with precision, it certainly accounts for a very small part of the concentration.

Third, vigorous prosecution of violations of law by corporations has been concentrated in the period since 1932. Budgets have been increased and additional assistants provided, so that violations were acted upon in the last decade which were neglected in the earlier decades. Probably both the enactment of laws and the enforcement of laws during this period are explained by the fact that businessmen lost much prestige in the depression which began in 1929. The increase in the number of decisions on restraint of trade and misrepresentation in advertising, especially, can be explained in this manner.

Fourth, businessmen are resorting to an increasing extent to "policies of social manipulation" in contrast with the earlier concentration on efficiency in production. With emphasis on advertising and salesmanship, as policies of social manipulation, have gone increased attention to lobbying and litigation. This is shown especially in the trend in decisions regarding infringements. Since these are civil suits, initiated by persons who regard their rights as infringed, they are not a direct reflection of governmental policies. They are, however, presumably affected somewhat by governmental policies in an indirect manner. The increase in the number of prosecutions on charges of restraint of trade, frequently involving patent manipulations, has given the general public and the owners of patents insight into the policies of these large corporations and has stimulated efforts of patent holders to protect their rights.

Of these possible explanations, the increased vigor of and facilities for prosecution are probably the most important. It is probable, also, that the frequency of violations of some of the laws has increased significantly, although this does not appear to be true of all laws.

Of the 70 corporations, 30 were either illegal in their origin or began illegal activities immediately after their origin, and 8 additional corporations were probably illegal in origin or in initial policies. Of the violations of law which appeared in these early activities, 27 were restraint of trade and 3 were patent infringements; of the 8 origins which were probably criminal, 5 involved restraint of trade, 2 patent infringements, and 1 fraud. The evidence for this appraisal of the origins of corporations consists in court decisions in 21 cases, and other historical evidence in the other cases.

4

Corporate Crime
Clarifying the Concept and Extending the Data
Marshall B. Clinard and Peter C. Yeager

The first large-scale comprehensive investigation of the law violations of major firms since Sutherland's pioneering work (1949) was carried out in connection with the study of corporate crime reported in this [essay]. The study involved a systematic analysis of federal administrative, civil, and criminal actions either initiated or completed by 25 federal agencies against the 477 largest publicly owned manufacturing (*Fortune* 500) corporations in the United States during 1975 and 1976. In addition, a more limited study was made of the 105 largest wholesale, retail, and service corporations, for a total sample of 582 corporations. The 1975 sales of the corporations studied ranged from $300 million to more than $45 billion, with an average of $1.7 billion for all 582 firms. Banking, insurance, transportation, communication, and utilities corporations were excluded.

It was not feasible to investigate the extent and nature of all corporate violations reported by consumers, competitors, and other injured parties. Nor was it possible to do so for violations discovered by government investigators but not formally charged. (The latter data would have been roughly equivalent to data on ordinary crimes known to the police as reported in *Uniform Crime Reports*.) In most cases the records are not publicly available unless violations have been charged; moreover, records on investigations are rarely available in an agency's national offices. For this reason, therefore, the study had to be restricted to *actions initiated* against corporations for violations (roughly equivalent to arrests or prosecutions)

From *Corporate Crime*, pp. 110–122. Copyright © 1980 by The Free Press, a Division of Macmillan Publishing Co., Inc. Reprinted by permission.

and *actions completed* (equivalent to convictions). Consequently, official actions taken against corporations are probably only the tip of the iceberg of total violations, but they do constitute an index of illegal behavior by the large corporations.

Ideally, one would include the violations of all subsidiaries in any compilation of enforcement actions involving parent corporations. Large corporations, however, frequently have many subsidiaries in numerous product lines. For this reason, therefore, in a study of this size it was not possible to gather necessary data on the large number of subsidiaries, particularly since violations of subsidiaries often are not reported with the name of the parent corporation.

Sources of Data

Data on enforcement actions against corporations were derived from four sources: federal agencies, law service reports, reports to the SEC, and newspaper articles. This variety of information assured greater coverage than a single source would have provided.

1. *Federal Agencies.* Data on enforcement actions taken against the corporations in the sample were obtained directly from some federal agencies. Most agency record systems are not adequate for such purposes for a variety of reasons, and could not furnish complete data.

2. *Law Service Reports.* These reports furnished data on decisions particularly in antitrust, consumer product safety, labor violations, and environmental pollution cases.

3. *Reports to the SEC.* Corporations submit annual financial reports (Form 10-K) to the Securities and Exchange Commission. These reports, which include a section on legal proceedings initiated and concluded against the firms, were often found to be incomplete.

4. *Newspaper Articles.* A computerized listing from a computer bank (Lockheed Dialogue System) of abstracts of every article concerning enforcement proceedings against corporations carried in the *New York Times,* the *Wall Street Journal,* and leading trade journals was used.

Actions Initiated against Corporations for Violations

Prior to any analysis of initiated federal actions and sanctions against corporations, several important considerations should be recognized. First of all, persons who are accustomed to thinking about the incidence of theft and burglary must reorient themselves when they examine corporate crime figures. Even if these acts are numerically few, the consequences of but a single corporate violation can be great. Usually, a corporate crime represents far more significant personal, social, and monetary damage than does an ordinary crime. Many corporate crimes involve tens of millions, even billions, of dollars: in fact, a million dollar loss would be regarded as small. Thus, corporate crimes must be viewed from a different perspective, particularly when they involve large national and multinational corporations.

Second, complete data on certain types of agency cases, such as most cases involving taxes, could not be obtained in spite of careful and systematic efforts. Not included also were detected violations responded to informally, for example, by telephone. *What is represented here, then, are minimal figures of government actions against major corporations:* the undercount may be as high as one-fourth to one-third. This undercount is, we hope, not biased and thus does not interfere with any of the general conclusions.

A third important consideration is that more than one violation may be charged in a legal case. For example, a legal case of OSHA may entail an inadequate safety guard on a machine and failure to discover that employees have removed safety guards from a conveyor. The 477 manufacturing corporations engaged in 1,724 violations involving 1,451 cases. Thus, two methods were used to analyze these data: first, we analyzed only the most serious violation in the charge and, second, occasionally we analyzed not cases but up to five violations per firm per case.

A total of 1,553 federal cases were begun against all 582 corporations during 1975 and 1976, or an average of 2.7 federal cases of violation each. Of the 582 corporations, 350 (60.1 percent) had at least one federal action brought against them, and for those firms that had at least one action brought against them, the average was 4.4 cases.

Approximately 40 percent of both the total group of 582 corporations and the 477 manufacturing firms were not charged with any violations by the 25 federal agencies during the two-year period. It might be concluded, therefore, that the world of the giant corporation does not require illegal behavior in order to compete successfully. This does not mean, however, that all of these corporations necessarily were "clean." Some simply might not have been caught, particular industries might not have been well policed, or their corporate counsels might have been more successful in preventing violations because of greater familiarity with the law or in preventing the lodging of formal charges.

Types of Violations

The violations of the corporations studied showed great range and varied characteristics. Six main types of corporate illegal behavior were found: administrative, environmental, financial, labor, manufacturing, and unfair trade practices.

Administrative violations involve noncompliance with the requirements of an agency or court, such as failure to obey an agency order (for example, an order to institute a recall campaign or to construct pollution control facilities) or a court order enforcing an agency order. Information violations included such "paperwork" violations as refusal to produce information (hindering investigations, denying access, inadequate record-keeping), failure to report information (failure to submit reports, to notify of pollution discharge, and to register with the agency), and failure to file, secure certification, or acquire permits.

Environmental violations include incidents of air and water pollution, including oil and chemical spills, as well as violations of air and water permits that require capital outlays by the corporations for construction of pollution control equipment. Only those oil and chemical spills of at least 500 gallons of substance were included in the analysis.

Financial violations include illegal payments or failure to disclose such violations (commercial domestic bribery, illegal domestic political contributions, payments to foreign officials, the conferring of illegal gratuities and benefits, violations of foreign currency laws). Examples of securities related violations are false and misleading proxy materials, misuse of nonpublic material information, and the issuance of false statements. Transaction violations involve the following: terms of sale (overcharging customers), exchange agreements (failure to apply increased prices equally to classes of purchasers, illegal changing of base lease conditions, illegal termination of base supplier-purchaser relationship, imposition of more stringent credit terms than those existing during the base period), and purchase conditions (failure to pay full price when due, issuing insufficient funds checks, making preferential payments). Also included are tax violations, involving fraudulent returns and deficiency in tax liability, and accounting malpractices, such as internal control violations (inadequate control over disbursement of funds or unaccounted funds, failure to record terms of transactions involving questionable pricing and promotional practices), false entries (borrowing against nonexistent receivables, recording fictitious sales), and improper estimates (improper accounting of costs, improper calculation of recoverable costs, misreporting of costs).

Labor violations fall into four major types: discrimination in employment (by race, sex, national origin, or religion), occupational safety and health hazards, unfair labor practices, and wage and hour violations. The four agencies responsible for initiating actions for these respective violations are the Equal Employment Opportunity Commission, the Occupational Safety and Health Administration, the National Labor Relations Board, and the Wage and Hour Division of the Department of Labor.

Manufacturing violations involve three government agencies. The Consumer Product Safety Commission responds to violations of the Federal Hazardous Substances Act, the Poison Prevention Packaging Act, the Flammable Fabrics Act, and the Consumer Product Safety Act. Such violations include electric shock hazards, chemical and environmental hazards (poisonings and other injuries that result from handling, using, or ingesting toxic or hazardous household substances, as well as chemicals and agents causing injuries initially discernible only years after exposure), and fire and thermal burn hazards (involving, for example, flammable fabrics, mattresses, carpeting, clothing, and ovens). The National Highway Traffic Safety Administration requires manufacturers of motor vehicles or parts to notify the agency and owners, purchasers, and dealers of defects related to motor vehicle safety. It also requires manufacturers to remedy such defects. Defects include mechanical hazards involving faulty parts installations, improper part installations, improper manufacture of parts, defective systems, and inadequate design. The main categories of manufacturing violations for infractions of Food and Drug Administration regulations are misbranding, mispackaging, and mislabeling (packaging in incorrect or defective containers, lack of adequate or correct content or ingredient statements, lack of adequate or correct directions for use on labels); contamination or adulteration (lack of assurance of sterility; product prepared, held, or stored under unsanitary conditions); lack of effectiveness of product (failure to meet U.S.P. standards, defect in product); inadequate testing procedures; and inadequate standards in blood or plasma collection and laboratory processing (improper procedures in choice and use of blood donors, equipment or materials not acceptable, inadequate supervision of collection and manufacturing processes, lack of assurance of sterility).

Unfair trade practices involve various abuses of competition (monopolization, misrepresentation, price discrimination, maintaining resale conditions with coercion, credit violations, and other abuses that restrain trade and prevent fair competition), vertical combinations (tying agreements), and horizontal combinations (price fixing, bid rigging, illegal merger activity, illegal interlocking directorates, fixing fees, agreements among competitors to allocate markets, jobs, customers, accounts, sales, and patents). False and misleading advertising represents an important unfair trade practice.

Just as some persons are not in positions of financial trust, as a bank teller is, and thus are not given an opportunity to embezzle funds (Cressey, 1953), so some corporations are not in "eligible" positions to commit certain types of violations.

> Blacks have a very low rate of embezzlement, as compared to whites, because they are seldom in the positions of financial trust that make embezzlement available to them as a crime. Restricted opportunity keeps United States Steel and General Motors from violating Pure Food and Drug laws. Armour, Swift, and Wilson, on the other hand, have many opportunities to violate those laws. (Cressey, 1976, p. 218)

Some corporations are not in the oil business, for example, and cannot violate laws regulating oil spills and oil pricing; many other corporations are not in the pharmaceutical business and therefore cannot be charged with the manufacture of unsafe drugs. On the other hand, all manufacturing corporations have the opportunity to violate environmental pollution standards and occupational safety and health regulations, as well as labor and most corporate tax laws.

More than three-fourths of the legal actions (cases) occurred in the manufacturing, environmental, and labor sectors; in each of these areas about one-fourth of the manufacturing corporations violated regulations at least once. In addition, two of every ten corporations had one or more administrative cases brought against them. Illegal corporate behavior was found least often in the financial and trade areas: one of ten had at least one trade action taken against them, while only one in twenty had financial actions charged against them.

Multiple Violators: The Most Deviant Firms

Although approximately three-fifths of the 477 manufacturing corporations had at least one action initiated against them, it is perhaps more notable that 200 corporations, or 42 percent of the total, had multiple cases charged against them during 1975–1976. In terms of the various violation types, it was found that 71 corporations (15 percent) had multiple environmental cases charged, while 61 firms (13 percent) had multiple manufacturing cases; for labor cases, the multiple violators numbered 37 (8 percent); administratives cases, 22 (5 percent); financial cases, 8 (2 percent); trade cases, 6 (1 percent).

A small percentage of violating corporations, moreover, committed a highly disproportionate share of all infractions cited (counting up to five violations per legal case). Our research found that only 38 of the 300 manufacturing corporations cited for violations, or 13 percent (8 percent of all corporations studied), accounted for 52 percent of all violations charged in 1975–1976, an average of 23.5 violations per firm. Disproportionate percentages were found for environmental, manufacturing, administrative, and labor violations, although not for financial and trade infractions. Some

22 percent of the corporations involved in environmental violations committed 60 percent of these violations; 20 percent of those involved in manufacturing violations accounted for two-thirds of such infractions; 19 percent of those in administrative violations committed 40 percent of the illegal acts, while 18 percent of the firms that violated the various labor laws accounted for 26 percent of all such violations. For these most frequent violators, the average number of violations was manufacturing, 17.7, environmental, 10.7, administrative, 3.9, and labor, 3.4. In terms of the *most* violative corporation in each area, one firm had 54 environmental cases brought against it, one had 49 manufacturing cases, 8 labor actions were initiated against one corporation, one had 6 administrative cases, one had 4 financial cases, and one had 3 trade cases.

When certain corporations are charged more than once with violations, it is possible, of course, that enforcement agencies, alerted to the possibility of repeat violations, have policed these particular firms more closely and thereby increased the odds that subsequent violations will be discovered. It is more likely, however, that some corporations, have developed a corporate atmosphere favorable to unethical and illegal behavior and that executives and other employees of these corporations may have become socialized to violate the law.

To this point the discussion has dealt only with total corporate violations. Some violations, however, are extremely serious and may cause large financial losses or injuries to consumers, to workers, or to the general public, while others are minor in respect to both financial impact and injurious effects. Some are only of a minor reporting or record-keeping nature. Although some broad distinctions are straightforward, the determination of the degree of seriousness in corporate crime is an unexplored area that challenges both research and policy efforts. For example, is a price-fixing scheme more harmful than fouling the environment or marketing untested or unsafe goods? And within a single regulatory area (trade regulation), is an illegal merger that affects commerce in five states more serious than a false advertising campaign conducted nationwide for a single product? Are strict liability offenses such as oil spills in any way comparable to corporate offenses in which individual or group blame is assessed? These questions largely do not arise with ordinary crime, where the seriousness is generally agreed upon and is usually reflected in the severity of the statutory penalty. In corporate cases, however, one generally cannot use the severity of the sanction as an indicator of seriousness of crime.

It was thus necessary to work out a classification by which to rank violations as serious, moderate, or minor if the criteria were not available from government agencies (only three agencies out of 25 had such criteria). The following criteria were selected.

1. Repetition of the same violation by the corporation
2. Knowledge that the action involved violation of law (intent)
3. Extent of the violation (i.e., whether it occurred company-wide or involved only a limited number of corporation facilities, especially in cases of discrimination and other unfair labor practices)
4. Size of monetary losses to consumers, competitors, or government
5. Unsafe products manufactured in large amounts that were actually reaching the consumer
6. Corporation refused to reinstate or rehire employees
7. Corporation refused to recall defective products
8. Corporation refused to honor agreements
9. Corporation threatened witnesses or employees
10. Length of time the violation took place

Serious and moderately serious corporate violations were extensive and, again, were concentrated among certain manufacturing corporations. The 682 actions initiated for serious or moderate violations against manufacturing corporations constituted almost half of all cases of violations, an average of 3.1 for those corporations (222, or 46.5 percent of the sample) with at least one serious or moderate violation.

Fully one-quarter of the 477 manufacturing corporations, or 120, had multiple cases of non-minor violations charged against them during 1975–1976; five or more such cases were brought against 32 firms. Forty-four corporations had more than one case charging serious or moderately serious manufacturing violations brought against them; and 16 of these "repeaters" had five or more cases, one firm being cited 34 times during the two-year period. For serious or moderately serious labor violations, the "repeaters" num-

bered 33, one corporation being cited seven times for such violations. Multiple environmental cases were brought against 12 firms;
against eight firms for financial violations, six firms for administrative violations, and five for trade infractions. These data suggest,
then, that the problem of recidivism—measured in terms of serious and moderately serious infractions—is more pronounced in
certain areas of corporate behavior than in others, specifically in
the areas of labor law and product quality. The primary victims of
such violations are employees and consumers, respectively.

Large Corporations the Chief Violators

Violations were far more likely to be committed by large corporations. Manufacturing corporations were divided on the basis of
annual sales into 30.5 percent small ($300–499 million), 27.2 per-
cent medium ($500–999 million), and 42.3 percent large ($1 billion or more). Small corporations accounted for only one-tenth of
the violations, medium-size for one-fifth, but large corporations for
almost three-fourths of all violations, nearly twice their expected
percentage. Large corporations, moreover, accounted for 72.1
percent of the serious and 62.8 percent of the moderately serious
violations. Large corporations averaged 5.1 total violations each,
3.0 of them serious or moderate.

Of the total enforcement actions taken against all corporations,
one in ten were against small, one-fifth against medium, and almost
three-fourths against large corporations, a distribution essentially
similar to the initiated actions. The 477 manufacturing corporations
had the same pattern. Likewise, large corporations had a widely
disproportionate share of the sanctions for serious and moderate
violations.

Violations Concentrated in Certain Industries

The oil, pharmaceutical, and motor vehicle industries were the most
likely to violate the law. The oil refining industry was charged in

one out of every five legal cases brought in 1975–1976, or one out of every 10 cases involving serious and moderate violations. Corporations in this particular industry had nearly three-fifths of all serious and moderately serious financial violations, almost half of the total environmental violations, and more than a third of the serious and moderately serious environmental violations. They accounted for almost one out of every six serious or moderately serious trade violations, and one of seven administrative violations. In the oil refining industry, 22 of the 28 companies violated the law at least once; 20 had one or more serious or moderately serious violations.

The motor vehicle industry was responsible for one out of every six cases of violation charged and one out of every five serious or moderately serious violations. For manufacturing violations, it was responsible for one-third of both the total and the serious or moderate infractions. One out of every 9 total and serious or moderate labor violations was committed by the motor vehicle industry, as was one of every 8 trade violations, regardless of seriousness level. Eighteen of the 19 firms in this industry had at least one violation; 17 had one or more serious or moderately serious violations. Four motor vehicle industry firms had 21 or more violations.

The pharmaceutical industry accounted for one out of every 10 cases of violation and one of eight serious or moderately serious violations. These firms had a fifth of both the total and the serious or moderate manufacturing cases, and one out of every seven of the total and the serious or moderately serious administrative violations. All 17 pharmaceutical corporations violated the law at least once in 1975 and 1976; 15 (88.2 percent) committed at least one serious or moderately serious violation. Two drug firms had 21 or more violations.

The motor vehicle industry had 3.9 times its share of total violations, five times its share of serious or moderately serious violations. The oil refining industry had 3.2 times its share of total violations, 1.7 times for serious or moderately serious violations. The pharmaceutical industry had 2.5 times its share of total violations, 3.2 times for serious or moderately serious infractions.

Within each violation type, the oil refining industry accounted for 9.7 times its share of financial violations and 9.6 times its share of serious or moderately serious financial violations. This industry had

7.3 times more environmental violations than its relative size would warrant and 5.7 times more serious or moderately serious environmental violations. It had 2.5 times its share of trade violations and 2.1 times more serious or moderately serious trade violations.

The motor vehicle industry had 7.7 times its share of total and of serious or moderately serious manufacturing violations. It had 3.8 times more administrative violations than expected from its relative size in the sample and two times more serious or moderately serious administrative violations. It had 5.0 times its share of total and of serious or moderately serious trade violations. It also had 2.6 times more labor violations than expected and 3.1 times more serious or moderately serious labor violations.

The pharmaceutical industry had 5.6 times its share of manufacturing violations; 5.8 times more serious or moderately serious violations. Finally, it had 3.9 times its share of both the total and the serious or moderately serious administrative violations.

In the more specific types of violations, 90.9 percent of financial violations and 70.6 percent of water pollution violations (a large proportion of which were oil spills) were committed by the oil refining industry. The motor vehicle industry had almost half of the violations involving the manufacture of hazardous products.

Likewise, generally the oil, auto, and pharmaceutical industries received the highest proportion of sanctions, regardless of whether total sanctions were considered or only the serious and moderately serious cases. The oil industry accounted for 17.3 percent of all sanctions; oil firms received 8 percent of the sanctions if the cases are restricted to serious or moderately serious violations and one out of five monetary penalties in such cases. The motor vehicle industry accounted for one out of every six sanctions; one out of every five in serious and moderately serious cases. These corporations also received one out of every four warnings issued in all cases and one out of every three warnings issued for serious and moderately serious violations. The pharmaceutical industry had one out of every 10 sanctions imposed on it; one out of eight for serious or moderately serious violations. It received one out of every five warnings for all violations and for all serious and moderately serious violations as well.

When corporations were compared by industry type in terms of the industry's proportion of sanctions received relative to the number of firms studied in the industry, the motor vehicle industry was found to have had 3.7 times more sanctions against it than expected, 4.4 times more in serious and moderately serious violations. The oil refining industry received 2.8 times more; 1.3 times more for serious and moderately serious violations. The pharmaceutical industry had 2.5 times more sanctions; 3.2 times more in serious and moderately serious cases. All other industry types had approximately their share or less of all sanctions imposed.

References

Cressey, Donald R. *Other People's Money*. New York: Free Press, 1953.
———. "Restraint of Trade, Recidivism, and Delinquent Neighborhoods." In *Delinquency, Crime, and Society*, James F. Short, Jr., ed. Chicago: University of Chicago Press, 1976.
Sutherland, Edwin H. *White Collar Crime*. New York: Holt, 1949.

5
Organizational Actors and the Irrelevance of Persons

James S. Coleman

[Organizational Actors]

[T]he law has facilitated, and technological developments have motivated, an enormous growth of a new kind of person in society, a person not like you and me, but one which can and does act, and one whose actions have extensive consequences for natural persons like you and me.

Something of the character and nature of that growth can be seen by a few charts. Figure 5.1 gives an indication of the growth in numbers of profit-making corporations in the United States since 1917. The chart shows the numbers of corporations paying taxes in each year since 1917, a growth from 1917 to 1969 of more than five times. There was, to be sure, population growth among natural persons in the United States during this period, but far less than the fivefold growth shown in the chart.

Two other charts show something about the actions of corporate actors and persons. The first of these, Figure 5.2, covering all actions in the New York State Appellate Court from 1853 to 1973, shows the proportion of persons—or agents of corporate actors (the two were combined, because it was difficult to tell whether a person was a party to a case as a natural person or as an agent of a corporation)—and the proportion that were corporate actors. The proportion was highly skewed in the direction of natural persons in

From *The Asymmetric Society*, pp. 9–30. Copyright © 1982 by Syracuse University Press. Reprinted by permission.

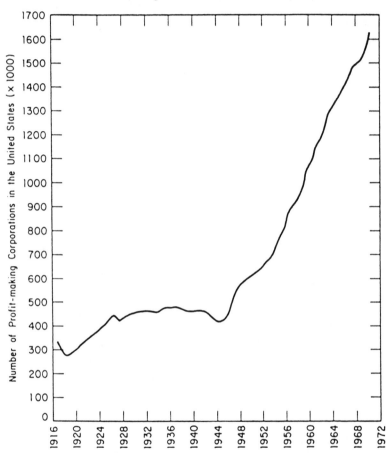

FIGURE 5.1

Growth in Numbers of Corporations in the United States, 1916–1968

Source: From Shi Chang Wu, "Distribution of Economic Resources in the United States," mimeographed (Chicago, Ill.: National Opinion Research Center, 1974).

FIGURE 5.2

Participation of Persons and Corporate Actors in Court Cases, New York State Court of Appeals, 1853–1973

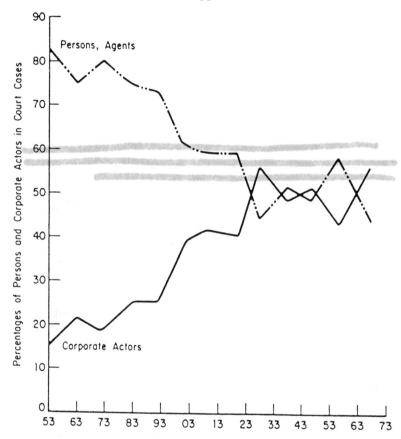

Source: From Naava Binder Grossman, "A Study of the Relative Participation of Persons and Corporate Actors in Court Cases," mimeographed (Chicago, Ill.: National Opinion Research Center, 1974).

1853 (85 percent to 15 percent); by 1930, it became about even and
has remained that way through 1973.

Figure 5.3 shows . . . actions reported on the front page of the
New York Times, over a portion of the same period, from 1876 to
1972. This chart shows the proportion of front page attention
given—either as the subject of the action or as the object of action—
to natural persons and the proportion of attention given to corporate actors—either the corporate actors or their agents. Again the
chart shows a reduction in the proportion of all attention on the
stage of the *New York Times* given to natural persons: from about
40 percent in 1876, down to about 20 percent in 1972.

What these changes suggest is a structural change in society over
the past hundred years in which corporate actors play an increasing role and natural persons play a decreasing role. It is as if there
has been extensive immigration over this period, not of persons
from Europe or Asia or Africa or South America, but of [people]

FIGURE 5.3

Attention to Persons and Corporate Actors on the Front Page
of the *New York Times,* 1876–1972

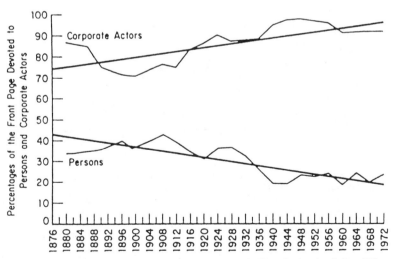

Source: From Ronald S. Burt, "Corporate Society: A Time Series Analysis of Network Structure," mimeographed (Chicago, Ill.: National Opinion Research Center,
1975).

from Mars—a race of persons unknown in history. And this new race of persons has come to crowd out natural persons from various points in the social structure—at least some of those points that take part in activities which end up in appellate court or on the front page of the *New York Times*.

Yet these new persons are not Martians. They employ natural persons as agents, they have natural persons as their chief executives, they are governed by boards of directors made up of natural persons,[1] natural persons are their owners. Or so it once was; not even all these things are now true. The stockholders are, with increasing frequency, themselves corporate actors, either other business corporations or other forms of corporate actors: pension funds or insurance companies. Members of their boards of directors may be agents of other corporate actors who are large stockholders.

These corporate actors are different from those that have gone before in a fundamental way. In the earlier structure of societies, the family was the nucleus of the corporate structure, and the component elements of the family were natural persons. The family had a place in the larger structure, and through the family, each person did as well. That person had a fixed station and was an intrinsic part of the structure of society. As Marc Bloch (1961) wrote about the manor in the Middle Ages, "In the days when vassalage was developing, or when it was in its prime, the manor was first and foremost a community of dependents who were by turns protected, commanded, and oppressed by their lord to whom many of them were bound by a sort of hereditary link, unconnected with possession of the soil or place of abode" (p. 279). There were, to be sure, various devices to cope with the fact that persons were mortal, and one person's function might have to be taken over by another. But the central and overriding fact was that all social organization was

1. The practice in industrial firms of having executives of other firms or of financial institutions as members of boards of directors does not involve agency. These persons are board members in their capacities as persons, and their other positions are relevant only as they have acquired skills or knowledge from those positions. This points to a central difficulty of sociological studies of "interlocking directorates," which show the "interlock" created by an executive officer of one firm being a member of a board of directors of another firm. Because the board member does not come as an agent but as a natural person, there is no interlock in the sense ordinarily meant. It is for this reason that such studies have never proved very useful for the study of the functioning of society. The end point of such studies is ordinarily simply a demonstration of the "interlocks," with the implicit assumption that the interlock has significance for the functioning of society.

organization of persons, and that those forms of organization which
were fruitfully conceptualized as corporate actors were structures
themselves composed of persons.

But the conception of the corporation as a legal person distinct
from natural persons, able to act and be acted on, and the reor-
ganization of society around corporate bodies made possible a radi-
cally different kind of social structure than before. So long as society was seen as a single fixed organic whole, then the existence of
social differentiation of activities as it was emerging in the Middle
Ages (merchants, crafts, agriculture, churches) implied a rigid differentiation of persons in fixed positions—as in caste India, but with
less continuity through generations. But as this differentiation of
activities increased, a new form of social organization slowly came
to be invented, and the law reflected this invention. This form
involved the corporation as a functional element in social organization; a juristic person which could substitute functionally for a
natural person. It could act in a unitary way, it could own resources,
it could have rights and responsibilities, it could occupy the fixed
functional position or estate which had been imposed on natural
persons (and later it too could be partially freed from that fixed
position). Natural persons, in turn, came to be free from the fixed
estates, gaining mobility, as the structural stability of society was
provided by the new fixed functional units, the corporations or
corporate bodies. Persons needed no longer to be "one dimen-
sional" but could occupy several positions in the structure at once
and could change positions freely. It was the positions, as components of the new elements of society, the corporate actors, which
provided the continuity and stability of structure.

The emergence of this new structure for society has had and
continues to have extensive consequences for the lives of the natural persons within it. . . .

The Asymmetry of Relations

The first and perhaps most compelling [consequence] is the *asymmetry* of a large portion of its relations. I can best describe this asymmetry to you by asking you to look at the diagram of Figure 5.4.

FIGURE 5.4

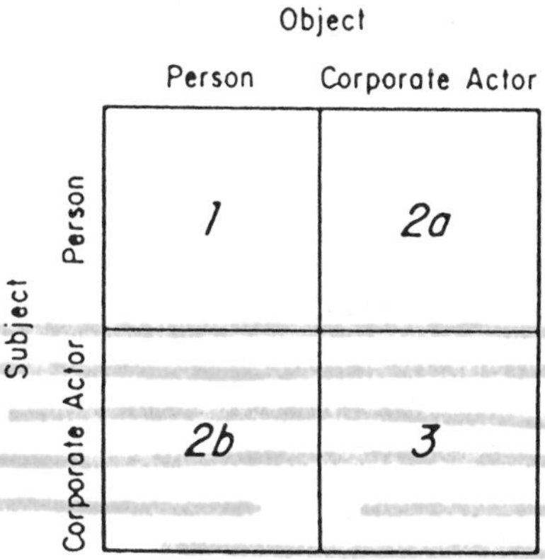

Object

Person   Corporate Actor

	Person	*1*	*2a*
Subject	Corporate Actor	*2b*	*3*

What I have done here is to start with the recognition that there
are two fundamentally distinct types of actors in modern society,
natural persons and corporate actors. Then I have classified actions
according to whether the *subject* of action is a person or corporate
actor, and according to whether the *object* of action is a person or
corporate actor. The result is four kinds of action, which I have labeled 1, 2a, 2b, and 3. Actions of type 1 are actions to which we
have all been socialized as children: actions of one person toward
another person. Actions of type 3 are actions of a corporate actor
toward another corporate actor, for example an action of one corporation toward another, or an action of the state (i.e., the government) toward a corporation or a trade union. Actions of types 2a
and 2b, however, are actions in which the two parties to an action
are of *different* types: one is a person and one is a corporate actor.
And because a relation involves both parties as subject and object
of action, we may speak of a relation of type 2, involving actions of
types 2a and 2b. This, in contrast to the other two types of relations, is asymmetric. And with the enormous growth in numbers
of corporate actors in modern society, this asymmetric form of
relation has come to proliferate throughout the social structure.
Some of the growth in appearances of corporate actors in court
cases which I presented earlier is growth in this kind of relation, a
person and a corporate actor opposed in court. Some of the growth

in attention to corporate actors in the *New York Times,* which I also presented earlier, is growth in this kind of relation, that is, articles involving some sort of interaction or relation between a person and a corporate actor. Yet either of these is only a pale reflection of the total growth that has taken place in these asymmetric relations.

Increasingly, there are . . . relations which at first glance appear to be between two persons, but in fact are between a person and a corporate actor, with the corporate actor represented by its agent. . . . [M]any of these relations are not only asymmetric in the types of parties they involve, but are asymmetric—often extremely so—in two other respects as well: in the relative *sizes* of the two parties, and in the *numbers* of alternative transaction partners on each side of the relation. Typically, the corporate actor is very large in resources, compared to the person on the other side of the relation. On one side may be the telephone company, a corporate actor, and on the other side, a customer, a person. Or on the one side may be the United Steelworkers' Union, a corporate actor, and on the other side a union member, a person. Or on the one side may be the U.S. government, a corporate actor, and on the other side, a citizen, a person.

And typically, on the corporate actor side there are only a few other parties as alternative transaction partners. . . . On the person side there are typically hundreds, thousands, or even millions. These two asymmetries have extensive consequences for the nature of the relation. One consequence is that the corporate actor nearly always controls most of the conditions surrounding the relation. The corporate actor controls much of the information relevant to the interaction—typically by advertising, propaganda, market research, public opinion research, credit ratings of customers, and dossiers of other sorts. Information expressly designed to serve the interests of the person is far less in evidence. And as with information, so with other of the conditions. The end result is that two parties beginning with nominally equal rights in a relation, but coming to it with vastly different resources, end with very different actual rights in the relation.

These asymmetries of power in relationships have led to extensive attempts by persons to redress the balance, using as their instrument the state. Thus the principle of *caveat emptor,* let the buyer beware, in a social structure which was not asymmetric between buyers and sellers, has been replaced, in the asymmetric society, with sharp restriction of the seller's rights and expansion of the means of redress for persons. The [1970s] alone saw a whole spate of such legislation at both the state and federal levels, ranging from truth in lending laws to privacy acts, designed to protect natural persons from corporate actors' use of information about them in ways antagonistic to their interests.

The asymmetry, however, has other consequences in the behavior of the two parties to the relation. The person, if unconstrained by internal moral constraints, may steal from or cheat a corporate actor, protected by the anonymity provided by numbers. A person angry at the telephone company might rip the cord from a public phone, or a customer or employee in a store may shoplift, or may fail to notify a cashier if too much change has been returned. Yet these same persons might never do any of these things in relations with other *persons,* where actions are subject to the other's constant surveillance.

In short, the asymmetry of the relation gives power to the corporate actor and at the same time gives opportunities for malfeasance to the person. On both counts, the relation functions less well than the personal relations of which social structures have long been composed, and for which normative systems of constraints have arisen. . . .

The Irrelevance of Persons

Persons have become, in a sense that was never before true, incidental to a large fraction of the productive activity in society. This is most evident when the person who occupies a position in a corporate actor is replaced not by another person but by a machine. Then the general irrelevance of persons is clear. But the invention which made this possible was not a technological invention which replaced [people with machines]; it was a social invention which created a structure that was independent of particular persons and consisted only of positions. Once this was done, it became merely a matter of ingenuity to devise machines that could carry out the activities which those positions required.

The irrelevance of persons in the structure is not a question of machines, it is a question of the *form* of the structure. In management training programs in many firms, there is a game that is used as part of the training program: the in-basket game. In this game [management trainees are] asked to assume that [they] unexpectedly replaced the previous plant manager over the weekend and [are] confronted with the unanswered mail in [their] predecessor's in-basket. The task is to respond appropriately to the various items of correspondence. A few are personal, and [they are] expected to distinguish between those and the correspondence that is intended for the plant manager as manager, that is, as agent of the firm. The aim of the in-basket exercise is to make the transition from one manager to the next unnoticeable—to make the manager *as a person* irrelevant to the functioning of the plant. This is good for the smooth functioning of the organization; but it takes away something of central importance to each of us: the sense of being *needed*. It is this which makes the family—which is an anachronism from another age in the modern social structure we have created—an important element in our lives. A family member is a part of that family as a person, not as an occupant of a position; and no answers to correspondence in an in-basket can make a family's loss of a member unnoticeable. . . .

Is this a desirable state of affairs for society? I think not. Yet it is a state of affairs which follows directly from the structure of corporate action which we have invented for ourselves and under which we live.

Reference

Bloch, Marc. *Feudal Society*, vol. 1. Chicago, Ill.: University of Chicago Press, 1961.

Editors' Postscript

The trends Professor Coleman identified continue. Among lawsuits filed in federal courts between 1985 and 1991, the largest number of them (191,000) involved business contract disputes between two or more firms. These suits were far more common than personal injury lawsuits filed by natural persons against companies. (See Milo Geyelin, "Suits by Firms Exceed Those by Individuals," *Wall Street Journal*, December 3, 1993, p. B1.)

III
Patterns

Editors' Introduction

Deviant patterns sometimes are a central part of business organizations and government agencies. External market conditions and internal pressures for performance can push employees in the direction of deviant actions. Universities and other organizations sometimes tolerate actions contrary to the best interests of organization members and the organization itself. Governmental bureaucracies and the armies and police forces representing government can provide resources, beliefs, and authorization that encourage genocide, murder, and torture. The readings in this section examine these and other patterns of corporate and governmental deviance.

Selection 6, Gilbert Geis's "The Heavy Electrical Equipment Antitrust Cases," is a classic description and analysis of an important and well-publicized instance of price-fixing where prosecutors actually went after major corporations. Professor Geis describes how over a 20-year period General Electric, Westinghouse, 27 other corporations, and many more individuals illegally conspired to decide which of them would offer the low bid, and what that bid would be, when selling heavy electrical equipment to public utilities for use to generate and transmit electricity.

Selection 7, "Beer and Circus," by Professor Murray Sperber details how big-time college sports is crippling undergraduate education. Professor Sperber argues that major sports, especially football and men's basketball, uses young athletes who receive no meaningful compensation for athletic efforts that make coaches and athletic directors rich. Further, football and men's basketball are revenue drains at nearly all universities, depsite pronouncements to the contrary. Most important, Professor Sperber argues that the beer and circus atmosphere that surrounds big-time athletics serves to entertain undergraduates and thereby keep them from recognizing that the education they are receiving is at best uneven. Professor Sperber's selection strikes us as a particularly chilling indictment of the types of institutions where one of the coeditors (Lundman) professes and some of you, our readers, are receiving your undergraduate education.

Selection 8, Kermit Vandivier's "Why Should My Conscience Bother Me?" details how and why B. F. Goodrich Company built and released an aircraft brake that many employees knew was unsafe. In addition to providing a vivid account of his personal involvement in corporate deviance, the author shows how Goodrich's organizational structure and climate made the deviance more likely. Mr. Vandivier's description of this case continues to be used in business and engineering ethics courses at many colleges and universities.

Selection 9, Raul Hilberg's "The Nazi Holocaust," focuses on the administrative and psychological obstacles that we might think would hinder participants in genocide. It explains how German bureaucracies and German people overcame these normal human obstacles. Agencies reformulated or ignored laws, bureaucrats wrote intentionally passionless memos, others sought to efficiently define and concentrate the people who were to be murdered, and the entire structure helped participants at all levels repress and rationalize the problems that their participation raised in their minds.

Selection 10, Suzanne Daley's "Apartheid Torturer," details the actions and rationalizations of one South African police officer during the white rule of South Africa that ended in 1994. The police officer, Jeffrey Benzien, was one of many government employees who sustained white rule with his daily acts of torture and his self-serving argument that he was a "nobody" who was simply doing his job. Like the Nazi government, the apartheid South African government readily found thousands of people like the police officer described in this selection.

Selection 11, "The My Lai Massacre," explains why U.S. soldiers murdered at least 300 and perhaps as many as 500 unarmed women, children, babies, and old men in My Lai, Vietnam. Professors Herbert Kelman and Lee Hamilton use this case to direct our attention to the organizational forces, especially authorization, routinization, and dehumanization, that lead to sanctioned massacres such as My Lai.

Annotated Bibliography

Adams, James Ring. *The Big Fix: Inside the S & L Scandal.* New York: Wiley, 1990. Why so many savings and loans went belly up.

Burnham, David. *A Law unto Itself: Power, Politics, and the IRS.* New York: Random House, 1990. Alleged misconduct by the Internal Revenue Service, ranging from cashing checks not its to cash, to helping presidents harass political enemies.

Burrough, Bryand, and John Helyar. *Barbarians at the Gate: The Fall and Rise of RJR Nabisco.* New York: Harper and Row, 1990. A richly textured account of the LBO (leveraged buyout) of the giant tobacco and food conglomerate.

Donner, Frank. *Protectors of Privilege: Red Squads and Police Repression in Urban America.* Berkeley: University of California Press, 1990. Repression by police in major U.S. cities.

Gamson, William A. "Hiroshima, the Holocaust, and the Politics of Exclusion." *American Sociological Review* 60 (1995): 1–20. Who we define as "we" and who we define as "they" set in motion processes that can culminate in genocide and other forms of mass destruction.

Hilberg, Raul. *Perpetrators Victims Bystanders: The Jewish Catastrophe, 1933–1945.* New York: Aaron Asher Books, 1992. More on the Holocaust by a leading scholar.

Jamieson, Katherine M. *The Organization of Corporate Crime: Dynamics of Antitrust Violation.* Thousand Oaks, Calif.: Sage, 1994. Price-fixing by Fortune 500 corporations between 1981 and 1985.

Jamieson, Kathleen Hall. *Dirty Politics: Deception, Distraction, and Democracy.* New York: Oxford University Press, 1992. "Attack campaigning" across time, with an especially compelling chapter on the 1988 presidential campaign and the Willie Horton episode.

Jones, James. *Bad Blood: The Tuskegee Syphilis Experiment.* New York: Free Press, 1993. The U.S. Public Health Service's racist "experiment" in which poor black men with syphilis were left untreated, ostensibly to assess the long-term effects of the disease.

Kohn, Howard. "Service With A Sneer." *The New York Times Magazine,* November 6, 1994, pp. 43ff. Explains racism at Denny's restaurants and what the company is doing to change things.

Kolodny, Annette. *Failing the Future: A Dean Looks at Higher Education in the Twenty-first Century.* Durham, N.C.: The University of North Carolina Press, 1998. What's wrong with and what can be done to make things better at major universities, by former dean of the College of Humanities at the University of Arizona.

Kutler, Stanley. *The Wars of Watergate: The Last Crisis of Richard Nixon.* New York: Knopf, 1990. The Watergate burglary and the cover-up that followed.

Perry, Susan, and Jim Dawson. *Nightmare: Women and the Dalkon Shield.*

New York: Macmillan, 1985. A. H. Robin's birth control device that killed and injured women.

Reverby, Susan, ed. *Tuskegee's Truths: Rethinking the Tuskegee Syphilis Study.* Chapel Hill, N.C.: The University of North Carolina Press, 2000. An anthology providing multiple and richly detailed perspectives on the racist Tuskegee Experiment.

Robins, Natalie. *Alien Ink: The FBI's War on Freedom of Expression.* New York: William Morrow, 1992. Description of FBI collection and use of information on prominent authors.

Rojstaczer, Stuart. *Gone for Good: Tales of University Life After the Golden Age.* New York: Oxford University Press, 2000. How and why undergraduate and graduate education and professing are changing for the worse, by a professor in the Division of Earth and Ocean Sciences at Duke University.

Rosenblatt, Roger. "How Do They Live With Themselves?" *The New York Times Magazine,* March 20, 1994, pp. 34ff. How the people inside the giant tobacco and food conglomerate Philip Morris rationalize making and selling Marlboro and other cigarettes.

Rothmiller, Mike, with Ivan G. Goldman. *L.A. Secret Police: Inside the LAPD Elite Spy Network.* New York: Pocket Books, 1992. Description of the Organized Crime Intelligence Division that spied on almost everybody, sometimes even members of organized crime.

Wilkinson, Alec. *Big Sugar: Seasons in the Cane Fields of Florida.* New York: Knopf, 1989. Description of the workers who keep things sweet for major sugar companies.

6

The Heavy Electrical Equipment Antitrust Cases

Price-Fixing Techniques and Rationalizations

Gilbert Geis

An inadvertent bit of humor by a defense attorney provided one of the major criminological motifs for "the most serious violation of the antitrust laws since the time of their passage at the turn of the century."[1] The defendants, including several vice-presidents of the General Electric Corporation and the Westinghouse Electric Corporation—the two largest companies in the heavy electrical equipment industry—stood somberly in a federal courtroom in Philadelphia on February 6, 1961. They were aptly described by a newspaper reporter as "middle-class men in Ivy League suits—typical business men in appearance, men who would never be taken for lawbreakers."[2] Several were deacons or vestrymen of their churches. One was president of his local chamber of commerce, another a hospital board member, another chief fund raiser for the community chest, another a bank director, another a director of the taxpayer's association, another an organizer of the local Little League.

The attorney for a General Electric executive attacked the government's demand for a jail sentence for his client, calling it "cold-blooded." The lawyer insisted that government prosecutors did not understand what it would do to his client, "this fine man," to be put "behind bars" with "common criminals who have been convicted of embezzlement and other serious crimes."[3]

From Marshall B. Clinard and Richard Quinnev (eds.), *Criminal Behavior Systems: A Typology*, pp. 140–51. Copyright © 1967 by Holt, Rinehart and Winston. Reprinted by permission.

1. Judge J. Cullen Ganey in "Application of the State of California," *Federal Supplement*, 195 (Eastern District, Pennsylvania, 1961), p. 39.

2. *New York Times*, February 7, 1961.

3. *New York Times*, February 7, 1961.

The difficulty of defense counsel in considering antitrust violations "serious crimes," crimes at least equivalent to embezzling, indicates in part why the 1961 prosecutions provide such fascinating material for criminological study. Edwin H. Sutherland, who originated the term "white collar crime" to categorize offenders such as antitrust violators, had lamented that his pioneering work was handicapped by the absence of adequate case histories of corporate offenders. "No firsthand research from this point of view has even been reported,"[4] Sutherland noted and, lacking such data, he proceeded to employ rather prosaic stories of derelictions by rather unimportant persons in small enterprises upon which to build an interpretative and theoretical structure for white collar crime.

To explain corporate offenses and offenders, Sutherland had to rely primarily upon the criminal biographies of various large companies, as these were disclosed in the annals of trial courts and administrative agencies. In the absence of information about human offenders, the legal fiction of corporate humanity, a kind of economic anthropomorphism, found its way into criminological literature. Factual gaps were filled by shrewd guesses, definitional and semantic strategies, and a good deal of extrapolation. It was as if an attempt were being made to explain murder by reference only to the listed rap sheet offenses of a murderer and the life stories and identification data of several lesser offenders.[5]

Sutherland was writing, of course, before the antitrust violations in the heavy electrical equipment industry became part of the public record. Though much of the data regarding them is tantalizingly incomplete, unresponsive to fine points of particular criminological concern, the antitrust offenses nonetheless represent extraordinary case studies of white-collar crime, that designation which, according to Sutherland, applies to behavior by "a person of high socioeconomic status who violates the laws designed to regulate his

---

4. Edwin H. Sutherland, *White Collar Crime.* New York: Holt, Rinehart and Winston, Inc., 1949, p. 240. Note: "Private enterprise remains extraordinarily private. . . . We know more about the motives, habits, and most intimate arcana of primitive peoples in New Guinea . . . than we do of the denizens of executive suites in Unilever House, Citroen, or General Electric (at least until a recent Congressional investigation)."—Roy Lewis and Rosemary Stewart, *The Managers.* New York: New American Library, 1961, pp. 111–112.

5. For an elaboration of this point, see Gilbert Geis, "Toward a Delineation of White-Collar Offenses," *Sociological Inquiry,* 32 (Spring 1962), pp. 160–171.

occupational activities"[6] and "principally refers to business managers and executives."[7] In particular, the antitrust cases provide the researcher with a mass of raw data against which to test and to refine earlier hunches and hypotheses regarding white-collar crime.

Facts of the Antitrust Violations

The most notable characteristic of the 1961 antitrust conspiracy was its willful and blatant nature. These were not complex acts only doubtfully in violation of a highly complicated statute. They were flagrant criminal offenses, patently in contradiction to the letter and the spirit of the Sherman Antitrust Act of 1890, which forbade price-fixing arrangements as restraints upon free trade.[8]

The details of the conspiracy must be drawn together from diverse secondhand sources because the grand jury hearings upon which the criminal indictments were based were not made public. The decision to keep the records closed was reached on the ground that the traditional secrecy of grand jury proceedings took precedence over public interest in obtaining information about the conspiracy and over the interest of different purchasers in acquiring background data upon which to base civil suits against the offending corporations for allegedly fraudulent sales.[9]

The federal government had initiated the grand jury probes in mid-1959, apparently after receiving complaints from officials of the Tennessee Valley Authority concerning identical bids they were getting from manufacturers of highly technical electrical equipment,

6. Edwin H. Sutherland in Vernon C. Branham and Samuel B. Kutash, *Encyclopedia of Criminology.* New York: Philosophical Library, Inc., 1949, p. 511.

7. Sutherland, *White Collar Crime*, p. 9, fn. 7.

8. *United States Statutes*, 26 (1890), p. 209; *United States Code,* 15 (1958), pp. 1, 2. See also William L. Letwin, "Congress and the Sherman Antitrust Law, 1887–1890," *University of Chicago Law Review,* 23 (Winter 1956), pp. 221–258, and Paul E. Hadlick, *Criminal Prosecutions under the Sherman Anti-Trust Act,* Washington, D.C.: Ransdell, 1939. The best interpretation of American antitrust law is A. D. Neale, *Antitrust Laws of the United States,* New York: Cambridge University Press, 1960.

9. Note, "Release of the Grand Jury Minutes to the National Deposition Program of the Electrical Equipment Cases," *University of Pennsylvania Law Review,* 112 (June 1964), pp. 1133–1145.

even though the bids were submitted in sealed envelopes.[10] Four grand juries were ultimately convened and subpoenaed 196 persons, some of whom obviously revealed the intimate details of the price-fixing procedures. A package of twenty indictments was handed down, involving 45 individual defendants and 29 corporations. Almost all of the corporate defendants pleaded guilty; the company officials tended to enter pleas of nolo contendere (no contest) which, in this case, might reasonably be taken to indicate that they did not see much likelihood of escaping conviction.

The pleas negated the necessity for a public trial and for public knowledge of the precise machinations involved in the offenses. At the sentencing hearing, fines amounting to $1,924,500 were levied against the defendants, $1,787,000 falling upon the corporations and $137,000 upon different individuals. The major fines were set against General Electric ($437,500) and Westinghouse ($372,500). Much more eye-catching were the jail terms of thirty days imposed upon seven defendants, of whom four were vice-presidents, two were division managers, and one was a sales manager.

The defendants sentenced to jail were handled essentially the same as other offenders with similar dispositions. They were handcuffed in pairs in the back seat of an automobile on their way to the Montgomery County Jail in Norristown, Pennsylvania, fingerprinted on entry, and dressed in the standard blue denim uniforms. During their stay, they were described as "model prisoners," and several were transferred to the prison farm. The remainder, working an eight-hour day for 30 cents, earned recognition from the warden as "the most intelligent prisoners" he had had during the year on a project concerned with organizing prison records. None of the seven men had visitors during the Wednesday and Saturday periods reserved for visiting; all indicated a desire not to be seen by their families or friends.[11]

Good behavior earned the men a five-day reduction in their sentence. Toward the end of the year, the remaining defendants, who had been placed on probation, were released from that status,

10. John Herling, *The Great Price Conspiracy*, Washington, D.C.: Robert B. Luce, 1962, pp. 1–12; John G. Fuller, *The Gentleman Conspirators*, New York: Grove Press, Inc., 1962, pp. 7–11. See also Myron W. Watkins, "Electrical Equipment Antitrust Cases—Their Implications for Government and Business," *University of Chicago Law Review*, 29 (August 1961) pp. 97–110.

11. United Press International, February 16, 1961; *New York Times*, February 25, 1961.

despite the strong protests of government officials. The judge, the same man who had imposed the original sentences, explained his action by noting that he "didn't think that this was the type of offense that probation lent itself readily to or was designed for." Supervision was seen as meaningless for men with such past records and such little likelihood of recidivism, particularly since the probation office was already "clogged to the gunwales" with cases.[12]

The major economic consequences to the corporations arose from civil suits for treble damages filed against them as provided in the antitrust laws. The original fines were, of course, negligible: For General Electric, a half-million dollar loss was no more unsettling than a $3 parking fine would be to a man with an income of $175,000 a year. Throughout the early stages of negotiations over the damage suits, General Electric maintained that it would resist such actions on grounds which are noteworthy as an indication of the source and the content of the rationale that underlay the self-justification of individual participants in the price-fixing conspiracy:

> We believe that the purchasers of electrical apparatus have received fair value by any reasonable standard. The prices which they have paid during the past years were appropriate to value received and reasonable as compared with the general trends of prices in the economy, the price trends for similar equipment and the price trends for materials, salaries, and wages. The foresight of the electrical utilities and the design and manufacturing skills of companies such as General Electric have kept electricity one of today's greatest bargains.[13]

By 1962, General Electric was granting that settlements totaling between $45 and $50 million would have to be arranged to satisfy claimants.[14] Municipalities and other purchasers of heavy electrical equipment were taking the period of lowest prices, when they assumed the price-rigging was least effective, using these prices as "legitimate," and calculating higher payments as products of the price conspiracy.[15] The initial G.E. estimate soon proved as untenable as its original thesis regarding value received. A mid-1964 calculation showed that 90

12. Telephone interview with Judge Ganey, Philadelphia, August 31, 1964; *New York Times*, December 20, 1961.

13. *New York Times*, February 7, 1961.

14. *New York Times*, July 27, 1962.

15. *New York Times*, March 14, 1961.

percent of some 1800 claims had been settled for a total of $160 million,[16] but General Electric could derive some solace from the fact that most of these payments would be tax-deductible.[17]

Techniques of the Conspiracy

The modus operandi for the antitrust violations shows clearly the awareness of the participants that their behavior was such that it had better be carried on as secretly as possible. Some comparison might be made between the antitrust offenses and other forms of fraud occurring in lower economic classes. It was one of Sutherland's most telling contentions that neither the method by which a crime is committed nor the manner in which it is handled by public agencies alters the essential criminal nature of the act and the criminal status of the perpetrator.[18] Selling faucet water on a street corner to a blind man who is led to believe that the product is specially prepared to relieve his ailment is seen as no different from selling a $50 million turbine to a city which is laboring under the misapprehension that it is purchasing the product at the best price possible from closed competitive bidding. The same may be said in regard to methods of treatment. Tuberculosis, for example, remains tuberculosis and its victim a tubercular whether the condition is treated in a sanitarium or whether it is ignored or even condoned by public authorities. So too with crime. As Miss Stein might have said: A crime is a crime is a crime.

Like most reasonably adept and optimistic criminals, the antitrust violators had hoped to escape apprehension: "I didn't expect to get caught and I went to great lengths to conceal my activities so that I wouldn't get caught," one of them said.[19] Another went into some

16. *New York Times*, April 29, 1964. Regarding Westinghouse, see *Wall Street Journal*, September 3, 1964.

17. *Wall Street Journal*, July 27, 1964.

18. Edwin H. Sutherland, "While-Collar Criminality," *American Sociological Review*, 5 (February 1940), pp. 1–12.

19. Senate Committee on the Judiciary, Subcommittee on Antitrust and Monopoly, 87th Cong., 2d Sess., 1961. "Administered Prices," *Hearings*, Pts. 27 and 28. Unless otherwise indicated, subsequent data and quotations are taken from these documents. Space considerations do not permit citation to the precise pages.

detail concerning the techniques of concealment: "it was considered discreet to not be too obvious and to minimize telephone calls, to use plain envelopes if mailing material to each other, not to be seen together on traveling, and so forth, . . . not to leave wastepaper, of which there was a lot, strewn around a room when leaving." The plans themselves, while there were some slight variations over time and in terms of different participants, were essentially similar. The offenders hid behind a camouflage of fictitious names and conspiratorial codes. The attendance roster for the meetings was known as the "Christmas card list" and the gatherings, interestingly enough, as "choir practice."[20] The offenders used public telephones for much of their communication, and they met either at trade association conventions, where their relationship would appear reasonable, or at sites selected for their anonymity. It is quite noteworthy, in this respect, that while some of the men filed false claims, so as to mislead their superiors regarding the city they had visited, they never asked for expense money to places more distant than those they had actually gone to—on the theory, apparently, that whatever else was occurring, it would not do to cheat the company.

At the meetings, negotiations centered about the establishment of a "reasonable" division of the market for the various products. Generally participating companies were allocated essentially that part of the market which they had previously garnered. If Company A, for instance, had under competitive conditions secured 20 percent of the available business, then agreement might be reached that it would be given the opportunity to submit the lowest bid on 20 percent of the new contracts. A low price would be established, and the remainder of the companies would bid at approximately equivalent, though higher, levels. It sometimes happened, however, that because of things such as company reputation, or available servicing arrangements, the final contract was awarded to a firm which had not submitted the lowest bid. For this, among other reasons, debate among the conspirators was often acrimonious about the proper division of spoils, about alleged failures to observe previous agreements, and about other intramural matters. Sometimes, depending upon the contract, the conspirators would draw

20. The quotation is from an excellent two-part article by Richard Austin Smith. "The Incredible Electrical Conspiracy," *Fortune*, 63 (April 1961), pp. 132–137, and 63 (May 1961), 161–164, which is reproduced in *Hearings*, Pt. 27, pp. 17094–17105 and 17172–17182.

lots to determine who would submit the lowest bid; at other times the appropriate arrangement would be determined under a rotating system conspiratorially referred to as the "phase of the moon."

Explanations of the Conspiracy

Attempts to understand the reasons for and the general significance of the price-fixing conspiracy have been numerous. They include re-examinations of the antitrust laws[21] as well as denunciations of the corporate ethos and the general pattern of American life and American values. For example, "This is the challenge of the grim outcome in Philadelphia. Can corporations outgrow the idea that employees must produce, whatever the moral cost, or lose their perquisites? Is it possible to create a business ethic favoring honesty even at the expense of profit? Can our society get away from its pervasive attitude that a little cheating is harmless? The electrical cases raise those questions not only in the antitrust field, but in others, especially taxation. And they are questions not only for large corporations and not only for business but for all of us."[22]

A not inconsiderable number of the defendants took the line that their behavior, while technically criminal, had really served a worthwhile purpose by "stabilizing prices" (a much-favored phrase of the conspirators). This altruistic interpretation almost invariably was combined with an attempted distinction among illegal, criminal, and immoral acts, with the offender expressing the view that what he had done might have been designated by the statutes as criminal, but either he was unaware of such a designation or he thought it unreasonable that acts with admirable consequences should be considered criminal. The testimony of a Westinghouse executive during hearings by the Senate Subcommittee on Antitrust and Monopoly clearly illustrates this point of view:

> *Committee Attorney:* Did you know that these meetings with competitors were illegal?

21. See, for instance, Leland Hazard, "Are Big Businessmen Crooks?" *Atlantic*, 208 (November 1961), pp. 57–61.

22. Anthony Lewis, *New York Times*, February 12, 1961.

Witness: Illegal? Yes, but not criminal. I didn't find that out until I read the indictment. . . . I assumed that criminal action meant damaging someone, and we did not do that. . . . I thought that we were more or less working on a survival basis in order to try to make enough to keep our plant and our employees.

This theme was repeated in essentially similar language by a number of witnesses. "It is against the law," an official of the Ingersoll-Rand Corporation granted, but he added: "I do not know that it is against public welfare because I am not certain that the consumer was actually injured by this operation." A Carrier Corporation executive testified that he was "reasonably in doubt" that the price-fixing meetings violated the antitrust law. "Certainly, we were in a gray area. I think the degree of violation, if you can speak of it that way, is what was in doubt." Another offender said: "We were not meeting for the purpose of getting the most that traffic could bear. It was to get a value for our product." Some of these views are gathered together in a statement by a former sales manager of the I-T-E Circuit Breaker Company:

> One faces a decision, I guess, at such times, about how far to go with company instructions, and since the spirit of such meetings only appeared to be correcting a horrible price level situation, that there was not an attempt to actually damage customers, charge excessive prices, there was no personal gain in it for me, the company did not seem actually to be defrauding. Corporate statements can evidence the fact that there have been poor profits during all these years. . . . So I guess morally it did not seem quite so bad as might be inferred by the definition of the activity itself.

For the most part, personal explanations for the acts were sought in the structure of corporate pressures rather than in the avarice or lack of law-abiding character of the men involved. The defendants almost invariably testified that they came new to a job, found price-fixing an established way of life, and simply entered into it as they did into other aspects of their job. The explanatory scheme fit into a pattern that Senator Philip A. Hart of Michigan during the subcommittee hearings labeled *imbued fraud.*[23]

There was considerable agreement concerning the precise method

23. Analysis of the relationship between occupational norms and legal violations could represent a fruitful line of inquiry. See Richard Quinney, "The Study of White Collar Crime: Toward a Reorientation in Theory and Research," *Journal of Criminal Law, Criminology and Police Science*, 55 (June 1964), pp. 208–214.

in which the man initially became involved in price-fixing. "My first actual experience was back in the 1930's," a General Electric official said. "I was taken there by my boss . . . to sit down and price a job." An Ingersoll-Rand executive said: "[My superior] took me to a meeting to introduce me to some of our competitors, none of whom I had met before, and at that meeting pricing of condensers was discussed with the competitors." Essentially the same comment is repeated by witness after witness. "I found it this way when I was introduced to competitive discussion and just drifted into it," a Carrier Corporation man noted. A General Electric officer echoed this point: "Every direct supervisor that I had directed me to meet with competition. . . . It had become so common and gone on for so many years that I think we lost sight of the fact that it was illegal." Price-fixing, whether or not recognized as illegal by the offenders, was clearly an integral part of their jobs. "Meeting with competitors was just one of the many facets of responsibility that was delegated to me," one witness testified, while an Allis-Chalmers executive responded to the question "Why did you go to the meetings?" with the observation: "I thought it was part of my duty to do so."

What might have happened to the men if, for reasons of conscience or perhaps through a fear of the possible consequences, they had objected to the "duty" to participate in price-fixing schemes? This point was raised only by the General Electric employees, perhaps because they alone had some actual evidence upon which to base their speculations. In 1946, General Electric had first issued a directive, number 20.5, which spelled out the company's policy against price-fixing, in terms stronger than those found in the antitrust laws. A considerable number of the executives believed, in the words of one, that the directive was only for "public consumption," and not to be taken seriously. One man, however, refused to engage in price-fixing after he had initialed the document forbidding it. A witness explained to the Senate subcommittee what followed: "[My superior] told me, 'This fellow is a fine fellow, he is capable in every respect except he was not broad enough for his job, that he was so religious that he thought in spite of what his superiors said, he thought having signed that, that he should not do any of this and he is getting us in trouble with competition.'"

The man who succeeded the troublesome official, one of the defendants in the Philadelphia hearing, said that he had been told that he "would be expected to do otherwise" and that this "was why I was offered that promotion to Philadelphia because this man would not do it." At the same time, however, the General Electric witnesses specified clearly that it was not their jobs with the company that would be in jeopardy if they failed to price-fix, but rather the particular assignment they had. "If I didn't do it, I felt that somebody else would," said one, with an obvious note of self-justification. "I would be removed and somebody else would do it."

Westinghouse and General Electric differed considerably in their reactions to the exposure of the offenses, with Westinghouse electing to retain in its employ persons involved in the conspiracy, and General Electric deciding to dismiss the employees who had been before the court. The reasoning of the companies throws light both on the case and on the relationship between antitrust offenses and the more traditionally viewed forms of criminal behavior.

Westinghouse put forward four justifications for its retention decision. First, it declared, the men involved had not sought personal aggrandizement: "While their actions cannot in any way be condoned, these men did not act for personal gain, but in the belief, misguided though it may have been, that they were furthering the company's interest." Second, "the punishment incurred by them already was harsh" and "no further penalties would serve any useful purpose." Third, "each of these individuals is in every sense a reputable citizen, a respected and valuable member of the community and of high moral character." Fourth, there was virtually no likelihood that the individuals would repeat their offense.[24]

General Electric's punitive line toward its employees was justified on the ground that the men had violated not only federal law but also a basic company policy, and that they therefore deserved severe punishment. The company's action met with something less than wholehearted acclaim; rather, it was often interpreted as an attempt to scapegoat particular individuals for what was essentially the responsibility of the corporate enterprise and its top executives. "I do not understand the holier-than-thou attitude in GE when your directions came from very high at the top," Senator Kefauver said during his committee's hearings, while Senator John A. Carroll of Colorado expressed his view through a leading question: "Do you

24. Sharon (Pa.) *Herald*, February 6, 1961.

think you were thrown to the wolves to ease the public relations situation . . . that has developed since these indictments?" he asked a discharged General Electric employee. The witness thought that he had.

Perhaps most striking is the fact that though many offenders quite clearly stressed the likely consequences for them if they failed to conform to price-fixing expectations, not one hinted at the benefits he might expect, the personal and professional rewards, from participation in the criminal conspiracy. It remained for the sentencing judge and two top General Electric executives to deliver the harshest denunciations of the personal motives and qualities of the conspirators to be put forth during the case.

The statement of Judge J. Cullen Ganey, read prior to imposing sentence, received widespread attention. In it he sharply criticized the corporations as the major culprits, but he also pictured the defendants in a light other than that they chose to shed upon themselves in their subsequent discussions of the offenses: "they were torn between conscience and an approved corporate policy, with the rewarding objective of promotion, comfortable security, and large salaries. They were the organization or company man, the conformist who goes along with his superiors and finds balm for his conscience in additional comforts and security of his place in the corporate set-up."[25]

The repeated emphasis on "comfort" and "security" constitutes the basic element of Judge Ganey's view of the motivations of the offenders. Stress on passive acquiescence occurs in remarks by two General Electric executives viewing the derelictions of their subordinates. Robert Paxton, the retired company president, called antitrust agreements "monkey business" and denounced in vitriolic terms one of his former superiors who, when Paxton first joined General Electric, had put him to work attempting to secure a bid on a contract that had already been prearranged by a price-fixing agreement. Ralph Cordiner, the president and board chairman of General Electric, thought that the antitrust offenses were motivated by drives for easily acquired power. Cordiner's statement is noteworthy for its dismissal of the explanations of the offenders as "rationalizations": "One reason for the offenses was a desire to be

25. *New York Times*, February 7, 1961.

'Mr. Transformer' or 'Mr. Switchgear'* . . . and to have influence over a larger segment of the industry. . . . The second was that it was an indolent, lazy way to do business. When you get all through with the rationalizations, you have to come back to one or the other of these conclusions."

There were other explanations as well. One truculent offender, the 68-year-old president of a smaller company who had been spared a jail sentence only because of his age and the illness of his wife, categorically denied the illegality of his behavior. "We did not fix prices," he said. "I can't agree with you. I am telling you that all we did was recover costs." Some persons blamed the system of decentralization in the larger companies, which they said placed a heavy burden to produce profit on each of the relatively autonomous divisions, particularly when bonuses—"incentive compensation" —were at stake, while others maintained that the "dog-eat-dog" business conditions in the heavy electrical equipment industry were responsible for the violations, Perhaps the simplest explanation came from a General Electric executive. "I think," he said, "the boys could resist everything but temptation."

Portrait of an Offender

The highest paid executive to be given a jail sentence was a General Electric vice-president, earning $135,000 a year—about $2600 every week. The details of his career and his participation in the conspiracy provide additional insight into the operations of white collar crime and white collar criminals.

The General Electric vice-president was one of the disproportionate number of Southerners involved in the antitrust violations. He had been born in Atlanta and was 46 years old at the time he was sentenced to jail. He had graduated with a degree in electrical engineering from Georgia Tech, and received an honorary doctorate degree from Sienna College in 1958, was married, and the father of three children. He had served in the Navy during the Second

---

*Earlier, a witness had quoted his superior as saying: "I have the industry under my thumb. They will do just about as I ask them." This man, the witness said, "was known as Mr. Switchgear in the industry."

World War, rising to the rank of lieutenant commander, was a director of the Schenectady Boy's Club, on the board of trustees of Miss Hall's School, and, not without some irony, was a member of Governor Rockefeller's Temporary State Committee on Economic Expansion.[26]

Almost immediately after his sentencing, he issued a statement to the press, noting that he was to serve a jail term "for conduct which has been interpreted as being in conflict with the complex antitrust laws." He commented that "General Electric, Schenectady, and its people have undergone many ordeals together and we have not only survived them, but have come out stronger, more vigorous, more alive than ever. We shall again." Then he voiced his appreciation for "the letters and calls from people all over the country, the community, the shops, and the offices . . . expressing confidence and support."[27]

The vice-president was neither so sentimental about his company nor so certain about the complexity of the antitrust regulations when he appeared before the Kefauver committee five months later. "I don't get mad, Senator," he said at one point, referring to his behavior during a meeting with competitors, but he took another line when he attempted to explain why he was no longer associated with General Electric: ". . . when I got out of being a guest of the government for 30 days, I had found out that we were not to be paid while we were there,* and I got, frankly, madder than hell."

Previously, he had been mentioned as a possible president of General Electric, described by the then president, as "an exceptionally eager and promising individual." Employed by the company shortly after graduation from college, he had risen dramatically through the managerial ranks, and passed that point, described by a higher executive, "where the man, if his work has been sufficiently promising, has an opportunity to step across the barrier out of his function into the field of general management." In 1946, he had his first contact with price-fixing, being introduced to competitors by his superior and told that he "should be the one to contact them as far as power transformers were concerned in the future."

---

26. *New York Times*, February 7, 1961.
27. *Schenectady Union-Star*, February 10, 1961.
*A matter of some $11,000 for the jail term.

The meetings that he attended ran a rather erratic course, with numerous squabbles between the participants. Continual efforts had to be made to keep knowledge of the meetings from "the manufacturing people, the engineers, and especially the lawyers," but this was achieved, the witness tried to convince the Kefauver committee, because commercial transactions remained unquestioned by managerial personnel so long as they showed a reasonable profit. The price-fixing meetings continued from 1946 until 1949. At that time, a federal investigation of licensing and cross-patent activities in the transformer industry sent the conspirators scurrying for shelter. "The iron curtain was completely down" for a year, and sales people at General Electric were forbidden to attend gatherings of the National Electrical Manufacturers' Association, where they had traditionally connived with competitors.

Meetings resumed, however, when the witness's superior, described by him as "a great communicator, a great philosopher, and, frankly, a great believer in stabilities of prices," decided that "the market was getting in chaotic condition" and that they "had better go out and see what could be done about it." He was told to keep knowledge of the meetings from Robert Paxton, "an Adam Smith Advocate," then the plant works manager, because Paxton "don't understand these things."

Promoted to general manager in 1954, the witness was called to New York by the president of General Electric and told specifically, possibly in part because he had a reputation of being "a bad boy," to comply with the company policy and with the antitrust laws, and to see that his subordinates did so too. This instruction lasted as long as it took him to get from New York back to Massachusetts, where his superior there told him: "Now, keep on doing the way that you have been doing but just . . . be sensible about it and use your head on the subject." The price-fixing meetings therefore continued unabated, particularly as market conditions were aggravated by overproduction which had taken place during the Korean War. In the late 1950s foreign competition entered the picture, and lower bids from abroad often forced the American firms to give up on particular price-fixing attempts.

In 1957, the witness was promoted to vice-president, and again brought to New York for a lecture from the company president on the evils of price-fixing. This time, his "air cover gone"—he now had to report directly to top management—he decided to abandon altogether his involvement in price-fixing. He returned to his plant and issued stringent orders to his subordinates that they were no longer to attend meetings with competitors. Not surprisingly, since he himself had rarely obeyed such injunctions, neither did the sales persons in his division.

The witness was interrogated closely about his moral feelings regarding criminal behavior. He fumbled most of the questions, avoiding answering them directly, but ultimately came to the point of saying that the consequences visited upon him represented the major reason for a re-evaluation of his actions. He would not behave in the same manner again because of what "I have been through and what I have done to my family." He was also vexed with the treatment he had received from the newspapers: "They have never laid off a second. They have used some terms which I don't think are necessary—they don't use the term price fixing. It is always price rigging or trying to make it as sensational as possible."[28] The taint of a jail sentence, he said, had the effect of making people "start looking at the moral values a little bit." Senator Hart drew the following conclusions from the witness's comments:

> Hart: This was what I was wondering about, whether absent the introduction of this element of fear, there would have been any re-examination of the moral implications.
> Witness: I wonder, Senator. That is a pretty tough one to answer.
> Hart: If I understand you correctly, you have already answered it. . . . After the fear, there came the moral re-evaluation.

Nevertheless, the former General Electric vice-president viewed his situation rather philosophically. Regarding his resignation from the company, it was "the way the ball has bounced." He hoped that he would have "the opportunity to continue in American industry and do a job," and he wished some of the other men who had been dismissed a lot of good luck. "I want to leave the company with no bitterness and go out and see if I can't start a new venture along the right lines." Eight days later, he accepted a job as assistant to the

28. A contrary view is expressed in Note, "Increasing Community Control over Corporate Crime—A Problem in the Law of Sanctions," *Yale Law Journal,* 71 (December 1961), footnoted material pp. 287–289. It has been pointed out that *Time* magazine (February 17, 1961, pp. 64ff) reported the conspiracy in its "Business" section, whereas it normally presents crime news under a special heading of its own—Donald R. Taft and Ralph W. England, Jr., *Criminology,* 4th ed., New York: The Macmillan Company, 1964, p. 203.

president in charge of product research in a large corporation located outside Philadelphia.[29] Slightly more than a month after that, he was named president of the company, at a salary reported to be somewhat less than the $74,000 yearly received by his predecessor.[30]

A Summing Up

The antitrust violations in the heavy electrical industry permit a reevaluation of many of the earlier speculations about white collar crime. The price-fixing behavior, flagrant in nature, was clearly in violation of the criminal provisions of the Sherman Act of 1890, which had been aimed at furthering "industrial liberty." Rather, the price-fixing arrangements represented attempts at "corporate socialism," and in the words of Senator Kefauver to a subcommittee witness: "It makes a complete mockery not only of how we have always lived and what we have believed in and have laws to protect, but what you were doing was to make a complete mockery of the carefully worded laws of the government of the United States, ordinances of the cities, rules of the REA's [Rural Electrification Administration], with reference to sealed secret bids in order to get competition."

The facts of the antitrust conspiracy would seem clearly to resolve in the affirmative debate concerning the criminal nature and the relevance for criminological study of such forms of white collar crime,[31] though warnings regarding an indefinite and unwarranted extension of the designation "crime" to all acts abhorrent to academic criminologists must remain in force.[32] Many of

29. *New York Times*, May 12, 1961.

30. *New York Times*, June 23, 1961.

31. See Edwin H. Sutherland, "Is 'White Collar Crime' Crime?" *American Sociological Review*, 10 (April 1945), pp. 132–139. Note: "It may be hoped that the Philadelphia electric cases have helped to dispel this misapprehension. . . . It should now be clear that a deliberate or conscious violation of the antitrust laws . . . is a serious offense against society which is as criminal as any other act that injures many in order to profit a few. Conspiracy to violate the antitrust laws is economic racketeering. Those who are apprehended in such acts are, and will be treated as criminals."—Lee Loevinger, "Recent Developments in Antitrust Enforcement," Antitrust Section, American Bar Association, 18 (1961), p. 102.

32. Paul W. Tappan, "Who Is the Criminal?" *American Sociological Review*, 12 (February 1947), pp. 96–102.

Sutherland's ideas concerning the behavior of corporate offenders also receive substantiation. His stress on learning and associational patterns as important elements in the genesis of the violations receives strong support.[33] So too does his emphasis on national trade conventions as the sites of corporate criminal conspiracies.[34]

Others of Sutherland's views appear to require overhaul. His belief, for example, that "those who are responsible for the system of criminal justice are afraid to antagonize businessmen"[35] seems less than totally true in terms of the electrical industry prosecutions. Sutherland's thesis that "the customary pleas of the executives of the corporation . . . that they were ignorant of and not responsible for the action of the special department . . . is akin to the alibi of the ordinary criminal and need not be taken seriously"[36] also seems to be a rather injudicious blanket condemnation, The accuracy of the statement for the antitrust conspiracy must remain moot, but it would seem important that traditional safeguards concerning guilty knowledge as a basic ingredient in criminal responsibility be accorded great respect.[37] Nor, in terms of the antitrust data, does Sutherland appear altogether correct in his view that "the public agencies of communication, which continually define ordinary violations of the criminal code in a very critical manner, do not make similar definitions of white collar crime."[38]

Various analytical schemes and theoretical statements in criminology and related fields provide some insight into elements of the price-fixing conspiracy. Galbraith's caustic observation regarding the traditional academic view of corporate price-fixing arrangements represents a worthwhile point of departure: "Restraints on competition and the free movement of prices, the principal source of uncertainty to business firms, have been principally deplored by

---

33. Sutherland, *White Collar Crime,* pp. 234–57.

34. Ibid., p. 70.

35. Ibid., p. 10.

36. Ibid., p. 54.

37. For an excellent presentation, see Sanford H. Kadish, "Some Observations on the Use of Criminal Sanctions in Enforcing Economic Regulations," *University of Chicago Law Review,* 30 (Spring 1963), pp. 423–449. See also Richard A. Whiting, "Antitrust and the Corporate Executive," *Virginia Law Review,* 47 (October 1961), pp. 929–987.

38. Sutherland, *White Collar Crime,* p. 247.

university professors on lifelong appointments. Such security of tenure is deemed essential for fruitful and unremitting thought."[39] It seems apparent, looking at the antitrust offenses in this light, that the attractiveness of a secure market arrangement represented a major ingredient drawing corporate officers to the price-fixing violations. The elimination of competition meant the avoidance of uncertainty, the formalization and predictability of outcome, the minimization of risks. It is, of course, this incentive which accounts for much of human activity, be it deviant or "normal," and this tendency that Weber found so pronounced in bureaucracies in their move from vital but erratic beginnings to more staid and more comfortable middle and old age.[40]

For the conspirators there had necessarily to be a conjunction of factors before they could participate in the violations. First, of course, they had to perceive that there would be gains accruing from their behavior. Such gains might be personal and professional, in terms of corporate advancement toward prestige and power, and they might be vocational, in terms of a more expedient and secure method of carrying out assigned tasks. The offenders also apparently had to be able to neutralize or rationalize their behavior in a manner in keeping with their image of themselves as law-abiding, decent, and respectable persons.[41] The ebb and flow of the price-fixing conspiracy also clearly indicates the relationship, often overlooked in explanations of criminal behavior, between extrinsic conditions and illegal acts. When the market behaved in a manner the executives thought satisfactory, or when enforcement agencies seemed particularly threatening, the conspiracy desisted. When market conditions deteriorated, while corporate pressures for achieving attractive profit-and-loss statements remained constant, and enforcement activity abated, the price-fixing agreements flourished.

39. John Kenneth Galbraith, *The Affluent Society*, Boston: Houghton Mifflin Co., 1958, p. 84. See also Richard Hofstadter, "Antitrust in America," *Commentary*, 38 (August 1964), pp. 47–53. An executive of one corporation is said lo have remarked regarding the collusive antitrust arrangements: "It is the only way business can be run. It's free enterprise." Quoted by Mr. Justice Clark to Antitrust Section, American Bar Association, St Louis, August 8, 1961, p. 4.

40. Max Weber, *The Theory of Social and Economic Organization*, translated by A. M. Henderson and Talcott Parsons. New York: Oxford University Press, 1947, pp. 367–373.

41. See Donald R. Cressey, *Other People's Money*. New York: The Free Press of Glencoe, 1953; Gresham M. Sykes and David Matza, "Techniques of Neutralization: A Theory of Delinquency," *American Sociological Review*, 22 (December 1957), pp. 664–670.

More than anything else, however, a plunge into the elaborate documentation of the antitrust cases of 1961, as well as an attempt to relate them to other segments of criminological work, points up the considerable need for more and better monographic field studies of law violators and of systems of criminal behavior, these to be followed by attempts to establish theoretical guidelines and to review and refine current interpretative viewpoints. There have probably been no more than a dozen, if that many, full-length studies of types of criminal (not delinquent) behavior in the past decade. The need for such work seems overriding, and the 1961 antitrust cases represent but one of a number of instances, whether in the field of white collar crime, organized crime, sex offenses, personal or property crimes, or similar areas of concern, where we are still faced with a less than adequate supply of basic and comparative material upon which to base valid and useful theoretical statements.

7

Beer and Circus
Big-Time College Sports and
the Crippling of Undergraduate Education
Murray Sperber

Ten years ago, the big-time college sports entertainment industry
could be termed College Sports Inc. Since that time, its revenue
has exploded, and it has become College Sports MegaInc.

> *Six Billion?*
> *Where's Mine?*
> Six billion dollars over 11 years [that's the new NCAA deal with CBS-
> TV]. It comes out to about $545 million per year. . . .
>   College basketball players watch the coach roaming the sidelines
> in his $1,500 custom-made suit. They read about his $500,000 sal-
> ary and $250,000 per [year] from some sneaker deal. They watch
> the schools sell jerseys with the players' [names and] numbers on
> them. . . . They see the athletic director getting rich and the college
> president getting rich and NCAA officials getting rich and the
> coach's dog getting rich. And you wonder why they might ask, "Hey,
> where's my share? What am I, a pack mule?"
>   There is no other show business in which the actual entertainers
> don't get any money. . . . Even our Olympic teams pay the athletes
> above the table now. Believe me, the NCAA is not getting six bil-
> lion dollars so we can watch [Duke University's] Mike Kryzewski
> coach a bunch of chem majors.
>   —Tony Kornheiser, sportswriter and broadcaster

Beyond the sarcasm and outrage, this writer makes a crucial
point: How can the NCAA and member schools continue the pretense of student-athlete amateurism when the people running big-
time college sports amass fortunes from this huge entertainment
business, whereas the actual performers—the young men and

women who put fans in the seats and viewers in front of their TVs—receive only athletic scholarships, the most generous of which top out at $30,000, with the majority below $20,000 per year? *USA Today* led its front-page story on the new NCAA/CBS-TV March Madness deal with, "Amateurism has never been more lucrative" for the NCAA. As Tony Kornheiser indicated, Division I basketball players are rarely "chem majors," but, most often, minor leaguers in training for the next pro level. And CBS-TV is not paying the NCAA for TV rights to games where the players take difficult majors, such as an Emory versus Rochester contest, which feature truly amateur athletes in action. Yet, the NCAA works hard to maintain the amateur facade of big-time college sports—without it, the association would lose its tax exemptions, and the IRS would place it in the same category as all other professional sports enterprises.

To maintain its nonprofit status, the NCAA employs full-time lobbyists in Washington, D.C., and it locates their office in a building on Dupont Circle that also houses the most reputable higher education associations in America. The NCAA's head lobbyist explained the decision to rent space at One Dupont Circle as a strategic move: "Because of our office location, we are perceived as and treated as one of the higher education associations."

But the NCAA emperor has no clothes: When *USA Today* and other media outlets discussed the new March Madness TV contract, they put it within the context of "professional sports TV rights deals," placing it third on the television contract list, behind the NFL and NBA, but ahead of Nascar, major league baseball, and the NHL. And when the TV deals of NCAA Division I-A football schools are added to the basketball money, the annual television revenue of "amateur" college sports surpasses that of every professional league in the world.

In addition, the athletic directors and coaches who work in big-time college sports tend to forget the NCAA's official line on amateurism, and they usually speak in sports business terms. In a typical comment in January 2000 the AD at North Carolina State justified his slow timetable on hiring a new football coach by arguing, "We are part of a corporate group bigger than N.C. State called the Atlantic Coast Conference," and we have to consider the collective corporate interests before acting on our own.

Mike Kryzewski, the men's basketball coach at Duke University, another part of the Atlantic Coast Corporation, uses similar language. He has long complained that "the marketing of our product [college basketball] is at a really low level," and has urged the NCAA to bring in top corporate marketers to sell the college game better. Kryzewski, with an annual income of over $1 million, has marketed himself into the elite level of college coaches and, ironically, part of his success is the image of his players as authentic students, placing their academic goals ahead of their athletic ambitions. (In recent years, as some of his best players left school early to enter the NBA, this marketing ploy has eroded.)

Many college sports fans, particularly those over thirty-five, enjoy the student-athlete trappings of intercollegiate athletics. However, as Tony Kornheiser and other journalists constantly point out, the "big bucks reality" is omnipresent, and fans increasingly require a willful innocence to ignore the dollar signs.

> Compare the BCS' [football Bowl Championship Series] $100 million [a year revenue] to the $545 million a year the NCAA basketball tournaments will get from CBS, and you can see why everyone's spinning in his boots. They [college sports administrators] say, "Wait a minute. I thought football was the king of college sports."
> —Jim Wheeler, vice president of an
> international sports marketing firm

One hundred million dollars a year revenue from the BCS bowls—Rose, Orange, Sugar, and Fiesta—is not "chump change"; however, according to Wheeler, if the bowls were reconfigured into a playoff system, culminating in a College Super Bowl, "you'd be looking at $250 million" a year for the final games. To back this argument, his company, Swiss-based International Sports and Leisure (ISL), has offered BCS football schools a multiyear, multibillion-dollar contract for the rights to produce and market the college football playoffs. (The BCS encompasses the top six conferences in Division I-A football and Notre Dame.)

Many of the opponents of the ISL proposal cloak their objections in the rhetoric of amateurism—they claim that a playoff will stretch the football season too far into January, and players will have trouble starting their second semester classes—but the real roadblock is money. BCS officials believe that the current system works fine, and that other formats would render all games but the championship match meaningless, hurting overall bowl attendance, TV ratings, and the money flow. That's exactly what occurred in late 1999 and early 2000 when the media focused primarily on the Sugar Bowl game between No. 1 Florida State and No. 2 Virginia Tech. Probably a sixteen-team playoff series would produce more positive results: it could include many bowl games and, like the NCAA basketball Sweet Sixteen and final rounds when every game counts, college football playoff games would fill the stands, earn excellent TV ratings, and generate maximum revenue.

If, in future years, the BCS format continues to hamper the lower-tier bowls, the main participants in those games—the runners-up in the BCS conferences—might support a playoff system. The BCS television contract extends through 2005; however, a TV network insider explained that the executive in charge of the Bowl Championship Series, Roy Kramer, is always receptive to new ideas for postseason college football, particularly when it involves billions of dollars: "Money is what drove Roy to put together the BCS, and money can drive him to a better version."

When that occurs, you can bet that no BCS or NCAA official will argue that "college football players should not suit up in late January." Indeed, as an alternative proposal to the sixteen-team play-off, ISL suggests that after the current bowl season ends, a four-team billion-dollar playoff take place, adding more weeks to the winter football season.

> [Bowl game] life is good—if you're part of the BCS. On the outside, rumbles of discontent remain. . . . Schools in the six major [BCS] conferences—the Atlantic Coast, Big East, Big Ten, Big 12, Pacific 10, and Southeastern—figure to pull in just under 94% of the total $144.6 million paid out by 23 bowls this season.
>
> —Steve Weiberg, *USA Today* reporter

More than 110 schools play Division I-A football; however, unless they reside within the BCS fold, they remain at home during the bowl season or collect spare change in such marginal contests as the Motor City Bowl and the Las Vegas Bowl. In addition, although more than 300 schools play Division I basketball, the six BCS conferences hog the largest proportion of payout dollars from March Madness. According to a recent analysis of the finances of big-time college sports, the average annual revenue of the BCS conferences was $63 million, whereas the amount for the other twenty-three leagues in Division I averaged less than $3 million per year. Those are the revenue totals in big-time intercollegiate athletics. But the expenses numbers are higher, resulting in the amazing fact that *most college sports programs lose money.* Most extraordinary of all, the losers include many schools in the BCS conferences, including those playing in the most lucrative bowl games and advancing deep into the final rounds of the NCAA basketball tournaments. In late 1999, the athletic director of the University of Michigan—a school with an always full 110,000-seat stadium and 20,000-seat basketball arena—acknowledged that "the Wolverines intercollegiate sports program . . . last year ran a deficit," more than $2 million dollars of red ink. If Big Blue loses money in college sports, what hope is there for smaller programs?

. . .

Historically, and contrary to popular myth, almost all colleges and universities have always lost money on their intercollegiate athletics programs. Moreover, athletic departments ran deficits long before the federal government's Title IX mandated equality for women's intercollegiate athletics, and male athletic directors seized upon their Title IX costs to excuse their overall money losses. Historically, the main causes of athletic department red ink were waste, mismanagement, and fraud, and this situation continues today.

Of course, these annual deficits preclude paying the players: journalists like Tony Kornheiser have logic and ethics on their side when they demand that the athletes receive their fair "share" of the TV payouts—except, after the athletic directors, coaches, and athletic department staff spend the revenue, nothing remains for the players. Before the athletes can obtain their share, the entire athletic department finance system must be overhauled. But the people who run intercollegiate athletics, and benefit so handsomely from the corrupt system in place, will not willingly overturn the red ink trough.

The NCAA, in its regular financial reports, provides an indication of the profit-and-loss situation in big-time college sports. The most recent edition revealed that a majority of Division I athletic departments lost money in the 1990s, running larger deficits at the end of the decade than at the beginning, even though their revenue increased every year. However, because of the accounting tricks used by almost all athletic departments, the NCAA reports are only partially accurate, and the actual annual deficit numbers are much higher than the NCAA and member schools admit publicly.

Some accounting experts multiply the NCAA's deficit numbers by a factor of three. They point out that almost all athletic departments routinely move many legitimate costs from their ledgers and place them on their universities' financial books. These items include the utilities, maintenance, and debt-servicing bills on their intercollegiate athletic facilities—multimillion-dollar annual expenses for most big-time programs. Economist Andrew Zimbalist, after in-depth research on the finances of intercollegiate athletics, recently concluded that, despite all the accounting maneuvers, "the vast majority of schools" still "run a significant deficit from their athletic programs," and "only a handful of schools consistently earn surpluses," often small ones.

Athletic department deficits impact on host universities in many negative ways. Not only are millions of dollars siphoned from schools when athletic departments move expenditures onto university books, but more millions depart when schools cover the annual athletic department deficits. At the end of each fiscal year, universities "zero out" athletic department books; to do so they divert money from their General Operating Funds and other financial resources to cover the college sports losses. Money that could go to academic programs, student scholarships and loans, and many other educational purposes annually disappears down the athletic department financial hole.

The bottom line is clear: Big-time intercollegiate athletics financially hurts NCAA Division I schools more than it helps them. For every dollar that a few of these institutions acquire through college sports phenomena like the Flutie Factor, many more Division I members annually lose millions of dollars as a result of their athletic department deficits and other negative college sports factors. One inescapable conclusion appears: *College Sports Megalnc. is the most dysfunctional business in America.*

But neither the media nor the public focuses on this fact. Even Tony Kornheiser, one of the savviest sportswriters in America, says that the schools, as well as the individuals in charge of intercollegiate athletics, amass fortunes from the fun and games. Other media personalities also state this loudly and frequently.

. . .

The myth of college sports profitability not only masks the deficits of intercollegiate athletic programs, but it generates other negative financial consequences:

> The public hears about the millions that universities rake in from the NCAA basketball tournaments and bowl games, and people conclude that higher education doesn't need their tax dollars or private contributions. They believe that universities are doing great from their big-time college sports teams. . . . At Illinois, it couldn't be further from the truth, and that's also the situation at most other schools.
>
> —Howard Schein, professor at the University of Illinois, Champaign-Urbana

During the last two decades, legislative and taxpayer support for higher education has declined considerably. The role of big-time intercollegiate athletics in this decline is difficult to ascertain, but some observers believe that the never-ending college sports recruiting and academic scandals have made the public cynical about intercollegiate athletics, and stingy toward the universities that promote it. Additional evidence suggests that the myth of college sports profitability also closes taxpayers' wallets. In interviews for this book, a number of respondents offered comments similar to Professor Schein's. Common sense suggests that the myth of college sports profitability is a factor, possibly an important one, in the decline of public support for higher education; it certainly appeared to be so in the state of Illinois in the 1980s and 1990s.

. . .

Not only is the public unaware of the financial reality of college sports, but it knows even less about the causes of this situation. The media trumpets the huge payouts from bowl games and the NCAA basketball tournaments, and the public sees the high dollar numbers, but rarely does the media go beyond the myths and explore the financial facts.

A discussion of the following myths and realities helps explain why College Sports MegaInc. is the most dysfunctional business in America. It also explains how and why the men and women who administer universities and supposedly control their schools' athletic departments are totally complicit in the deficit financing of College Sports MegaInc.

. . .

Myth: Schools make millions of dollars when their teams play in football bowl games.

Reality: Most universities lose money when their football teams appear in bowl games. In a typical case, the University of Wisconsin received $1.8 million for participating in the 1999 Rose Bowl, but racked up almost $2.1 million in expenses on this event, close to $300,000 of rose-colored ink. The Rose Bowl payout could have helped the UW athletic department balance its books—its announced deficit at the end of the 1998–99 fiscal year was $1.1 million—but its excessive spending on this trip turned potential profit into real loss.

The cost of flying the football team, the coaches, and the team's support staff to and from Los Angeles, and housing and feeding them while there came to $831,400. In addition to this cost, like all schools going to bowl games, Wisconsin took along the families of the coaches, as well as baby-sitters (six) for the coaches' kids. Also a large number of other athletic department personnel and their spouses made the junket. Also on the "gravy plane" were members of the University of Wisconsin Board of Regents and spouses, school administrators and spouses, plus the so-called Faculty Board of Control of Intercollegiate Athletics and their spouses, and many hangers-on (termed "friends of the program") and their spouses. Then there was the marching band and cheerleaders, and not one but *three Bucky Badger mascots*—possibly in case the school-sponsored New Year's Eve celebration, costing $34,400, incapacitated one or two Buckys and the third one had to suit up on January 1.

The official Wisconsin traveling party numbered 832 people, including well over one hundred university officials and spouses. The Wisconsin group journeyed in the usual athletic department deluxe-class-for-all style, staying at a very expensive Beverly Hills hotel, wining and dining in an extravagant manner. After the UW athletic department paid all the bills from the trip, the expenses totaled $2,093,500. The travel manager of a major corporation, after examining a breakdown of the Wisconsin expenses, concluded:

> They could have done this trip for at least a fifth the cost and still stayed at nice hotels and eaten well. And that's with all the extra people—I've never seen so many free-loaders on a trip before and it appears completely unjustified. . . . These athletic department administrators could give lessons to drunken sailors on how to throw money around.

In the amazing world of college sports finances, Wisconsin's losses were not an anomaly: most athletic departments lose money on their bowl game excursions, and often they incur greater losses than Wisconsin's because few payouts equal or top the $1.8 million the Badgers received from the Rose Bowl Corporation.

. . .

With bowl paydays so fat, why do athletic directors pass up these excellent opportunities to help balance their books? The answer is twofold: Despite all the corporate jargon that ADs spout, their management style has never been lean and mean. Because Big-time U's always sop up the red ink at the end of the fiscal year, most ADs spend in an extravagant and wasteful manner and allow many of their employees, particularly their football and men's basketball coaches, to do the same.

The other reason ADs sanction lavish bowl trips is self-protection: Long ago, they learned that by spending money on university officials and faculty boards of control, taking them and their spouses to bowl games and on other junkets (as well as providing them with free skyboxes or excellent seats to all home football and basketball games), athletic departments obtained insurance policies—they persuaded the people within the university who have direct oversight over intercollegiate athletics to back it enthusiastically. The potential critics of the financial and other abuses of big-time college sports climb onto the gravy planes and become complicit in the wasting of large sums of money. As a result, these university officials rarely question the specific expenses or the general financial operations of their athletic departments, nor do they hesitate to cover the annual deficits.

Not only are most university officials intimidated by powerful ADs and coaches and fear displeasing them, but, in the current era, many administrators seem to believe the NCAA and athletic department propaganda about the wonderful benefits that College Sports MegaInc. bestows upon the university.

Is this the total explanation? It accounts for athletic department behavior—ADs and coaches are merely doing what comes naturally—but beyond the obvious causes of administrative complicity in the deficit spending, a more complex reason for their official conduct exists. Many Big-time U officials, knowing that their schools cannot provide the vast majority of undergraduates with meaningful educations, try to distract and please these consumers with ongoing entertainment in the form of big-time college sports. For all of its high expenses, an intercollegiate athletics program costs far less than a quality undergraduate education program. University officials deny employing this strategy, but their denials are less important than the current reality: Many Big-time U's supply their students with an abundance of college sports events and accept the drinking culture that accompanies the fun and games; meanwhile, these schools offer their undergraduates few quality educational opportunities, reserving those for the honors students (usually a single-digit percentage of the student body).

An administrator of a Sunbelt university, when presented with this thesis, replied:

> There's certainly no plot or conspiracy by school officials on this. You have to remember that most universities are always in a money bind. We sure as hell can't get enough money our of our state legislature or anyone else to turn our undergraduate education program into one big honors college. But we need every undergraduate tuition dollar we can get . . . and we can swallow the million bucks a year that the athletic department costs us. . . . Maybe that's how it all happens. I can assure you that we never thought any of this out beforehand, nor did any other school.

He also mentioned, somewhat defensively:

> Yes, I've been to bowl games and the NCAA tourney with our teams, and I'm not going to apologize for enjoying those trips. I see them as rewards for me working hard on behalf of the athletic department. . . .

He concluded:

> I don't know how it all happened, how our athletic department never stops growing, and how this school always rates high on the "Party School" lists in the college guides, but I'm not going to carry the can for it, and my president sure wouldn't. Anyway, he's mainly concerned with our research and graduate programs which have really improved under his leadership.

Finally, in an age of accepting personal responsibility, college presidents and administrators at beer-and-circus schools should assume some of the blame for the current situation. They make frequent pronouncements on "refocusing student life" and "curtailing drinking" on their campuses, but they sanction, promote, and sometimes even participate in the beer-and-circus culture out of which student sports fandom and partying comes. Remarkably, they never acknowledge their hypocrisy, even when they tailgate with alums before and after college sports events.

In the 1960s, rebel students often accused university administrators of "selling out" undergraduate education to gain power and perks for themselves, and to keep their institutions running efficiently. Thirty-plus years later, the activities of university officials in charge of beer-and-circus schools adds a new dimension to the term *selling out.*

Another illustration of presidential and administrative misconduct concerns their dealings with the NCAA. Deconstructing a popular myth about the March Madness money provides a way into this subject.

· · ·

Myth: Thanks to the NCAA's billion-dollar TV contract for its Division I basketball tournaments, schools make millions when their teams participate in March Madness, and college officials put this money into academic programs.

Reality: The association distributes the tournament revenue through a complicated formula that sends most of it to the conferences of the participating schools. Because the BCS football conferences also form the big-time college basketball leagues and dominate the NCAA tourney, they receive the highest percentage of the money. As a result, when a school in a minor conference makes a brief appearance in the men's tourney—thirty-two of sixty-four teams lose in the first round—it receives a low-six-figure check.

On the other hand, if several teams from the same conference enter and reach the final rounds, they and their fellow conference members gain low-seven-figure payouts. With more than three hundred schools in NCAA Division I men's basketball, the minority who receive the million-dollar checks resemble lottery winners. But, like addicted gamblers, all three-hundred-plus schools spend big bucks to enter the Division I basketball season lottery, and most end up holding losing tickets. Athletic directors and coaches drive this process, and university presidents and administrators approve it.

But financial reality never deters fanatic lottery players, especially when they are playing with other people's—in this case, their school's—money. After the announcement of the recent NCAA/

CBS television deal, a national newspaper predicted that the increased payout will prompt "a continued migration of schools from lower divisions into the NCAA's Division I to more fully share the wealth." Probably the migration will occur, but the NCAA wealth is a mirage. Economist Andrew Zimbalist states bluntly: The new "CBS contract will have precious little impact on the economics of college sports." According to this expert, of the three-hundred-plus athletic departments in Division I basketball operating under the current miltimillion-dollar CBS contract, a tiny percentage "generate black ink in any given year." The prudent bet is that college sports will be in the same financial mess or worse in 2003," when the new NCAA/CBS deal begins, and that the red ink will continue to flow for the length of the contract until 2013.

But, thanks to the media, the public only hears about the NCAA's fabulous deals with CBS, and it considers March Madness a financial bonanza for American higher education. The public also believes that the colleges and universities who belong to the NCAA run the association, and they use the TV money to help their academic missions. In reality, the NCAA is a large, autonomous bureaucracy acting primarily out of self-interest, and because almost all members lose money on their college sports programs, they rarely have excess revenue to put into academic programs.

Finally, the March Madness money is not an NCAA share-the-wealth plan with higher education, but trickle-down economics in a slow-drip phase. The bottom line for almost all NCAA members is simple: *Belonging to the NCAA costs much more money annually than they receive from the association.*

. . .

Every year, the largest financial drain on NCAA members results from the association's requirement that schools field a minimum number of teams to remain in good standing—for Division I, at least fourteen teams in seven sports. This is a compulsory stake in a very expensive poker game. The motive behind this rule is self-interest: NCAA executives, mainly former athletic directors and coaches, regard the NCAA as a trade association, in business to promote college sports; they are empire-builders, they want athletic programs to be as large as possible, and to employ as many athletic administrators and coaches as possible.

Because, throughout Division I, almost all of a school's fourteen teams lose money every year, the minimum team requirement locks athletic departments and universities into huge annual expenses. Within the context of American higher education, this NCAA rule is an anomaly—no other outside agency forces universities to spend money in this way. Only the NCAA, with its minimum team requirements, totally ignores the financial autonomy of colleges and universities. Currently, this situation occurs during a period of severe financial constraints within higher education, when many parts of the university are experiencing drastic cutbacks.

Ironically, the presidents and administrators who wield the sharpest financial axes at their schools, slashing undergraduate programs and services, are often the men and women on the gravy planes to NCAA events. When these administrators cut academic programs, and then underwrite ever-escalating athletic department costs, they weaken the educational fabric of their schools and increase the beer-and-circus aspects. Furthermore, in the last decade, not one of these officials asked the NCAA to consider changing its team minimum rules, allowing schools to spend less money on their college sports programs. This sends a signal to people inside and out of the university system that, at many Big-time U's, intercollegiate athletics comes before undergraduate education.

. . .

Beyond the NCAA minimum team requirements, a huge part of the stake in the association's poker game concerns facilities, not only stadiums and arenas but training structures and state-of-the-art equipment. For a school to remain in Division I-A, the NCAA requires it to have large stadiums and arenas, and to meet attendance levels. In the 1990s, many athletic departments either upgraded their facilities or built new ones, often moving the expenses, including the debt-servicing, off their books and onto university ledgers. As always, athletic directors and coaches pressured presidents and administrators to approve the construction—whether the institution could afford the costs or not. Often the ADs and coaches enlisted the sports media and fans in their campaigns.

In 1999, University of Minnesota football coach Glen Mason lobbied for a new stadium for his team, arguing that his program needed to keep up with the recent stadium upgrades at Penn State and Ohio State ($100 million each), and new structures at other schools: "When you look at what is happening nationally with the amount of investments these great academic institutions are making in athletics and football, it's mind-boggling." It is particularly mind-boggling when these investments are compared to the proportionally lower ones that these supposedly "great academic institutions" put into their undergraduate education programs.

Virginia Tech AD Jim Weaver was more honest than Glen Mason about his department's construction spree, not bothering to put academic ribbons on it: "If you are not upgrading your facilities, you are going backward. In college athletics today . . . we're in the game of keeping up with the Joneses. I don't like it, but it's a fact."

Sociologist Harry Edwards calls this the "Athletics Arms Race," and although the Cold War competition ended, College Sports MegaInc. has intensified its version. According to ADs, coaches, and the executives who run their trade association, the NCAA, athletic departments must never stop expanding, and should never reach a spending equilibrium—even though they run continual deficits. A former athletic official at the University of Nebraska explained:

> When we won the national [football} championship at Nebraska in 1994, what we did instantly was continue to expand. That's when we started the project to build skyboxes and expand the stadium and continue to improve facilities.

Colossal new football stadiums and basketball arenas, as well as luxury skyboxes, are the most visible symbol of College Sports MegaInc. In addition, in many college towns, big-name coaches build enormous mansions, part of the harvest from their million-dollar annual incomes. As Tony Kornheiser indicated, every coach and administrator in big-time college sports is "getting rich," if not already enormously wealthy. Predictably, the association in charge of College Sports MegaInc. also takes care of its own, and overpays its personnel, particularly its top officials. For example, NCAA executive director Cedric Dempsey receives an annual salary of $650,000, plus multiple perks: his pay is about $450,000 more per year than the average salary of CEOs at America's two hundred largest nonprofit organizations, and his perks far exceed most of theirs.

The only consistent financial losers are the schools that belong to the NCAA and furnish the stadiums, arenas, and facilities for its operations. Contrary to one of the most tenacious myths in American society, *the vast majority of colleges and universities do not make money in big-time intercollegiate athletics.* But the myth will never die as long as university officials use it to justify their affection and need for beer-and-circus, particularly as a substitute for quality undergraduate education.

Editors' Postscript

One of the coeditors (Lundman) spent four hours observing parts of the October 14, 2000, homecoming football game at The Ohio State University through the lense of Professor Sperber's *Beer and Circus.* Here is what he saw:

I arrived on campus at 8:00 A.M., some four hours before the start of the game against the University of Minnesota. Save for the high school marching bands assembling for the homecoming parade, and the parents of the band members taking pictures, there were very few people on campus. Only an anticipation of circus and no beer in sight.

The parade began at 9:00 A.M. and I walked its entire length twice in 90 minutes. It was the stuff of politicians, campus organizations, marching bands, and couples, kids, coffee, doughnuts, orange juice, and bottled water. Among several thousand people, only two with beer.

The sidewalks, commercial establishments, and parking lots to the north of the football stadium along Lane Avenue were a very different story before the start of the game. Nearly every adult was drinking and most of what they were drinking was beer. Some carried 12- or 24-packs as they walked. In the parking lots, nearly all of the people, most of whom were middle-aged and older, were enjoying food, and here as well nearly all were drinking beer. In two hours, I saw much beer and much circus, more than I have ever seen before, although I confess I probably was not looking very carefully previously.

It is worth noting that while students were clearly among the drinkers, equal numbers were not of university age. These were the parents and grandparents, the neighbors. friends, and employers of the university students, the ones who helped teach them to drink the beer and participate in the circus that was central to the 2000 homecoming at Ohio State.

8
Why Should My Conscience Bother Me?
Hiding Aircraft Brake Hazards
Kermit Vandivier

The B. F. Goodrich Co. is what business magazines like to speak of as "a major American corporation." It has operations in a dozen states and as many foreign countries, and of these far-flung facilities, the Goodrich plant at Troy, Ohio, is not the most imposing. It is a small, one-story building, once used to manufacture airplanes. Set in the grassy flatlands of west-central Ohio, it employs only about six hundred people. Nevertheless, it is one of the three largest manufacturers of aircraft wheels and brakes, a leader in a most profitable industry. Goodrich wheels and brakes support such well-known planes as the F111, the C5A, the Boeing 727, the XB70 and many others. Its customers include almost every aircraft manufacturer in the world.

Contracts for aircraft wheels and brakes often run into millions of dollars, and ordinarily a contract with a total value of less than 570,000, though welcome, would not create any special stir of joy in the hearts of Goodrich sales personnel. But purchase order P-23718, issued on June 18, 1967, by the LTV Aerospace Corporation, and ordering 202 brake assemblies for a new Air Force plane at a total price of $69,417, was received by Goodrich with considerable glee. And there was good reason. Some ten years previously, Goodrich had built a brake for LTV that was, to say the least, considerably less than a rousing success. The brake had not lived up to Goodrich's promises, and after experiencing considerable difficulty, LTV had written off Goodrich as a source of brakes. Since that time, Goodrich salesmen had been unable to sell so much as a shot of brake fluid to LTV. So in 1967, when LTV requested bids on wheels and brakes for the new A7D light attack aircraft it proposed to build for the Air Force, Goodrich submitted a bid that was absurdly low, so low that LTV could not, in all prudence, turn it down.

Goodrich had, in industry parlance, "bought into the business." Not only did the company not expect to make a profit on the deal; it was prepared, if necessary, to lose money. For aircraft brakes are not something that can be ordered off the shelf. They are designed for a particular aircraft, and once an aircraft manufacturer buys a brake, he is forced to purchase all replacement parts from the brake manufacturer. The $70,000 that Goodrich would get for making the brake would be a drop in the bucket when compared with the cost of the linings and other parts the Air Force would have to buy from Goodrich during the lifetime of the aircraft. Furthermore, the company which manufactures brakes for one particular model of an aircraft quite naturally has the inside track to supply other brakes when the planes are updated and improved.

Thus, that first contract, regardless of the money involved, is very important, and Goodrich, when it learned that it had been awarded the A7D contract, was determined that while it may have slammed the door on its own foot ten years before, this time, the second time around. things would be different. The word was soon circulated throughout the plant: "We can't bungle it this time. We've got to give them a good brake, regardless of the cost."

There was another factor which had undoubtedly influenced LTV. All aircraft brakes made today are of the disk type, and the bid submitted by Goodrich called for a relatively small brake, one containing four disks and weighing only 106 pounds. The weight of any aircraft part is extremely important. The lighter a part is, the heavier the plane's payload can be. The four-rotor, 106-pound brake promised by Goodrich was about as light as could be expected, and this undoubtedly had helped move LTV to award the contract to Goodrich.

The brake was designed by one of Goodrich's most capable engineers, John Warren. A tall, lanky blond and a graduate of Purdue, Warren had come from the Chrysler Corporation seven years before and had become adept at aircraft brake design. The happy-go-lucky manner he usually maintained belied a temper which exploded whenever anyone ventured to offer any criticism of his work, no matter how small. On these occasions, Warren would turn red in the face, often throwing or slamming something and then stalking from the scene. As his co-workers learned the consequences of criticizing him, they did so less and less readily, and when he submitted his preliminary design for the A7D brake, it was accepted without question.

Warren was named project engineer for the A7D, and he, in turn, assigned the task of producing the final production design to a newcomer to the Goodrich engineering stable, Searle Lawson. Just turned twenty-six, Lawson had been out of the Northrup Institute of Technology only one year when he came to Goodrich in January 1967. Like Warren, he had worked for a while in the automotive industry, but his engineering degree was in aeronautical and astronautical sciences, and when the opportunity came to enter his special field, via Goodrich, he took it. At the Troy plant, Lawson had been assigned to various "paper projects" to break him in, and after several months spent reviewing statistics and old brake designs, he was beginning to fret at the lack of challenge. When told he was being assigned to his first "real" project, he was elated and immediately plunged into his work.

The major portion of the design had already been completed by Warren, and major assemblies for the brake had already been ordered from Goodrich suppliers. Naturally, however, before Goodrich could start making the brakes on a production basis, much testing would have to be done. Lawson would have to determine the best materials to use for the linings and discover what minor adjustments in the design would have to be made.

Then, after the preliminary testing and after the brake was judged ready for production, one whole brake assembly would undergo a series of grueling, simulated braking stops and other severe trials called qualification tests. These tests are required by the military, which gives very detailed specifications on how they are to be conducted, the criteria for failure, and so on. They are performed in the Goodrich plant's test laboratory, where huge machines called dynamometers can simulate the weight and speed of almost any aircraft. After the brakes pass the laboratory tests, they are approved for production, but before the brakes are accepted for use in military service, they must undergo further extensive flight tests.

Searle Lawson was well aware that much work had to be done before the A7D brake could go into production, and he knew that LTV had set the last two weeks in June, 1968, as the starting dates for flight tests. So he decided to begin testing immediately. Goodrich's suppliers had not yet delivered the brake housing and other parts, but the brake disks had arrived, and using the housing from a brake similar in size and weight to the A7D brake, Lawson built a prototype. The prototype was installed in a test wheel and placed on one of the big dynamometers in the plant's test laboratory. The dynamometers was adjusted to simulate the weight of the A7D and Lawson began a series of tests, "landing" the wheel and brake at the A7D's landing speed, and braking it to a stop. The main purpose of these preliminary tests was to learn what temperatures would develop within the brake during the simulated stops and to evaluate the lining materials tentatively selected for use.

During a normal aircraft landing the temperatures inside the brake may reach 1000 degrees, and occasionally a bit higher. During Lawson's first simulated landings, the temperature of his prototype brake reached 1500 degrees. The brake glowed a bright cherry-red and threw off incandescent particles of metal and lining material as the temperature reached its peak. After a few such stops, the brake was dismantled and the linings were found to be almost completely disintegrated. Lawson chalked this first failure up to chance and, ordering new lining materials, tried again.

The second attempt was a repeat of the first. The brake became extremely hot, causing the lining materials to crumble into dust.

After the third such failure, Lawson, inexperienced though he was, knew that the fault lay not in defective parts or unsuitable lining material but in the basic design of the brake itself. Ignoring Warren's original computations, Lawson made his own, and it didn't take him long to discover where the trouble lay—the brake was too small. There simply was not enough surface area on the disks to stop the aircraft without generating the excessive heat that caused the linings to fail.

The answer to the problem was obvious but far from simple— the four-disk brake would have to be scrapped, and a new design, using five disks, would have to be developed. The implications were not lost on Lawson. Such a step would require the junking of all the four-disk-brake subassemblies, many of which had now begun to arrive from the various suppliers. It would also mean several weeks of preliminary design and testing and many more weeks of waiting while the suppliers made and delivered the new subassemblies.

Yet, several weeks had already gone by since LTV's order had arrived, and the date for delivery of the first production brakes for flight testing was only a few months away.

Although project engineer John Warren had more or less turned the A7D over to Lawson, he knew of the difficulties Lawson had been experiencing. He had assured the young engineer that the problem revolved around getting the right kind of lining material. Once that was found, he said, the difficulties would end.

Despite the evidence of the abortive tests and Lawson's careful computations, Warren rejected the suggestion that the four-disk brake was too light for the job. Warren knew that his superior had already told LTV, in rather glowing terms, that the preliminary tests on the A7D brake were very successful. Indeed, Warren's superiors weren't aware at this time of the troubles on the brake. It would have been difficult for Warren to admit not only that he had made a serious error in his calculations and original design but that his mistakes had been caught by a green kid, barely out of college.

Warren's reaction to a five-disk brake was not unexpected by Lawson, and, seeing that the four-disk brake was not to be abandoned so easily, he took his calculations and dismal test results one step up the corporate ladder.

At Goodrich, the man who supervises the engineers working on projects slated for production is called, predictably, the projects manager. The job was held by a short, chubby and bald man named Robert Sink. A man truly devoted to his work, Sink was as likely to be found at his desk at ten o'clock on Sunday night as ten o'clock on Monday morning. His outside interests consisted mainly of tinkering on a Model-A Ford and an occasional game of golf. Some fifteen years before, Sink had begun working at Goodrich as a lowly draftsman. Slowly, he worked his way up. Despite his geniality, Sink was neither respected nor liked by the majority of the engineers, and his appointment as their supervisor did not improve their feelings about him. They thought he had only gone to high school. It quite naturally rankled those who had gone through years of college and acquired impressive specialties such as thermodynamics and astronautics to be commanded by a man whom they considered their intellectual inferior. But, though Sink had no college training, he had something even more useful: a fine working knowledge of company politics.

Puffing upon a Meerschaum pipe, Sink listened gravely as young Lawson confided his fears about the four-disk brake. Then he examined Lawson's calculations and the results of the abortive tests. Despite the fact that he was not a qualified engineer, in the strictest sense of the word, it must certainly have been obvious to Sink that Lawson's calculations were correct and that a four-disk brake would never have worked on the A7D.

But other things of equal importance were also obvious. First, to concede that Lawson's calculations were correct would also mean conceding that Warren's calculations were incorrect. As projects manager, he not only was responsible for Warren's activities but, in admitting that Warren had erred, he would have to admit that he had erred in trusting Warren's judgment. It also meant that, as projects manager, it would be he who would have to explain the whole messy situation to the Goodrich hierarchy, not only at Troy but possibly on the corporate level at Goodrich's Akron offices. And, having taken Warren's judgment of the four-disk brake at face value (he was forced to do this since, not being an engineer, he was unable to exercise any engineering judgment of his own), he had assured LTV, not once but several times, that about all there was left to do on the brake was pack it in a crate and ship it out the back door.

There's really no problem at all, he told Lawson. After all, Warren was an experienced engineer, and if he said the brake would work, it would work. Just keep on testing and probably, maybe even on the very next try, it'll work out just fine.

Lawson was far from convinced. but without the support of his superiors there was little he could do except keep on testing. By now, housings for the four-disk brake had begun to arrive at the plant, and Lawson was able to build up a production model of the brake and begin the formal qualification tests demanded by the military.

The first qualification attempts went exactly as the tests on the prototype had. Terrific heat developed within the brakes and, after a few, short, simulated stops, the linings crumbled. A new type of lining material was ordered and once again an attempt to qualify the brake was made. Again, failure.

Experts were called in from lining manufacturers, and new lining "mixes" were tried, always with the same result. Failure.

It was now the last week in March 1968, and flight tests were scheduled to begin in seventy days. Twelve separate attempts had been made to formally qualify the brake, and all had failed. It was no longer possible for anyone to ignore the glaring truth that the brake was a dismal failure and that nothing short of a major design change could ever make it work.

In the engineering department, panic set in. A glum-faced Lawson prowled the test laboratory dejectedly. Occasionally, Warren would witness some simulated stop on the brake and, after it was completed, troop silently back to his desk. Sink, too, showed an unusual interest in the trials, and he and Warren would converse in low tones while poring over the results of the latest tests. Even the most inexperienced of the lab technicians and the men who operated the testing equipment knew they had a "bad" brake on their hands, and there was some grumbling about "wasting time on a brake that won't work."

New menaces appeared. An engineering team from LTV arrived at the plant to get a good look at the brake in action. Luckily, they stayed only a few days, and Goodrich engineers managed to cover the true situation without too much difficulty.

On April 4, the thirteenth attempt at qualification was begun. This time no attempt was made to conduct the tests by the methods and techniques spelled out in the military specifications. Regardless of how it had to be done, the brake was to be "nursed" through the required fifty simulated stops.

Fans were set up to provide special cooling. Instead of maintaining pressure on the brake until the test wheel had come to a complete stop, the pressure was reduced when the wheel had decelerated to around 15 mph, allowing it to "coast" to a stop. After each stop, the brake was disassembled and carefully cleaned, and after some of the stops, internal brake parts were machined in order to remove warp and other disfigurations caused by the high heat.

By these and other methods, all clearly contrary to the techniques established by the military specifications, the brake was coaxed through the fifty stops. But even using these methods, the brake could not meet all the requirements. On one stop the wheel rolled for a distance of 16,000 feet, nearly three miles, before the brake could bring it to a stop. The normal distance required for such a stop was around 3500 feet.

. . .

On April 11, the day the thirteenth test was completed, I became personally involved in the A7D situation.

I had worked in the Goodrich test laboratory for five years, starting first as an instrumentation engineer, then later becoming a data analyst and technical writer. As part of my duties, I analyzed the reams and reams of instrumentation data that came from the many testing machines in the laboratory, then transcribed it to a more usable form for the engineering department. And when a new-type brake had successfully completed the required qualification tests, I would issue a formal qualification report.

Qualification reports were an accumulation of all the data and test logs compiled by the test technicians during the qualification tests, and were documentary proof that a brake had met all the requirements established by the military specifications and was therefore presumed safe for flight testing. Before actual flight tests were conducted on a brake, qualification reports had to be delivered to the customer and to various government officials.

On April 11, I was looking over the data from the latest A7D test, and I noticed that many irregularities in testing methods had been noted on the test logs.

Technically, of course, there was nothing wrong with conducting tests in any manner desired, so long as the test was for research purposes only. But qualification test methods are clearly delineated by the military, and I knew that this test had been a formal qualification attempt. One particular notation on the test logs caught my eye. For some of the stops, the instrument which recorded the brake pressure had been deliberately miscalibrated so that, while the brake pressure used during the stops was recorded as 1000 psi (the maximum pressure that would be available on the A7D aircraft), the pressure had actually been 1100 psi!

I showed the test logs to the test lab supervisor, Ralph Gretzinger, who said he had learned from the technician who had miscalibrated the instrument that he had been asked to do so by Lawson. Lawson, said Gretzinger, readily admitted asking for the miscalibration, saying he had been told to do so by Sink.

I asked Gretzinger why anyone would want to miscalibrate the data-recording instruments.

"Why? I'll tell you why," he snorted. "That brake is a failure. It's way too small for the job, and they're not ever going to get it to work. They're getting desperate, and instead of scrapping the damned thing and starting over, they figure they can horse around down here in the lab and qualify it that way."

An expert engineer, Gretzinger had been responsible for several innovations in brake design. It was he who had invented the unique brake system used on the famous XB70. A graduate of Georgia Tech, he was a stickler for detail and he had some very firm ideas about honesty and ethics. "If you want to find out what's going on," said Gretzinger, "ask Lawson, he'll tell you."

Curious, I did ask Lawson the next time he came into the lab. He seemed eager to discuss the A7D and gave me the history of his months of frustrating efforts to get Warren and Sink to change the brake design. "I just can't believe this is really happening," said Lawson, shaking his head slowly. "This isn't engineering, at least not what I thought it would be. Back in school, I thought that when you were an engineer, you tried to do your best, no matter what it cost. But this is something else."

He sat across the desk from me, his chin propped in his hand. "Just wait," he warned. "You'll get a chance to see what I'm talking about. You're going to get in the act too, because I've already had the word that we're going to make one more attempt to qualify the brake, and that's it. Win or lose, we're going to issue a qualification report!"

I reminded him that a qualification report could only be issued after a brake had successfully met all military requirements, and therefore, unless the next qualification attempt was a success, no report would be issued.

"You'll find out," retorted Lawson. "I was already told that regardless of what the brake does on test, it's going to be qualified." He said he had been told in those exact words at a conference with Sink and Russell Van Horn.

This was the first indication that Sink had brought his boss, Van Horn, into the mess. Although Van Horn, as manager of the design engineering section, was responsible for the entire department, he was not necessarily familiar with all phases of every project, and it was not uncommon for those under him to exercise the what-he-doesn't-know-won't-hurt-him philosophy. If he was aware of the full extent of the A7D situation, it meant that matters had truly reached a desperate stage—that Sink had decided not only to call for help but was looking toward that moment when blame must be borne and, if possible, shared.

Also, if Van Horn had said, "regardless what the brake does on test, it's going to be qualified," then it could only mean that, if necessary, a false qualification report would be issued! I discussed this possibility with Gretzinger, and he assured me that under no circumstances would such a report ever be issued.

"If they want a qualification report, we'll write them one, but we'll tell it just like it is," he declared emphatically. "No false data or false reports are going to come out of this lab."

On May 2, 1968, the fourteenth and final attempt to qualify the brake was begun. Although the same improper methods used to nurse the brake through the previous tests were employed, it soon became obvious that this too would end in failure.

When the tests were about half completed, Lawson asked if I would start preparing the various engineering curves and graphic displays which were normally incorporated in a qualification report. "It looks as though you'll be writing a qualification report shortly," he said.

I flatly refused to have anything to do with the matter and immediately told Gretzinger what I had been asked to do. He was furious and repeated his previous declaration that under no circumstances would any false data or other matter be issued from the lab.

"I'm going to get this settled right now, once and for all," he declared. "I'm going to see Line [Russell Line, manager of the Goodrich Technical Services Section, of which the test lab was a part] and find out just how far this thing is going to go!" He stormed out of the room.

In about an hour, he returned and called me to his desk. He sat silently for a few moments, then muttered, half to himself, "I wonder what the hell they'd do if I just quit?" I didn't answer and I didn't ask him what he meant. I knew. He had been beaten down. He had reached the point when the decision had to be made. Defy them now while there was still time—or knuckle under, sell out.

"You know," he went on uncertainly, looking down at his desk, "I've been an engineer for a long time, and I've always believed that ethics and integrity were every bit as important as theorems and formulas, and never once has anything happened to change my beliefs. Now this. . . . Hell, I've got two sons I've got to put through school and I just . . ." His voice trailed off.

He sat for a few more minutes, then, looking over the top of his glasses, said hoarsely, "Well, it looks like we're licked. The way it stands now, we're to go ahead and prepare the data and other things for the graphic presentation in the report, and when we're finished, someone upstairs will actually write the report."

"After all," he continued, "we're just drawing some curves, and what happens to them after they leave here, well, we're not responsible for that."

He was trying to persuade himself that as long as we were concerned with only one part of the puzzle and didn't see the completed picture, we really weren't doing anything wrong. He didn't believe what he was saying, and he knew I didn't believe it either. It was an embarrassing and shameful moment for both of us.

I wasn't at all satisfied with the situation and decided that I too would discuss the matter with Russell Line, the senior executive in our section.

Tall, powerfully built, his teeth flashing white, his face tanned to a coffee-brown by a daily stint with a sun lamp, Line looked and acted every inch the executive. He was a crossword-puzzle enthusiast and an ardent golfer, and though he had lived in Troy only a short time, he had been accepted into the Troy Country Club and made an official of the golf committee. He had been transferred from the Akron offices some two years previously, and an air of mystery surrounded him. Some office gossips figured he had been sent to Troy as the result of some sort of demotion. Others speculated that since the present general manager of the Troy plant was due shortly for retirement, Line had been transferred to Troy to assume that job and was merely occupying his present position to "get the feel of things." Whatever the case, he commanded great respect and had come to be well liked by those of us who worked under him.

He listened sympathetically while I explained how I felt about the A7D situation, and when I had finished, he asked me what I wanted him to do about it. I said that as employees of the Goodrich Company we had a responsibility to protect the company and its reputation if at all possible. I said I was certain that officers on the corporate level would never knowingly allow such tactics as had been employed on the A7D.

"I agree with you," he remarked, "but I still want to know what you want me to do about it."

I suggested that in all probability the chief engineer at the Troy plant, H. C. "Bud" Sunderman, was unaware of the A7D problem and that he, Line, should tell him what was going on.

Line laughed, good-humoredly. "Sure, I could, but I'm not going to. Bud probably already knows about this thing anyway, and if he doesn't, I'm sure not going to be the one to tell him."

"But why?"

"Because it's none of my business, and it's none of yours. I learned a long time ago not to worry about things over which I had no control. I have no control over this."

I wasn't satisfied with this answer, and I asked him if his conscience wouldn't bother him if, say, during flight tests on the brake, something should happen resulting in death or injury to the test pilot.

"Look," he said, becoming somewhat exasperated, "I just told you I have no control over this thing. Why should my conscience bother me?"

His voice took on a quiet, soothing tone as he continued. "You're just getting all upset over this thing for nothing. I just do as I'm told, and I'd advise you to do the same."

He had made his decision, and now I had to make mine.

I made no attempt to rationalize what I had been asked to do. It made no difference who would falsify which part of the report or whether the actual falsification would be by misleading numbers or misleading words. Whether by acts of commission or omission, all of us who contributed to the fraud would be guilty. The only question left for me to decide was whether or not I would become a party to the fraud.

Before coming to Goodrich in 1963, I had held a variety of jobs, each a little more pleasant, a little more rewarding than the last. At forty-two, with seven children, I had decided that the Goodrich Company would probably be my "home" for the rest of my working life. The job paid well, it was pleasant and challenging, and the future looked reasonably bright. My wife and I had bought a home and we were ready to settle down into a comfortable, middle-age, middle-class rut. If I refused to take part in the A7D fraud, I would have to either resign or be fired. The report would be written by someone anyway, but I would have the satisfaction of knowing I had had no part in the matter. But bills aren't paid with personal satisfaction, nor house payments with ethical principles. I made my decision. The next morning, I telephoned Lawson and told him I was ready to begin on the qualification report.

In a few minutes, he was at my desk, ready to begin. Before we started, I asked him, "Do you realize what we are going to do?"

"Yeah," he replied bitterly, "we're going to screw LTV. And speaking of screwing," he continued, "I know now how a whore feels, because that's exactly what I've become, an engineering whore. I've sold myself. It's all I can do to look at myself in the mirror when I shave. I make me sick."

I was surprised at his vehemence. It was obvious that he too had done his share of soul-searching and didn't like what he had found. Somehow, though, the air seemed clearer after his out-burst, and we began working on the report.

I had written dozens of qualification reports, and I knew what a "good" one looked like. Resorting to the actual test data only on occasion, Lawson and I proceeded to prepare page after page of elaborate, detailed engineering curves, charts, and test logs, which purported to show what had happened during the formal qualification tests. Where temperatures were too high, we deliberately chopped them down a few hundred degrees, and where they were too low, we raised them to a value that would appear reasonable to the LTV and military engineers. Brake pressure, torque values, distances, times, everything of consequence was tailored to fit the occasion.

Occasionally, we would find that some test either hadn't been performed at all or had been conducted improperly. On those occasions, we "conducted" the test—successfully, of course—on paper.

For nearly a month we worked on the graphic presentation that would be part of the report. Meanwhile, the fourteenth and final qualification attempt had been completed, and the brake, not unexpectedly, had failed again.

During that month, Lawson and I talked of little else except the enormity of what we were doing. The more involved we became in our work, the more apparent became our own culpability. We discussed such things as the Nuremberg trials and how they related to our guilt and complicity in the A7D situation. Lawson often expressed his opinion that the brake was downright dangerous and that, once on flight tests, "anything is liable to happen."

I saw his boss, John Warren, at least twice during that month and needled him about what we were doing. He didn't take the jibes too kindly but managed to laugh the situation off as "one of those things." One day I remarked that what we were doing amounted to fraud, and he pulled out an engineering handbook and turned to a section on laws as they related to the engineering profession.

He read the definition of fraud aloud, then said, "Well, technically I don't think what we're doing can be called fraud. I'll admit it's not right, but it's just one of those things. We're just kinda caught in the middle. About all I can tell you is, do like I'm doing. Make copies of everything and put them in your SYA file."

"What's an 'SYA' file?" I asked.

"That's a 'save your ass' file." He laughed.

Although I hadn't known it was called that, I had been keeping an SYA file since the beginning of the A7D fiasco. I had made a copy of every scrap of paper connected even remotely with the A7D and had even had copies of 16 mm movies that had been made during some of the simulated stops. Lawson, too, had an SYA file, and we both maintained them for one reason: Should the true state of events on the A7D ever be questioned, we wanted to have access to a complete set of factual data. We were afraid that should the question ever come up, the test data might accidentally be "lost."

We finished our work on the graphic portion of the report around the first of June. Altogether, we had prepared nearly two hundred pages of data, containing dozens of deliberate falsifications and misrepresentations. I delivered the data to Gretzinger, who said he had been instructed to deliver it personally to the chief engineer, Bud Sunderman, who in turn would assign some one in the engineering department to complete the written portion of the report. He gathered the bundle of data and left the office. Within minutes, he was back with the data, his face white with anger.

160   PATTERNS

"That damned Sink's beat me to it," he said furiously. "He's
already talked to Bud about this, and now Sunderman says no one
in the engineering department has time to write the report. He
wants us to do it, and I told him we couldn't."

The words had barely left his mouth when Russell Line burst in
the door. "What the hell's all the fuss about this damned report?"
he demanded loudly.

Patiently, Gretzinger explained. "There's no fuss. Sunderman just
told me that we'd have to write the report down here, and I said
we couldn't. Russ," he went on, "I've told you before that we weren't
going to write the report. I made my position clear on that a long
time ago."

Line shut him up with a wave of his hand and, turning to me,
bellowed, "I'm getting sick and tired of hearing about this damned
report. Now, write the goddam thing and shut up about it!" He
slammed out of the office.

Gretzinger and I just sat for a few seconds looking at each other.
Then he spoke.

"Well, I guess he's made it pretty clear, hasn't he? We can either
write the thing or quit. You know, what we should have done was
quit a long time ago. Now, it's too late."

Somehow, I wasn't at all surprised at this turn of events, and it
didn't really make that much difference. As far as I was concerned,
we were all up to our necks in the thing anyway, and writing the
narrative portion of the report couldn't make me any more guilty
than I already felt myself to be.

Still, Line's order came as something of a shock. All the time
Lawson and I were working on the report, I felt, deep down, that
somewhere, somehow, something would come along and the whole
thing would blow over. But Russell Line had crushed that hope.
The report was actually going to be issued. Intelligent, law-abiding
officials of B. F. Goodrich, one of the oldest and most respected of
American corporations, were actually going to deliver to a customer
a product that was known to be defective and dangerous and which
could very possibly cause death or serious injury.

Within two days, I had completed the narrative, or written portion of the report. As a final sop to my own self-respect, in the conclusion of the report I wrote, "The B. F. Goodrich P/N 2-1162-3
brake assembly does not meet the intent or the requirements

of the applicable specification documents and therefore is not qualified."

This was a meaningless gesture, since I knew that this would certainly be changed when the report went through the final typing process. Sure enough, when the report was published, the negative conclusion had been made positive.

One final and significant incident occurred just before publication.

Qualification reports always bear the signature of the person who has prepared them. I refused to sign the report, as did Lawson. Warren was later asked to sign the report. He replied that he would "when I receive a signed statement from Bob Sink ordering me to sign it."

The engineering secretary who was delegated the responsibility of "dogging" the report through publication, told me later that after I, Lawson, and Warren had all refused to sign the report, she had asked Sink if he would sign. He replied, "On something of this nature, I don't think a signature is really needed."

· · ·

On June 5, 1968, the report was officially published and copies were delivered in person to the Air Force and LTV. Within a week, flight tests were begun at Edwards Air Force Base in California. Searle Lawson was sent to California as Goodrich's representative. Within approximately two weeks, he returned because some rather unusual incidents during the tests had caused them to be canceled.

His face was grim as he related stories of several near crashes during landings—caused by brake troubles. He told me about one incident in which, upon landing, one brake was literally welded together by the intense heat developed during the test stop. The wheel locked, and the plane skidded for nearly 1500 feet before coming to a halt. The plane was jacked up and the wheel removed. The fused parts within the brake had to be pried apart.

Lawson had returned to Troy from California that same day, and that evening, he and others of the Goodrich engineering department left for Dallas for a high-level conference with LTV.

That evening I left work early and went to see my attorney. After I told him the story, he advised that, while I was probably not actually guilty of fraud, I was certainly part of a conspiracy to defraud. He advised me to go to the Federal Bureau of Investigation and offered to arrange an appointment. The following week he took

me to the Dayton office of the FBI, and after I had been warned
that I would not be immune from prosecution, I disclosed the A7D
matter to one of the agents. The agent told me to say nothing about
the episode to anyone and to report any further incident to him.
He said he would forward the story to his superiors in Washington.

A few days later, Lawson returned from the conference in Dallas and said that the Air Force, which had previously approved the
qualification report, had suddenly rescinded that approval and was
demanding to see some of the raw test data taken during the tests.
I gathered that the FBI had passed the word.

Omitting any reference to the FBI, I told Lawson I had been to
an attorney and that we were probably guilty of conspiracy.

"Can you get me an appointment with your attorney?" he asked.
Within a week, he had been to the FBI and told them of his part in
the mess. He too was advised to say nothing but to keep on the job
reporting any new development.

Naturally, with the rescinding of Air Force approval and the
demand to see raw test data, Goodrich officials were in a panic. A
conference was called for July 27, a Saturday morning affair at which
Lawson, Sink, Warren and myself were present. We met in a tiny
conference room in the deserted engineering department. Lawson
and I, by now openly hostile to Warren and Sink, ranged ourselves
on one side of the conference table while Warren sat on the other
side. Sink, chairing the meeting, paced slowly in front of a blackboard, puffing furiously on a pipe.

The meeting was called, Sink began, "to see where we stand on
the A7D." What we were going to do, he said, was to "level" with
LTV and tell them the "whole truth" about the A7D. "After all," he
said, "they're in this thing with us, and they have the right to know
how matters stand."

"In other words," I asked, "we're going to tell them the truth?"

"That's right," he replied. "We're going to level with them and
let them handle the ball from there."

"There's one thing I don't quite understand," I interjected.
"Isn't it going to be pretty hard for us to admit to them that we've
lied?"

"Now, wait a minute," he said angrily. "Let's don't go off half-
cocked on this thing. It's not a matter of lying. We've just interpreted
the information the way we felt it should be."

"I don't know what you call it," I replied, "but to me it's lying, and it's going to be damned hard to confess to them that we've been lying all along."

He became very agitated at this and repeated his "We're not lying," adding, "I don't like this sort of talk."

I dropped the matter at this point, and he began discussing the various discrepancies in the report.

We broke for lunch, and afterward, I came back to the plant to find Sink sitting alone at his desk, waiting to resume the meeting. He called me over and said he wanted to apologize for his outburst that morning. "This thing has kind of gotten me down," he confessed, "and I think you've got the wrong picture. I don't think you really understand everything about this."

Perhaps so, I conceded, but it seemed to me that if we had already told LTV one thing and then had to tell them another, changing our story completely, we would have to admit we were lying.

"No," he explained patiently, "we're not really lying. All we were doing was interpreting the figures the way we knew they should be. We were just exercising engineering license."

During the afternoon session, we marked some forty-three discrepant points in the report: forty-three points that LTV would surely spot as occasions where we had exercised "engineering license."

After Sink listed those points on the blackboard, we discussed each one individually. As each point came up, Sink would explain that it was probably "too minor to bother about," or that perhaps it "wouldn't be wise to open that can of worms," or that maybe this was a point that "LTV just wouldn't understand." When the meeting was over, it had been decided that only three points were "worth mentioning."

Similar conferences were held during August and September, and the summer was punctuated with frequent treks between Dallas and Troy, and demands by the Air Force to see the raw test data. Tempers were short and matters seemed to grow worse.

Finally, early in October 1968, Lawson submitted his resignation, to take effect on October 25. On October 18, I submitted my own resignation, to take effect on November 1. In my resignation, addressed to Russell Line, I cited the A7D report and stated: "As you are aware, this report contained numerous deliberate and willful misrepresentations which, according to legal counsel, constitute fraud and expose both myself and others to criminal charges of conspiracy to defraud. . . . The events of the past seven months have created an atmosphere of deceit and distrust in which it is impossible to work. . . ."

On October 25, I received a sharp summons to the office of Bud Sunderman. As chief engineer at the Troy plant, Sunderman was responsible for the entire engineering division. Tall and graying, impeccably dressed at all times, he was capable of producing a dazzling smile or a hearty chuckle or immobilizing his face into marble hardness, as the occasion required.

I faced the marble hardness when I reached his office. He motioned me to a chair. "I have your resignation here," he snapped, "and I must say you have made some rather shocking, I might even say irresponsible, charges. This is very serious."

Before I could reply, he was demanding an explanation. "I want to know exactly what the fraud is in connection with the A7D and how you can dare accuse this company of such a thing!"

I started to tell some of the things that had happened during the testing, but he shut me off saying, "There's nothing wrong with anything we've done here. You aren't aware of all the things that have been going on behind the scenes. If you had known the true situation, you would never have made these charges." He said that in view of my apparent "disloyalty" he had decided to accept my resignation "right now," and said it would be better for all concerned if I left the plant immediately. As I got up to leave he asked me if I intended to "carry this thing further."

I answered simply, "Yes," to which he replied, "Suit yourself." Within twenty minutes, I had cleaned out my desk and left. Forty-eight hours later, the B. F. Goodrich Company recalled the qualification report and the four-disk brake, announcing that it would replace the brake with a new, improved, five-disk brake at no cost to LTV.

Ten months later, on August 13, 1969, I was the chief government witness at a hearing conducted before Senator William Proxmire's Economy in Government Subcommittee of the Congress's Joint Economic Committee. I related the A7D story to the committee, and my testimony was supported by Searle Lawson, who followed me to the witness stand. Air Force officers also testified, as well as a four-man team from the General Accounting Office, which had conducted an investigation of the A7D brake at the request of Senator Proxmire. Both Air Force and GAO investigators declared that the brake was dangerous and had not been tested properly.

Testifying for Goodrich was R. G. Jeter, vice-president and general counsel of the company, from the Akron headquarters. Representing the Troy plant was Robert Sink. These two denied any wrongdoing on the part of the Goodrich Company, despite expert testimony to the contrary by Air Force and GAO officials. Sink was quick to deny any connection with the writing of the report or of directing any falsifications, claiming to be on the West Coast at the time. John Warren was the man who supervised its writing, said Sink.

As for me, I was dismissed as a high-school graduate with no technical training, while Sink testified that Lawson was a young, inexperienced engineer. "We tried to give him guidance," Sink testified, "but he preferred to have his own convictions."

About changing the data and figures in the report, Sink said: "When you take data from several different sources, you have to rationalize among those data what is the true story. This is part of your engineering know-how." He admitted that changes had been made in the data, "but only to make them more consistent with the over-all picture of the data that is available."

Jeter pooh-poohed the suggestion that anything improper occurred, saying: "We have thirty-odd engineers at this plant . . . and I say to you that it is incredible that these men would stand idly by and see reports changed or falsified. . . . I mean you just do not have to do that working for anybody. . . . Just nobody does that."

The four-hour hearing adjourned with no real conclusion reached by the committee. But, the following day the Department of Defense made sweeping changes in its inspection, testing and reporting procedures. A spokesman for the DOD said that changes were a result of the Goodrich episode.

The A7D is now in service, sporting a Goodrich-made five-disk brake, a brake that works very well, I'm told. Business at the Goodrich plant is good. Lawson is now an engineer for LTV and has been assigned to the A7D project. And I am now a newspaper reporter.

At this writing [1972], those remaining at Goodrich are still secure in the same positions, all except Russell Line and Robert Sink. Line has been rewarded with a promotion to production superintendent, a large step upward on the corporate ladder. As for Sink, he moved up into Line's old job.

Editors' Postscript

In the years since he wrote about his experiences at Goodrich, Mr. Vandivier has been a newspaper reporter. He retired from the *Troy Daily News* (Troy, Ohio) in 1993 but still submits a column.

Mr. Vandivier reports that he has met occasionally with all of the principals involved in the aircraft brake episode. There do not seem to be any hard feelings, and their relationships with him have been consistently "cordial." All are gone from Goodrich themselves, in many cases the victims of corporate downsizing, what Mr. Vandivier terms "the corporate deviance of the 90s."

If he had to do it all over again, Mr. Vandivier says he would, because "it had to be done." He wishes the whole thing had never happened, though, and notes that Goodrich was an exciting company involved in his main line of interest, which was electronics.

Faulty parts continue to put military personnel at risk. In 1995, a small firm pleaded guilty to supplying F-18 gearboxes that caused 71 emergency landings and the loss of one airplane. Also in 1995, engineers for the giant Phillips Electronic firm pleaded guilty to secretly replacing missile system electrical capacitors during testing so they could pass. Boeing currently continues to fight charges that it knowingly installed and then concealed substandard helicopter transmission parts that may have caused multiple accidents. See William Carley, "Bombs Away: A Defense Contractor Gets Tough Scrutiny for Defective Products," *Wall Street Journal*, February 27, 1996, p. 1, and John Davison, "Boeing Kept Helicopter Faults Secret," *The Independent* (London), September 14, 1999, p. 5.

9

The Nazi Holocaust
Using Bureaucracies and Overcoming Psychological Barriers to Genocide
Raul Hilberg

[During the 12 years of Nazi rule,] the Germans killed five million Jews. The onslaught did not come from the void; it was brought into being because it had meaning to its perpetrators. It was not a narrow strategy for the attainment of some ulterior goal, but an undertaking for its own sake, an event experienced as *Erlebnis*–lived and lived through by its participants.

The German bureaucrats who contributed their skills to the destruction of the Jews all shared in this experience, some in the technical work of drafting a decree or dispatching a train, others starkly at the door of a gas chamber. They could sense the enormity of the operation from its smallest fragments. At every stage they displayed a striking pathfinding ability in the absence of directives, a congruity of activities without jurisdictional guidelines, a fundamental comprehension of the task even when there were no explicit communications. One has the feeling that when Reinhard Heydrich and the ministerial *Staatssekretäre* met on the morning of January 20, 1942 to discuss the "Final Solution of the Jewish Question in Europe," they understood each other.

In retrospect it may be possible to view the entire design as a mosaic of small pieces, each commonplace and lusterless by itself. Yet this progression of everyday activities, these file notes, memoranda, and telegrams, embedded in habit, routine, and tradition, were fashioned into a massive destruction process. Ordinary men were to perform extraordinary tasks. A phalanx of functionaries in public offices and private enterprises was reaching for the ultimate. . . .

The Destructive Expansion

. . . The destruction of the Jews was a total process, comparable in its diversity to a modern war, a mobilization, or a national reconstruction. . . .

An administrative process of such range cannot be carried out by a single agency, even if it is a trained and specialized body like the Gestapo or a commissariat for Jewish affairs, for when a process cuts into every phase of human life, it must ultimately feed upon the resources of the entire organized community. That is why we find among the perpetrators the highly differentiated technicians of the armament inspectorates, the remote officials of the Postal Ministry, and—in the all-important operation of furnishing records for determination of descent—the membership of an aloof and withdrawn Christian clergy. The machinery of destruction, then, was structurally no different from organized German society as a whole; the difference was only one of function. The machinery of destruction *was* the organized community in one of its special roles.

Established agencies rely on existing procedures. In his daily work the bureaucrat made use of tried techniques and tested formulas with which he was familiar and which he knew to be acceptable to his superiors, colleagues, and subordinates. The usual practices were applied also in unusual situations. The Finance Ministry went through condemnation proceedings to set up the Auschwitz complex, and the German railroads billed the Security Police for the transport of the Jews, calculating the one-way fare for each deportee by the track kilometer. Swift operations precipitated greater complications and necessitated more elaborate adjustments. In the course of the roundup of the Warsaw Jews during the summer of 1942, the ghetto inhabitants left behind their unpaid gas and electricity bills, and as a consequence the German offices responsible for public utilities and finance in the city had to marshal all their expertise to restore an administrative equilibrium. . . .

Oral orders were given at every level. Höss was told to build his death camp at Auschwitz in a conversation with Himmler. Stangl received instructions about Sobibór from Globocnik on a park bench in Lublin. A railroad man in Kraków, responsible for scheduling death trains, recalls that he was told by his immediate supervisor to run the transports whenever they were requested by the SS.

In essence, then, there was an atrophy of laws and a corresponding multiplication of measures for which the sources of authority were more and more ethereal. Valves were being opened for a decision flow. The experienced functionary was coming into his own. A middle-ranking bureaucrat, no less than his highest superior, was aware of currents and possibilities. In small ways as well as large, he recognized what was ripe for the time. Most often it was he who initiated action.

Thousands of proposals were introduced in memoranda, presented at conferences, and discussed in letters. The subject matter ranged from dissolution of mixed marriages to the deportation of the Jews of Liechtenstein or the construction of some "quick-working" device for the annihilation of Jewish women and children at Lódź and the surrounding towns of the Warthegau. At times it was assumed that the moment had come, even if there was no definite word from above. Hans Globke wrote anti-Jewish provisions in a decree on personal names in December 1932, before there was a Nazi regime or a Führer. The Trusteeship Office in Warsaw began to seize Jewish real property "in expectation" of a "lawful regulation," meanwhile performing the "indispensable" preparatory work.

. . .

A destruction process has an inherent pattern. There is only one way in which a scattered group can effectively be destroyed. Three steps are organic in the operation:

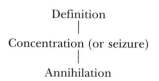

$$\text{Definition}$$
$$|$$
$$\text{Concentration (or seizure)}$$
$$|$$
$$\text{Annihilation}$$

This is the invariant structure of the basic process, for no group can be killed without a concentration or seizure of the victims, and no victims can be segregated before the perpetrator knows who belongs to the group.

There are additional steps in a modern destructive undertaking. These measures are required not for the annihilation of the victim but for the preservation of the economy. Basically, they are all expropriations. In the destruction of the Jews, expropriatory decrees were introduced after every organic step. Dismissals and Aryanizations came after the definition, exploitation and starvation measures followed concentration, and the confiscation of personal belongings was incidental to the killing operation. In its completed form a destruction process in a modern society will thus be structured as shown in this chart:

Definition
|
Dismissals of employees and expropriations of
business firms
|
Concentration
|
Exploitation of labor and starvation measures
|
Annihilation
|
Confiscation of personal effects

The sequence of steps in a destruction process is thus determined. If there is an attempt to inflict maximum injury upon a group of people, it is therefore inevitable that a bureaucracy—no matter how decentralized its apparatus or how unplanned its activities—should push its victims through these stages.

The expansion of destruction did not stop at this point. As the machine was thrown into high gear and as the process accelerated toward its goal, German hostility became more generalized. The Jewish target became too narrow; other targets were added. This development is of the utmost importance, for it casts a revealing light upon the perpetrators' fundamental aim.

If a group seeks merely the destruction of hostile institutions, the limit of its most drastic action would be drawn with the complete destruction of the bearers of the institution. The Germans, however, did not draw the line with the destruction of Jewry. They attacked still other victims, some of whom were thought to be like Jews, some of whom were quite unlike Jews, and some of whom were Germans. The Nazi destruction process was, in short, not aimed at institutions; it was targeted at people. The Jews were only the first victims of the German bureaucracy; they were only the first caught in its path. That they should have been chosen first is not accidental. Historical precedents, both administrative and conceptual, determined the selection of the people that for centuries had been the standby victim of recurring destructions. No other group could fill this role so well. None was so vulnerable. But the choice was not confined to the Jews. The following are three illustrations.

Example I. The destruction process engulfed a group classified as a parasitic people leading a parasitic life: the Gypsies. There were 34,000 to 40,000 Gypsies in the Reich. In accordance with a Himmler directive, the Criminal Police was empowered to seize all persons who looked like Gypsies or who wandered around in "Gypsy-like" manner. Those who were seized were classified as follows:

Z	Full Gypsy
ZM+	Gypsy Mischling, predominantly Gypsy
ZM	Gypsy Mischling with equal Gypsy and German "bloodshares"
ZM–	Gypsy Mischling, predominantly German
NZ	Free of Gypsy blood

The victims in the first three categories were subjected to special wage regulations, taxes, and movement restrictions. Special provisions were made for "privileged Gypsy mixed marriages," and so on. In the 1940's the Germans went one step further. Mobile units of the Security Police in Russia killed roving Gypsies, the military commander in Serbia concentrated Gypsies and shot them, and the SS and Police rounded up Gypsies inside and outside the Reich for deportation to ghettos, concentration camps, and killing centers.

Example II. The Poles in the territories incorporated by the Reich were in a rather precarious position. It had been planned to shove them into the Generalgouvernement, while the incorporated provinces to the west were to have become purely German. But that program, like the forced emigration of the Jews from Europe, collapsed. In the back of some people's minds, a "terrible solution" now loomed for these Poles. On May 27, 1941, an interministerial conference took place under the chairmanship of Staatssekretär

Conti of the Interior Ministry. The subject of discussion was the reduction of the Polish population in the incorporated territories. The following proposals were entertained: (1) no Pole to be allowed to marry before the age of twenty-five; (2) no permission to be granted unless the marriage was economically sound; (3) a tax on illegitimate births; (4) sterilization following illegitimate birth; (5) no tax exemptions for dependents; (6) permission to submit to abortion to be granted upon application of the expectant mother.

One year later, on May 1, 1942, Gauleiter Greiser of the incorporated Wartheland reported to Himmler that the "special treatment" of 100,000 Jews in his Gau would be completed in another two or three months. Greiser then proceeded in the same paragraph to request Himmler's permission for the use of the experienced Sonderkommando at Kulmhof in order to liberate the Gau from still another danger that threatened "with each passing week to assume catastrophic proportions." Greiser had in his province 35,000 tubercular Poles. He wanted to kill them. The suggestion was passed on to health expert Blome (Conti's deputy), who wanted to refer the matter to Hitler. Months passed without a decision. Finally, Greiser expressed his disappointment to Himmler in words that recall the analogy principle: "I for my person do not believe that the Führer has to be bothered with this question again, especially since he told me only during our last conversation, with reference to the Jews, that I may deal with those in any way I pleased."

Example III. In consequence of an agreement between Himmler and Justice Minister Thierack, so-called asocials were transferred from prisons to concentration camps. On November 16, 1944, after the transfer of the "asocials" had largely been completed, the judiciary met to discuss a weird subject: ugliness. The phrase on the agenda was "gallery of outwardly asocial prisoners." The summary of that conference states:

> During various visits to the penitentiaries, prisoners have always been observed who—because of their bodily characteristics—hardly deserve the designation human: they look like miscarriages of hell. Such prisoners should be photographed. It is planned that they too shall be eliminated. Crime and sentence are irrelevant. Only such photographs should be submitted which clearly show the deformity.

The Obstacles

A destructive development unparalleled in history had surfaced in Nazi Germany. The bureaucratic network of an entire nation was involved in these operations, and its capabilities were being expanded by an atmosphere facilitating initiatives in offices at every level. Destruction was brought to its logical, final conclusion, and even as this fate overtook the Jews, a veritable target series was established to engulf yet other groups.

The German bureaucracy, however, did not always move with unencumbered ease. From time to time barriers appeared on the horizon and caused momentary pauses. Most of these stoppages were occasioned by those ordinary difficulties encountered by every bureaucracy in every administrative operation: procurement difficulties, shortages, mixups, misunderstandings, and all the other annoyances of the daily bureaucratic process. We shall not be concerned with these occurrences here. But some of the hesitations and interruptions were the products of extraordinary administrative and psychological obstacles. These blocks were peculiar to the destruction process alone, and they must therefore claim our special attention.

Administrative Problems

The destruction of the Jews was not a gainful operation. It imposed a strain upon the administrative machine and its facilities. In a wider sense, it became a burden that rested upon Germany as a whole.

One of the most striking facts about the German apparatus was the sparseness of its personnel, particularly in those regions outside the Reich where most of the victims had to be destroyed. Moreover, that limited manpower was preoccupied with a bewildering variety of administrative undertakings. Upon close examination, the machinery of destruction turns out to have been a loose organization of part-timers. There were at most a handful of bureaucrats who could devote all their time to anti-Jewish activities. There were the "experts" on Jewish affairs in the ministries, the mobile killing units of the Reich Security Main Office, the commanders of the killing centers. But even an expert like Eichmann had two jobs: the deportation of Jews and the resettlement of ethnic Germans. The mobile killing units had to shoot Jews, Gypsies, commissars, and partisans alike, while a camp commander like Höss was host to an industrial complex next to his gas chambers.

In the totality of the administrative process, the destruction of the Jews presented itself as an additional task to a bureaucratic machine that was already straining to fulfill the requirements of the battlefronts. One need think only of the railroads, which served as the principal means for transporting troops, munitions, supplies, and raw materials. Every day, available rolling stock had to be allocated, and congested routes assigned for trains urgently requested by military and industrial users. Notwithstanding these priorities, no Jew was left alive for lack of transport to a killing center. The German bureaucracy was not deterred by problems, never resorting to pretense, like the Italians, or token measures, like the Hungarians, or procrastinations, like the Bulgarians. German administrators were driven to accomplishment. Unlike their collaborators, German decision makers never contented themselves with the minimum. They always did the maximum.

Indeed there were moments when an agency's eagerness to participate in the decision making led to bureaucratic competition and rivalry. Such a contest was in the offing when Unterstaatssekretär Luther concluded an agreement with the Reich Security Main Office to preserve the Foreign Office's power to negotiate with Axis satellites on Jewish matters. Again, within the SS itself, a jealous struggle was waged between two technocrats of destruction, Obersturmbannführer Höss and Kriminalkommissar Wirth, over the replacement of carbon monoxide with Zyklon B in the death camps. We have observed this bureaucratic warfare also in the attempt of the judiciary to conserve its jurisdiction in Jewish affairs. When that attempt was finally given up, Justice Minister Thierack wrote to his friend Bormann: "I intend to turn over criminal jurisdiction against Poles, Russians, Jews, and Gypsies to the Reichsführer-SS. In doing so, I base myself on the principle that the administration of justice can make only a small contribution to the extermination of these peoples." This letter reveals an almost melancholy tone. The judiciary had done its utmost; it was no longer needed. . . .

Psychological Problems

The most important problems of the destruction process were not administrative but psychological. The very conception of the drastic Final Solution was dependent on the ability of the perpetrators to cope with weighty psychological obstacles and impediments. The psychological blocks differed from the administrative difficulties in one important respect. An administrative problem could be solved and eliminated, but the psychological difficulties had to be dealt with continuously. They were held in check but never removed. Commanders in the field were ever watchful for symptoms of psychological disintegration. In the fall of 1941 Higher SS and Police Leader Russia Center von dem Bach shook Himmler with the remark: "Look at the eyes of the men of this Kommando, how deeply shaken they are. These men are finished for the rest of their lives. What kind of followers are we training here? Either neurotics or savages!" Von dem Bach was not only an important participant in killing operations. He was also an acute observer. With this remark he pointed to the basic psychological problem of the German bureaucracy, namely that the German administration had to make determined efforts to prevent the breakdown of its men into either "savages" or "neurotics." This was essentially a dual task—one part disciplinary, the other part moral.

The disciplinary problem was understood clearly. The bureaucrats were fully aware of the dangers of plundering, torture, orgies, and atrocities. Such behavior was first of all wasteful from an administrative point of view, for the destruction process was an organized undertaking which had room only for organized tasks. Moreover, "excesses" attracted attention to aspects of the destruction process that had to remain secret. Such were the activities of Brigadeführer Dirlewnager, whose rumored attempts to make human soap drew the attention of the public to the killing centers. Indeed, atrocities could bring the entire "noble" work into disrepute.

What was wasteful administratively was dangerous psychologically. Loose behavior was an abuse of the machine, and a debauched administration could disintegrate. That was why the German administration had a certain preference for quick-blow-type action. Maximum destructive effect was to be achieved with minimum destructive effort. The personnel of the machinery of destruction were not supposed to look to the right or to the left. They were not allowed to have either personal motives or personal gains. An elaborate discipline was introduced into the machine of destruction. The first and most important rule of conduct of this discipline was that all Jewish property belonged to the Reich. So far as Himmler was concerned, the enforcement of this rule was a success. In 1943 he told his Gruppenführer:

> The riches which they [the Jews] owned we have taken from them. I have given strict orders, which Obergruppenführer Pohl has carried out, that this wealth should naturally be delivered to the Reich. We have taken nothing. Individuals who have transgressed are being punished in accordance with an order which I gave in the beginning and which threatened that anyone who takes just one mark is a condemned man. A number of SS men—not many—have transgressed against that order, and they will be condemned to death mercilessly. We had the moral right vis-à-vis OUR people to annihilate THIS people which wanted to annihilate us. But we have no right to take a single fur, a single watch, a single mark, a single cigarette, or anything whatever. We don't want in the end, just because we have exterminated a germ, to be infected by that germ and die from it. I will not stand by while a slight infection forms. Whenever such an infected spot appears, we will burn it out. But on the whole we can say that we have fulfilled this heavy task with love for our people, and we have not been damaged in the innermost of our being, our soul, our character.

There is, of course, considerable evidence that more than a few individuals "transgressed" against the discipline of the destruction process. No estimate can be formed of the extent to which transport Kommandos, killing units, the ghetto and killing center personnel, and even Kommando 1005—the grave destruction Kommando—filled their pockets with the belongings of the dead. Moreover, we should note that Himmler's rule dealt only with *unauthorized* takings by participating personnel in the field. It did not deal with *authorized* distributions to the participants.

The essence of corruption is to reward people on the basis of their proximity to the loot—in a corrupt system the tax collectors become rich. In the course of the destruction process, many distributions were made to the closest participants. We need remind ourselves only of the Finance Ministry's appropriation of fine furniture during the deportation of Jews from Germany; the distribution of better apartments to civil servants; the cuts taken by the railways, SS and Police, and postal service in the allocation of the furniture of the Dutch, Belgian, and French Jews; the "gifts" of watches and "Christmas presents" to SS men and their families. The destruction process had its own built-in corruption. Only unauthorized corruption was forbidden.

The second way in which the Germans sought to avoid damage to "the soul" was in the prohibition of unauthorized killings. A sharp line was drawn between killings pursuant to order and killings induced by desire. In the former case a man was thought to have overcome the "weaknesses" of "Christian morality"; in the latter case he was overcome by his own baseness. That was why in the occupied USSR both the army and the civil administration sought to restrain their personnel from joining the shooting parties at the killing sites.

Perhaps the best illustration of the official attitude is to be found in an advisory opinion by a judge on Himmler's Personal Staff, Obersturmbannführer Bender. Bender dealt with procedure to be followed in the case of unauthorized killings of Jews by SS personnel. He concluded that if purely political motives prompted the killing, if the act was an expression of idealism, no punishment was necessary unless the maintenance of order required disciplinary action or prosecution. However, if selfish, sadistic, or sexual motives were found, punishment was to be imposed for murder or for manslaughter, in accordance with the facts.

The German disciplinary system is most discernible in the mode of the killing operation. At the conclusion of the destruction process, Hitler remarked in his testament that the Jewish "criminals" had "atoned" for their "guilt" by "humane means." The "humaneness" of the destruction process was an important factor in its success. It must be emphasized, of course, that this "humaneness" was evolved not for the benefit of the victims but for the welfare of its perpetrators. Time and again, attempts were made to reduce opportunities for "excesses" of all sorts. Much research was expended for the development of devices and methods that arrested propensities for uncontrolled behavior and at the same time lightened the crushing psychological burden on the killers. The construction of gas vans and gas chambers, the employment of Ukranian, Lithuanian, and Latvian auxiliaries to kill Jewish women and children, the use of Jews for the burial and burning of bodies—all these were efforts in the same direction. Efficiency was the real aim of all that "humaneness."

So far as Himmler was concerned, his SS and Police had weathered the destruction process. In October 1943, when he addressed his top commanders, he said to them:

> Most of you know what it means when 100 corpses lie there, or 500 lie there, or 1000 lie there. To have gone through this and—apart from the exceptions caused by human weakness—to have remained decent, that has hardened us. That is a page of glory in our history never written and never to be written.

However, the descent into savagery was not nearly so important a factor in the destruction process as the feeling of growing uneasiness that pervaded the bureaucracy from the lowest strata to the highest. That uneasiness was the product of moral scruples—the lingering effect of two thousand years of Western morality and ethics. A Western bureaucracy had never before faced such a chasm between moral precepts and administrative action; an administrative machine had never been burdened with such a drastic task. In a sense the task of destroying the Jews put the German bureaucracy to a supreme test. The German technocrats solved also that problem and passed also this test.

To grasp the full significance of what these men did we have to understand that we are not dealing with individuals who had their own separate moral standards. The bureaucrats who were drawn into the destruction process were not different in their moral makeup from the rest of the population. The German perpetrator was not a special kind of German. What we have to say here about his morality applies not to him specially but to Germany as a whole. How do we know this?

We know that the very nature of administrative planning, of the jurisdictional structure, and of the budgetary system precluded the special training of personnel. Any member of the Order Police could be a guard at a ghetto or on a train. Every lawyer in the Reich Security Main Office was presumed to be suitable for leadership in the mobile killing units; every finance expert to the Economic-Administrative Main Office was considered a natural choice for service in a death camp. In other words, all necessary operations were accomplished with whatever personnel were at hand. However one may wish to draw the line of active participation, the machinery of destruction was a remarkable cross-section of the German population. Every profession, every skill, and every social status was represented in it. We know that in a totalitarian state the formation of an opposition movement outside the bureaucracy is next to impossible. However, if there is very serious opposition in the population, if there are insurmountable psychological obstacles to a course of action, such impediments reveal themselves *within* the bureaucratic apparatus. We know what such barriers will do, for they emerged clearly in the Italian Fascist state. Again and again the Italian generals and consuls, prefects and police inspectors refused to cooperate in the deportations. The destruction process in Italy and the Italian-controlled areas was carried out against unremitting Italian opposition. No such opposition is to be found in the German area. No obstruction stopped the German machine of destruction. No moral problem proved insurmountable. When all participating personnel were put to the test, there were very few lingerers and almost no deserters. The old moral order did not break through anywhere along the line. This is a phenomenon of the greatest magnitude.

How did the German bureaucrat cope with his moral inhibitions? He did so in an inner struggle, recognizing the basic truth that he had a choice. He knew that at crucial junctures every individual makes decisions, and that every decision is individual. He knew this fact as he faced his own involvement and while he went on and on. At the same time he was not psychically unarmed. When he wrestled with himself, he had at his disposal the most complex psychological tools fashioned during centuries of German cultural development. Fundamentally, this arsenal of defenses consisted of two parts: a mechanism of repressions and a system of rationalizations.

First of all, the bureaucracy wanted to hide its deeds. It wanted to conceal the destructive process not only from all outsiders but also from the censuring gaze of its own conscience. The repression proceeded through five stages.

As we might expect, every effort was made to hide the ultimate aim of the destruction process from Axis partners and from the Jews. Inquiries such as Hungarian Prime Minister Kállay put to the Foreign Office about the disappearance of European Jewry or questions that foreign journalists in Kiev asked army authorities about mass shootings could obviously not be answered. Rumors, which could spread like wildfire, had to be smothered. "Plastic" evidence, such as "souvenir" photographs of killings, mass graves, and the wounded Jews who had risen from their graves, had to be destroyed. . . .

[T]he first stage in the repression was to shut off the supply of information from all those who did not have to know it. Whoever did not participate was not supposed to know.

The second stage was to make sure that whoever knew would participate. There was nothing so irksome as the realization that someone was watching over one's shoulder, that someone would be free to talk and accuse because he was not himself involved. This fear was the origin of what Leo Alexander called the "blood kit," the irresistible force that drew every official "observer" into the destruction process. The "blood kit" explains why so many office chiefs of the Reich Security Main Office were assigned to mobile killing units and why staff officers with killing units were ordered to participate in the killing operations. The "blood kit" also explains why Unterstaatssekretär Luther of the Foreign Office's Abteilung Deugschland insisted that the Political Division countersign all instructions to embassies and legations for the deportation of Jews. Finally, the "blood kit" explains the significant words spoken by Generalgouverneur Frank at the conclusion of a police conference in Kraków: "We want to remember that we are, all of us assembled here, on Mr. Roosevelt's war-criminals list. I have the honor of occupying first place on that list. We are therefore, so to speak, accomplices in a world-historical sense."

The third stage in the process of repression was the prohibition of criticism. Public protests by outsiders were extremely rare. The criticisms were expressed, if at all, in mutterings on the rumor circuit. It is sometimes hard even to distinguish between expressions of sensationalism and real criticism, for often the two were mixed. One example of such mixed reactions is to be found in the circulation of rumours in Germany about the mobile killing operations in Russia. The Party Chancellery, in confidential instructions to its regional machinery, attempted to combat these rumors. Most of the reports, the chancellery stated, were "distorted" and "exaggerated." "It is conceivable," the circular continued, "that not all of our people—especially people who have no conception of the Bolshevik terror—can understand sufficiently the necessity for these measures." In their very nature, "these problems," which were some-

times "very difficult," could be solved "in the interest of the security of our people" only with "ruthless severity.". . .

In its fourth stage the repressive mechanism eliminated the destruction process as a subject of social conversation. Among the closest
participants, it was considered bad form to talk about the killings.
This is what Himmler had to say on the subject in his speech of
October 4, 1943:

> I want to mention here very candidly a particularly difficult chap-
> ter. Among us it should be mentioned once, quite openly, but in
> public we will never talk about it. Just as little as we hesitated on
> June 30, 1934, to do our duty and to put comrades who had trans-
> gressed [the brownshirts] to the wall, so little have we talked about
> it and will ever talk about it. It was with us, thank God, an inborn
> gift of tactfulness, that we have never conversed about this matter,
> never spoken about it. Every one of us was horrified, and yet every
> one of us knew that we would do it again if it were ordered and if
> it were necessary. I am referring to the evacuation of the Jews, to
> the extermination of the Jewish people.

This then was the reason why that particular "page of glory" was
never to be written. There are some things that can be done only
so long as they are not discussed, for once they are discussed they
can no longer be done. . . .

The fifth and final stage in the process of repression was to omit
mention of "killings" or "killing installations" even in the secret
correspondence in which such operations had to be reported. The
reader of these reports is immediately struck by their camouflaged
vocabulary: *Endlösung der Judenfrage* ("final solution of the Jewish
question"), *Lösungsmöglichkeiten* ("solution possibilities"), *Sonder-
behandlung* or *SB* ("special treatment"), *Evakuierung* ("evacuation"),
Aussiedlung (same), *Umsiedlung* (same), *Spezialeinrichtungen* ("special
installations"), *durchgeschleusst* ("dragged through"), and many
others.

There is one report that contains a crude cover story. In 1943
the Foreign Office inquired whether it would be possible to exchange
30,000 Baltic and White Russian Jews for Reich Germans in Allied
countries. The Foreign Office representative in Riga replied that
he had discussed the matter with the Security Police commander
in charge. The Commander of Security Police had felt that the
"interned" Jews could not be sent away for "weighty Security Police
reasons." As was known, a large number of Jews had been "done

away with" in "spontaneous actions." In some places these actions
had resulted in "almost total extermination." A removal of the remaining Jews would therefore give rise to "anti-German atrocity
propaganda."...

The process of repression was continuous, but it was never completed. The killing of the Jews could not be hidden completely,
either from the outside world or from the inner self. Therefore the
bureaucracy was not spared an open encounter with its conscience.
It had to pit argument against argument and philosophy against
philosophy. Laboriously, and with great effort, the bureaucracy had
to justify its activities....

[Rationalization]

Psychological justification is called rationalization. The Germans
employed two kinds of rationalizations. The first was an attempt
to justify the destruction process as a whole. It was designed to
explain why the Jews had to be destroyed. It was focused on the
Jew. The other explanations served only to justify individual participation in the destruction process—a signature on a piece of paper
or the squeeze of a trigger. They were focused entirely on the
perpetrator. Let us consider first the broad rationalizations that
encompassed the whole destruction process. In the formation of
these justifications, old conceptions about the Jew, reinforced and
expanded by new propaganda, played an important role. Precisely
how did German propaganda function in this process?

The Germans had two kinds of propaganda. One was designed
to produce action. It exhorted people to come to a mass meeting,
to boycott Jewish goods, or to kill Jews. This type of propaganda
does not concern us here since it was confined, on the whole,
to the incitement of demonstrations and pogroms, the so-called
Einzelaktionen. But the Germans also engaged in a campaign that
consisted of a series of statements implying that the Jew was evil.
This propaganda had a very important place in the arsenal of psychological defense mechanisms.

Repeated propagandistic allegations may be stored and drawn
upon according to need. The statement "The Jew is evil" is taken

from the storehouse and is converted in the perpetrator's mind into a complete rationalization: "I kill the Jew because the Jew is evil." To understand the function of such formulations is to realize why they were being constructed until the very end of the war. Propaganda was needed to combat doubts and guilt feelings wherever they arose, whether inside or outside the bureaucracy, and whenever they surfaced, before or after the perpetration of the acts.

In fact, we find that in April 1943, after the deportations of the Jews from the Reich had largely been completed, the press was ordered to deal with the Jewish question continuously and without letup. In order to build up a storehouse, the propaganda had to be turned out on a huge scale. "Research institutes" were formed, doctoral dissertations were written, and volumes of propaganda literature were printed by every conceivable agency. Sometimes a scholarly investigation was conducted too assiduously. One economic study, rich in the common jargon but uncommonly balanced in content, appeared in Vienna with the notation "Not in the book trade"—the author had discovered that the zenith of Jewish financial power had been reached in 1913.

. . .

What did all this propaganda accomplish? How was the Jew portrayed in this unending flow of leaflets and pamphlets, books, and speeches? How did the propaganda image of the Jew serve to justify the destruction process?

First of all, the Germans drew a picture of an international Jewry ruling the world and plotting the destruction of Germany and German life. "If international-finance Jewry," said Adolf Hitler in 1939, "inside and outside of Europe should succeed in plunging the nations into another world war, then the result will not be the Bolshevization of the earth and with it the victory of the Jews, but the annihilation of the Jewish race in Europe." In 1944 Himmler said to his commanders: "This was the most frightening order which an organization could receive—the order to solve the Jewish question," but if the Jews had still been in the rear, the front line could not have been held, and if any of the commanders were moved to pity, they had only to think of the bombing terror, "which after all is organized in the last analysis by the Jews."

The theory of world Jewish rule and of the incessant Jewish plot against the German people penetrated into all offices. It became interwoven with foreign policy and sometimes led to preposterous results. Thus the conviction grew that foreign statesmen who were not very friendly toward Germany were Jews, part-Jews, married to Jews, or somehow dominated by Jews. Streicher did not hesitate to state publicly that he had it on good Italian authority that the Pope had Jewish blood. Similarly, Staatssekretär Weizsäcker of the Foreign Office once questioned the British chargé d'affaires about the percentage of "Aryan" blood in Mr. Rublee, an American on a mission in behalf of refugees. . . .

However, the Jews were portrayed not only as a world conspiracy but also as a criminal people. This is the definition of the Jews as furnished in instructions to the German press:

> *Stress:* In the case of the Jews there are not merely a few criminals (as in every other people), but all of Jewry rose from criminal roots, and in its very nature it is criminal. The Jews are no people like other people, but a pseudo-people welded together by hereditary criminality. . . . The annihilation of Jewry is no loss to humanity, but just as useful as capital punishment or protective custody against other criminals.

And this is what Streicher had to say: "Look at the path which the Jewish people has traversed for millenia: Everywhere murder; everywhere mass murder!"

A Nazi researcher, Helmut Schramm, collected all the legends of Jewish ritual murder. The book was an immediate success with Himmler. "Of the book *The Jewish Ritual Murders*," he wrote to Kaltenbrunner, "I have ordered a large number. I am distributing it down to Standartenführer [SS colonel]. I am sending you several hundred copies so that you can distribute them to your Einsatzkommandos, and above all to the men who are busy with the Jewish question." *The Ritual Murders* was a collection of stories about alleged tortures of Christian children. Actually, hundreds of thousands of Jewish children were being killed in the destruction process. Perhaps that is why *The Ritual Murders* became so important. In fact, Himmler was so enthusiastic about the book that he ordered Kaltenbrunner to start investigations of "ritual murders" in Romania, Hungary, and Bulgaria. He also suggested that Security Police people be put to work tracing British court records and police descriptions of missing children, "so that we can report in our radio broadcasts to England that in the town of XY a child is missing and that it is probably another case of Jewish ritual murder.". . .

A third rationalization that focused on the Jew was the conception of Jewry as a lower form of life. Generalgouverneur Frank was given to the use of such phrases as "Jews and lice." In a speech delivered on December 19, 1940, he pointed out that relatives of military personnel surely were sympathizing with men stationed in Poland, a country "which is so full of lice and Jews." But the situation was not so bad, he continued, though of course he could not rid the country of lice and Jews in a year. On July 19, 1943, the chief of the Generalgouvernement Health Division reported during a meeting that the typhus epidemic was subsiding. Frank remarked in this connection that the "removal" of the "Jewish element" had undoubtedly contributed to better health in Europe. He meant this not only in the literal sense but also politically: the reestablishment of sound living conditions on the European continent. In a similar vein, Foreign Office Press Chief Schmidt once declared during a visit to Slovakia, "The Jewish question is no question of humanity, and it is no question of religion; it is solely a question of political hygiene." . . .

[Individual Rationalizations]

In addition to the formulations that were used to justify the whole undertaking as a war against "international Jewry," as a judicial proceeding against "Jewish criminality," or simply as a "hygienic" process against "Jewish vermin," there were also rationalizations fashioned in order to enable the individual bureaucrat to justify his individual task in the destruction process. It must be kept in mind that most of the participants did not fire rifles at Jewish children or pour gas into gas chambers. A good many, of course, also had to perform these very "hard" tasks, but most of the administrators and most of the clerks did not see the final, drastic link in these measures of destruction.

Most bureaucrats composed memoranda, drew up blueprints, signed correspondence, talked on the telephone, and participated in conferences. They could destroy a whole people by sitting at their desks. Except for inspection tours, which were not obligatory, they never had to see "100 bodies lie there, or 500, or 1,000." However, these men were not naive. They realized the connection between their paperwork and the heaps of corpses in the East, and they also realized the shortcomings of arguments that placed all evil on the Jew and all good on the German. That was why they were compelled to justify their individual activities. The justifications contain the implicit admission that the paperwork was to go on regardless of the actual plans of world Jewry and regardless of the actual behavior of the Jews who were about to be killed. . . .

The oldest, the simplest, and therefore the most effective rationalization was the doctrine of superior orders. First and foremost there was discipline. First and foremost there was duty. No matter what objections there might be, orders were given to be obeyed. A clear order was like absolution. Armed with such an order, a perpetrator felt that he could pass his responsibility and his conscience upward. When Himmler addressed a killing party in Minsk, he told his men that they need not worry. Their conscience was in no way impaired, for they were soldiers who had to carry out every order unconditionally.

Every bureaucrat knows, of course, that open defiance of orders is serious business, but he also knows that there are many ingenious ways of evading orders. In fact, the opportunities for evading them increase as one ascends in the hierarchy. Even in Nazi Germany orders were disobeyed, and they were disobeyed even in Jewish matters. We have mentioned the statement of Reichsbankdirektor Wilhelm, who would not participate in the distribution of "second-hand goods." Nothing happened to him. A member of the Reich Security Main Office, Sturmbannführer Hartl, simply refused to take over an Einsatzkommando in Russia. Nothing happened to this man, either. Even Generalkommissar Kube, who had actually frustrated a killing operation in Minsk and who had otherwise expressed himself in strong language, was only warned.

The bureaucrat clung to his orders not so much because he feared his superior (with whom he was often on good terms) but because he feared his own conscience. The many requests for "authorization," whether for permission to mark Jews with a star or to kill them, demonstrate the true nature of these orders. When they did not exist the bureaucrats had to invent them.

The second rationalization was the administrator's insistence that he did not act out of personal vindictiveness. In the mind of the bureaucrat, duty was an assigned path; it was his "fate." The German bureaucrat made a sharp distinction between duty and personal feelings. He insisted that he did not "hate" Jews, and sometimes he even went out of his way to perform "good deeds" for Jewish friends and acquaintances. When the trials of war criminals started, there was hardly a defendant who could not produce evidence that he had helped some half-Jewish physics professor, or that he had used his influence to permit a Jewish symphony conductor to conduct a little while longer, or that he had intervened on behalf of some couple in mixed marriage in connection with an apartment. While these courtesies were petty in comparison with the destructive conceptions that these men were implementing concurrently, the "good deeds" performed an important psychological function. They separated "duty" from personal feelings. They preserved a sense of "decency." The destroyer of the Jews was no "anti-Semite.". . .

The third justification was the rationalization that one's own activity was not criminal, that the next fellow's action was the criminal act. The Ministerialrat who was signing papers could console himself with the thought that he did not do the shooting. But that was not enough. He had to be sure that *if* he were ordered to shoot, he would not follow orders but would draw the line right then and there.

The following exchange took place during a war crimes trial. A Foreign Office official, Albrecht von Kessel, was asked by defense counsel (Dr. Becker) to explain the meaning of "final solution."

ANSWER: This expression "final solution" was used with various meanings. In 1936 "final solution" meant merely that all Jews should leave Germany. And, of course, it was true that they were to be robbed; that wasn't very nice, but it wasn't criminal.

JUDGE MAGUIRE: Was that an accurate translation?

DR. BECKER: I did not check on the translation. Please repeat the sentence.

ANSWER: I said it was not criminal; it was not nice, but it was not criminal. That is what I said. One didn't want to take their life; one merely wanted to take money away from them. That was all.

The most important characteristic of this dividing line was that it could be *shifted* when the need arose. . . .

There was a fourth rationalization that implicitly took cognizance of the fact that all shifting lines are unreal. It was a rationalization that was built on a simple premise: No man alone can build a bridge and no man alone can destroy the Jews. The participant in the destruction process was always in company. Among his superiors he could always find those who were doing more than he; among his subordinates he could always find those who were ready to take his place. No matter where he looked, he was one among thousands. His own importance was diminished, and he felt that he was replaceable, perhaps even dispensable. . . .

When Werner von Tippelskirch, a Foreign Office official, was interrogated after the war, he pointed out that he had never protested against the killing of Jews in Russia because he had been "powerless." His superiors, Erdmannsdorff, Wörmann, and Weizsäcker, had also been "powerless." All of them had waited for a "change of regime." Asked by Prosecutor Kempner whether it was right to wait for a change of regime "and in the meantime send thousands of people to their death," von Tippelskirch replied, "A difficult question." For Staatssekretär von Weizsäcker himself the question of what he could have done was circular. If he had had influence he would have stopped measures altogether. But the "if" presupposed a fairyland. In such a land he would not have had to use his influence.

10
Apartheid Torturer
Evil Shows Its Banal Face
Suzanne Daley

Jeffrey Benzien was one of the many minor but effective functionaries who made apartheid work for South Africa's white Government.

Every day, the paunchy, graying police officer left his home in this city's tidy suburbs and went to a police barracks where he extracted confessions with torture.

Mr. Benzien was particularly adept at the use of the "wet bag," in which a cloth placed over victims' heads took them to the brink of asphyxiation, over and over again. Few withstood more than half an hour.

Questioned at a hearing of South Africa's Truth and Reconciliation Commission by one of his victims, Peter Jacobs, Mr. Benzien said he simply could not recall exactly what he had done to whom.

"If I say to Mr. Jacobs I put the electrodes on his nose I may be wrong," he testified. "If I say I attached them to his genitals, I may be wrong. If I say I put a probe in his rectum, I may be wrong. I could have used any one of those methods."

As the commission continues its work, the brutality of South Africa's past is being itemized, not in the grand sweep of a history book, but in the individual stories of victims and torturers, of murderers and mothers of the murdered, of high commanders who made their decisions over tea trays and foot soldiers who made theirs beside fresh bloodstains.

Mr. Benzien's story has gripped the country partly because of photographs of him demonstrating his technique during hearings, and partly because until he testified he was a nobody.

He did not have the nickname "Prime Evil" like Eugene de Kock, who commanded a whole unit of killers but has never been photographed doing anything more active than wringing his hands. The press did not call him a superspy, as it does Craig Williamson, who mailed bombs in letters and earphones to anti-apartheid activists.

Mr. Benzien, now 50, was just a middle-level officer whose only distinction may be that he came forward to talk about his job as a torturer. He is the only member of his unit to have done so. Whether the others will ever be tracked down and prosecuted remains an open question, as South Africa's justice system is already struggling just to deal with today's crime wave.

He has cried and confessed that he has no explanation for what he did—that he wonders what kind of a person can do such things. His psychiatrist, Ria Kotze, who was called to testify on his behalf, has described a man who saw himself as a good policeman, who at the end of the day went home to his family and never discussed what he did at work. Nowadays, she said, he is full of self-loathing and suffers acutely. His memory has become patchy. He takes antidepressants.

During four days before the commission, his victims took turns attacking the veracity of his amnesty application, which contained only the barest of details. In writing, Mr. Benzien admitted only to use of the wet-bag treatment on six victims and said he had worked alone, to make it easier to deny the torture in court later, if he is not granted amnesty.

But pressed, at times relentlessly, he admitted that he had used electric shocks as well. One victim said Mr. Benzien had shoved a broomstick up his rectum. There were beatings, too, and some people were hung for hours by handcuffs attached to the window bars in their cells.

Yet if much of South Africa has focused on Mr. Benzien as the ultimate torturer, his victims say he was only one of many officers who went home to their wives and children after making prisoners howl and writhe and beg for their lives. They say he gained prominence only because some of his victims are now prominent—one of them, Tony Yengeni, a Member of Parliament.

Only One of Many Just Following Orders

Indeed, at his hearing it became clear that while Mr. Benzien's victims screamed, other officers helped to hold them down or moved in and out of the room indifferent to what was happening. Mr. Benzien's story, they say, offers nothing more than a glimpse into the day-to-day workings of the elite security police—who routinely used torture and routinely denied doing so.

Through his lawyer, Mr. Benzien declined to be interviewed. But much of his life and even his feelings were laid bare by the proceedings. He remains in the police force, albeit relegated to an obscure job at the Cape Town International Airport.

Mr. Jacobs, now a police officer himself, says many officers shun Mr. Benzien. At a recent police conference, Mr. Jacobs said, he found that during a cigarette break outside a building, he alone was willing to talk to Mr. Benzien.

"It was strange," Mr. Jacobs said. "Everyone just disappeared."

The two men talked about their current assignments, and Mr. Jacobs noted that Mr. Benzien now referred to him as Superintendent, an acknowledgment of Mr. Jacobs's higher rank.

Mr. Benzien joined the force in 1977 and barely a year later was transferred to the detective branch. He soon went on to a murder-and-robbery squad, one of the units notorious for torturing ordinary criminals. In 1986, he was plucked to join the far more prestigious security branch, which investigated political activists and which, under the watchful eye of international human rights groups, tortured more carefully.

"They didn't take him because he was a brute," Mr. Jacobs said. "They took him for his suaveness."

To grant him amnesty, the panel must rule that his acts had a political motive and that he has confessed everything. Mr. Benzien says he was an enthusiastic supporter of the National Party, which ran the Government, and was following explicit or implicit orders. His commanding officer also testified, acknowledging that he had known about Mr. Benzien's torture sessions and had once helped pin a prisoner down.

His job with the security branch, Mr. Benzien told the commission, was to trace a person, arrest him and get him to reveal weapons caches before they could be moved.

In describing his work, Mr. Benzien seemed at times to take pride in his accomplishments. "I believe that due to my expeditious and unorthodox conduct," he said at one point, "we made a big difference in combating terror."

But at other times, he expressed bitterness about the role he had played in the apartheid machinery of the white Government, which ruled until Nelson Mandela was elected President in 1994 in the country's first nonracial election.

"I can sit here and tell you in all honesty that I was used by the then security branch," he said. "When it came down to getting the job done, I was the person who did it. Maybe I was too patriotic, too naive or anything else that you want to call it."

Early in the hearings he appealed for sympathy, saying he, too, had paid a price for apartheid.

"My house windows had to be barricaded with cupboards," he said. "Every night a wet blanket had to be put in the bath, available where my younger children could get hold of that in the case of grenade attacks. You are surely aware that I was transferred as the station commander at Stanford because not only were my nerves shot, my wife threatened divorce if I did not get out of Cape Town."

"That was after the African Youth League threatened to have demonstrations on my front lawn," he added. Then, in a reference to Mr. Mandela's African National Congress party, he said, "I did terrible things, I did terrible things to members of the A.N.C., but as God is my witness, believe me, I have also suffered."

His victims did not seem moved. It was Mr. Yengeni, the legislator, who insisted that Mr. Benzien demonstrate, for panel members and photographers, how the wet-bag method had worked. After all these years, Mr. Yengeni said, he wanted to see exactly what had been done to him.

Angst-Ridden Words, Unmoved Victims

Mr. Yengeni also wanted to know what kind of man could listen to the moans and cries and take people so near to death so many times.

The policeman was in tears when he answered.

"Mr. Yengeni," he said, "not only you have asked me that question. I, I, Jeff Benzien, have asked myself that question to such an extent that I voluntarily, and it is not easy for me to say this in a full court with a lot of people who do not know me, approached psychiatrists to have myself evaluated, to find out what type of person am I."

But the pathetic officer before the commission presented a sharp contrast to the images the victims evoked as they hammered at him.

"When I was arrested," one victim asked, "do you remember saying to me that you were able to treat me like an animal or a human being?"

"I concede I may have said it," Mr. Benzien said.

"Do you remember when you used the wet bag I was undressed and my pants were pulled to my ankles?"

"I cannot remember specifically, but I can concede, yes."

"Do you remember saying that you are going to break my nose and then putting both your thumbs into my nostrils and pulling it until the blood came out of my nose?"

"I know you had a nosebleed. I thought it was the result of a smack I gave you."

Mr. Benzien said he had never been trained in torture, although officers had talked about which methods worked best. And he insisted that Mr. Jacobs had been his first victim.

Mr. Jacobs found this hard to believe.

"You appeared very effective, yet you had no experience," he said. "How come? Are you a natural talent?"

"I wouldn't know," Mr. Benzien answered wearily. "It's not a very nice talent to have."

Mr. Benzien's psychiatrist, Ms. Kotze, said she had first met him in 1994 through his wife, whom she was treating for depression. Mr. Benzien was refusing to discuss his work with his wife but was clearly agitated and "verbally aggressive" toward her.

Earlier this year he had a breakdown whose symptoms included hearing voices. He started seeing Ms. Kotze on his own then. She reported that he found it hard to describe what he had done and sometimes had to stop in the middle of sessions. He has nightmares, she said, and forgets details of events.

A Psychiatrist Describes the Ravages of Guilt

He is not without a sense of moral outrage. He seemed hurt as he vigorously denied a victim's claim that he brought his wet bag when he visited one of his prisoners in the hospital.

In explaining his decision to come forward, he said he was still trying to serve his country and wanted to "see if we can't build and forget about hardships."

He also apologized repeatedly to his victims.

The commission's decision on him could take months. Some of his victims are opposing amnesty, saying he did not implicate everyone who had helped him and did not volunteer all he knew.

And the reaction of Mr. Jacobs. who is now at once his victim, his interrogator and his superior?

Mr. Jacobs says he is ambivalent about the man and in a strange way feels sorry for him.

"He came out and we exposed him," Mr. Jacobs said. "What's it really going to serve now, not to give him amnesty? What strategic value would be served? I can't see it."

Editors' Postscript

Mr. Benzien was granted amnesty by the Truth and Reconciliation Commission in February 1999. See "World in Brief," *The Washington Post*, February 18, 1999, p. A16.

11

The My Lai Massacre
Crimes of Obedience and Sanctioned Massacres
Herbert C. Kelman and V. Lee Hamilton

March 16, 1968, was a busy day in U.S. history. Stateside, Robert F. Kennedy announced his presidential candidacy, challenging a sitting president from his own party—in part out of opposition to an undeclared and disastrous war. In Vietnam, the war continued. In many ways, March 16 may have been a typical day in that war. We will probably never know. But we do know that on that day a typical company went on a mission—which may or may not have been typical—to a village called Son (or Song) My. Most of what is remembered from that mission occurred in the subhamlet known to Americans as My Lai 4.

The My Lai massacre was investigated and charges were brought in 1969 and 1970. Trials and disciplinary actions lasted into 1971. Entire books have been written about the army's year-long cover-up of the massacre (for example, Hersh, 1972), and the cover-up was a major focus of the army's own investigation of the incident. Our central concern here is the massacre itself—a crime of obedience—and public reactions to such crimes, rather than the lengths to which many went to deny the event. Therefore this account concentrates on one day: March 16, 1968.

Many verbal testimonials to the horrors that occurred at My Lai were available. More unusual was the fact that an army photographer, Ronald Haeberle, was assigned the task of documenting the anticipated military engagement at My Lai—and documented a massacre instead. Later, as the story of the massacre emerged, his photographs were widely distributed and seared the public con-

From *Crimes of Obedience: Toward a Social Psychology of Authority and Responsibility*, pp. 1–20. Copyright © 1989 by Yale University Press. Reprinted by permission.

science. What might have been dismissed as unreal or exaggerated was depicted in photographs of demonstrable authenticity. The dominant image appeared on the cover of *Life*: piles of bodies jumbled together in a ditch along a trail—the dead all apparently unarmed. All were Oriental, and all appeared to be children, women, or old men. Clearly there had been a mass execution, one whose image would not quickly fade.

So many bodies (over twenty in the cover photo alone) are hard to imagine as the handiwork of one killer. These were not. They were the product of what we call a crime of obedience. Crimes of obedience begin with orders. But orders are often vague and rarely survive with any clarity the transition from one authority down a chain of subordinates to the ultimate actors. The operation at Son My was no exception.

"Charlie" Company, Company C, under Lt. Col. Frank Barker's command, arrived in Vietnam in December of 1967. As the army's investigative unit, directed by Lt. Gen. William R. Peers, characterized the personnel, they "contained no significant deviation from the average" for the time. Seymour S. Hersh (1970) described the "average" more explicitly: "Most of the men in Charlie Company had volunteered for the draft; only a few had gone to college for even one year. Nearly half were black, with a few Mexican-Americans. Most were eighteen to twenty-two years old. The favorite reading matter of Charlie Company, like that of other line infantry units in Vietnam, was comic books" (p. 18). The action at My Lai, like that throughout Vietnam, was fought by a cross-section of those Americans who either believed in the war or lacked the social resources to avoid participating in it. Charlie Company was indeed average for that time, that place, and that war.

Two key figures in Charlie Company were more unusual. The company's commander, Capt. Ernest Medina, was an upwardly mobile Mexican-American who wanted to make the army his career, although he feared that he might never advance beyond captain because of his lack of formal education. His eagerness had earned him a nickname among his men: "Mad Dog Medina." One of his admirers was the platoon leader Second Lt. William L. Calley, Jr., an undistinguished, five-foot-three-inch junior-college dropout who had failed four of the seven courses in which he had enrolled his first year. Many viewed him as one of those "instant officers" made possible only by the army's then-desperate need for manpower. Whatever the cause, he was an insecure leader whose frequent claim was "I'm the boss." His nickname among some of the troops was "Surfside 5½," a reference to the swashbuckling heroes of a popular television show, "Surfside 6."

The Son My operation was planned by Lieutenant Colonel Barker and his staff as a search-and-destroy mission with the objective of rooting out the Forty-eighth Viet Cong Battalion from their base area of Son My village. Apparently no written orders were ever issued. Barker's superior, Col. Oran Henderson, arrived at the staging point the day before. Among the issues he reviewed with the assembled officers were some of the weaknesses of prior operations by their units, including their failure to be appropriately aggressive in pursuit of the enemy. Later briefings by Lieutenant Colonel Barker and his staff asserted that no one except Viet Cong was expected to be in the village after 7 A.M. on the following day. The "innocent" would all be at the market. Those present at the briefings gave conflicting accounts of Barker's exact orders, but he conveyed at least a strong suggestion that the Son My area was to be obliterated. As the army's inquiry reported: "While there is some conflict in the testimony as to whether LTC Barker ordered the destruction of houses, dwellings, livestock, and other foodstuffs in the Song My area, the preponderance of the evidence indicates that such destruction was implied, if not specifically directed, by his orders of 15 March" (Peers Report, in Goldstein et al., 1976, p. 94).

Evidence that Barker ordered the killing of civilians is even more murky. What does seem clear, however, is that—having asserted that civilians would be away at the market—he did not specify what was to be done with any who might nevertheless be found on the scene. The Peers Report therefore considered it "reasonable to conclude that LTC Barker's minimal or nonexistent instructions concerning the handling of noncombatants created the potential for grave misunderstandings as to his intentions and for interpretation of his orders as authority to fire, without restriction, on all persons found in target area" (Goldstein et al., 1976, p. 95). Since Barker was killed in action in June 1968, his own formal version of the truth was never available.

Charlie Company's Captain Medina was briefed for the operation by Barker and his staff. He then transmitted the already vague orders to his own men. Charlie Company was spoiling for a fight, having been totally frustrated during its months in Vietnam—first by waiting for battles that never came, then by incompetent forays led by inexperienced commanders, and finally by mines and booby traps. In fact, the emotion-laden funeral of a sergeant killed by a booby trap was held on March 15, the day before My Lai. Captain Medina gave the orders for the next day's action at the close of that funeral. Many were in a mood for revenge.

It is again unclear what was ordered. Although all participants were still alive by the time of the trials for the massacre, they were either on trial or probably felt under threat of trial. Memories are often flawed and self-serving at such times. It is apparent that Medina relayed to the men at least some of Barker's general message—to expect Viet Cong resistance, to burn, and to kill live-stock. It is not clear that he ordered the slaughter of the inhabit-ants, but some of the men who heard him thought he had. One of those who claimed to have heard such orders was Lt. William Calley.

As March 16 dawned, much was expected of the operation by those who had set it into motion. Therefore a full complement of "brass" was present in helicopters overhead, including Barker, Colonel Henderson, and their superior, Major General Koster (who went on to become commandant of West Point before the story of My Lai broke). On the ground, the troops were to carry with them one reporter and one photographer to immortalize the anticipated battle.

The action for Company C began at 7:30 as their first wave of helicopters touched down near the subhamlet of My Lai 4. By 7:47 all of Company C was present and set to fight. But instead of the Viet Cong Forty-eighth Battalion, My Lai was filled with the old men, women, and children who were supposed to have gone to market. By this time, in their version of the war, and with whatever orders they thought they had heard, the men from Company C were never-theless ready to find Viet Cong everywhere. By nightfall, the offi-cial tally was 128 VC killed and three weapons captured, although later unofficial body counts ran as high as 500. The operation at Son My was over. And by nightfall, as Hersh reported: "The Viet Cong were back in My Lai 4, helping the survivors bury the dead. It took five days. Most of the funeral speeches were made by the Communist guerrillas. Nguyen Bat was not a Communist at the time of the massacre, but the incident changed his mind. 'After the shooting,' he said, 'all the villagers became Communists'" (1970, p. 74). To this day, the memory of the massacre is kept alive by markers and plaques designating the spots where groups of villagers were killed, by a large statue, and by the My Lai Museum, established in 1975 (Williams, 1985).

But what could have happened to leave American troops reporting a victory over Viet Cong when in fact they had killed hundreds of noncombatants? It is not hard to explain the report of victory; that is the essence of a cover-up. It is harder to understand how the killings came to be committed in the first place, making a cover-up necessary.

Mass Executions and the Defense of Superior Orders

Some of the atrocities on March 16, 1968, were evidently unofficial, spontaneous acts: rapes, tortures, killings. For example, Hersh (1970) describes Charlie Company's Second Platoon as entering "My Lai 4 with guns blazing" (p. 50); more graphically, Lieutenant "Brooks and his men in the second platoon to the north had begun to systematically ransack the hamlet and slaughter the people, kill the livestock, and destroy the crops. Men poured rifle and machine-gun fire into huts without knowing—or seemingly caring—who was inside" (pp. 49–50).

Some atrocities toward the end of the action were part of an almost casual "mopping-up," much of which was the responsibility of Lieutenant LaCross's Third Platoon of Charlie Company. The Peers Report states: "The entire 3rd Platoon then began moving into the western edge of My Lai (4), for the mop-up operation. . . . The squad . . . began to burn the houses in the southwestern portion of the hamlet" (Goldstein et al., 1976, p. 133). They became mingled with other platoons during a series of rapes and killings of survivors for which it was impossible to fix responsibility. Certainly to a Vietnamese all GIs would by this point look alike: "Nineteen-year-old Nguyen Thi Ngoc Tuyet watched a baby trying to open her slain mother's blouse to nurse, A soldier shot the infant while it was struggling with the blouse, and then slashed it with his bayonet." Tuyet also said she saw another baby hacked to death by GIs wielding their bayonets. "Le Tong, a twenty-eight-year-old rice farmer, reported seeing one woman raped after GIs killed her children. Nguyen Khoa, a thirty-seven-year-old peasant, told of a thirteen-year-old girl who was raped before being killed. GIs then attacked Khoa's wife, tearing off her clothes. Before they could rape her, however, Khoa said, their six-year-old son, riddled with bullets, fell and saturated her with blood. The GIs left her alone" (Hersh, 1970, p. 72). All of Company C was implicated in a pattern of death and destruction throughout the hamlet, much of which seemingly lacked rhyme or reason.

But a substantial amount of the killing was *organized* and traceable to one authority: the First Platoon's Lt. William Calley. Calley was originally charged with 109 killings, almost all of them mass executions at the trail and other locations. He stood trial for 102 of these killings, was convicted of 22 in 1971, and at first received a life sentence. Though others—both superior and subordinate to Calley—were brought to trial, he was the only one convicted for the My Lai crimes. Thus, the only actions of My Lai for which *anyone* was ever convicted were mass executions, ordered and committed. We suspect that there are commonsense reasons why this one type of killing was singled out. In the midst of rapidly moving events with people running about, an execution of stationary targets is literally a still life that stands out and whose participants are clearly visible. It can be proven that specific people committed specific deeds. An execution, in contrast to the shooting of someone on the run, is also more likely to meet the legal definition of an act resulting from intent—with malice aforethought. Moreover, American military law specifically forbids the killing of unarmed civilians or military prisoners, as does the Geneva Convention between nations. Thus common sense, legal standards, and explicit doctrine all made such actions the likeliest target for prosecution.

When Lieutenant Calley was charged under military law it was for violation of the Uniform Code of Military Justice (UCMJ) Article 118 (murder). This article is similar to civilian codes in that it provides for conviction if an accused:

> without justification or excuse, unlawfully kills a human being, when he—
> 1. has a premeditated design to kill;

2. intends to kill or inflict great bodily harm;

3. is engaged in an act which is inherently dangerous to others and evinces a wanton disregard of human life; or

4. is engaged in the perpetration or attempted perpetration of burglary, sodomy, rape, robbery, or aggravated arson. (Goldstein et al., 1976, p. 507)

For a soldier, one legal justification for killing is warfare; but warfare is subject to many legal limits and restrictions, including, of course, the inadmissibility of killing unarmed noncombatants or prisoners whom one has disarmed. The pictures of the trail victims at My Lai certainly portrayed one or the other of these. Such an action would be illegal under military law; ordering another to commit such an action would be illegal; and following such an order would be illegal.

But following an order may provide a second and pivotal justification for an act that would be murder when committed by a civilian. . . . American military law assumes that the subordinate is inclined to follow orders, as that is the normal obligation of the role. Hence, legally, obedient subordinates are protected from unreasonable expectations regarding their capacity to evaluate those orders:

> An order requiring the performance of a military duty may be inferred to be legal. An act performed manifestly beyond the scope of authority, or pursuant to an order that a man of ordinary sense and understanding would know to be illegal, or in a wanton manner in the discharge of a lawful duty, is not excusable. (Par. 216, Subpar. *d*, Manual for Courts Martial, United States, 1969 Rev.)

Thus what *may* be excusable is the good-faith carrying out of an order, as long as that order appears to the ordinary soldier to be a legal one. In military law, invoking superior orders moves the question from one of the action's consequences—the body count—to one of evaluating the actor's motives and good sense.

In sum, if anyone is to be brought to justice for a massacre, common sense and legal codes decree that the most appropriate targets are those who make themselves executioners. This is the kind of target the government selected in prosecuting Lieutenant Calley with the greatest fervor. And in a military context, the most promising way in which one can redefine one's undeniable deeds into acceptability is to invoke superior orders. This is what Calley did in attempting to avoid conviction. Since the core legal issues involved points of mass execution—the ditches and trail where America's image of My Lai was formed—we review these events in greater detail.

The day's quiet beginning has already been noted. Troops landed and swept unopposed into the village. The three weapons eventually reported as the haul from the operation were picked up from three apparent Viet Cong who fled the village when the troops arrived and were pursued and killed by helicopter gunships. Obviously the Viet Cong did frequent the area. But it appears that by about 8:00 A.M. no one who met the troops was aggressive, and no one was armed. By the laws of war Charlie Company had no argument with such people.

As they moved into the village, the soldiers began to gather its inhabitants together. Shortly after 8:00 A.M. Lieutenant Calley told Pfc. Paul Meadlo that "you know what to do with" a group of villagers Meadlo was guarding. Estimates of the numbers in the group ranged as high as eighty women, children, and old men, and Meadlo's own estimate under oath was thirty to fifty people. As Meadlo later testified, Calley returned after ten to fifteen minutes: "He [Calley] said, 'How come they're not dead?' I said, 'I didn't know we were supposed to kill them.' He said, 'I want them dead.' He backed off twenty or thirty feet and started shooting into the people—the Viet Cong—shooting automatic. He was beside me. He burned four or five magazines. I burned off a few, about three. I helped shoot 'em" (Hammer, 1971, p. 155). Meadlo himself and others testified that Meadlo cried as he fired; others reported him later to be sobbing and "all broke up." It would appear that to Lieutenant Calley's subordinates something was unusual, and stressful, in these orders.

At the trial, the first specification in the murder charge against Calley was for this incident; he was accused of premeditated murder of "an unknown number, not less than 30, Oriental human beings, males and females of various ages, whose names are unknown, occupants of the village of My Lai 4, by means of shooting them with a rifle" (Goldstein et al., 1976, p. 497).

Among the helicopters flying reconnaissance above Son My was that of CWO Hugh Thompson. By 9:00 or soon after Thompson had noticed some horrifying events from his perch. As he spotted wounded civilians, he sent down smoke markers so that soldiers on the ground could treat them. They killed them instead. He reported to headquarters, trying to persuade someone to stop what was going on. Barker, hearing the message, called down to Captain Medina. Medina, in turn, later claimed to have told Calley that it was "enough for today." But it was not yet enough.

At Calley's orders, his men began gathering the remaining villagers—roughly seventy-five individuals, mostly women and children—and herding them toward a drainage ditch. Accompanied by three or four enlisted men, Lieutenant Calley executed several batches of civilians who had been gathered into ditches. Some of the details of the process were entered into testimony in such accounts as Pfc. Dennis Conti's: "A lot of them, the people, were trying to get up and mostly they were just screaming and pretty bad shot up. . . . I seen a woman tried to get up. I seen Lieutenant Calley fire. He hit the side of her head and blew it off" (Hammer, 1971, p. 125).

Testimony by other soldiers presented the shooting's aftermath. Specialist Four Charles Hall, asked by Prosecutor Aubrey Daniel how he knew the people in the ditch were dead, said: "There was blood coming from them. They were just scattered all over the ground in the ditch, some in piles and some scattered out 20, 25 meters perhaps by the ditch. . . . They were very old people, very young children, and mothers. . . . There was blood all over them" (Goldstein et al., 1976, pp. 501–02). And Pfc. Gregory Olsen corroborated the general picture of the victims: "They were—the majority were women and children, some babies. I distinctly remember one middle-aged Vietnamese male dressed in white right at my feet as I crossed. None of the bodies were mangled in any way. There was blood. Some appeared to be dead, others followed me with their eyes as I walked across the ditch" (Goldstein et al., 1976, p. 502).

The second specification in the murder charge stated that Calley did "with premeditation, murder an unknown number of Oriental human beings, not less than seventy, males and females of various ages, whose names are unknown, occupants of the village of My Lai 4, by means of shooting them with a rifle" (Goldstein et al., 1976, p. 497). Calley was also charged with and tried for shootings of individuals (an old man and a child); these charges were clearly supplemental to the main issue at trial—the mass killings and how they came about.

It is noteworthy that during these executions more than one enlisted man avoided carrying out Calley's orders, and more than one, by sworn oath, directly refused to obey them. For example, Pfc. James Joseph Dursi testified, when asked if he fired when Lieutenant Calley ordered him to: "No. I just stood there. Meadlo turned to me after a couple of minutes and said 'Shoot! Why don't you shoot! Why don't you fire!' He was crying and yelling. I said, 'I can't! I won't!' And the people were screaming and crying and yelling. They kept firing for a couple of minutes, mostly automatic and semiautomatic" (Hammer, 1971, p. 143).

Specialist Four Ronald Grzesik reported an even more direct confrontation with Calley, although under oath he hedged about its subject:

GRZESIK: Well, Lieutenant Calley—I walked past the ditch. I was called back by someone, I don't recall who. I had a discussion with Lieutenant Calley. He said to take the fire team back into the village and help the second platoon search.
DANIEL: Did Lieutenant Calley say anything before he gave you that order?
GRZESIK: He said, "Finish them off." I refused.
DANIEL: What did you refuse to do?
GRZESIK: To finish them off.
DANIEL: What did he mean? Who did he mean to finish off?
GRZESIK: I don't know what he meant or who he meant by them.
(Hammer, 1971, p. 150)

In preceding months, not under oath, Grzesik had indicated that he had a good idea what was meant but that he simply would not comply. It is likely that the jury at Calley's trial did not miss the point.

Disobedience of Lieutenant Calley's own orders to kill represented a serious legal and moral threat to a defense *based* on superior orders, such as Calley was attempting. This defense had to assert that the orders seemed reasonable enough to carry out, that they appeared to be legal orders. Even if the orders in question were not legal, the defense had to assert that an ordinary individual could not and should not be expected to see the distinction. In short, if what happened was "business as usual," even though it might be bad business, then the defendant stood a chance of acquittal. But under direct command from "Surfside 5½," some ordinary enlisted men managed to refuse, to avoid, or at least to stop doing what they were ordered to do. As "reasonable men" of "ordinary sense and understanding," they had apparently found something awry that morning; and it would have been hard for an officer to plead successfully that he was more ordinary than his men in his capacity to evaluate the reasonableness of orders.

Even those who obeyed Calley's orders showed great stress. For example, Meadlo eventually began to argue and cry directly in front of Calley. Pfc. Herbert Carter shot himself in the foot, possibly because he could no longer take what he was doing. We were not destined to hear a sworn version of the incident, since neither side at the Calley trial called him to testify.

The most unusual instance of resistance to authority came from the skies. CWO Hugh Thompson, who had protested the apparent carnage of civilians, was Calley's inferior in rank but was not in his line of command. He was also watching the ditch from his helicopter and noticed some people moving after the first round of slaughter—chiefly children who had been shielded by their mothers' bodies. Landing to rescue the wounded, he also found some villagers hiding in a nearby bunker. Protecting the Vietnamese with his own body, Thompson ordered his men to train their guns on the Americans and to open fire if the Americans fired on the Vietnamese. He then radioed for additional rescue helicopters and stood between the Vietnamese and the Americans under Calley's command until the Vietnamese could be evacuated. He later returned to the ditch to unearth a child buried, unharmed, beneath layers of bodies. In October 1969, Thompson was awarded the Distinguished Flying Cross for heroism at My Lai, specifically (albeit inaccurately) for the rescue of children hiding in a bunker "between Viet Cong forces and advancing friendly forces" and for the rescue of a wounded child "caught in the intense crossfire" (Hersh, 1970, p. 119). Four months earlier, at the Pentagon, Thompson had identified Calley as having been at the ditch.

By about 10:00 A.M., the massacre was winding down. The remaining actions consisted largely of isolated rapes and killings, "clean-up" shootings of the wounded, and the destruction of the village by fire. We have already seen some examples of these more indiscriminate and possibly less premeditated acts. By the 11:00 A.M. lunch break, when the exhausted men of Company C were relaxing, two young girls wandered back from a hiding place only to be invited to share lunch. This surrealist touch illustrates the extent to which the soldiers' action had become dissociated from its meaning. An hour earlier, some of these men were making sure that not even a child would escape the executioner's bullet. But now the job was done and it was time for lunch—and in this new context it seemed only natural to ask the children who had managed to escape execution to join them. The massacre had ended. It remained only for the Viet Cong to reap the political rewards among the survivors in hiding.

The army command in the area knew that something had gone wrong. Direct commanders, including Lieutenant Colonel Barker, had firsthand reports, such as Thompson's complaints. Others had such odd bits of evidence as the claim of 128 Viet Cong dead with a booty of only three weapons. But the cover-up of My Lai began at once. The operation was reported as a victory over a stronghold of the Viet Cong Forty-eighth.

My Lai might have remained a "victory" but for another odd twist. A soldier who had not even been at the massacre, Ronald Ridenhour, talked to several friends and acquaintances who had been. As he later wrote: "It was late in April 1968 that I first heard of 'Pinkville' [a nickname reflecting the villagers' reputed Communist sympathies] and what allegedly happened there. I received that first report with some skepticism, but in the following months I was to hear similar stories from such a wide variety of people that it became impossible for me to disbelieve that something rather dark and bloody did indeed occur sometime in March 1968 in a village called 'Pinkville' in the Republic of Viet Nam" (Goldstein et al., 1976, p. 34). Ridenhour's growing conviction that a massacre—or something close to it—had occurred was reinforced by his own travel over the area by helicopter soon after the event. My Lai was desolate. He gradually concluded that someone was covering up the incident within the army and that an independent investigation was needed.

At the end of March 1969, he finally wrote a letter detailing what he knew about "Pinkville." The letter, beginning with the paragraph quote above, was sent to thirty individuals—the president, Pentagon officials, and some members of the Senate and House. Ridenhour's congressman, fellow Arizonan Morris Udall, gave it particular heed. The slow unraveling of the cover-up began. During the following months, the army in fact initiated an investigation but carried it out in strict secrecy. Ridenhour, convinced that the cover-up was continuing, sought journalistic help and finally, by coincidence, connected with Seymour Hersh. Hersh followed up and broke the story, which eventually brought him a Pulitzer Prize and other awards for his investigative reporting. The cover-up collapsed, leaving only the question of the army's resolve to seek justice in the case: Against whom would it proceed, with how much speed and vigor, and with what end in mind?

William Calley was not the only man tried for the events at My Lai. The actions of over thirty soldiers and civilians were scrutinized by investigators; over half of these had to face charges or disciplinary action of some sort. Targets of investigation included Captain Medina, who was tried, and various higher-ups, including General Koster. But Lieutenant Calley was the only person convicted, the only person to serve time.

The core of Lieutenant Calley's defense was superior orders. What this meant to him—in contrast to what it meant to the judge and jury—can be gleaned from his responses to a series of questions from his defense attorney, George Latimer, in which Calley sketched out his understanding of the laws of war and the actions that constitute doing one's duty within those laws:

> LATIMER: Did you receive any training . . . which had to do with the obedience to orders?
>
> CALLEY: Yes, sir.
>
> LATIMER: . . . [W]hat were you informed [were] the principles involved in that field?
>
> CALLEY: That all orders were to be assumed legal, that the soldier's job was to carry out any order given him to the best of his ability.
>
> LATIMER: . . . [W]hat might occur if you disobeyed an order by a senior officer?
>
> CALLEY: You could be court-martialed for refusing an order and refusing an order in the face of the enemy, you could be sent to death, sir.
>
> LATIMER: [I am asking] whether you were required in any way, shape or form to make a determination of the legality or illegality of an order?
>
> CALLEY: No, sir. I was never told that I had the choice, sir.
>
> LATIMER: If you had a doubt about the order, what were you supposed to do?
>
> CALLEY: . . . I was supposed to carry the order out and then come back and make my complaint. (Hammer, 1971, pp. 240–41)

Lieutenant Calley steadfastly maintained that his actions within My Lai had constituted, in his mind, carrying out orders from Captain Medina. Both his own actions and the orders he gave to others (such as the instruction to Meadlo to "waste 'em") were entirely in response to superior orders. He denied any intent to kill individuals and any but the most passing awareness of distinctions among the individuals: "I was ordered to go in there and destroy the enemy. That was my job on that day. That was the mission I was given. I did not sit down and think in terms of men, women, and children. They were all classified the same, and that was the classification that we dealt with, just as enemy soldiers." When Latimer asked if in his own opinion Calley had acted "rightly and according to your understanding of your directions and orders," Calley replied, "I felt then and I still do that I acted as I was directed, and I carried out the orders that I was given, and I do not feel wrong in doing so, sir" (Hammer, 1971, p. 257).

His court-martial did not accept Calley's defense of superior orders and clearly did not share his interpretation of his duty. The jury evidently reasoned that, even if there had been orders to destroy everything in sight and to "waste the Vietnamese," any reasonable person would have realized that such orders were illegal and should have refused to carry them out. The defense of superior orders under such conditions is inadmissible under international and military law. The U.S. Army's *Law of Land Warfare* (Dept. of the Army, 1956), for example, states that "the fact that the law of war has been violated pursuant to an order of a superior authority, whether military or civil, does not deprive the act in question of its character of a war crime, nor does it constitute a defense in the trial of an accused individual, unless he did not know and could not reasonably have been expected to know that the act was unlawful" and that "members of the armed forces are bound to obey only lawful orders" (in Falk et al., 1971, pp. 71–72).

The disagreement between Calley and the court-martial seems to have revolved around the definition of the responsibilities of a subordinate to obey, on the one hand, and to evaluate, on the other. This tension . . . runs through the analyses and empirical studies. . . . For now, it can best be captured via the charge to the jury in the Calley court-martial, made by the trial judge, Col. Reid Kennedy. The forty-one pages of the charge include the following:

> Both combatants captured by and noncombatants detained by the
> opposing force . . . have the right to be treated as prisoners. . . .

Summary execution of detainees or prisoners is forbidden by law. . . . I therefore instruct you . . . that if unresisting human beings were killed at My Lai (4) while within the effective custody and control of our military forces, their deaths cannot be considered justified. . . . Thus if you find that Lieutenant Calley received an order directing him to kill unresisting Vietnamese within his control or within the control of his troops, *that order would be an illegal order.*

A determination that an order is illegal does not, of itself, assign criminal responsibility to the person following the order for acts done in compliance with it. Soldiers are taught to follow orders, and special attention is given to obedience of orders on the battlefield. Military effectiveness depends on obedience to orders. On the other hand, the obedience of a soldier is not the obedience of an automaton. A soldier is a reasoning agent, obliged to respond, not as a machine, but as a person. The law takes these factors into account in assessing criminal responsibility for acts done in compliance with illegal orders.

The acts of a subordinate done in compliance with an unlawful order given him by his superior are excused and impose no criminal liability upon him unless the superior's order is one which a man of *ordinary sense and understanding* would, under the circumstances, know to be unlawful, or if the order in question is actually known to the accused to be unlawful. (Goldstein et al., 1976, pp. 525–526; emphasis added)

By this definition, subordinates take part in a balancing act, one tipped toward obedience but tempered by "ordinary sense and understanding."

A jury of combat veterans proceeded to convict William Calley of the premeditated murder of no less than twenty-two human beings. (The army, realizing some unfortunate connotations in referring to the victims as "Oriental human beings," eventually referred to them as "human beings.") Regarding the first specification in the murder charge, the bodies on the trail, he was convicted of premeditated murder of not less than one person. (Medical testimony had been able to pinpoint only one person whose wounds as revealed in Haeberle's photos were sure to be immediately fatal.) Regarding the second specification, the bodies in the ditch, Calley was convicted of the premeditated murder of not less than twenty human beings. Regarding additional specifications that he had killed an old man and a child, Calley was convicted of premeditated murder in the first case and of assault with intent to commit murder in the second.

Lieutenant Calley was initially sentenced to life imprisonment. That sentence was reduced: first to twenty years, eventually to ten (the latter by Secretary of Defense Callaway in 1974).[1] Calley served three years before being released on bond. The time was spent under house arrest in his apartment, where he was able to receive visits from his girlfriend. He was granted parole on September 10, 1975.

Sanctioned Massacres

The slaughter at My Lai is an instance of a class of violent acts that can be described as sanctioned massacres (Kelman, 1973): acts of indiscriminate, ruthless, and often systematic mass violence, carried out by military or paramilitary personnel while engaged in officially sanctioned campaigns, the victims of which are defenseless and unresisting civilians, including old men, women, and children. Sanctioned massacres have occurred throughout history. Within American history, My Lai had its precursors in the Philippine war around the turn of the century (Schirmer, 1971) and in the massacres of American Indians. Elsewhere in the world, one recalls the Nazis' "final solution" for European Jews, the massacres and deportations of Armenians by Turks, the liquidation of the kulaks and the great purges in the Soviet Union, and more recently the massacres in Indonesia and Bangladesh, in Biafra and Burundi, in South Africa and Mozambique, in Cambodia and Afghanistan, in Syria and Lebanon. Sanctioned massacres may vary on a number of dimensions. For present purposes, however, we want to focus on features they share. Two of these are the *context* and the *target* of the violence.

---

1. The involvement of President Nixon in the case may have had something to do with these steadily lower sentences. Immediately after the Calley conviction, Nixon issued two presidential edicts. The president first announced that Calley was to stay under house arrest until appeals were settled, rather than in the stockade. The subsequent announcement was that President Nixon would personally review the case. These edicts received wide popular support. The latter announcement in particular brought sharp criticism from Prosecutor Daniel and others, on grounds that Nixon was interfering inappropriately with the process of justice in the case. Nevertheless, the president's interest and intention to review the case could have colored the subsequent appeals process or the actions of the secretary of defense. By the time of Secretary Callaway's action, of course, the president was himself fighting to avoid impeachment.

Sanctioned massacres tend to occur in the context of an overall policy that is explicitly or implicitly genocidal: designed to destroy all or part of a category of people defined in ethnic, national, racial, religious, or other terms. Such a policy may be deliberately aimed at the systematic extermination of a population group as an end in itself, as was the case with the Holocaust during World War II. In the Nazis' "final solution" for European Jewry, a policy aimed at exterminating millions of people was consciously articulated and executed (see Levinson, 1973), and the extermination was accomplished on a mass-production basis through the literal establishment of a well-organized, efficient death industry. Alternatively, such a policy may be aimed at an objective other than extermination—such as the pacification of the rural population of South Vietnam, as was the case in U.S. policy for Indochina—but may include the deliberate decimation of large segments of a population as an acceptable means to that end.

We agree with Bedau's (1974) conclusion from his carefully reasoned argument that the charge of U.S. genocide in Vietnam has not been definitively proven, since such a charge requires evidence of a specific genocidal *intent*. Although the evidence suggests that the United States committed war crimes and crimes against humanity in Indochina (see Sheehan, 1971; Browning and Forman, 1972), it does not show that extermination was the conscious purpose of U.S. policy. The evidence reviewed by Bedau, however, suggests that the United States did commit genocidal acts in Vietnam as a means to other ends. Central to U.S. strategy in South Vietnam were such actions as unrestricted air and artillery bombardments of peasant hamlets, search-and-destroy missions by ground troops, crop destruction programs, and mass deportation of rural populations. These actions (and similar ones in Laos and Cambodia) were clearly and deliberately aimed at civilians and resulted in the death, injury, and/or uprooting of large numbers of that population and in the destruction of their countryside, their source of livelihood, and their social structure. These consequences were anticipated by policymakers and indeed were intended as part of their pacification effort; the actions were designed to clear the countryside and deprive guerrillas of their base of operations, even if this meant destroying the civilian population. Massacres of the kind that occurred at My Lai were not deliberately planned, but they took place in an atmosphere in which the rural Vietnamese population was viewed as expendable and actions that resulted in the killing of large numbers of that population as strategic necessities.

A second feature of sanctioned massacres is that their targets have not themselves threatened or engaged in hostile actions toward the perpetrators of the violence. The victims of this class of violence are often defenseless civilians, including old men, women, and children. By all accounts, at least after the first moments at My Lai, the victims there fit this description, although in guerrilla warfare there always remains some ambiguity about the distinction between armed soldiers and unarmed civilians. As has often been noted, U.S. troops in Vietnam had to face the possibility that a woman or even a child might be concealing a hand grenade under clothing.

There are, of course, historical and situational reasons particular groups become victims of sanctioned massacres, but these do not include their own immediate harmfulness or violence toward the attackers. Rather, their selection as targets for massacre at a particular time can ultimately be traced to their relationship to the pursuit of larger policies. Their elimination may be seen as a useful tool or their continued existence as an irritating obstacle in the execution of policy.

The genocidal or near-genocidal context of this class of violence and the fact that it is directed at a target that—at least from an observer's perspective—did not provoke the violence through its own actions has some definite implications for the psychological environment within which sanctioned massacres occur. It is an environment almost totally devoid of the conditions that usually provide at least some degree of moral justification for violence. Neither the reason for the violence nor its purpose is of the kind that is normally considered justifiable. Although people may disagree about the precise point at which they would draw the line between justifiable and unjustifiable violence, most would agree that violence in self-defense or in response to oppression and other forms of strong provocation is at least within the realm of moral discourse. In contrast, the violence of sanctioned massacres falls outside that realm.

In searching for a psychological explanation for mass violence under these conditions, one's first inclination is to look for forces that might impel people toward such murderous acts. Can we identify, in massacre situations, psychological forces so powerful that they outweigh the moral restraints that would normally inhibit unjustifiable violence?

The most obvious approach—searching for psychological dispositions within those who perpetrate these acts—does not yield a satisfactory explanation of the phenomenon, although it may tell us something about the types of individuals most readily recruited for participation. For example, any explanation involving the attackers' strong sadistic impulses is inadequate. There is no evidence that the majority of those who participate in such killings are sadistically inclined. Indeed, speaking of the participants in the Nazi slaughters, Arendt (1964) points out that they "were not sadists or killers by nature; on the contrary, a systematic effort was made to weed out all those who derived physical pleasure from what they did" (p. 105). To be sure, some of the commanders and guards of concentration camps could clearly be described as sadists, but what has to be explained is the existence of concentration camps in which these individuals could give play to their sadistic fantasies. These opportunities were provided with the participation of large numbers of individuals to whom the label of sadist could not be applied.

A more sophisticated type of dispositional approach seeks to identify certain characterological themes that are dominant within a given culture. An early example of such an approach is Fromm's (1941) analysis of the appeals of Nazism in terms of the prevalence of sadomasochistic strivings, particularly among the German lower middle class. It would be important to explore whether similar kinds of characterological dispositions can be identified in the very wide range of cultural contexts in which sanctioned massacres have occurred. However general such dispositions turn out to be, it seems most likely that they represent states of readiness to participate in sanctioned massacres when the opportunity arises rather than major motivating forces in their own right. Similarly, high levels of frustration within a population are probably facilitators rather than instigators of sanctioned massacres, since there does not seem to be a clear relationship between the societal level of frustration and the occurrence of such violence. Such a view would be consistent with recent thinking about the relationship between frustration and aggression (see, for example, Bandura, 1973).

Could participation in sanctioned massacres be traced to an inordinately intense hatred toward those against whom the violence is directed? The evidence does not seem to support such an interpretation. Indications are that many of the active participants in the extermination of European Jews, such as Adolf Eichmann (Arendt, 1964), did not feel any passionate hatred of Jews. There is certainly no reason to believe that those who planned and executed American policy in Vietnam felt a profound hatred of the Vietnamese population, although deeply rooted racist attitudes may conceivably have played a role.

To be sure, hatred and rage *play a part* in sanctioned massacres. Typically, there is a long history of profound hatred against the groups targeted for violence—the Jews in Christian Europe, the Chinese in Southeast Asia, the Ibos in northern Nigeria—which helps establish them as suitable victims. Hostility also plays an important part at the point at which the killings are actually perpetrated, even if the official planning and the bureaucratic preparations that ultimately lead up to this point are carried out in a passionless and businesslike atmosphere. For example, Lifton's (1973) descriptions of My Lai, based on eyewitness reports, suggest that the killings were accompanied by generalized rage and by expressions of anger and revenge toward the victims. Hostility toward the target, however, does not seem to be the *instigator* of these violent actions. The expressions of anger in the situation itself can more properly be viewed as outcomes rather than causes of the violence. They serve to provide the perpetrators with an explanation and rationalization for their violent actions and appropriate labels for their emotional state. They also help reinforce, maintain, and intensify the violence, but the anger is not the primary source of the violence. Hostility toward the target, historically rooted or situationally induced, contributes heavily toward the violence, but it does so largely by dehumanizing the victims rather than by motivating violence against them in the first place.

In sum, the occurrence of sanctioned massacres cannot be adequately explained by the existence of psychological forces—whether these be characterological dispositions to engage in murderous violence or profound hostility against the target—so powerful that they must find expression in violent acts unhampered by moral restraints. Instead, the major instigators for this class of violence derive from the policy process. The question that really calls for psychological analysis is why so many people are willing to formulate, participate in, and condone policies that call for the mass killings of defenseless civilians. Thus it is more instructive to look not at the motives for violence but at the conditions under which the usual moral inhibitions against violence become weakened. Three social processes that tend to create such conditions can be identified: authorization, routinization, and dehumanization. Through authorization, the situation becomes so defined that the individual is absolved of the responsibility to make personal moral choices. Through routinization, the action becomes so organized that there is no opportunity for raising moral questions. Through dehumanization, the actors' attitudes toward the target and toward themselves become so structured that it is neither necessary nor possible for them to view the relationship in moral terms.

Authorization

Sanctioned massacres by definition occur in the context of an authority situation, a situation in which, at least for many of the participants, the moral principles that generally govern human relationships do not apply. Thus, when acts of violence are explicitly ordered, implicitly encouraged, tacitly approved, or at least permitted by legitimate authorities, people's readiness to commit or condone them is enhanced. That such acts are authorized seems to carry automatic justification for them. Behaviorally, authorization obviates the necessity of making judgments or choices. Not only do normal moral principles become inoperative, but—particularly when the actions are explicitly ordered—a different kind of morality, linked to the duty to obey superior orders, tends to take over.

In an authority situation, individuals characteristically feel obligated to obey the orders of the authorities, whether or not these correspond with their personal preferences. They see themselves as having no choice as long as they accept the legitimacy of the orders and of the authorities who give them. Individuals differ considerably in the degree to which—and the conditions under which—they are prepared to challenge the legitimacy of an order on the grounds that the order itself is illegal, or that those giving it have overstepped their authority, or that it stems from a policy that violates fundamental societal values. Regardless of such individual differences, however, the basic structure of a situation of legitimate authority requires subordinates to respond in terms of their role obligations rather than their personal preferences; they can openly disobey only by challenging the legitimacy of the authority. Often people obey without question even though the behavior they engage in may entail great personal sacrifice or great harm to others.

An important corollary of the basic structure of the authority situation is that actors often do not see themselves as personally responsible for the consequences of their actions. Again, there are individual differences, depending on actors' capacity and readiness to evaluate the legitimacy of orders received. Insofar as they see themselves as having had no choice in their actions, however, they do not feel personally responsible for them. They were not personal agents, but merely extensions of the authority. Thus, when their actions cause harm to others, they can feel relatively free of guilt. A similar mechanism operates when a person engages in antisocial behavior that was not ordered by the authorities but was tacitly encouraged and approved by them—even if only by making it clear that such behavior will not be punished. In this situation, behavior that was formerly illegitimate is legitimized by the authorities' acquiescence.

In the My Lai massacre, it is likely that the structure of the authority situation contributed to the massive violence in both ways—that is, by conveying the message that acts of violence against Vietnamese villagers were *required,* as well as the message that such acts, even if not ordered, were *permitted* by the authorities in charge. The actions at My Lai represented, at least in some respects, responses to explicit or implicit orders. Lieutenant Calley indicated, by orders and by example, that he wanted large numbers of villagers killed. Whether Calley himself had been ordered by his superiors to "waste" the whole area, as he claimed, remains a matter of controversy. Even if we assume, however, that he was not explicitly ordered to wipe out the village, he had reason to believe that such actions were expected by his superior officers. Indeed, the very nature of the war conveyed this expectation. The principal measure of military success was the "body count"—the number of enemy soldiers killed—and any Vietnamese killed by the U.S. military was commonly defined as a "Viet Cong." Thus, it was not totally bizarre for Calley to believe that what he was doing at My Lai was to increase his body count, as any good officer was expected to do.

Even to the extent that the actions at My Lai occurred spontaneously, without reference to superior orders, those committing them had reason to assume that such actions might be tacitly approved of by the military authorities. Not only had they failed to punish such acts in most cases, but the very strategies and tactics that the authorities consistently devised were based on the proposition that the civilian population of South Vietnam—whether "hostile" or "friendly"—was expendable. Such policies as search-and-destroy missions, the establishment of free-shooting zones, the use of antipersonnel weapons, the bombing of entire villages if they were suspected of harboring guerrillas, the forced migration of masses of the rural population, and the defoliation of vast forest areas helped legitimize acts of massive violence of the kind occurring at My Lai.

Some of the actions at My Lai suggest an orientation to authority based on unquestioning obedience to superior orders, no matter how destructive the actions these orders call for. Such obedience is specifically fostered in the course of military training and reinforced by the structure of the military authority situation. It also reflects, however, an ideological orientation that may be more widespread in the general population, as some of the data presented . . . demonstrate.

Routinization

Authorization processes create a situation in which people become involved in an action without considering its implications and without really making a decision. Once they have taken the initial step, they are in a new psychological and social situation in which the pressures to continue are powerful. As Lewin (1947) has pointed out, many forces that might originally have kept people out of a situation reverse direction once they have made a commitment (once they have gone through the "gate region") and now serve to keep them in the situation. For example, concern about the criminal nature of an action, which might originally have inhibited a person from becoming involved, may now lead to deeper involvement in efforts to justify the action and to avoid negative consequences.

Despite these forces, however, given the nature of the actions involved in sanctioned massacres, one might still expect moral scruples to intervene; but the likelihood of moral resistance is greatly reduced by transforming the action into routine, mechanical, highly programmed operations. Routinization fulfills two functions. First, it reduces the necessity of making decisions, thus minimizing the occasions in which moral questions may arise. Second, it makes it easier to avoid the implications of the action, since the actor focuses on the details of the job rather than on its meaning. The latter effect is more readily achieved among those who participate in sanctioned massacres from a distance—from their desks or even from the cockpits of their bombers.

Routinization operates both at the level of the individual actor and at the organizational level. Individual job performance is broken down into a series of discrete steps, most of them carried out in automatic, regularized fashion. It becomes easy to forget the nature of the product that emerges from this process. When Lieutenant Calley said of My Lai that it was "no great deal," he probably implied that it was all in a day's work. Organizationally, the task is divided among different offices, each of which has responsibility for a small portion of it. This arrangement diffuses responsibility and limits the amount and scope of decision making that is necessary. There is no expectation that the moral implications will be considered at any of these points, nor is there any opportunity to do so. The organizational processes also help further legitimize the actions of each participant. By proceeding in routine fashion—processing papers, exchanging memos, diligently carrying out their assigned tasks—the different units mutually reinforce each other in the view that what is going on must be perfectly normal, correct, and legitimate. The shared illusion that they are engaged in a legitimate enterprise helps the participants assimilate their activities to other purposes, such as the efficiency of their performance, the productivity of their unit, or the cohesiveness of their group (see Janis, 1972).

Normalization of atrocities is more difficult to the extent that there are constant reminders of the true meaning of the enterprise. Bureaucratic inventiveness in the use of language helps to cover up such meaning. For example, the SS had a set of *Sprachregelungen,* or "language rules," to govern descriptions of their extermination program. As Arendt (1964) points out, the term *language rule* in itself was "a code name; it meant what in ordinary language would be called a lie" (p. 85). The code names for killing and liquidation were "final solution," "evacuation," and "special treatment." The war in Indochina produced its own set of euphemisms, such as "protective reaction," "pacification," and "forced-draft urbanization and modernization." The use of euphemisms allows participants in sanctioned massacres to differentiate their actions from ordinary killing and destruction and thus to avoid confronting their true meaning.

Dehumanization

Authorization processes override standard moral considerations; routinization processes reduce the likelihood that such considerations will arise. Still, the inhibitions against murdering one's fellow human beings are generally so strong that the victims must also be stripped of their human status if they are to be subjected to systematic killing. Insofar as they are dehumanized, the usual principles of morality no longer apply to them.

Sanctioned massacres become possible to the extent that the victims are deprived in the perpetrators' eyes of the two qualities essential to being perceived as fully human and included in the moral compact that governs human relationships: *identity*—standing as independent, distinctive individuals, capable of making choices and entitled to live their own lives—and *community*—fellow membership in an interconnected network of individuals who care for each other and respect each other's individuality and rights (Kelman, 1973; see also Bakan, 1966, for a related distinction between "agency" and "communion"). Thus, when a group of people is defined entirely in terms of a category to which they belong, and when this category is excluded from the human family, moral restraints against killing them are more readily overcome.

Dehumanization of the enemy is a common phenomenon in any war situation. Sanctioned massacres, however, presuppose a more extreme degree of dehumanization, insofar as the killing is not in direct response to the target's threats or provocations. It is not what they have done that marks such victims for death but who they are— the category to which they happen to belong. They are the victims of policies that regard their systematic destruction as a desirable end or an acceptable means. Such extreme dehumanization becomes possible when the target group can readily be identified as a separate category of people who have historically been stigmatized and excluded by the victimizers: often the victims belong to a distinct racial, religious, ethnic, or political group regarded as inferior or sinister. The traditions, the habits, the images, and the vocabularies for dehumanizing such groups are already well established and can be drawn upon when the groups are selected for massacre. Labels help deprive the victims of identity and community, as in the epithet "gooks" that was commonly used to refer to Vietnamese and other Indochinese peoples.

The dynamics of the massacre process itself further increase the participants' tendency to dehumanize their victims. Those who participate as part of the bureaucratic apparatus increasingly come to see their victims as bodies to be counted and entered into their reports, as faceless figures that will determine their productivity rates and promotions. Those who participate in the massacre directly—in the field, as it were—are reinforced in their perception of the victims as less than human by observing their very victimization. The only way they can justify what is being done to these people—both by others and by themselves—and the only way they can extract some degree of meaning out of absurd events in which they find themselves participating (see Lifton, 1971, 1973) is by coming to believe that the victims are subhuman and deserve to be rooted out. And thus the process of dehumanization feeds on itself.

References

Arendt, H. 1964. *Eichmann in Jerusalem: A report on the banality of evil.* New York: Viking Press.

Bakan, D. 1966. *The duality of human existence.* Chicago: Rand McNally.

Bandura, A. 1973. Social learning theory of aggression. In J. F. Knutson (Ed.), *Control of aggression: Implications from basic research.* Chicago: Aldine-Atherton.

Bedau, H. A. 1974. Genocide in Vietnam. In V. Held, S. Morgenbesser, & T. Nagel (Eds.), *Philosophy, morality, and international affairs* (pp. 5–46). New York: Oxford University Press.

Browning, F., & Forman, D. (Eds.). 1972. *The wasted nations: Report of the International Commission of Enquiry into United States Crimes in Indochina, June 20–25, 1971.* New York: Harper & Row.

Department of the Army. 1956. *The law of land warfare* (Field Manual, No. 27-10). Washington, D.C.: U.S. Government Printing Office.

Falk, R. A.; Kolko, G.; & Lifton, R. J. (Eds.). 1971. *Crimes of war.* New York: Vintage Books.

Fromm, E. 1941. *Escape from freedom.* New York: Rinehart.

Goldstein, J.; Marshall, B.; & Schwartz, J. (Eds.). 1976. *The My Lai massacre and its cover-up: Beyond the reach of law?* (The Peers report with a supplement and introductory essay on the limits of law). New York: Free Press.

Hammer, R. 1971. *The court-martial of Lt. Calley.* New York: Coward, McCann, & Geoghegan.

Hersh, S. 1970. *My Lai 4: A report on the massacre and its aftermath.* New York: Vintage Books.

Hersh, S. 1972. *Cover-up.* New York: Random House.

Janis, I. L. 1972. *Victims of groupthink: A psychological study of foreign-policy decisions and fiascoes.* Boston: Houghton Mifflin.

Kelman, H. C. 1973. Violence without moral restraint: Reflections on the dehumanization of victims and victimizers. *Journal of Social Issues,* 29(4), 25–61.

Lewin, K. 1947. Group decision and social change. In T. M. Newcomb & E. L. Harley (Eds.), *Readings in social psychology.* New York: Holt.

Lifton, R. J. 1971. Existential evil. In N. Sanford, C. Comstock, & Associates, *Sanctions for evil: Sources of social destructiveness.* San Francisco: Jossey-Bass.

Lifton, R. J. 1973. *Home from the war—Vietnam veterans: Neither victims nor executioners.* New York: Simon & Schuster.

Schirmer, D. B. 1971, April 24. My Lai was not the first time. *New Republic,* pp. 18–21.

Sheehan, N. 1971, March 28. Should we have war crime trials? *The New York Times Book Review,* pp. 1–3, 30–34.

Williams, B. 1985, April 14–15. "I will never forgive," says My Lai survivor. *Jordan Times* (Amman), p. 4.

Editors' Postscript

On March 6, 1998, some 30 years after the My Lai Massacre, the U.S. Army awarded the Soldier's Medal to helicopter pilot Hugh Thompson and the two members of his crew. As Professors Kelman and Hamilton detailed, Mr. Thompson and his crew reported the massacre, landed to rescue wounded civilians, and protected them with their own bodies until additional rescue helicopters arrived. The Solider's Medal is the highest award for bravery when not involved in conflict with an enemy. In presenting the award, an officer speaking at the ceremony, which was held at the Vietnam Veterans Memorial in Washington, D.C., noted that it was the ability of Mr. Thompson and his crew to "do the right thing even at the risk of their personal safety that guided these soldiers to do what they did." See Associated Press, "3 Honored for Saving Lives at My Lai," *The New York Times*, March 7, 1998, p. A9.

IV
Reactions

Editors' Introduction

Before any audience will define a given governmental or corporate act as deviant, a sequence of events typically takes place. The obvious first step is that audience members learn about the action, and one of the common ways this occurs is when people inside an organization become whistle-blowers. Audience members and others outside the organization then react in a number of different ways. Sometimes those reacting are members of law enforcement organizations who respond by launching investigations and promising to put an end to the behavior in question. Whether an action becomes common knowledge and widely defined as deviant frequently then depends upon media and investigative commission descriptions and assessments. And, at least on occasion, additional and more careful research reveals that initial reactions that labeled organizational behavior as deviant were wrong.

Selection 12, "Ten Whistleblowers" by Professor Myron Glazer, examines the experiences of people who went public with evidence of their organizations' wrongdoing. He tells us why these people blew the whistle and shows how personal and occupational consequences unfold for these whistle-blowers. Although publicly exposing deviant organizational acts is difficult and allows no going back, Professor Glazer notes that it is not the end of the road for the careers of many of these people.

Selection 13, "The Los Angeles Police Department Rampart Division Scandal," is drawn from the *Report of the Rampart Independent Review Panel*, and describes the scandal that continues to rock the Los Angeles Police Department. The scandal began when a trial of an alleged gang member and subsequent investigations revealed that a large number of police officers, especially in the Rampart Division, routinely lied to obtain convictions, sold drugs, and used unnecessary force. Judges and prosecutors were aware of these police actions and tolerated them as a price to be paid to get people they, and police officers, believed needed to be removed from the street. In the wake of the Rampart Division scandal, the Los Angeles Police Department signed a consent decree with the federal government that mandated appointment of an outside federal monitor to oversee the department. The department also has undertaken efforts to reform the organizational norms and practices that nourished and sustained the widespread police misconduct.

Selection 14, "Chained Factory Fire Exits," examines newspaper coverage of a chicken processing plant fire that killed 25 workers and injured 56 others. The authors evaluate how a cross-section of the nation's major newspapers covered the tragedy and shifted their focus over time when describing and explaining the killing fire. The authors then show opposing views about when the media should have labeled the deaths as manslaughter.

Selection 15, "Pinto Madness," is by Matthew Lee and M. David Ermann. This new paper takes a careful look at the Ford Pinto, a small car that is widely assumed to "light up" when hit from the rear by other vehicles. The authors reveal fundamental flaws in the generally accepted landmark narrative of the Pinto episode, especially those arguments grounded in the belief that the Pinto was the product of amoral financial calculation. In place of this conventional but incorrect wisdom, the authors argue that the Pinto was the product of routine organizational procedures inside Ford and elsewhere.

Selection 16, "The Challenger Space Shuttle Disaster" by Diane Vaughan, probes conventional understandings of the factors that led to the *Challenger* space shuttle disaster in January 1986. Professor Vaughan also rejects conventional amoral calculation explanations of the disaster and argues that "revisionist accounts" are in order. Professor Vaughan then advances and carefully documents these alternative explanations, arguing that the *Challenger* disaster is best understood as the result of the interplay of the organizational environment surrounding the National Aeronautics and Space Administration with the simple fact that putting people in shuttles and launching them into space is very risky technology that inevitably fails on occasion. When failures such as these occur, they have next to nothing to do with intent and everything to do with the nature of life inside large organizations.

Annotated Bibliography

Braithwaite, John. *To Punish or Persuade: Enforcement of Coal Mine Safety.* Albany, N.Y.: State University of New York Press, 1985. Data and argument that efforts to persuade and educate usually reduce violations and increase safety more effectively than efforts grounded exclusively in punishment.

Cannon, Lou. *Official Negligence: How Rodney King and The Riots Changed Los Angeles and the LAPD.* New York: Times Books, 1997. Effects of the police beating of Mr. King on the city and its police department, by a leading investigative journalist and author.

——. "One Bad Cop." *The New York Times Sunday Magazine,* October 1, 2000, pp. 32ff. More on the LAPD Rampart Division scandal.

Ermann, M. David, and William H. Clements II. "The Interfaith Center on Corporate Responsibility and Its Campaign Against Marketing Infant Formula in the Third World." *Social Problems* 32 (1984): 185–96. The deviance-defining process as illustrated by a church group's effective campaign against the marketing of infant formula in the Third World.

Fisse, Brent, and John Braithwaite. *The Impact of Publicity on Corporate Offenders.* Albany, N.Y.: State University of New York Press, 1983. What happens when corporations are caught in the unwelcome glare of negative publicity.

Grabosky, P. N., J. B. Braithwaite, and P. R. Wilson. "The Myth of Community Tolerance Toward White-Collar Crime." *Australian and New Zealand Journal of Criminology* 20 (1987): 33–41. Clear evidence from Australia, the United States, and elsewhere that members of the general public view white-collar crime as more serious and more deserving of serious punishment than most ordinary crimes.

Landy, Marc K., Marc J. Roberts, and Stephen R. Thomas. *The Environmental Protection Agency: Asking the Wrong Questions.* New York: Oxford University Press, 1990. A history of the EPA, with special attention to major issues and cases.

Macey, Jonathan R. "Agency Theory and the Criminal Liability of Organizations." *Boston University Law Review* 58 (1993): 315–40. Legal review of Sentencing Commission guidelines for corporations, in light of some theories of organizational behavior.

Magnuson, Jay C., and Gareth C. Leviton. "Policy Considerations in Corporate Criminal Prosecutions After People v. Film Recovery Systems, Inc." *Notre Dame Law Review* 62 (1987): 913–39. Review of the impact of an important and well-publicized case.

Mann, Kenneth. *Defending White-Collar Crime: A Portrait of Attorneys at Work.* New Haven: Yale University Press, 1985. How white-collar crime specialists defend clients by helping them control information flows to prosecutors.

Mokhiber, Russell. *Corporate Crime and Violence: Big Business Power and the Abuse of the Public Trust*. San Francisco: Sierra Club Books, 1988. Thirty-six clearly written case summaries, and more than 50 suggestions for reform and control.

Nichols, Lawrence T. "Social Problems as Landmark Narrative: Bank of Boston, Mass Media and Money Laundering." *Social Problems* 44 (1997): 324–41. How news media used information to level charges of money laundering against a major bank, and how policy makers used these charges to push for new laws.

Scott, Wilbur J. "Competing Paradigms in the Assessment of Latent Disorders: The Case of Agent Orange." *Social Problems* 35 (1988): 145–61. A description and analysis of the deviance-defining process as it applies to the effects of the herbicide Agent Orange.

Sherman, Lawrence W. *Scandal and Reform: Controlling Police Corruption*. Berkeley and Los Angeles: University of California Press, 1978. The healing power of scandal examined through the lense of police corruption.

Simpson, Ida Harper, and Richard L. Simpson, eds. *Deviance in the Workplace: Research in the Sociology of Work*. Vol. 8. Stamford, Conn.: JAI Press, 1999. Collection of 11 papers by leading scholars focusing on reactions to and control of corporate and governmental deviance.

Szasz, Andrew. "The Process and Significance of Political Scandals: A Comparison of Watergate and the 'Sewergate' Episode at the Environmental Protection Agency." *Social Problems* 33 (1986): 202–17. Asserts that most political scandals are like professional wrestling because "political bodies fly through the air, mete out incredible punishments, and crash noisily to the canvas" with no lasting consequences.

Vaughan, Diane. *Controlling Unlawful Organizational Behavior: Social Structure and Corporate Misconduct*. Chicago: University of Chicago Press, 1983. Control of an episode of corporate deviance.

Wheeler, Stanton, Kenneth Mann, and Austin Sarat. *Sitting in Judgment: The Sentencing of White-Collar Criminals*. New Haven: Yale University Press, 1988. Factors shaping the sentencing of white-collar criminals.

Winters, Paul A., ed. *Policing the Police*. San Diego: Greenhaven Press, 1995. Overview of efforts and ideas to control and reform deviant police organizations.

Yeager, Peter. *The Limits of Law*. Cambridge: Cambridge University Press, 1991. Thorough study of water pollution, legislation, and legal liability.

12
Ten Whistleblowers
What They Did and How They Fared
Myron Peretz Glazer

In 1959, Frank Serpico joined the New York City police force. For Serpico, the police had always represented the meshing of authority and service. His early days on the force propelled him into the conflict between the norms governing police behavior set by department regulations and the actual "code" generated by the police. Formal regulations precluded the taking of any items from neighborhood stores and sanctioned the acceptance of bribes. In the station house and out on patrol a different set of rules applied. "Shopping" for items of food at local stores was clearly acceptable and taking money to pardon a lawbreaker became standard fare. Serpico was caught in a dilemma that faces many rookie police. Which set of norms should he uphold?[1]

Like many other whistleblowers in industry, government, and the academic world, initially Serpico was caught between his desire to follow his moral beliefs and the organizational pressures to conform. How do workers handle such a conflict? And what happens to their personal lives and their careers once they have blown the whistle? In an effort to understand the dynamics of the process, I have interviewed or exchanged letters with nine prominent whistleblowers and have corresponded with the wife of a tenth, who

From "Ten Whistleblowers and How They Fared," *The Hastings Center Report,* December 1983, pp. 33–41. Copyright © 1983 by The Hastings Center. Reprinted by permission.

1. Peter Maas, *Serpico* (New York: The Viking Press, 1973). For a participant observation account of police training, see Richard Harris, *The Police Academy: An Inside View* (New York: John Wiley, 1973). Other studies of the police support Serpico's experiences and observations. See Lawrence W. Sherman, *Police Corruption* (New York: Anchor, 1974).

is deceased.[2] Their cases portray three distinct paths through which individuals move toward public disclosure:

Unbending resisters protest within the organization about unethical or illegal behavior that they have observed. They maintain a strict commitment to their principles, despite efforts to cajole or coerce them. Ultimately, as a consequence of neglect and retaliation within the organization, they take a public stand.

Implicated protesters speak out within their organizations, but acquiesce when they are ordered to conform. They find themselves drawn into illegal or unethical behavior, which they expose when they fear legal liability.

Reluctant collaborators become deeply involved in acts they privately condemn. They seek public remedy and personal expiation only when they leave the organization.

Once an employee has blown the whistle, the responses of his or her superiors can take two broad forms. There are "degradation ceremonies" to punish and alienate resisters and protesters, and "ceremonies of status elevation," which reinforce the whistleblower's feeling that what he or she is doing is right. Whether and when someone will blow the whistle will depend on the peculiar mixture of sustenance and punishment, as well as the person's courage and the circumstances of his or her life. My observations also reveal that the whistleblower's fate need not be grim.

Blowing the Whistle

Like Serpico, Bob Leuci, the protagonist of *The Prince of the City*, was also caught in a net of conflicting loyalties. He has aptly de-

---

2. In those instances where the whistleblowers lived beyond driving distance, I exchanged letters with them and did a lengthy, taped, telephone interview during the summer of 1982. Unless otherwise noted all quoted material is from the interviews or letters. Since I was interested in the whistleblowers' perceptions of their experience, I did not interview other people involved in the cases. The material on Frank Serpico derives from published sources.

Three of the whistleblowers discussed in this article—Joseph Rose, Grace Pierce, and Frank Camps—also described their experiences in Alan Westin, ed. *Whistle Blowing? Loyalty and Dissent in the Corporation* (New York: McGraw-Hill, 1981).

For a study that reports on 51 cases of whistleblowers, see Lea P. Stuart, "'Whistle Blowing: Implications for Organizational Communication," *Journal of Communication* 30:4 (Autumn 1980), 90–101. For an intensive case study, read Robert M. Anderson, Robert Perrucci, Dan D. Schendel, and Leon E. Tractman, *Divided Loyalties: Whistle-Blowing at BART* (West Lafayette, Ind.: Purdue University, 1980).

scribed to me the "erosion process" by which young police officers became "bent":

> I remember the first time I was in a situation that scared me. We were in a police car and there was a fight in the street. I was working with this big, strong guy. I was nervous when I got out of the car and approached the fight. "Am I good enough to handle this kind of thing?" Two guys were going at each other with knives. I backed off a bit, but one guy came at me. My partner pushed me aside. "You move toward my partner again, and I'll kill you." And all of a sudden I got this feeling. He didn't say "You move toward me," but he said, "You move toward my partner." Whether he would have killed this guy or not, had the guy come at him, I don't know. But he would have killed him if the guy came at me. When hearing that, in that sort of context, you have this feeling of something very, very special about working with someone when your life may be in danger. So I was with a guy who was fifteen years my senior and a wonderful policeman. The first time he went in to get dinner, and came out with a sandwich I asked, "Did you pay for it?" He answered, "No, it's okay." It was in fact okay coming from him. It *was* okay. This man would not do anything wrong; he would not do anything criminal certainly, and what was so terrible about this? But what happens is that emotionally things are going on that you don't realize. There is an erosion process that is taking place, and it is changing you. That is something that I certainly didn't notice for many years. But it was happening to me—happening to a lot of people around me.[3]

Serpico felt similar pulls of loyalty born of comparable experiences. Yet he began to drift from the others on the force as he tired of the endless shoptalk. In a search for outside interests he took courses for a degree in sociology and moved to Greenwich Village where he spent time with aspiring women artists and dancers. Serpico's disenchantment peaked when, as a plainclothes officer, he accidentally received a $300 payoff, which he immediately took to one of the top men in the New York City Department of Investigation. The captain told Serpico that he could go before the grand jury, but that word would get out that he had been the chief witness and he might end "face down in the East River." Or, the captain continued, Serpico could forget the whole thing.

3. Bob Leuci's experiences are recounted by Robert Daly, *Prince of the City* (Boston: Houghton Mifflin, 1978). This statement is taken from a class visit to Smith College, March 12, 1981. Since then, I have had numerous other discussions with Leuci.

This is a crucial decision for the whistleblower. The organization counts on the threat of punishment to exercise control. But this can often backfire. Serpico's alienation toward the police force intensified. He felt powerless to require others to live up to their responsibilities. Doubting his own belief in the honesty of his comrades and leaders and knowing that serious rule-breaking was endemic at all levels of the department, he felt increasingly isolated from those whose trust was essential for his survival. He refused, however, to complete the cycle of self-alienation by turning his back on his own beliefs of proper police conduct. Serpico resisted the temptation to go along with the group, even though the pressure increased markedly when he transferred to the South Bronx with assurances by high-level police officials that it was free of corruption.

The combination of blatant police wrongdoing and the extreme poverty of the neighborhood aggravated his dilemma. In desperation, he bluffed to a superior that he had gone to "outside sources" about police payoffs. This threat generated an investigation and eight of his peers were eventually tried. But no higher-ups were indicted, despite promises from the district attorney. Ostracized by most police after testifying and feeling increasingly vulnerable, Serpico convinced his immediate superior to accompany him to the *New York Times*. This led to a series of front-page articles on police corruption and ultimately to the establishment of the Knapp Commission. Its lengthy, independent investigation verified all of Serpico's charges and led to important changes in the New York City Police Department. Serpico would leave his mark.[4]

Several months later, Serpico was shot and seriously wounded during a drug raid. Had he been set up by his comrades? He retired, received a pension, and left the country for a time. Serpico still maintains that a principled officer must resist. Serpico reappeared in 1981 and reported on a television news program that he was writing a book. Since Serpico's experiences, another police officer, detective Robert Ellis, has assisted investigators in the apprehension of corrupt fellow police. He reports the difficulty of his activities and the subsequent threats made upon his wife and daughter. "I don't want my friends in other commands to think that for eight years

---

4. David Burnham, "Graft Paid to Police Said to Run into Millions, *New York Times*, April 25, 1970. New York City, *The Knapp Commission Report on Police Corruption* (New York: George Braziller, 1973).

they were dealing with a spy," he said. "I want it simply to be said that I am an honest cop" (*New York Times,* July 3, 1977, p. 1).

The experience of other unbending resisters shows similar links between initial protest, retaliation against the whistleblower from one's superiors, and a continuing search for affirmation of professional ideals. In 1973 Joseph Rose, an experienced lawyer, joined the Associated Milk Producers Incorporated (AMPI) as an in-house attorney. Rose quickly became aware of illegal political payments to the Nixon reelection campaign, which were part of the Watergate investigation. In a phone interview in 1982, he told me:

> My assignment in the corporation included fiduciary responsibilities. When I found out that so much money had gone under the table, I might have been able to take a moral posture of "All right—that's a past offense that I can indeed defend." But the criminal conspiracy was ongoing, and the law concerning criminal conspirators states that you don't have to participate in the original crime to be indicted as a coconspirator later. All you need is to know about it and take steps to cover it up or otherwise further the conspiracy. Second, money was misused. The Watergate televised proceedings had started. An airline retrieved money that it had paid for similar purposes. When that broke, I went to the law books and became convinced of the duty to recover these assets. A whole chain of events led me more and more to believe that the current executives were in very deep themselves. I talked to a lawyer and former judge here in San Antonio named Joe Frazier Brown. He urged me to start keeping notes on everything I did. He also urged me to gather all of the documents that supported my position, to bypass the general manager, and to take the evidence to the board of directors. I was never allowed to do that. My attempt [to talk to the board] happened on a weekend during their convention in Minneapolis. Labor Day followed, and then Tuesday I went into work. I found a guard posted at my door; locks had been changed. The general manager demanded to see me. My services had become very, very unsatisfactory. When I was fired, I felt virtually a sense of relief. I was glad to be out of it, and I planned to keep my mouth shut. Then I had a call from one of the lawyers involved in an antitrust case against AMPI. He said, "They are really slandering you—making some very vicious attacks on you." I had indicated to AMPI executives that if the board would not listen to me, I would go right to the dairy farmers and they obviously felt my career and credibility had to be completely destroyed to protect their own tails. After I was terminated, I had a call both from the Watergate Special Prosecutor's office and from the Congressional Committee's Subcommittee, wanting to know if they could fly down and talk to me. My

answer was absolutely, unequivocally not. They both said they had subpoena power, and I said, "You have it. I suggest you use it if you want to talk to me." Of course, I was subpoenaed, first to Congress and then to Mr. Cox's grand jury.

Unlike Serpico who came forth on his own, Joseph Rose correctly feared he would be charged with breaking attorney-client privilege if he testified voluntarily. For Rose the path to public disclosure had been triggered by a series of events–his refusal to engage in illegal and unethical actions, corporate retaliation, and the government requirement that he testify against his former associates. Afterwards Rose was forced to confront the shame of being disreputable in the eyes of others, for as a result of his testimony he remained underemployed for eight years. Potential employers, who accepted AMPI's explanation that Rose had been disloyal, were unwilling to hire him. His father died believing that his son had irrevocably lost his ability to earn a living. A once-successful attorney and his family were forced to live on food stamps.

Rose's career opportunities began to improve appreciably only after the *Wall Street Journal* publicized his case. In the meantime, the AMPI was found guilty and heavily fined, and two of its officers were convicted and sentenced to prison terms. Its finance officers sought and received immunity from prosecution to testify against others.

Rose now looks at American society with cold cynicism.

> I believe I can make a contribution to the young people in this country by continuing to respond with a strong warning that all of the public utterances of corporations and indeed our own government concerning "courage, integrity, loyalty, honesty, and duty" are nothing but the sheerest hogwash that disappear very rapidly when it comes to the practical application of these concepts by strict definition. The reason that there are very few Serpicos or Roses is that the message is too clearly out in this society that white-collar crime, or nonviolent crime, should be tolerated by the public at large, so long as the conduct brings a profit or a profitable result to the institution committing it. . . .

Public disclosure can also come about in an effort to clear one's personal reputation and establish the legitimacy of professionals to resist what they see as their superiors' unethical directives. Dr. Grace Pierce joined the Ortho Pharmaceutical Corporation, a division of Johnson & Johnson, in 1971 after eleven years in private medical practice, service in the Food and Drug Administration, and experience with another drug firm. In 1975 she was assigned to direct a research team attempting to develop Loperamide, a drug for the relief of acute and chronic diarrhea. The liquid Loperamide formulation originated with Janssen, a Johnson & Johnson company in Belgium, and had a very high saccharin content to hide the bitter taste. Dr. Pierce and all the Ortho team members agreed that there was a need to reformulate the drug to diminish the saccharin concentration, particularly with the ongoing controversy over its carcinogenic potential. While her colleagues ultimately acceded to management pressures to accept the high saccharin formulation, Dr. Pierce refused. As the only medical person on the team, she would not agree to begin clinical trials with what she considered a questionable formulation.

After her refusal, Dr. Pierce charged that her immediate superior questioned her judgment, loyalty, and competence. Later, he accused her of misusing company funds on a research trip and of taking an unauthorized vacation. Although she rejected and refuted the accusations, the critique was a clear signal of her diminished prospects.

> When the situation came up and I couldn't get other people to go along with me, I asked my superior whether we could get three objective consultants outside the company. If they say it's okay, I'll do it. Or if you'll permit me to go to the FDA and put the situation to them openly and they say okay, I'll do it. I think I offered alternatives for a reasonable compromise. He refused. Use of saccharin remains a question yet. Nobody knows where this problem of carcinogens is heading. It probably won't be resolved soon, if ever. I was on the spot. I had to get with it or get out. I hated that. I was cornered. There was no compromise. Nobody from higher up came and said, "Why don't we do that or do this." They were just riding roughshod all over me. I always like to feel I'm a person, not a cog in a machine. . . . One of my colleagues said, "Grace, you're nuts. Why not write a lengthy memo for the files, make sure you're on record. They're responsible." If I do the research, I'm responsible. I feel responsibility as a physician first. My responsibility to the corporation is second. I think my colleagues' attitude is commonplace. People salve their conscience. They keep the benefits of the job. This memo gives them an escape hatch.

Pierce resigned. Unlike Joseph Rose, she was quickly approached by a colleague to affiliate in a group medical practice, which she joined on a part-time basis. Later the vice president of Personal Products, another subsidiary of Johnson & Johnson, invited her to join his research staff although she alerted him that she might sue Ortho. Within six months she had become director of research. While Dr. Pierce felt vindicated of charges against her integrity and competence, her work situation changed dramatically when she actually filed her suit for "damage to her professional reputation, dissipation of her career, loss of salary, as well as seniority and retirement benefits."[5]

Despite their excellent relationship, the vice president's attitude cooled. Not unexpectedly, he summoned her at the end of one work day.

> I was fired. He said it was unconscionable that any one working for Personal Products would sue a sister company. I said I didn't think so. He had been aware of the legal thing with Ortho. He was dejected and hurt by the whole thing. The next morning he seemed very sad about seeing me go. . . . I haven't seen him since.

Dr. Pierce carried her suit to the New Jersey Supreme Court, which broke constitutional ground by affirming a professional's right to challenge superiors where professional ethics are at stake. In Grace Pierce's case, however, five of the six judges for the New Jersey Supreme Court ruled that her judgment and Ortho's were simply at variance. Professional ethics were not the issue, according to the court, which sustained Ortho's actions.

Postponing the Whistle

Some professionals delay taking a path of direct confrontation and, as a result, they become involved in unethical or illegal behavior. Implicated protesters include those who have spoken up within their organizations, have capitulated and gone along with the policies of their superiors, and have subsequently publicized inappropriate actions when they have become fearful of the consequences of their own involvement.

5. Alfred G. Feliu, "Discharge of Professional Employees: Protecting Against Dismissal for Acts Within a Professional Code of Ethics," *Columbia Human Rights Law Review*, 11 (1979–1980). See especially pp. 186–187.

In the late 1960s, Kermit Vandivier, a technician, assisted in the production of an airplane brake whose faulty design could have endangered Air Force test pilots. He asserted that, despite his repeated pleas and those of several engineers including his supervisor, other engineers and managers in the Goodrich Corporation pushed a false report. When Air Force pilots tested the brakes with near fatal results, Vandivier approached a lawyer who advised him to go to the FBI.

Though Vandivier's account has been reprinted many times in the last decade,* he recently provided additional insight. Note how—as a relatively uneducated technician—he felt alienated and powerless. Note also his sense of anomie as people he trusted simply backed off, and his anxiety over his isolation.

> At the time of the Goodrich fiasco I had six children of school age at home. My salary, if I remember correctly, was around $125–$135 per week. My only outside source of income was the pay I received from the *Troy Daily News* [TDN]—$15 for the three columns per week I wrote. High principles notwithstanding, I couldn't—at that time—subject myself and my family to "retaliation." Please note I said "at that time," because I think there is one factor which I perhaps have not made entirely clear in the Goodrich story. I don't think anyone within the Goodrich organization really believed—until the moment it actually happened—that the report was going to be issued to the Air Force. Until such time as it was published and delivered to the Air Force, none of us who actually had a part in preparing the phony report was guilty of any criminal act. True, my attorney offered his opinion that we might be guilty of conspiracy to defraud, but qualified that opinion by adding there would have to be proof we knew at the outset a fraud would ultimately be committed. I can't describe the sense of incredulity I (and I'm sure others) experienced when I learned the report had really been issued, that Goodrich was actually going to try and pull this thing off. . . . Naturally, my editors at TDN knew what was going on right from the start. When the situation had developed sufficiently we considered whistleblowing in the TDN, but TDN attorneys were concerned that there was simply not enough proof of any wrongdoing at that time and felt that a libel suit could be certain. Meanwhile, I was gathering incriminating data, photographs, charts, movie film, notes of meetings and telephone conversations. I smuggled them out of the plant each day, copied them at night, and returned the originals the following day. Altogether, I amassed more than 1,000 documents and other items

*ED. NOTE: See Selection 8 in this volume.

(I still have them), which were invaluable evidence at the Senate hearing. When I finally was ready to blow the whistle I had all the evidence necessary to make a strong case. No one was indicted or charged in connection with the hearing, but the day following the hearing the Department of Defense quietly initiated sweeping changes in its inspection and procurement procedures. A DOD official later confirmed the changes were made as a direct result of the hearing. . . .

Vandivier's testimony underscores that the ties of loyalty can be broken and public criticism undertaken when the dangers of continued inaction appear more serious than the fears of retaliation. Under such circumstances, those who contemplate blowing the whistle have a potentially powerful and omnipresent ally in the weight of the law, which holds companies and individuals responsible for the production of faulty products.[6] Many implicated protesters might resist the orders of their superiors were there greater likelihood of apprehension, conviction, and severe punishment for white-collar crimes.[7]

In the early 1970s another serious breach of professional and managerial ethics unfolded. Frank Camps, a senior principal design engineer, was directly involved in the development of the Ford Pinto, which proved to have an unsafe windshield and a gas tank that might explode on impact. He questioned the design and testing procedure and later charged publicly that his superiors who knew of this danger were so anxious to produce a lightweight and cheap car to compete with the imports that they were determined to overlook serious design problems. Camps's level of anxiety grew as he contemplated the consequences of his own involvement.

> We were still in the development stage. I had a certain degree of resentment; these people were not listening although we were having problems with the car. I can remember I went into my manager's office. He said, "Look, we're in the business of selling cars and every time we barrier crash a car and it causes problems, then we have one failure. If we get another car to crash, to see how the first failure happened, we may have two failures. This would compound

6. For a discussion of the recent legislation to protect and encourage whistleblowing, see Westin, *Whistle Blowing?* pp. 131–167.

7. For a pertinent instance, see Eberhard Faber, "How I Lost Our Great Debate about Corporate Ethics," *Fortune*, November 1976, pp. 180–188.

itself until my bonus would be reduced." Now this was the kind of thinking—the corporate attitude—that my immediate superior had. He didn't say anything about crashing for occupant safety. He just didn't want his bonus to be cut down. I said to my wife, "This guy is a bad actor. This guy is going to get me in trouble if I don't start documenting and protecting myself." This was colossal arrogance, callous indifference toward the safety of people. It bothered me even if only one person should die or be disfigured because of something that I was responsible for.

Camps was a respected and longtime member of Ford's engineering staff and thus not totally without influence. Yet he felt powerless to affect company policy. To avoid complete absorption into a system of relationships and definitions that calibrated human life on a scale of company costs and to protect himself against legal liability, he sued the company.

Camps described the response of fellow engineers, a response that mitigated his sense of isolation.

> Most of the working engineers were very supportive of me at that time. They are still supportive of me. I can recall, right after I filed the suit, other engineers said—"Go get 'em, we wish we could do it, there goes a man with brass balls." While I had tacit support, I was looking for an honest man to stand with me. I found that these guys were suddenly given promotions, nice increases in salary. Next thing I knew, I did not have the support any more.

Camps wasn't alone in his agony over the Pinto. From 1971 to 1978 fifty lawsuits were filed against Ford because of gas-tank explosions in rear-end accidents. In 1980 Ford was brought to trial on a criminal charge in the death of three Indiana girls. The case created national headlines and featured the testimony of a former high-ranking Ford engineer whose statements were similar to those made by Frank Camps within the company.[8] While Ford was found innocent in this trial, the Pinto has come to symbolize management's drive for profits over customer safety. Had Camps been treated as a voice to be heeded rather than a protester to be ignored and punished, Ford might have avoided fatalities and serious injuries, years of litigation, and the stigma of corporate irresponsibility.

---

8. Richard T. DeGeorge, "Ethical Responsibilities of Engineers in Large Organizations: The Pinto Case," *Business Professional Ethics Journal* 1 (Fall 1981), 1–17.

Whistling Late in the Game

Many professionals who participate in illegal or unethical acts only blow the whistle once they have left the organization and have reestablished their careers in other companies or fields of work. They seek to make up for their past timidity and to ease their consciences.

The late Arthur Dale Console studied at Cornell Medical College and later practiced neurosurgery. In search of less strenuous work after a serious illness, he joined the E. R. Squibb and Sons pharmaceutical company in 1949 as associate director of research. He found Squibb an ethical company, still run by its founder and maintaining an orientation in which the physician in charge of research was defined as a "physician's physician." During the ensuing years, according to Dr. Console, much changed in the pharmaceutical industry. Larger companies bought out the smaller ones and the search for profit became more intense. The transformation affected all members of the company staff including the director of research, a position that Dr. Console had by then assumed. As he worked, he experienced an increasing tension between his sense of what was appropriate medical decision making and what was required by his more business-oriented superiors. He was particularly disturbed by those instances in which he had pressured physicians to certify drugs that they had not sufficiently tested. He resigned from his position in 1956 after six and a half years in the drug industry, and soon after began to train for a new career as a psychiatrist.

During the 1960s, Console's continuing sense of self-estrangement led him to take the initiative and testify several times before congressional committees. At one hearing he was asked why he had left Squibb. His answer captures the process of capitulating to the pressures of multi-national corporations and the disillusionment that follows.

> I believe that the best answer can be found in my unfinished essay of *The Good Life of a Drug Company Doctor*. Toward the end I said: "These are only some of the things a drug company doctor must learn if he is to be happy in the industry. After all, *it is a business*, and there are many more things he must learn to rationalize. He must learn the many ways to deceive the FDA and, failing in this, how to seduce, manipulate or threaten the physician assigned to the New Drug Application into approving it even if it is incomplete. He must learn that anything that helps to sell a drug is valid even if it

is supported by the crudest testimonial, while anything that decreases sales must be suppressed, distorted and rejected because it is not absolutely conclusive proof. He will find himself squeezed between businessmen who will sell anything and justify it on the basis that doctors ask for it and doctors who demand products they have been taught to want through the advertising and promotion schemes contrived by businessmen. If he can absorb all this, and more, and still maintain any sensibilities he will learn the true meaning of loneliness and alienation." During my tenure as medical director I learned the meaning of loneliness and alienation. I reached a point where I could no longer live with myself. I had compromised to the point where my back was against a wall and I had to choose between resigning myself to total capitulation, or resigning as medical director. I chose the latter course.[9]

After he left the pharmaceutical industry, Dr. Console received a grant from Squibb to train for a career in psychiatry, which placed him outside the authority of all corporate structures. Console's widow, a respected psychiatrist in her own right, has provided additional insight into Dr. Console's background, his commitment to Squibb, and his ultimate decision to blow the whistle several years after entering private practice.

He was one of two surviving brothers who both carried out their father's ambitions to complete medical school. Arthur did so with great distinction. . . . In spite of two bouts of tuberculosis during this period he went on and completed a neurosurgical residency—the first resident chosen in this separate specialty considered the most prestigious in surgery. Trouble really began when, in attempting to establish a practice, he fell ill a third time, necessitating complete bed rest at home. We had an infant son with club feet requiring frequent surgical intervention and casts, absolutely no income except mine from an also newly established practice, and the resulting pressure on me from multiple conflicting responsibilities was overwhelming. It was apparent that he had to find a less physically demanding and an economically sound alternative. It was at this time he accepted the offer to join Squibb as an associate medical director. The decision to give up neurosurgery as a career was a bitter and lasting defeat. The coincidence of Dr. Console's tenure as medical director of Squibb with its changeover from an ethical drug house to a competitive business-oriented company

9. "A. Dale Console," in Ralph Nader, Peter J. Petkas, and Kate Blackwell, eds., *Whistle Blowing* (New York: Bantam, 1972), pp. 122–123. Also see Hearings before the Subcommittee on Monopoly of the Select Committee on Small Business, United States Senate, Ninety-first Congress, First Session on Present Status of Competition in the Pharmaceutical Industry, Part II, March 13, 1959, pp. 44–84.

could not have been foreseen, but his sense of having been condemned to second-class medicine then became more and more intolerable. Because of Dr. Console's increasing and outspoken alienation from the drug industry it was clear that an open break was pending. It was imperative for him to look elsewhere for the future. The choice of psychiatry was made after considerable discussion together. . . . When the opportunity arose to testify in the Kefauver hearings, Dr. Console had already distanced himself from almost all his former colleagues. . . . The real problem was one of conflict from some sense of loyalty to Squibb, which had been very generous to him, and the pressure of his need to speak out. I did not share this intensity and had some misgivings but felt that he had to follow his own conviction. His moments of "speaking out" appeared then to be an opportunity to vindicate himself in his own eyes before the world.

Dr. Console *chose* to reveal his own complicity in a large-scale effort to profit from unethical marketing procedures. Whistleblowing of this kind can result when people believe deeply that they should have acted earlier to resist illegitimate authority.[10] Although Dr. Console testified over a decade ago, recent scholarship reveals that many of the problems he highlighted continue to characterize the drug industry, particularly in its relationship with Third World countries.[11]

Taboos and Degradation Ceremonies

Those willing to breach the taboo against informing face potent challenges.[12] Their superiors have the power to harass them by questioning their competence and judgment, to terminate their employment, and to blacklist them from other positions. Attorney Joseph Rose learned that the extensive influence of the Associated Milk Producers could bring his career to a standstill.

10. Other reluctant collaborators now have become international figures. See Philip Agee, *Inside the Company* (New York: Bantam Books, 1976). His decision to identify publicly CIA agents makes him the country's most controversial whistleblower. For a debate on his actions, see "On Naming C.I.A. Agents," *The Nation* (March 14, 1981), pp. 295–301.

11. See Ray H. Elling, "The Political Economy of International Health with a Focus on the Capitalist World-System," in Michael Lewis, ed. *Social Problems and Public Policy*, Vol. II (Stamford, Conn.: JAI Press, 1982).

12. For a recent and illuminating study of the role of the informer, see Victor Navasky, *Naming Names* (New York: Viking, 1980).

After I left AMPI, they weren't content with the firing, they wanted to call my ex-employers and completely ruin me. There was an attorney up in New York and I answered one of his ads. It turned out that he was a friend of an executive of AMPI, and indeed his secretary was one of the executive's nieces. I accepted the job and he and I went out on one case. He said right in front of a client, "He doesn't know it yet, but at Christmas time, I am going to fire him." I thought he was kidding, and I didn't pay any attention to it, and then lo and behold, right at Christmas time, right on target before Christmas, he fired me. After he dismissed me, I had been under fire so long that I was about to have a damned nervous breakdown. I did a very peculiar thing. President Ford was in office, and I wrote Ford and said, "This is happening to me, because I wouldn't be a crook." The next thing I knew, John Sales of the Watergate prosecutor's office called me and he said, "How are you?" and the clear implication was "Are you keeping your sanity?" And I said, "John, I'm holding on, but it sure as hell isn't easy." And he said, "Well, we've got an interview for you with the Department of Labor in Dallas." I thought, all of a sudden, there is justice in the world, maybe somebody does care. So I drove to Dallas, and I interviewed with the guy who was the head of the Department of Labor there, and I'll be damned if he didn't know some of the AMPI people. He made the comment, "I didn't request to interview you, as far as I am concerned, I can throw your resume up to the ceiling and hope it sticks there."

AMPI's influence seemed also to extend into religious organizations. Rose, a devout man, was particularly hurt by this.

My wife and I were attending Castle Hills First Baptist Church in town. I was in very bad emotional shape. I mean *very* bad and one of the high guys at AMPI attended the same church. I went to talk to the leader of the church. I guess I just wanted somebody to talk to, to get this thing out of my system. The man literally turned his back on me and started talking to other people. I felt that I certainly was not abandoning Jesus Christ by abandoning the specific church building.

As Joseph Rose learned through bitter experience, those who break the taboo will experience degradation, which recasts the social identity of whistleblowers, labeling them as unreliable, of poor judgment, and of dangerous character.

Joseph Rose worked in private industry. What of the government employees? A prime example is Ernest A. Fitzgerald, a staff analyst in the Pentagon. In 1969, he appeared before Proxmire's Senate subcommittee investigating the production of the C5A air transport. Fitzgerald "committed truth" by answering affirmatively that there had been a two-billion-dollar overrun in the plane's development.[13] He could have sidestepped the question or lied to the Senator. Had he done so, Fitzgerald would have avoided being labeled as someone who no longer had a future at the Pentagon. Such a designation came from the highest levels of government, including the Secretary of the Air Force and the President of the United States, Richard M. Nixon.

A statement by Alexander Butterfield, White House aide (and the man who later revealed the existence of the secret Nixon tapes), best summed up the official view toward Fitzgerald.

> Fitzgerald is no doubt a top-notch cost expert, but he must be given very low marks in loyalty, and after all loyalty is the name of the game. Only a basic "nogoodnik" would take his official grievances so far from normal channels. We should let him bleed for a while at least.[14]

While such retaliation did not break Fitzgerald, it extracted a heavy price from him and his family. In a recent conversation he has spoken of the impact on his children as comparable to radiation—difficult to measure but potentially very damaging.

Butterfield's statement implicitly highlights some of the central characteristics of "successful degradation ceremonies" that Harold Garfinkel has identified: the whistleblower's actions are "out of the ordinary" and in contrast to those of a loyal employee or peer; the actions are not accidental and reflect on the entire person of the whistleblower; the denunciation reinforces the values of the group, which stress silence and loyalty.[15] The message is clear. Whether in industry or government or academia, the whistleblower who is determined to reject self-estrangement despite the attacks of superiors must be able to withstand the charge of being labeled incompetent and disloyal.

13. A. Ernest Fitzgerald, *The High Priests of Waste* (New York: W. W. Norton, 1972). For a pertinent study, see Mark Ryter, *A Whistle-blower's Guide to the Federal Bureaucracy* (Washington: Institute for Policy Studies, 1977).

14. Media Transcripts Incorporated Program 20/20. December 18, 1980, p. 14.

15. Harold Garfinkel, "Conditions of Successful Degradation Ceremonies," *The American Journal of Sociology* 61 (January 1956), 420–424; Victor W. Turner, *The Ritual Process* (Chicago: Aldine, 1969), pp. 168–203.

Ceremonies of Status Elevation

New York City detective Bob Leuci received crucial encouragement from government prosecutors Scoppetta and Shaw in his decision to do undercover work against racketeers and corrupt police. Note how Leuci's sense of self is directly tied to his identification with these two men.

> I undertook this investigation because of the support that I received from Scoppetta and Shaw, incredible support. It was the same kind of support that I received from my partners when I was working out on the street. You have a sense that there is somebody who truly cares about you.

The experiences of James Boyd and Marjorie Carpenter offer a sharp example of the way in which efforts toward status elevation can alleviate the pressures toward self-estrangement. Boyd and Carpenter are credited with exposing and bringing down the powerful Senator Thomas Dodd of Connecticut in the late 1960s. Boyd, Dodd's assistant for twelve years, and Carpenter, Dodd's secretary, suspected that the Senator was pocketing large amounts of campaign funds.[16] According to Boyd, Dodd sensed their suspicions, fired them both, and spread the word that they were disreputable employees who were dismissed when he discovered that they were engaged in a sordid love affair. Boyd suspected that the Senator also intended to blacklist him from employment in Washington.

> I didn't come to the decision to really go at it, tooth and nail, until I saw him trying to keep me from getting a job. I didn't want to go back with him. I was trying to get away from him for some time, but he tried to use the power to keep me from getting a job, and then, in a roundabout way, boasting to me what he was doing, toying with me as if I were some kind of a creature, instead of a partner as we had started out.

Boyd had decided to expose Senator Dodd but could not act until he was approached by Drew Pearson and Jack Anderson.[17] The two

16. James Boyd, *Above the Law* (New York: New American Library, 1968).

17. Drew Pearson and Jack Anderson, "Portraits of a Senator," in *The Case Against Congress* (New York: Simon and Schuster, 1968). The Dodd case was one among other factors leading to the Senate's ultimate reconsideration of its principles of behavior and the revision of its own code of ethics. See the special section entitled "Revising the U.S. Senate Code of Ethics," *Hastings Center Report* (February 1981), pp. 1–28.

journalists assessed his suspicion, and encouraged him to act against Dodd with their explicit promise that they would define the case as their highest priority, would never back off no matter how great the heat, and would continue to demand an investigation by the Senate and other legal authorities.

After this careful agreement, Boyd and Carpenter obtained keys to Dodd's office, and removed and copied thousands of documents that contained evidence of Dodd's financial dealings with major corporations and others who sought his intervention on their behalf. Boyd and Carpenter had taken bold and controversial action, which resulted in Dodd's eventual censure by the Senate.

Healing the Wounds

The available literature on whistleblowers often emphasizes the dead end that awaits those who break with peers and superiors. My evidence provides a more intricate mosaic. Virtually all the individuals discussed here have been able to rebuild their careers and belief in their competence and integrity. They found an escape hatch in private practice, consulting, and the media. Ironically perhaps the diversity of American economic and social institutions provides opportunities to those who have dared defy the authority of the established ones.

Although Frank Serpico never sought to develop a new career, he is a national figure who continues to be respected for his courageous stand. His name is synonymous with police integrity. Bob Leuci completed his twenty years in the New York City Police Department, is a popular speaker on college campuses, and is currently writing a novel about police work.

Joseph Rose is a successful attorney in San Antonio. Former colleagues who avoided him and believed the accusation that he had betrayed AMPI now treat him with respect. Some clients seek him out expressly because they know of his past difficulties and admire his toughness. When we spoke in the winter of 1983 his practice was flourishing.

Grace Pierce works exclusively in clinical medicine. She has expanded her work in the group clinic by opening an office in her home, believes she provides an important service to local patients, and has time to enjoy her garden.

"I really lucked out," she says. Her skills, the support of the medical community, and the receptiveness of her patients have provided an up-beat continuity to her work and personal life. She does, however, harbor many troubling questions about whistleblowing and its effectiveness in changing organizational policies. . . .

> And now that the "whistleblowers" have been re-established or resettled into other pursuits of living what has happened to the persons, institutions or corporations that created these dilemmas? Have there been corrective steps taken to avoid similar episodes of employee disenchantment? Have those offenders to the whistleblowers changed in any way—have there been any recriminations? Is there less deception or corruption or is it better concealed? Have the pathways of whistleblowers been kept open, or even broadened for other employees who may be confronted with similar ethical issues? Are the courts any more or less supportive? Were these struggles really worth it? Have our little pieces of the world actually improved because of these actions? Are there other ways and means available to resolve the whistleblower's conflicts—perhaps more effectively and perhaps less painfully with less personal sacrifice? Is there still a place for "idealists" in a world quite full of "realists"?

Unique opportunities arose for both Kermit Vandivier and Frank Camps after their break with former superiors. Vandivier has built a new career at the *Troy Daily News.*

> Looking back, I would say probably the best thing that ever happened to me was the Goodrich thing. That gave me the push I probably wouldn't have had otherwise. When you have six kids and you've got a job that looks fairly secure, and you like it—which I did—I liked the Goodrich job—and you feel like you're accomplishing something —you don't feel like quitting or starting a new career. I went into a different field. I would never have gotten a job at Goodyear or Bendix, the other two brake manufacturers. I don't think anyone in private industry would touch me. I am a troublemaker, you know. I went to work for the *Troy Daily News* the day following my abrupt departure from BFG. I have served as a general assignment reporter and have covered a variety of beats, including the police, city hall and political beats. . . . Two years ago the TDN became involved in cable television. I was named cable news director and given the responsibility of organizing and implementing the project.

Like Vandivier, Frank Camps found that others were interested in his skills and eager to hire him. Camps now serves as a consult-

ant to attorneys involved in product liability litigations. He underscores how important those relationships have become in recreat-
ing his career and his sense of himself.

> When I filed my suit, six months before I left Ford, it gained wide
> publicity, not only in the Detroit papers but in many papers and in
> many television outlets in the cities where the Ford plants were
> located. It also got into the *Wall Street Journal.* I began getting calls
> from attorneys all over the country, and I couldn't quite compre-
> hend what they were driving at until one of the attorneys said he
> would like me to help him on a case. He came up with an hourly
> figure and a retainer that was absolutely staggering, based on what
> I was making at Ford. He became my mentor. . . . All of those feel-
> ings I had—the anxiety, resentment, anger, helplessness, that's all
> gone, because of what I now accomplish. I am doing what I want to
> do, when I want to do it. I can speak my mind truthfully and openly
> in a court of law. There is nothing more gratifying than to know
> that you are now involved in due process. Incidentally, in all of the
> cases I have been involved in, I have not been on the losing side
> even one time.

Ernest Fitzgerald has spent more than a decade in litigation to
secure his former position. He has defeated a bureaucracy committed to his expulsion and banishment. An out-of-court settlement
with former President Richard Nixon, the return to previous duties,
and the court-directed government payment of his legal fees have
all provided clear evidence for his complete and public vindication.
Fitzgerald has survived as the nation's best-known whistleblower.

Finally, James Boyd has taken a more circuitous route. He has
published a book about his experiences in the Dodd case, has directed
the Fund for Investigation Journalism, has written for the *New York
Times Magazine,* and has completed several projects with Jack
Anderson. He and Marjorie Carpenter Boyd live with their two
children in a rural area far from Washington. She continues to
believe that they acted appropriately and were guided by their need
for a sense of inner satisfaction, which she finds characteristic of
many whistleblowers. As Boyd reflects on the last fifteen years, he
can count some of the costs and gains of his decision to take on a
United States Senator.

> I have friends from that period of my life who are now retired. If I
> had done that, I would have been retired now for three years, and
> I would have been getting $35,000 a year. I realize that there is a

tremendous material loss involved. Also you lose something—there's something in an institution, various supports—professional, friendship, life-support type things—that you lose when you are separated from that institution. What I have gained is a whole new outlook on life—a feeling of independence—of "being my own man"—working at my own hours—and all that sort of thing, which I find enormously attractive. . . .

In a recent note Rose aptly summarized his views.

Gandhi said that noncooperation with evil is as much a duty as cooperation with good; Burke said the only thing necessary for the triumph of evil is for good men to do nothing. Both concepts are still viable . . . although expensive.

For each of these whistleblowers there was no going back. Yet there was a future.[18] That message is as vital as the severe price they paid.

18. These findings are confirmed by a recent government report. The U.S. Merit Systems Protection Board, *Whistle Blowing and the Federal Employee* (Washington, D.C.: U.S. Government Printing Office, October 1981), particularly p. 41.

13
The Los Angeles Police Department Rampart Division Scandal
Exposing Police Misconduct and Responding to It
The Rampart Independent Review Panel

Los Angeles, long home to one of the country's leading police departments, is now struggling to address one of the worst police scandals in American history. Any effort to understand that scandal and to learn from it must start with the allegations at its heart—allegations of corruption and widespread police abuses that have generated almost daily headlines in Los Angeles describing the activities of a special anti-gang unit assigned to the Los Angeles Police Department's Rampart Area.

Rampart Area is located just west of downtown Los Angeles, covers 7.9 square miles, and is one of the busiest and largest operational commands within the LAPD, with more than 400 sworn and civilian personnel assigned. The Area has the highest population density in Los Angeles, with approximately 33,790 people per square mile, and the crime rate has always been among the highest in Los Angeles.

When Rampart Station opened in 1966, there were few street gangs in the area. By the mid-1980s, however, gangs and gang membership in the Rampart Area had increased alarmingly. So had narcotics trafficking and violent crimes associated with gangs. As elsewhere in Los Angeles, gangs in Rampart Area had easy access to weapons and were repeatedly implicated in a multitude of "gang-related crimes," including murders, assaults, robberies, rapes, arsons, and incidents of witness intimidation.

The Los Angeles Police Department responded with CRASH—"Community Resources Against Street Hoodlums." CRASH was created and funded by a grant in the early 1970s to combat the

From *Report of the Rampart Independent Review Panel,* November 16, 2000, pp. 1–11.

violent gang problem plaguing Los Angeles. There were two original CRASH units—one for Operation–South Bureau and one for Operation–Central Bureau. Both CRASH units worked gang problems in all Areas in the Bureau until they were decentralized a few years later. For years, CRASH was in the forefront of the LAPD's efforts to combat criminal activity by Los Angeles street gangs.

The Rampart CRASH unit was comprised of one to two sergeants and up to 24 CRASH officers. Prior to 1995, all Rampart officers were stationed in a single location. In 1995, the Rampart Area split into two stations due to overcrowding and poor conditions, such as inadequate lighting, few lockers, and lack of parking at the main station. Both CRASH and Detective operations were relocated from the main Rampart Station on Temple Street to a new station at 3rd and Union.

Determined to cut crime, LAPD gave Rampart CRASH officers wide latitude to aggressively fight gangs. According to the LAPD, gang-related crimes in Rampart Area fell from 1,171 in 1992 to 464 for 1999,[1] a reduction that exceeded the city-wide decline in violent crime over the same period.

This "success" of CRASH, however, came at a great price. Rampart CRASH officers developed an independent subculture that embodied a "war on gangs" mentality where the ends justified the means, and they resisted supervision and control and ignored LAPD's procedures and policies. As stated in the Board of Inquiry into the Rampart Corruption Incident Report (Board of Inquiry report), "Rampart CRASH had developed its own culture and operated as an entity unto itself. It routinely made up its own rules and, for all intents and purposes, was left with little or no oversight.[2] As a result, Los Angeles is now faced with a police corruption scandal of historic proportions that involves allegations of not just widespread perjury, false arrest reports, and evidence planting, but also incidents of attempted murder and the beating of suspects. The misconduct of CRASH officers went undetected because the Department's managers ignored warning signs and failed to pro-

---

1. LAPD Summary of Crimes and Arrests for the City of Los Angeles, Information Resources Division.

2. Los Angeles Police Department, Board of Inquiry Into the Rampart Corruption Incident Report at 62 (March 1, 2000).

vide the leadership, oversight, management and supervision necessary to control this specialized unit.

The consequences of the Rampart scandal cannot be overstated. The scandal has undermined the credibility of individual officers who testify in court and in their dealing with the public they serve. This lack of credibility potentially has dire consequences to effective law enforcement and the successful prosecution of crimes in Los Angeles. The public's willingness to cooperate with the LAPD and to believe the testimony of its officers has been directly impacted by the Rampart scandal. The scandal also has exposed a deep rift between the LAPD and the Los Angeles County District Attorney's Office (District Attorney or DA) and severely impacted the credibility of the entire criminal justice system in Los Angeles.

Finally, the scandal has damaged the LAPD leadership and the Los Angeles Board of Police Commissioners (Police Commission) to such an extent that there is widespread support for the agreed-upon consent decree and for the appointment of an outside federal monitor backed by the enforcement powers of the federal courts. Many officials and others simply do not believe that the Police Commission can effectively oversee the Department, or that the Department will submit voluntarily to civilian oversight. Questions also have been raised about the Department's ability to investigate uses of force by its officers; its handling of public complaints; its commitment to community policing; its failure to develop a system to track problem officers; and, above all, its willingness to institute the reforms necessary to restore its credibility in the eyes of the community it serves. Very few doubt that it will take years for the City and the Department to recover from this scandal.

The Origins and Dimensions of the Rampart Scandal

By early 1999, three separate criminal incidents, all having ties to Rampart CRASH officers, caused the LAPD to focus on and investigate Rampart CRASH. A bank robbery by LAPD Officer David Mack, the theft of narcotics from an LAPD evidence locker by Officer Rafael Perez, and allegations of excessive force against

Officer Brian Hewitt and others led to the creation of the LAPD Rampart Task Force.

On November 6, 1997, Officer Mack and others robbed the Bank of America branch located at 985 Jefferson Boulevard. Using a gun, the bank robbers confronted three bank employees and escaped with $722,000. The LAPD arrested Mack, who was indicted and ultimately convicted of federal bank robbery charges. Mack was sentenced to over 14 years, which he is currently serving in a federal prison in Illinois.[3]

On February 26, 1998, Rampart CRASH Officers Brian Hewitt and Daniel Lujan detained two 18th Street gang members for alleged parole violations and took them to the Rampart Substation where Hewitt allegedly choked and beat one of the men until he vomited blood because he refused to cooperate with them. Lujan and another officer, Ethan Cohan, allegedly knew about the beating, but failed to report it and allowed the man to be released without providing medical treatment. LAPD conducted an investigation and thereafter brought administrative charges against the three officers. Officers Hewitt and Cohan were found guilty at a Board of Rights hearing and fired by the Department. Officer Lujan was cleared at a second Board hearing.[4]

On March 27, 1998, LAPD Property Division discovered that three kilograms of cocaine had been checked out for court and were missing. LAPD initiated an investigation and determined that the court case for which the cocaine had been checked out had already been adjudicated. The Department then conducted an extensive audit of both the Property and Scientific Investigation Divisions, and suspicion soon focused upon Officer Rafael Perez. A handwriting expert concluded that there was a "high probability" that Perez had signed the request to check out the missing cocaine and there were a number of suspicious phone calls made by Perez on the day the missing cocaine was checked out.

---

3. Two days after the bank robbery, Mack went to Las Vegas with Rampart Officer Rafael Perez and another officer. Mack and Perez at one time worked together as a narcotics buy team and Mack reportedly saved Perez's life during a shooting during an undercover narcotics buy operation.

4. LAPD has sought on two occasions to obtain a criminal filing against Hewitt. The District Attorney's Special Investigations Division has rejected the filings due to insufficient evidence. The District Attorney's Office is now considering the case for a third time. LAPD also sought a criminal filing against Hewitt from the California Attorney General, which was also rejected.

On August 17, 1998, the District Attorney filed a complaint for one count of Possession of Cocaine for Sale, one count of Grand Theft, and one count of Forgery against Perez, who was arrested on August 25, 1998. Perez's first trial began on December 7, 1998, and a mistrial was declared after the jury deadlocked eight to four in favor of a guilty verdict. Thereafter LAPD investigators uncovered new evidence against Perez that resulted in additional charges being filed against him for thefts of additional cocaine from LAPD's Property Division.

Immediately before the scheduled start of the retrial on September 8, 1999, Perez pled guilty to eight felony counts, including four counts of Grand Theft for stealing the cocaine, and four counts of Possessing Cocaine for Sale. Perez agreed to cooperate in the investigation in exchange for a sentence of five years in prison.[5] On February 25, 2000, Perez was sentenced to five years in prison based on the representation of the District Attorney's Office that he had complied with the terms and conditions of the plea agreement.

Perez initially implicated 28 present and former members of the Rampart CRASH Unit in criminal activities and serious acts of misconduct. According to Perez, several of the officers he identified seemed to have the attitude that "they were LAPD and could do whatever they wished." According to Perez, this included attempted murder, planting evidence, false imprisonment, beatings, theft of money and drugs, unauthorized searches, obstruction of justice, false police reports and perjury.

Among the allegations made by Perez are that he and other officers lied in arrest reports about observing defendants engage in narcotics transactions, about defendants consenting to searches, and about the probable cause for arrests. According to Perez, they also shot and killed or wounded unarmed suspects[6] and innocent

---

5. Under the terms of the agreement Perez could be sentenced to the maximum of 12 years in prison if he lies to investigators. Initially, Perez was not given immunity for any crimes involving unlawful police shootings. The District Attorney then agreed to grant immunity for his testimony regarding the alleged unlawful police shooting of Javier Francisco Ovando. . . . To date, Perez has not implicated himself in any shootings other than the Ovando shooting.

6. In *People v. Durden*, Officer Nino Durden has been charged with attempted murder, assault with a deadly weapon, filing a false police report, and obstruction of justice in connection with the shooting of Javier Ovando, who was sentenced to over 23 years in prison based on false testimony by Perez and others. Durden is also accused of armed robbery in a separate incident, and perjury in a third incident for his role in the October 23, 1996 arrest of Miguel Hernandez, who was allegedly framed on a weapons offense.

bystanders, planted guns on suspects after shooting them, fabricated evidence,[7] framed defendants,[8] and delayed calling an ambulance to give them time to fabricate a story to justify a shooting.

Responses to the Rampart Scandal

The immediate impact of the Rampart scandal has been staggering. To date, the District Attorney has filed criminal charges against six former Rampart CRASH officers, and criminal investigations by the District Attorney's Office, the United States Attorney's Office, the LAPD and the Federal Bureau of Investigation are on-going.

Based largely on Perez's revelations, the District Attorney "lost confidence" in the evidence supporting the convictions of more than 100 people, and either initiated or joined in writs of habeas corpus filed by those defendants to dismiss their casess.[9] Most of the cases dismissed by the District Attorney's Office rested on Perez's statement that a defendant had been framed. In many of the cases, the defendant was located and interviewed by the Rampart Task Force and confirmed Perez's statements. Without apparent knowledge of Perez's version of events, they have given accounts consistent with Perez's statements. To date, however, no police officer has directly corroborated Perez's allegations of serious misconduct.

No sworn, tenured member of LAPD can be suspended without pay for more than twenty-two days or be fired or demoted without a Board of Rights hearing. In a Board of Rights, the burden on the

7. In *People v. Ortiz*, Michael Buchanan, and Sergeants Edward Ortiz and Brian Liddy are charged with perjury and conspiracy stemming from the 1996 arrests of Raul Munoz and Caesar Natividad for assaulting officers by striking two officers with their pickup truck as they sped through an alley.

8. In *People v. Ortiz*, Sergeants Edward Ortiz and Brian Liddy and Officer Paul Harper are charged with framing Allan Lobos.

9. The degree of corroboration for dismissal of cases by the District Attorney via a writ of habeas corpus is low. Thus, if the District Attorney has lost confidence in the evidence supporting the conviction, he moves to dismiss the case. Perez's word alone, or a defendant's word alone, if believed by the District Attorney, would be sufficient. The Department identified 99 cases it believed to be tainted based on Perez's testimony and referred those cases to the District Attorney for dismissal.

LAPD is to prove each charge by a preponderance of the evidence. Therefore, an officer may be found guilty of administrative misconduct more readily than criminal misconduct, which requires proof beyond a reasonable doubt. Further, the decision need not be unanimous and only requires a majority vote of the Board. If the officer is found guilty, the Board decides an appropriate punishment ranging from an official reprimand, suspension or demotion to termination, subject to a reduction by the Chief of Police.

To date, there have been 76 Boards of Rights hearings for 37 officers based upon Perez's allegations. About half resulted in acquittals because Perez was either insufficiently corroborated or impeached by independent facts. For example, an officer was found not guilty of misconduct in a gun possession case after it was disclosed that Perez testified incorrectly about the identity of a key informant in the case. Three officers have been fired as a result of the Rampart scandal, six other officers have resigned rather than face a Board of Rights hearing, and 25 have been relieved of duty pending a Board of Rights.

As of the time of this report, according to the City Attorney's Office, there are approximately 95 cases and 81 claims pending in which Rampart misconduct is alleged, and these numbers are expected to grow. In order to effectively handle these Rampart-related cases, the City Attorney's Office set up a special Rampart Team. The team is comprised of seven attorneys who interact with the Rampart Task Force, receiving briefings and assistance in gathering discovery. The City Attorney's Office reports that the City has paid so far approximately $880,000 in settlements in cases relating to Perez's allegations, but no civil jury has yet to return a verdict based upon Perez's allegations.

The Los Angeles Police Department responded to the Rampart scandal in various ways, including the formation of a Task Force in May 1998 to investigate possible criminal and administrative violations. By January 2000, the Task Force had 21 full-time personnel. In conjunction with the LAPD's Internal Affairs Group, the Task Force is continuing its investigation. The Task Force is investigating 50 to 100 "priority" case files at this time.

On September 21, 1999, Chief of Police Bernard C. Parks convened a Board of Inquiry (BOI) to look into the Rampart scandal independent of the LAPD Task Force and the Internal Affairs

Group. On March 1, 2000, the BOI produced an extensive Public Report that listed 108 conclusions and recommendations for consideration by the Board of Police Commissioners.

Because the Rampart corruption allegations centered on the CRASH Unit, the LAPD reviewed the structure and effectiveness of these special anti-gang CRASH units. On March 6, 2000, in Special Order No. 6, Chief Parks ordered the CRASH units disbanded and created Special Enforcement Units (SEU) in each Area.

Making Sense of the Rampart Scandal

Specialized police units are designed to support patrol functions and to focus on specific crime problems that require special law enforcement efforts such as narcotics, gangs and vice. Officers assigned to these specialized units receive additional training focused on their area of specialization. They tend to develop a greater sense of camaraderie within each unit as a natural result of their specialized responsibilities, training, and close working relationships. On the negative side, the officers in these specialized units, by virtue of their insularity, are subject to the risk, if they are not strongly supervised, of becoming overly zealous, and losing focus on their sworn duty to serve as impartial enforcers of the criminal laws.

In the early 1990's, Rampart CRASH was a prized assignment for the Department's most promising young officers. For example, one of the officers implicated by Perez had received 63 commendations and community letters of appreciation for outstanding arrests, outstanding field tactics, gang expertise, aggressive police street work, dedication to duty, commitment, teamwork, initiative and professionalism. Rampart CRASH has been described as a tight, hard working unit with perhaps too much work and too little support from its chain of command. The BOI recounts that many of the line officers were disrespectful, resistant and unreceptive to suggestions from officers, management and training personnel outside Rampart Area. In place of appropriate respect for the police department they served, Rampart CRASH officers developed an enhanced loyalty to each other and to the unit's way of doing things.

This disrespect for the command structure is partially attributable to the command's lack of attention to the practices and procedures of Rampart CRASH. Supervisors effectively deferred to CRASH to monitor itself. This lack of control over Rampart CRASH sent a clear message to its officers that they were a police force unto themselves, governed only by their own rules, and free to take the law into their own hands if that would further the mission of CRASH. At Rampart, the failure to impose adequate supervision and controls over CRASH officers resulted in a heightened sense of insularity which reinforced and perpetuated an "us versus them" mentality among Rampart CRASH officers.

This set the stage for the siege mentality that appears to have taken hold among Rampart CRASH officers as they battled gang activity in Los Angeles. These officers, who were assigned the task of responding to the burgeoning gang problem plaguing the area, succumbed to the temptation to win the war on crime at any cost, to sacrifice civil liberties in order to reduce the danger posed by street gangs, and to imprison suspects likely to have committed unknown and unprovable crimes rather than allow them to remain at large where they might have the opportunity to commit such crimes in the future. These systematic abuses of authority at Rampart, and LAPD's failure to recognize and respond to "the end justifies the means" mentality that gave rise to it, underscores the need for routine transfers among specially assigned officers, as well as a careful monitoring of the attitudes and tactics of the officers assigned to such specialized units.

Responsibility for the Rampart misconduct doesn't lie with a single individual, but with a relatively small group of renegade police officers whose misdeeds went unchecked as a result of a systematic failure of supervision and leadership throughout the chain of command. Ironically, it was the very effectiveness of Rampart CRASH that planted the seeds for its eventual corruption. Focused on arrest statistics and the inroads made by CRASH into the Rampart crime problem, commanding officers and supervisors neglected their oversight duties, and the LAPD simply stopped policing its own. Thus, they failed to detect:

- A high number of arrest reports containing similar or identical language describing probable cause for the arrest.

- A high number of CRASH officers reporting that suspects were discarding weapons or drugs in plain view, just a few feet away from them.
- The use of informants in violation of LAPD policy.
- CRASH officers approving their own bookings and arrest reports.
- The inclusion of less than 50% of arrests in the Rampart CRASH arrest book, a document reviewed by the unit supervisor for auditing purposes.

In interviews of LAPD officers, members of the Panel were told that many of the sergeants at Rampart CRASH lacked sufficient experience prior to their arrival at Rampart and often did not stay in the assignment long enough to receive appropriate training. Thus, the sergeants failed to adequately supervise, question and audit officers who produced outstanding statistics. Beyond the sergeants, however, lieutenants and captains failed to detect patterns of misconduct, and staff officers ignored warning signs and failed to insist on the necessary oversight.

Rampart is a densely populated, gang-infested, high-crime area. Rampart CRASH was exceedingly productive as measured by the number of felony arrests, drug and weapon seizures, prosecutions, convictions, and resulting reduced crime statistics. Rampart lieutenants and captains were keenly aware of these impressive statistics. At the same time, they failed to conduct frequent unannounced field inspections, or to spend sufficient time in the field monitoring CRASH officers. Instead, there was an over-emphasis on field productivity in the form of arrests and contraband seizures. Coupled with a failure throughout the chain of command to perform essential supervision, oversight, and meaningful audits/verifications necessary to ensure compliance with existing rules, this led to an atmosphere in which the Rampart misconduct could occur and ultimately result in the systematic violation of the public's rights.

Rampart CRASH was not audited for a period of two years between 1995 and 1997. The Operations–Central Bureau lieutenant who was responsible for auditing Rampart CRASH made it known at the time that Rampart detectives refused to provide him with statistics and sergeant's log books necessary to complete an audit. When the detectives' refusal was brought to the attention of a Ram-

part lieutenant, nothing was done. Thereafter, the Central Bureau
lieutenant reported this failure to cooperate to the deputy chief in
charge of the Central Bureau. Yet again the complaint fell on deaf
ears. In the words of one interviewee, "[t]he Department simply
didn't have the will to manage properly."

It does not appear that command and staff officers have accepted
any responsibility for the Rampart scandal. A captain who has since
been promoted to commander stated that it would be unfair to hold
commanding officers responsible for the stations because they are
simply too busy. No one at the Bureau apparently was concerned
that Rampart CRASH had not been audited for two years, even
though, as one high-ranking official noted, it was generally known
throughout the Department that Rampart CRASH was difficult to
supervise and had developed its own culture and aggressive approach to the gang problem.

The Rampart scandal thus raises broad questions about the
LAPD. The failure of field officers to follow standard procedures,
the failure of sergeants to audit field officers who produced outstanding statistics, the failure of lieutenants and captains to ensure
that proper auditing procedures were followed, and the failure of
staff officers to insist upon adequate auditing procedures collectively resulted in an absence of fundamental management controls
that should have revealed evidence of systematic abuses of power
by Rampart CRASH officers. To prevent these failures from recurring, it is imperative that they be addressed energetically and imagi-
natively, by both the Department and by the City as a whole.

Reform in the Wake of the Rampart Scandal

The most serious allegations of police misconduct and corruption
in the Rampart scandal are based primarily on allegations made by
Officer Perez. His statements must necessarily be viewed with caution. He has admitted having repeatedly committed perjury and
having prepared false police reports in order to obtain convictions
against gang members in drug and weapons cases, and to cover up
his own thefts. Further, Perez had a strong incentive to implicate
other officers to satisfy the conditions of his plea agreement. By

pleading guilty and cooperating against other officers, Perez reduced his prison sentence from twelve years to five years.

Ultimately, it may be impossible to determine whether Rafael Perez is telling the truth in all respects and the nature and extent of police misconduct on the part of Rampart CRASH officers. Some of the questions about the specific crimes allegedly committed by LAPD officers will be dealt with under the microscope of civil lawsuits and criminal prosecutions in the future. What Perez and Rampart did was open the eyes of the LAPD, public officials, and the community to fundamental issues about the Los Angeles Police Department. . . . Officer-Involved Shooting (OIS) teams . . . [that] . . . failed to find out that Rampart CRASH officers . . . shot unarmed suspects and then planted guns to justify the shootings. . . . officers . . . [who failed] . . . to come forward to report misconduct by other officers, including the misconduct that Perez has now admitted he committed. . . . the Department's risk management systems . . . [that] . . . failed to . . . respond to "clearly identifiable patterns"; . . . [and] the LAPD's ethics and culture . . . [and] . . . the recruitment and training of its officers that allowed this scandal to occur. . . .

Editors' Postscript

In mid-November 2000, the first LAPD Rampart Division criminal trial ended with a jury finding three of four former officers guilty of framing gang members and planting evidence. One month later, the judge in that case overturned the convictions because her own error caused some jurors to be confused by irrelevant police jargon. The district attorney is appealing her latest ruling. See James Sterngold, "3 of 4 Officers Convicted in Police Corruption Case," *The New York Times*, November 16, 2000, p. A18; Twila Decker and Henry Weinstein, "D. A. Seeks to Reinstate Rampart Case Convictions," *The Los Angeles Times*, January 12, 2001, p. B1.

14

Chained Factory Fire Exits

Media Coverage of a Corporate Crime
That Killed 25 Workers

John P. Wright, Francis T. Cullen, and Michael B. Blankenship

The news media are frequently chastised for presenting a misleading portrayal of crime (Graber 1980; Lotz 1991; Marsh 1989). In
this view, the media function as a "carnival mirror" (Reiman 1990)
who distort reality by focusing disproportionately on street crime,
particularly violent offenses. The media thus neglect other types
of crime, especially corporate lawlessness (Garofalo 1981; Marsh
1989; Reiman 1990). This omission, the argument goes, helps to
reproduce inequality by directing public attention away from the
enormous costs—including violent costs—associated with the "crimes
of the powerful" (Hills 1987; Reiman 1990).

Although criminologists have argued that corporate illegality has
largely been ignored by the media, it is possible that this situation
is changing. Over the past 15 years, observe various commentators,
there has been a social movement against white-collar and corporate crime (Cullen, Maakestad, and Cavender 1987; Katz 1980;
Kramer 1989). This movement arguably has altered public sentiment against—and aroused interest in—acts of corporate crime. In
this context, the media not only may have provided an outlet for
the dissemination of information about corporate lawlessness but
also may have facilitated the continuation of the social movement.

These considerations raise the issue of the extent to which the
media have changed their coverage of corporate violence. Do they
continue to present distorted images of crime or are they in fact
contributing to the continued social movement against corporate

From "The Social Construction of Corporate Violence: Media Coverage of the
Imperial Food Products Fire," *Crime and Delinquency*, Vol. 41, pp. 20–36. Copyright © 1995 by Sage Publications. Reprinted by permission.

misconduct? In particular, are they defining corporate harms—including violence—as criminal? . . .

Building on previous research, our study attempts to address these issues by exploring newspaper coverage of an incident of corporate violence: the deaths and injuries resulting from the fire at the North Carolina plant of Imperial Food Products, Inc. As a case study, the generalizability of our research is inherently limited. Even so, the features of this case may make it especially useful in discerning the extent to which the news media are willing to construct corporate violence as criminal. . . .

Death in the Workplace

Chicken processing plants dot the southern region of the United States. The Imperial Food Products, Inc., plant was no exception to this pattern. Located in Hamlet, North Carolina, close to the state's southern border, the plant was the primary employer in the community.

On September 3, 1991, the plant caught fire. After workers had repaired a hydraulic line located above a large vat of grease, the line burst, spraying a flammable liquid into the 400° oil in the vat. The fire spread rapidly, and thick soot-filled smoke engulfed the plant. Of the plant's 230 workers, 90 were in the plant at the time the fire started. Of these, 25 died and 56 were injured. The plant suffered extensive damage, and the community lost its largest employer (see Aulette and Michalowski 1993).

Immediately, survivors reported that exit doors had been either locked or blocked and that their escape from the plant had been severely hampered. Apparently, the firm's owner, Emmett Roe, had authorized the doors to be padlocked due to suspected employee's pilferage of chicken parts.

The locked doors, however, were only part of the problem. The building, which was over 100 years old, did not have a plantwide sprinkler system. The plant had no windows to provide an alternate escape route and too few exit doors in critical areas. In its 11 years of operation, the plant had never been inspected by the state's Occupational Safety and Health Administration (OSHA).

An inquiry into the plant fire was initiated almost immediately—on September 4—under the direction of the State Bureau of Investigation. A week later, the AFL-CIO petitioned the federal OSHA to withdraw North Carolina's approval to operate independently from federal OSHA. After a series of meetings, the labor department did just that, taking over part of the state's workplace safety program on October 24, 1991. In response, the state agreed to hire 27 new safety inspectors, and, in August of 1992, the state legislature, amid controversy, enacted 12 workplace safety bills. Federal OSHA withdrew its threats to take over the state's OSHA program.

In the interim period, however, the State Department of Insurance found that the plant was in violation of nine sections of building codes and six state laws. In response, the state labor department fined Imperial Food Products, Inc., $808,150 for its willful and serious violations. Concurrently, on March 10, 1992, Emmett Roe, his son Brad, and the plant manager, James N. Hair were indicted on 25 counts each of involuntary manslaughter. If convicted, each man could have been sentenced to 250 years in prison.

After a series of negotiations with the state, Emmett Roe pleaded guilty to 25 counts of involuntary manslaughter. Under the plea agreement, Brad Roe and James N. Hair were not prosecuted. Emmett Roe received a 19-year, 6-month sentence but could be paroled in 2½ years.

Method

Sample

To assess coverage of the Imperial Food Products case, we conducted a content analysis of 10 newspapers: the *Boston Globe,* the *Chicago Tribune,* the *Los Angeles Times,* the *New York Times,* the *Wall Street Journal,* the *Washington Post,* the *Cincinnati Post,* the *Cincinnati Enquirer,* the *Cleveland Plain Dealer,* and the *Louisville Courier Journal.* These newspapers represent a cross-section of the United States and include several newspapers with national readership. . . .

Content Categories

After reviewing the literature on corporate crime, we developed content categories that measured important dimensions of the case: cause, harm, intent, responsibility, and sanctions. These were used to code the stories on the case. Each line of each story was coded by the first author and a trained assistant. In case of disagreement, which occurred infrequently, an impartial third party was used to solve the disagreement.

Cause. Early reports questioned whether the fire could have been prevented if the workers had followed more rigorous safety standards. Thus, the content category *cause* is divided into three dimensions: worker negligence of safety an issue, worker negligence not an issue, and none or no discussion of cause. The two categories gauge how the cause of the fire was portrayed. References to improper maintenance were coded as worker negligence an issue. Characterizations of the cause of the fire as an accident were coded as worker negligence not an issue.

Harm. Swigert and Farrell (1980) found that the personalization of harm played an important role in media depictions of the Ford Pinto trial. As a result, we analyzed stories for reference to three types of harm. First, direct harm refers to reports on those killed in the fire. Second, residual harm relates to references to the negative effects experienced by the victims' families and friends. Third, community harm covers depictions of the harm suffered by the community, such as the loss of jobs and the subsequent fiscal impact. Finally, a subcategory labeled "none" measured the absence of any reference to harm.

Intent. Traditionally, intent has played a pivotal role in the criminal prosecution of corporate crimes (Cullen et al. 1987). By using the term *intent,* we do not mean to infer that those responsible maliciously calculated the deaths of their employees. Instead, intent refers to the circumstances surrounding the incident that were responsible for the case being defined as manslaughter and not as an accident. We therefore constructed the intent category using two dimensions: references to overt intent, such as padlocked doors, and references to indirect intent, such as no sprinkler system and general plant conditions. A subcategory labeled "none" measured the absence of any reference to intent.

Responsibility.   Morash and Hale (1987) and Evans and Lundman (1983) both found that the media concentrates on the acts of individuals and largely neglects the context within which the acts take place. To construct this category, we used three dimensions that reflect different realms of responsibility. First, management refers to instances in which responsibility for the workers' deaths was placed on individual plant owners and managers. Second, company refers to references that the company (Imperial Food Products, Inc.) was responsible for the deaths. Third, given the importance of regulatory agencies in this story, we included a dimension labeled regulatory. This dimension includes instances in which regulatory agencies were held responsible for the workers' deaths. A subcategory labeled "none" measured the absence of any reference to responsibility.

Sanctions.   This category was composed of three elements. First, the criminal element relates to references to possible or actual criminal charges. Second, civil relates to instances in which stories made reference to the possibility of civil sanctions. Third, regulatory refers to possible or actual sanctions leveled by regulatory agencies. A subcategory labeled "none" measured the absence of any reference to sanctions.

Time intervals.   As illustrated by Swigert and Farrell (1980), news coverage is a dynamic process that changes over time. We therefore categorized three distinct time intervals that corresponded to important happenings (see Table 14.1). The first time interval began on the first day of coverage, September 4, 1991, and ended 1 week later. This period was chosen to allow newspapers time to cover the incident. The second interval began at the end of Interval 1 and continued through to the day before the criminal conviction was announced, September 13, 1992. During this time, the prosecutor announced indictments of the plant owner and managers on manslaughter charges. The third interval began on the day the conviction was announced and ended 1 week later. This method allowed us to gauge the evolution of the story and to provide the basis for comparisons in the degree of coverage.

Results

Coverage

Of the 10 newspapers in the sample, 9 covered the plant fire. Of these, 5 ran the initial news of the fire on the front page. Over the course of the week, however, the priority of the story faded as follow-up reports were placed further back in the paper. This finding holds across time intervals. As seen in Table 14.1, the mean page number for Interval 1 is page 6, the mean page number for Interval 2 is page 14, and the mean page number for Interval 3 is page 15. It is clear that as the story continued to unfold, newspapers accorded it less priority. This is especially noteworthy given that the sentence was handed down in Interval 3, the interval with the least amount of coverage.

The mean number of lines and paragraphs per story reflects a qualitative shift in reporting styles. Interval 1 encompassed most of the coverage, with 68% ($n = 34$) of the 50 total stories falling within the first week after the fire. The mean number of lines per story (111.4) and paragraphs (17.2), however, do not reflect the wide

TABLE 14.1
Newspaper Coverage of the Imperial Food Products Fire

| Characteristic of coverage | Time interval | | |
	First week	After first week and before conviction	Criminal conviction
Mean page number	6.0	14.0	15.0
Mean number of lines	111.4	125.0	61.8
Mean number of paragraphs	17.2	20.0	10.5
Number of newspapers covering story	9.0	3.0	4.0
Total number of stories	34.0	10.0	6.0

variation in reporting length. For instance, the number of lines per story ranged from 17 to 312; the number of paragraphs ranged from 1 to 44.

Table 14.1 indicates that in Interval 2, there was a substantial reduction in the number of stories ($n = 10$), but an increase in mean line and paragraph length. In short, stories were fewer, but those that were written were lengthier than in Interval 1. Again, however, variation in coverage is apparent, with the number of lines ranging from 38 to 435 and number of paragraphs from 5 to 68.

In Interval 3, we see a further reduction in the number of stones ($n = 6$). Not only were there fewer stories, but also the mean length of the stories was substantially reduced. As we will discuss later, the ramifications of the lack of coverage may have important implications for social policy.

Harm

Table 14.2 indicates that the media focused quite heavily on the harm produced by the fire. References of direct harm to victims outpaced all other subcategories in each time interval. Significant differences exist, however, in the media's portrayal of both residual and community harm between Interval 1 and Interval 2. During Interval 1, the newspapers focused primarily on the victims of the blaze. In Interval 2, however, references to residual and community harm significantly increased. Interval 2 can be characterized by a qualitative shift in reporting. Stories in this period concentrated on the damage done by the fire, on the lives of the survivors, and on the memories of the deaths of family and friends.

Culpability

Cause. As seen in Table 14.2, the origin of the fire was largely ignored in news reports (i.e., whether or not worker negligence caused the hydraulic line to burst and set the plant on fire). Of the stories in Interval 1, 47% ($n = 16$) did not mention the cause of the fire. This pattern holds across intervals. For example, 50% ($n = 5$) of the stories in Interval 2 and 33% of the stories in Interval 3 did not mention the cause of the fire.

TABLE 14.2
Incident Characteristics by Time Interval

Incident characteristic	Time interval		
	First week	After first week and before conviction	Criminal conviction
Harm			
Direct	10.9	11.2	4.0
Residual	3.0	8.3	3.0
Community	1.5	7.5	1.2
Number of stories not mentioning harm	0.0	0.0	0.0
Immediate cause of fire			
Worker negligence—not an issue	3.9	3.2	1.5
Worker negligence—an issue	0.0	2.1	1.0
Number of stories not mentioning cause	16.0	5.0	2.0
Intent			
Overt	7.3	5.4	3.2
Indirect	7.4	8.3	1.7
Number of stories not mentioning intent	1.0	0.0	0.0
Responsibility			
Management	1.5	3.0	2.2
Company	0.3	0.4	0.3
Regulatory	6.9	6.8	1.2
Number of stories not mentioning responsibility	8.0	0.0	0.0
Sanction			
Criminal	0.9	3.0	5.2
Civil	0.1	1.6	0.8
Regulatory	0.0	2.4	1.3
Number of stories not mentioning sanction	23.0	1.0	0.0

Note: Mean number of lines per story reported unless otherwise indicated.

Intent. A distinctive feature of this industrial tragedy was that a number of the plant's exit doors had been padlocked. Table 14.2 indicates that such "overt intent" was widely depicted in the media. However, the media did not limit its coverage to the doors being locked; they also focused on the unsafe conditions of the plant. As seen in Table 14.2, in the first two intervals, indirect intent, such as plant conditions, was focused on as much if not more than the doors being locked. It was not until Interval 3, the time of the criminal conviction, that the media focused more attention on the importance of the locked doors.

These findings suggest that the media attempted to bring to light the excessive risks associated with working in this particular plant. The padlocking of the doors was typically portrayed as part of a larger problem of management indifference and/or of lax regulatory oversight. In other words, the reports did not exclude the context in which the event transpired, a finding that differs from past research. We should note, however, that the final shift in the proportion of attention given to the locked doors occurred in Interval 3, exactly when coverage was at its lowest.

Responsibility. Again, past research suggests that the media will focus on the acts of individuals and remove them from the context in which the acts took place (Evans and Lundman 1983; Morash and Hale 1987). Our data, however, do not support such a contention. Early on, blame for the fire was assigned to the state's regulatory agency. The state of North Carolina OSHA had never inspected the plant in its 11 years of operation, even though the building was over 100 years old and lacked modern safety equipment, such as a sprinkler system.

Table 14.2 indicates that coverage critical of the actions of regulatory agencies emerged immediately and continued through Interval 2. In Interval 1, coverage attributing the plant fire to lax regulation was over four times more likely than coverage blaming a lack of management accountability. Even in Interval 2, coverage of regulatory responsibility was twice as likely as coverage of management culpability. It was not until Interval 3, when the conviction of the defendant was announced, that a shift occurred in assessing blame. In short, throughout much of its initial coverage, the media primarily laid blame for the fire on a lack of state regulatory oversight and inspection that allowed unsafe and hazardous conditions to exist.

Sanctions

Overall, Table 14.2 indicates that coverage of possible or actual sanctions was minimal across all time periods. In Interval 1, for example,72% of the stories failed to mention any sort of possible sanctions. When they did, the coverage amounted to an average of 1 line. Even though this incident was potentially criminal, and even in the wake of numerous deaths and injuries, the media did not initially define the act as criminal. It was not until the second interval, when manslaughter indictments were announced, that discussions of criminal sanctions emerged in the stories. And only in the third interval did discussions of criminal penalties receive a strong priority. It is instructive, however, that as depictions and definitions of criminal penalties emerged in the latter time periods, coverage became even more limited.

It appears that the media are hesitant to label acts of corporate violence as criminal—or are not conscious of this possibility—even with the clear presence of aggravating circumstances. Instead, the reports did not define the deaths as criminal until the government deemed the act as a potential and then an actual criminal violation. Of course, this stands in contrast to forms of traditional violence where the press immediately ask if criminal charges will be filed.

We should also note that when the plea agreement was reached, and the sentence was handed down, only 40% of the newspapers covered the story. Further, the coverage can be characterized as minimal, with only 5 stories highlighting the sentence. Not only was the mean page number pushed back to page 15, but also the mean number of lines and paragraphs was significantly reduced from previous time intervals. The newspapers in our sample did not see the event as a priority for coverage, even though the criminal penalty was one of the most severe sentences ever given to a corporate executive.

Discussion

. . . The newspaper coverage of the Imperial Food Products case clearly detailed the enormous harm from the fire: the deaths and injuries, the suffering of family members and relatives, and the damage to the social fabric and economy of the community. It is noteworthy, moreover, that the newspaper reports did not define the case simply as an industrial accident or as being due to worker negligence. In short, the reports readily depicted corporate violence and did not seek to localize responsibility in terms of bad luck (accident) or blaming the victim (the workers).

Even so, the newspapers showed little consciousness that corporate violence might be seen as a crime. The reports did not initially define the deaths as homicides, nor did they raise the possibility that the corporation or individual executives might be eligible for prosecution. In essence, the media was not proactive, but reactive: It was not until the government announced the manslaughter indictments and, in particular, the plea bargain that the criminality of the violence was reported. This attention, however, occurred after the first time interval, during which the coverage was the least extensive and least prominently placed in the newspapers.

Instead of a potential criminal offense, the news reports socially constructed the worker deaths as a breakdown in government safety regulation. The reports thus focused not only on the padlocked doors, which might have served as a safety exit, but also on the plant's general hazardous conditions and the failure of OSHA to conduct an inspection of working conditions.

This construction of corporate violence likely was not inconsequential. Although we do not know how media coverage influenced subsequent policy decisions, it is instructive that, under pressure from OSHA in Washington, DC, substantive regulatory reform was undertaken in North Carolina. As noted, the legislature enacted 12 new workplace safety laws and 27 additional safety inspectors were hired. If nothing else, the media coverage served to reinforce, not question, these policy initiatives.

Yet, again, the newspaper reports did not serve to transform the consciousness of the public and business community so that corporate violence would be seen as criminal—a transformation that scholars since Ross (1907) have argued is necessary (Hills 1987; Mokhiber 1988). Even though the violence was enormous and the grounds for a prosecution were apparent (e.g., locked safety exits), and even though precedents existed for prosecuting workplace deaths (Cullen et al. 1987; Farber and Green 1988; Frank 1985), the national media did not focus on the potential criminality of the corporate managers.

The lack of coverage devoted to the outcome of the case—the manslaughter convictions—also is noteworthy. Again, although it was a major case of corporate violence, the criminal conviction of the company's owner either was not covered or was conveyed in a relatively short report placed deep within the pages of the newspaper. This coverage thus limited the power this conviction might have had to exert educative or deterrent effects; that is, to have educated the public about the moral boundaries of corporate risk-taking and to have shown corporate managers that creating or tolerating safety hazards can make them criminally liable (Cullen et al. 1987; Swigert and Farrell 1980).

In short, although the role of the media might vary under other circumstances, the Imperial Food Products case suggests that reporters—including those at the nation's most influential newspapers—are unlikely to be instrumental in defining corporate violence as criminal and, more broadly, of leading efforts to implement policies that would make the use of the criminal law against corporate personnel more prevalent. Instead, as in this case of workplace violence, which saw the district attorney file manslaughter charges, it seems that local prosecutors, not the media, may be the key actors in socially constructing corporate violence as lawlessness.

· · ·

Although we have endeavored to analyze the data objectively, the discerning reader will detect that a prescriptive message informs our discussion: the news media *should* have been more proactive in criminalizing the harms of the Imperial Food Products fire and, more generally, should play a role in the movement against corporate violence. This critical appraisal of the media is value-laden but is not idiosyncratic: It reflects three themes common to the criminological literature.

First, as noted above, the news media have not traditionally treated corporate violence as criminal despite the enormous costs this form of violence imposes on society. Arguably, a duty exists for them to do so (see Linsky 1988). Second, because the media often distort the reality of crime—street as well as corporate law-lessness—they have a shaky claim to objectivity, "to merely reporting the facts." The issue is not if the media will construct a reality about crime, but rather which reality they will set forth (Elias 1994; Fishman 1978, 1980; Marsh 1989). Third, the reality constructed by the media frequently does not serve noble ends but is shaped by occupational/organizational self-interest (e.g., advancing careers, boosting ratings) and by larger power structures in society (Barak 1988; Leiber, Jamieson, and Krohn 1993). With these themes as a background, the failure of the press to criminalize the plant workers' deaths in North Carolina is seen not as judicious reporting but as part of an institutional pattern detrimental to the commonweal.

In fairness, a more sympathetic assessment of newspaper coverage of the Imperial Food Products fire is possible. Reporters legitimately could be praised for exercising restraint in not criminalizing this incident and in providing local prosecutors with the space to weigh the existing evidence and to let justice run its course (restraint that seems in short supply in cases involving rock stars and football heroes). Prematurely portraying corporate managers as crass criminals may have caused these individuals unfair public shame and spurred their unwarranted prosecution. Before casting accusations against corporations, moreover, reporters also must weigh whether they will expose their employers to legal liability and public embarrassment (Weiser 1993).

This perspective is weakened, however, by two considerations emphasized previously. First, the reporters covering the plant fire did not remain neutral compilers of facts but rather quickly developed as their angle—their paradigm for explaining the fire—the theme of regulatory breakdown. In short, they socially constructed the case, not as a crime in and of itself. Second, and perhaps most important, the newspapers can be criticized for the lack of coverage given when the case officially became a crime (i.e., when the plea agreement and prison sentence were announced). This disinterest undoubtedly is not peculiar to corporate violence—"journalists take to heart the old saying that yesterday's newspaper wraps today's fish" (Linsky 1988, p. 215)—but nonetheless, it is consequential. Although many citizens across the nation may have heard about the tragic loss of life in the chicken-processing plant, how many ever were informed that the workers' deaths were manslaughters? . . .

Whether the media had a duty to raise the prospect that the deaths at the Imperial Food Products plant were "criminal" is a value question of consequence. Admittedly, in cases involving corporate violence, criminologists—and we are no exceptions—may be overly ideological and perhaps too quick to criticize when news reporters do not immediately define such harms as criminal. At the same time, criminologists may well serve the commonweal when they unmask the implicit biases of reporters and challenge the media to join the public discourse concerning the seriousness and potential criminality of corporate violence.

References

Aulette, Judy R. and Raymond Michalowski. 1993. "Fire in Hamlet: A Case Study of a State-Corporate Crime." Pp. 171–206 in *Political Crime in Contemporary America,* edited by K. D. Tunnell. New York: Garland.

Barak, Gregg. 1988. "Newsmaking Criminology: Reflections on the Media, Intellectuals, and Crime." *Justice Quarterly* 5:565–87.

Cullen, Francis T., William J. Maakestad, and Gray Cavender. 1987. *Corporate Crime Under Attack: The Ford Pinto Case and Beyond.* Cincinnati, OH: Anderson.

Elias, Robert. 1994. "Official Stories: Media Coverage of American Crime Policy." *The Humanist* 54:3–8.

Evans, Sandra S. and Richard J. Lundman. 1983. "Newspaper Coverage of Corporate Price-Fixing." *Criminology* 21:529–41.

Farber, Stephan and Marc Green. 1988. *Outrageous Conduct: Art, Ego, and the Twilight Zone Case.* New York: Morrow.

Fishman, Mark. 1978. "Crime Waves as Ideology." *Social Problems* 25:531–43.

———. 1980. *Manufacturing News.* Austin: University of Texas Press.

Frank, Nancy. 1985. *Crimes Against Health and Safety.* New York: Harrow & Heston.

Garofalo, James. 1981. "Crime and the Mass Media: A Selective Review of Research." *Journal of Research in Crime and Delinquency* 18:319–50.

Graber, Doris A. 1980. *Crime News and the Public.* New York: Praeger.

Hills, Stuart L. 1987. *Corporate Violence: Injury and Profit for Death.* Totowa, NJ: Rowman and Littlefield.

Katz, Jack. 1980. "The Social Movement Against White-Collar Crime." Pp. 161–84 in *Criminology Review Yearbook,* edited by E. Bittner and S. Messinger. Beverly Hills, CA: Sage.

Kramer, Ronald C. 1989. "Criminologists and the Social Movement Against Corporate Crime." *Social Justice* 16:146–64.

Leiber, Michael J., Katherine M. Jamieson, and Marvin D Krohn. 1993. "Newspaper Reporting and the Production of Deviance: Drug Use Among Professional Athletes." *Deviant Behavior* 14:317–39.

Linsky, Martin. 1988. "The Media and Public Deliberation." Pp. 205–27 in *The Power of Public Ideas,* edited by R. Reich. Cambridge: Harvard University Press.

Lotz, Roy. 1991. *Crime and the American Press.* New York: Praeger.

Lynch, Michael J., Mahesh K. Nalla, and Keith W. Miller. 1989. "Cross-Cultural Perceptions of Deviance: The Case of Bhopal." *Journal of Research in Crime and Delinquency* 26:7–35.

Marsh, Harry L. 1989. "Newspaper Crime Coverage in the U.S.: 1893–1988." *Journal of Criminal Justice* 19:67–78.

Mokhiber, Russell. 1988. *Corporate Crime and Violence: Big Business Power and the Abuse of the Public Trust.* San Francisco: Sierra Club Books.

Morash, Merry and Donna Hale. 1987. "Unusual Crime or Crime as Unusual? Images of Corruption at the Interstate Commerce Commission." Pp. 129–49 in *Organized Crime in America: Concepts and Controversies,* edited by T. S. Bynum. Monsey, NY: Criminal Justice Press.

Reiman, Jeffery. 1990. *The Rich Get Richer and the Poor Get Prison.* 3rd ed. New York: Wiley.

Swigert, Victoria L. and Ronald A. Farrell. 1980. "Corporate Homicide: Definitional Processes in the Creation of Deviance." *Law and Society Review* 15:161–82.

Weiser, Benjamin. 1993. "TV's Credibility Crunch: NBC's Staging of a GM Truck Crash Puts the Focus on Television News Ethics." *Washington Post National Weekly Edition,* March 8–14, pp. 6–8.

Editors' Postscript

The plant's owner, Emmett Roe, was paroled in April 1997 after serving four and one-half years of his 20-year sentence. Mr. Roe is in his early 70s, lives in Atlanta, and visits North Carolina only to see his oncologist. His company is bankrupt and he reportedly works menial jobs to cover his expenses. See John Coutlakis, "Roe Freed From Prison," *Asheville Citizen-Times* (North Carolina), April 19, 1997, p. B2, and North Carolina State Government News Service, *The Insider* V. 5 No. 74 (April 18, 1997): 6.

15
Pinto Madness
Flaws in the Generally Accepted Landmark Narrative
Matthew T. Lee and M. David Ermann

Conventional wisdom holds that Ford Motor Company decided to rush the Pinto into production in 1970 to compete with compact foreign imports, despite internal pre-production tests that showed gas tank ruptures in low-speed rear-end collisions would produce deadly fires. This decision purportedly derived from an infamous seven-page cost-benefit analysis (the "Grush/Saunby Report" [1973]) that valued human lives at $200,000. Settling burn victims' lawsuits would have cost $49.5 million, far less than the $137 million needed to make minor corrections. According to this account, the company made an informed, cynical, and impressively coordinated decision that "payouts" (Kelman and Hamilton 1989:311) to families of burn victims were more cost-effective than improving fuel tank integrity. This description provides the unambiguous foundation on which the media and academics have built a Pinto gas tank decision-making narrative.

The Pinto as Landmark Narrative

The Pinto story has become a "landmark narrative" (Nichols 1997:324), a definitive story used to support the construction of amoral corporate behavior as a pervasive social problem, This narrative was first stated publicly by investigative journalist Mark Dowie

From "Pinto 'Madness' as a Flawed Landmark Narrative: An Organizational and Network Analysis," *Social Problems,* Vol. 46, pp. 30–47. Copyright © 1999 by Society for the Study of Social Problems. Reprinted by permission.

(1977) in a scathing Pulitzer Prize-winning exposé, "Pinto Madness," published in *Mother Jones* magazine. Dowie essentially makes three claims about the distinctiveness of the Pinto case: 1) the car had unique safety problems, 2) key decision-makers understood these problems, and 3) those decision-makers made explicit, clearly unethical decisions based on the goal of profit maximization.

The first claim was that the Pinto was more dangerous than other cars, directly producing "hundreds" (Kramer 1982:76) of excess deaths. Three facts reinforce the Pinto's distinctiveness: a Pinto burn victim was awarded a record $125 million in punitive damages in a civil trial; the Pinto was the subject of the largest recall in automobile history at its time; and Ford was the subject of an unprecedented criminal trial over an issue of product safety. In his book on the Pinto case, *Chicago Tribune* reporter Lee Strobel (1980:169) aptly characterized the Pinto as the "most controversial car ever built."

Second, Ford decision makers were allegedly well-aware of the Pinto's apparently dangerous defect. Dowie's (1977:20) conspiratorial account refers to crash tests at a "top-secret site" that conclusively demonstrated the Pinto's safety problem. He claims Ford collected and then systematically suppressed data proving that the Pinto was a "firetrap" (Dowie 1977:18). Presumably, if such data had become available to government agencies or public interest groups, Ford would have been forced to fix the gas tank.

The third claim infers a "deliberate" (Kramer 1982:75) and unethical decision to cover up rather than fix the Pinto's defect. This decision flowed from an amoral, economic calculation and was justified in terms of "Ford's need for profit" (Clarke 1988:297). According to Dowie (1977:20, emphasis in the original) Ford did not fix the defect for eight years (until forced to do so by federal regulation) "because its internal 'cost-benefit analysis,' *which places a dollar value on human life*, said it wasn't profitable to make the changes sooner."[1] This "smoking gun"—a table from an allegedly internal Ford document (the Grush/Saunby cost-benefit analysis)—has since been reprinted countless times in academic discussions as the epitome of the "cold-blooded

---

1. Dowie (1977) accurately explains in part of his *Mother Jones* article that Ford employees wrote this document as part of an on-going lobbying effort to influence NHTSA (24, 28). But his readers have relied exclusively on his other claim, that it was the "internal" (20, 24) memo on which Ford based its decision to market the dangerous Pinto and settle the few inevitable lawsuits (31).

calculus" (Mokhiber 1989:376) at the heart of most deviant corporate actions (see also Anderson 1989; Birsch and Fielder 1994; Coleman 1985; Cullen, Maakestad and Cavender 1984, 1987; Fisse and Braithwaite 1987; Gioia 1992; Simon 1999; Simon and Eitzen 1990; Skolnick and Currie 1979; Strobel 1980).

This is how the Pinto case is taught to students. At an organizational level of analysis, Simon and Eitzen (1990:5; see also Simon 1999) describe the Pinto as the "most notorious" example of a corporation "willfully" marketing a product "known to be dangerous." The capitalist imperative of profit maximization is the dominant explanatory variable. A typical summary from a criminology textbook: "Choosing profit over human lives, the company continued to avoid and lobby even eight years later against federal safety standards that would have forced modification of the gas tank" (Hagan 1994:376). Individual level explanations adopt a similar tone. One social problems text explains Pinto decisions in terms of Ford president Lee Iacocca's "insatiable desires" (Doob 1995:35), while an edited reader points to "sociopathic" (Greenberg 1993:88) executives.

The Pinto narrative is a sociological benchmark by which other organizational deviance cases are judged (cf. Kelman and Hamilton 1989; Vaughan 1996, 1998). It has been repeated so often that contemporary academic discussions of the case often occur without citations (e.g., Nichols 1997:327). Jackall (1988:5) uses it to illustrate vocabularies which "have become so institutionalized . . . that whole sets of assumptions and taken for granted analyses, often complete with settled moral judgments, are often invoked simply by cryptic references to, say, the 'Pinto Case'" . . . (Jackall 1988:5).[2]

---

2. The Pinto narrative is well-known outside academia as well. A Dow Corning employee's 1980 memo, cited in a 1996 *Frontline* documentary, shows how the Pinto case infiltrated the business community and the media up to the present: "to put a questionable lot of [unsafe breast implants] on the market is inexcusable. I don't know who is responsible for this decision, but is has to rank right up there with the Pinto gas tank." A Pinto-like case was the subject of 20th Century Fox's 1991 movie *Class Action*. *The Dilbert Principle* (Adams 1996:189) lists the Pinto among seven "examples of bad press for engineers" (others included the *Hindenberg* and *Titanic*). Correspondent Mike Wallace (1978: 7) suggested in a 1978 *Sixty Minutes* segment that Ford management must have reasoned that "we'll buy 2,000 deaths, 10,000 injuries because we want to make some money. . . ." Eighteen years later, Wallace (1996:10) repeated the story that Ford executives knowingly let people die because it "cost less to settle the lawsuits than to fix the dangerous gas tank."

Flaws in the Pinto Narrative

We argue that the Pinto narrative suffers from three basic flaws. First, available data at the time suggested to Ford engineers and government regulators alike that the Pinto had a safety profile comparable to other vehicles in its class (see Schwartz 1991). Ford employees did not use cost-benefit analyses to balance potential lawsuits against the cost of fixing an unsafe gas tank. Nor did work groups at Ford conclude that company crash tests suggested that the Pinto was "unsafe." *Established safety priorities, supplemented by long-standing industry norms and a change-resistant legal culture, helped define possible fuel tank ruptures as socially-legitimate "acceptable risks"* (see Lowrance 1976).

Second, the accepted narrative misinterprets organizational structures at Ford. Ford was not a monolithic entity with a single objective and universally shared knowledge. Like most organizations, it was "a constellation of loosely allied decision making units (e.g., a marketing group, a manufacturing division, a research and development staff), each with primary responsibility for a narrow range of problems" (Kriesberg 1976:1101). Outcomes did not trace back to explicit decisions and goals of an "amoral calculator" (see Kagan and Scholz 1984). Banal actions and inaction, not callous conspiracies by people preoccupied with profit-maximization, resulted in outcomes that could have had safety implications. Ford's sub-units were loosely coupled" (Weick 1995). Not atypically (Vaughan 1996), one set of Ford employees committed the organization to a particular Pinto design, and an entirely separate groups of employees (often in other departments) later acted in ways that were constrained by the earlier design actions. The incomplete and fuzzy information available to these employees drew relatively limited attention to potential Pinto gas tank problems.

In addition to this temporal issue, work activities were loosely coupled. Communication and coordination were unavoidably sporadic between actors involved in the "technical core" (who actually designed the Pinto) and those who were "boundary spanners" (who interfaced with regulators and others in the larger environment). Boundary spanners sought to buffer the technical core from environmental forces so that the core would focus on the organization's central tasks, in this case producing cars.

Although boundary spanners never completely sealed off the technical core from the environment, boundary spanners did control environmental inputs by "symbolic coding" (e.g., classifying regulations as unreasonable government "red tape") and modifying the inputs themselves (e.g., lobbying to keep regulations weak [Scott 1998:211]). Boundary spanners' documents used by critics to condemn Ford were actually banal exchanges in ongoing auto safety negotiations with federal regulators, produced years after technical core work had been completed.

Third, the Pinto narrative ignores Ford's social and institutional environment. The dominant "focal organization perspective" (Hannan and Freeman 1989:xii) has framed analyses of organizational deviance around specific cases involving a single organization. The legal system's "case motif" (Cullen, Maakestad and Cavender 1987:21) and media exposés of particular instances of deviance have reinforced this perspective. But Ford's use of cost-benefit analysis and the safety characteristics of the Pinto's fuel tank were both normal outcomes of the interorganizational *network* that existed in the late 1960s and early 1970s. Ford was embedded in a network of other auto makers, the court system, auto safety organizations, and the National Highway Transportation Safety Administration (NHTSA) and other government agencies. Ford's actions were typical and reflect forces in this network.

Scholars have only recently examined the relationship between "institutional logics" and organizational action (Friedland and Alford 1991; Jackall 1988; Vaughan 1998). Yet even the most sophisticated analyses of organizational deviance continue to focus on a "deviant" organization. The following quote is illustrative:

> The Ford Pinto case study, often cited to support [explanations based on] amoral calculation, also suggests that an *internal* normative environment developed where deviance became normalized *within the organization*. (Vaughan 1998:49, emphasis added)

The Present Study

Our analysis addresses knowledge and motives at Ford and NHTSA about the Pinto, and the resulting action generated in diverse organizational subunits. We first explore the meanings that real Ford employees working in both technical core and boundary functions gave to Pinto events—*at the time they occurred.* We conclude that ordinary Ford employees' perceptions and behaviors were shaped by organizational, industry, and legal/regulatory contexts. Each subunit's actions reflected its available information, its mundane organizational processes, and the norms and routines of the inter-organizational network.

Second, we show that NHTSA's promulgation of the fuel tank integrity standard, and its Pinto investigation, were based on limited information and contingencies in its own social environment. NHTSA waited eight years to promulgate its fuel integrity standard, not because of "capture" by the auto industry, but because of uncertain information about the standard's societal benefits and the prevailing conservative court system's probable rejection of it. Eventually, NHTSA acted to restore its credibility as the nation's traffic safety enforcer in the face of criticism over its initial inaction on the Pinto issue by forcing the largest automotive recall at the time.

Our reading of the case suggests that the defining characteristic of the Pinto narrative is its misplaced emphasis on individual amoral calculation within a focal organization. Drawing on recent work in the sociology of organizations (see Powell and DiMaggio 1991), we argue that institutionalized norms and conventional modes of communication at the organizational and network level better explain the available data. We agree with Vaughan (1998:29) that:

> . . . outcomes are products of external contingencies, political battles, unacknowledged cultural beliefs, and formal and informal internal pathologies that undercut both the determination of goals and their achievement.

Thus, our study of the Pinto as a normal outcome of organizational and institutional processes compliments Vaughan's (1996, and especially 1998) excellent analysis of mistakes in the *Challenger* space shuttle disaster. Unlike the *Challenger*, the Pinto's design was no accident, but both clearly demonstrate the complexity inherent in cases of organizational deviance.

Data

Our "historical ethnography" (Vaughan 1996:61) uses context-specific richly detailed documents produced in the course of daily work routines. We studied thousands of unnumbered pages of contemporaneously generated internal Ford and NHTSA documents, including interorganizational correspondence between Ford and NHTSA, the Grush/Saunby cost-benefit analysis, and Pinto crash test results prepared by both Ford and NHTSA. These documents were collected by NHTSA during the course of its 1977–78 defect investigation of the Pinto and the Chevrolet Vega (see NHTSA C7-38). Many of the internal Ford documents were classified, thus unavailable to the public, for years after the investigation. We also studied all testimony in the *Grimshaw v. Ford Motor Company* (1981) civil trial. These trial transcripts offered insights into the thoughts of participants we were unable to interview. A vast secondary literature also helped us to piece together participants' accounts of what happened.

We then interviewed all available participants to clarify their earlier public assertions and to place internal documents in contemporaneous contexts. When informants had previously given ambiguous public descriptions of the Pinto's safety, we probed for more precise statements and supporting evidence. Three former Ford employees, who had testified in Pinto trials and/or published articles about the Pinto case, helped us understand Ford documents and their own public comments. All three (an engineer, an engineer/manager, and a recall coordinator) had been publicly critical of Ford's safety practices. An official who led NHTSA's investigation helped us understand the agency's investigatory process and (along with several clerks in NHTSA's technical reference library) the organization and substance of its Pinto file. Two assistant prosecutors from Ford's criminal trial and a civil attorney who sued Ford explained legal issues. Finally, five scholars who had researched the case answered our questions about their writings and Pinto data.

Ironically, analysis of corporate outcomes can be most productive a decade or two after the occurrence. Passions of critics and defensiveness of the accused have subsided, documents are more readily available, participants are more willing to talk, and quite importantly the environmental context of the acts in question is better understood. Despite the passage of time, participants have an incentive in framing their actions in a positive light. Yet consistent descriptions by people with diverse interests and histories does enhance their credibility. Additionally, we have given greater weight to statements critical of the Pinto case by Ford supporters and the justifications offered by Ford's critics. All statements were checked against the documentary record for accuracy and reliability.

Organizational Action at Ford

Before we discuss the actions of specific Ford subunits, we must sketch the Pinto's historical context. The Pinto was designed at a time when vehicle crashworthiness was a newly identified public concern. Prior to the passage of the Motor Vehicle Safety Act of 1966 (Pinto design began in 1967), the federal government lacked authority to regulate vehicle design. For decades, the auto industry had successfully promoted an ideology that traffic fatalities were caused by unsafe drivers or roads, not uncrashworthy cars (Gusfield 1980; Nader 1965). The year the MVSA passed, a federal court opined:

> The intended purpose of an automobile does not include its participation in collisions with other objects, despite the manufacturer's ability to foresee the possibility that such collisions may occur . . . the defendant also knows that its automobiles may be driven into bodies of water, but it is not suggested that defendant has a duty to equip them with pontoons. (*Evans v. General Motors Corporation* 1966:825)

Although the MVSA rendered this decision obsolete, the long-standing assumption that the industry's obligations were limited to safety during "normal operations," of which collisions were not a part, was only reluctantly and partially abandoned by auto makers (Mashaw and Harfst 1990).

In addition, unchallenged industry norms provided rationalizations for accepting lower safety levels for smaller and cheaper cars, and for offering proven safety devices on them as optional rather than standard equipment (Eastman 1984). For example, Triumph

Motors argued in a formal petition filed with NHTSA in 1974 that a proposed rear-end fuel tank integrity standard would "discriminate against small vehicles" (U.S. Department of Transportation 1974:10589) because small cars could not withstand crash test collisions to the same degree as large cars.

Thus, throughout its development phase in the late 1960s, the Pinto was not expected to be as crashworthy as bigger, more expensive cars. In the next section, we explore this point further. We demonstrate that Pinto engineers' determinations of "acceptable risk" were outcomes of regulatory environments, negotiated in the absence of a clear federal safety standard and shaped by industry-wide practices and beliefs.

Technical Core Beliefs and Actions (1967–1973)

To explain what employees in Ford's technical core subunits believed, when they believed it, and how corporate structures influenced them to communicate and act on their beliefs, we separate design from marketing stages. During the design stage (1967–1970). Ford technical core employees did not view their actions as taking calculated risks with consumers' lives. Even Harley Copp, the outspoken Ford safety whistle-blower, never asserted that informed Ford participants believed the car was unsafe. Furthermore, they were not thinking about potential lawsuits when making design decisions (Feaheny 1997; Gioia 1996). And they did not refuse to correct perceived problems because settling lawsuits would be cheaper (NHTSA C7-38; Strobel 1980).

Although technical core work groups were not informed by explicit cost-benefit analyses (we explain these analyses below), they did recognize that unavoidable cost and time constraints make safety trade-offs inevitable for all product designs (see Lowrance 1976). For the auto industry, with its long history of subordinating safety to styling (Eastman 1984; Nader 1965), implicit safety compromises were particularly common. In the Pinto case, Lee Iacocca and others wanted to compete with foreign imports with a car that weighed less than 2,000 pottnds and cost less than $2,000 (Camps 1997; Dowie 1977; Strobel 1980). Other car manufacturers were building cars under similar or more stringent guidelines (Davidson 1983).

Commentators on the Pinto case (writing in a later era with different beliefs) assume that fuel tank leakage in rear-end crash tests *must have* alarmed both engineers and managers. They didn't, because the tests were not sufficiently convincing at the time (or even today). Crash tests during that era were novel procedures. Both the auto industry and NHTSA were more concerned with the reliability and validity of the tests than with safety data generated by a particular car's tests. Harold MacDonald, the engineer in charge of the Pinto's design, and every other engineer charged with interpreting crash-test data at the time—all of whom whistle-blower Harley Copp considered "safety-conscious individuals" (Strobel 1980:183)—doubted that the tests accurately represented real-world conditions (Feaheny 1997). After all, they reasoned, a car slamming backwards into a wall at twenty to thirty miles per hour in a crash test is only a rough approximation of a real-world car-to-car crash. Results that seemed "troubling" (Schwartz 1991:1028) to later writers seemed less problematical at the time and were neutralized by participants' background assumptions about small cars and crashworthiness. NHTSA validated the engineers' skepticism by asking the auto industry to help develop reliable and cost-effective ways to approximate real-world conditions (Strobel 1980).

Thus, engineers in the design stage were still trying "to find out how to conduct crash tests" (Feaheny 1997; see also Lacey 1986:613). For example, an internal Pinto test report dated November, 1970 listed as its objective "To develop a test procedure to be used to provide baseline data on vehicle fuel system integrity" (NHTSA C7-38-Al.5, Final Test Report #T-0738). In this test, a Pinto sedan exhibited "excessive fuel tank leakage" when towed rearward into a fixed barrier at 21.5 miles per hour, considered roughly equivalent to a car-to-car impact at 35 miles per hour.

Nothing in this, or any other, Ford test report indicates that participants felt cause for concern or organizational action. Although some Ford engineers were not especially pleased, they felt that the data were inconclusive or the risks acceptable (Feaheny 1997; Strobel 1980), or they kept their concerns to themselves (Camps 1997). Some felt that cars would rarely be subjected to the extreme forces generated in a fixed-barrier test in real-world collisions (Feaheny 1997; Devine 1996). NHTSA apparently agreed and ultimately replaced the proposed fixed-barrier test with a less-stringent moving-barrier test in its final standard (U.S. Department of Transportation 1988).

Occupational caution encouraged engineers to view many design adjustments that improved test performance as "unproven" in real-world accidents (Devine 1996; Feaheny 1997; Schwartz 1991; Strickland 1996; Strobel 1980). Engineers, who typically value "uncertainty avoidance" (Allison 1971:72), chose to stick with an existing design rather than face uncertainties associated with novel ones (Devine 1996; Strobel 1980). One series of tests, for instance, showed that Pintos equipped with pliable foam-like gas tanks would not leak in 30 mile-per-hour crashes. But some engineers feared that such a tank might melt and disagreed with others who felt it was safer than the existing metal design (Devine 1996, see also Strobel 1980). Other engineers believed that rubber bladders improved performance in tests, but anticipated problems under real-world conditions (Strobel 1980).[3]

Ford whistle-blower Harley Copp's argument—that the Pinto would have been safer had its gas tank been placed above the axle rather than behind it—is often cited in Pinto narratives as an example of safety being sacrificed to profits, or at least trunk space, in the design stage (Cullen, Maakestad and Cavender 1987; Dowie 1977; Strobel 1994). Yet Copp did not reach this conclusion until 1977 (Strobel 1980). And other engineers were considerably less certain about it, even though the above-the-axle design did perform better in one set of crash tests. The engineer overseeing the Pinto's design, Harold MacDonald (whose father died in a fuel tank fire when his Model A Ford exploded after a frontal collision with a tree), felt that the above-the-axle placement was less safe under real-world conditions because the tank was closer to the passenger com-

---

3. Documents often used to infer amoral calculation at Ford can only be understood in the context of these unavoidable ambiguities and disagreements. A memo dated April 22, 1971, for example, suggested that Ford wait until 1976 (when NHTSA's proposed fuel tank integrity standard was expected to take effect) before incorporating design changes such as a rubber bladder "to realize a design cost savings of $20.9 million compared to incorporation in 1974" (cited in Strobel 1994:50). Corporate memo-writing conventions, as in this example, favored rationales framed in financial terms among non-engineers. By contrast, "acceptable risk" understandings were used by engineers. Rubber bladders were not added to the Pinto even after the safety standard took effect. Two knowledgeable auto safety informants, who wished to remain anonymous, believe that no passenger car has ever incorporated rubber bladders (personal communications on October 26 and 27, 1998).

partment and more likely to be punctured by items in the trunk (Strobel 1980).

Additionally, after making a judgment that the Pinto was acceptably safe, most participants readily devalued subsequent competing definitions (Feaheny 1997). Lou Tubben, an engineer "with a genuine concern for safety" (Dowie 1977:23), did not press his concerns until 1971—after the car's release. Frank Camps (1981, 1997), another concerned engineer, did not formally object to the Pinto's windshield and *frontal-impact* fuel tank design problems until 1973, and never objected to rear-end fuel tank integrity. Tom Feaheny (1997) was worried about the lack of safety glass on all Ford models, and viewed the Pinto gas tank as a "non-issue" by comparison.

In sum, the design stage was *not* characterized by an engineering consensus that the Pinto was "unsafe." The value of crash tests was unclear. The Pinto's specific "problem" (e.g., frontal fuel tank integrity, safety glass) varied among those few engineers troubled by the car's safety performance. A "safe" placement of the gas tank was not identified, and the safety value of potential design changes was subject to disagreement. Additionally, engineers believed that the crash test performance of other small cars, particularly imports, was "terrible" (Feaheny 1997). Given this background and the host of other safety issues confronting engineers as a result of the recently passed MVSA, it is not surprising that many Pinto engineers and their family members (e.g., the chief systems engineer's wife) drove Pintos (Strobel 1980).

In the design stage (1967–1970), no company or government standard on rear-end fuel tank integrity existed to guide the engineers, but their actions were consistent with the taken-for-granted, industry-wide tradition of building lower levels of crashworthiness into small cars. This situation changed in the marketing stage (post 1970). Shortly after the 1971 model year Pintos were released, Ford adopted an internal 20 mile-per-hour moving barrier standard for the 1973 model year—the only manufacturer to do so (Gioia 1996; Strobel 1994). The extant legal/regulatory environment reinforced engineers' beliefs that this standard was "quite reasonable" since it was the same one recommended at that time by the federal General Services Administration; the Canadian equivalent of the GSA; the Society of Automotive Engineers; and a private consulting firm hired by NHTSA . . ." and by NHTSA itself in 1969

(Strobel 1980:205). This standard would constrain future debates by certifying the Pinto as "safe" to Ford's subunit charged with evaluating potential recallable safety problems.

Most Ford technical core personnel became less involved with Pinto safety during the marketing stage. One exception was Dennis Gioia, who began a new job in another part of Ford's technical core in the summer of 1972. A self-described "child of the '60s," Gioia (1992:379) hoped to change an industry he saw as insensitive to safety concerns. Within one year, this inexperienced recent MBA graduate was promoted to Field Recall Coordinator and charged with coordinating all active safety recall campaigns and identifying potential safety problems. Thus Ford had at least one individual in its technical core with the inclinations and authority, though little experience or organizational power, for taking a stand on the Pinto gas tank issue.

When Gioia became Recall Coordinator, he inherited about 100 active recall campaigns, half of them safety-related. As with most jobs, the enormous workload required him to use "standard operating procedures" (SOPs) to organize and manage information for decision making (cf. Kriesberg 1976:1102). SOPs increase organizational efficiency by operating as cognitive scripts that transform decision-making opportunities into largely predetermined action patterns. Existing SOPs required that, to be "recallable," problems needed either high frequency or a directly traceable causal link to a design defect.

When reports began to trickle in to Gioia that Pintos were "lighting up" in relatively low speed accidents, and after viewing the burned wreckage of a Pinto, he initiated a meeting to determine if this represented a recallable problem. His work group voted unanimously not to recall the Pinto because the weak data did not meet SOP criteria (Gioia 1996). The work group was unaware of any cost-benefit analyses or Pinto crash test results.

Reports of Pinto fires continued to trickle in, and eventually Gioia did become aware of, and concerned about, the crash test results. Again he wondered if the Pinto had a recallable problem, so he initiated a second meeting to convince his co-workers that crash tests showed a possible design flaw. But others again saw no design flaws—after all, the Pinto met internal company standards, and no contradictory external standard existed. The work group conceived the tank leak "problem" not as a defect, but as a fundamental and unalterable design feature: the car's small size, the use of light metals, and unibody construction produced a tendency for Pintos (and others in its class) to "crush up like an accordion" in rear-end collisions (Gioia 1996). In light of what they believed, work group members felt they would become the "laughing stock" of the company if they recommended a recall (Giola 1996). But fear of ridicule did not motivate their vote. They doubted a recall's legitimacy, or its chances of approval.

Boundary Spanners' Beliefs and Actions (1970–1977)

The Grush/Saunby Report. Having considered the meanings of one set of Pinto events at the technical core, we now examine the meanings of a different set of events for boundary spanners. All of these events occurred well into the marketing stage. Our primary concern in this section is the cost-benefit analysis (known as the "Grush/Saunby report," see Figure 15.1) that became the "smoking gun" in the Pinto narrative.

This analysis was written by Ford's boundary spanners to influence regulators (see also Kunen 1994; Schwartz 1991). It did not affect activities at the company's technical core. It was *not* prepared for internal consumption. It was never sent to Ford's design engineers or recall decision-makers. Ford employees responsible for making technical design and safety decisions (e.g., Camps 1997; Giola 1996) did not even know of the Grush/Saunby report or its rationale until Dowie's story broke in 1977. It could not have affected design decisions because it was written three years *after* the first vehicles were sold. The Pinto was designed in 1967–1970, but Grush/Saunby was written in 1973.

This analysis was *not* about the Pinto; it explicitly concerned all 12.5 million new American cars and light trucks sold annually by all companies in the United States. It never mentioned the Pinto, which sold less than 1.5 million total units up to the time it was recalled in 1977. Nor did it concern fuel tank integrity or rear-end crashworthiness. It addressed only a proposed federal standard requiring the installation of a special valve in all cars and light trucks to prevent fuel leakage from the carburetor and elsewhere during a rollover (Camps 1997; Davidson 1983; Kunen 1994). Finally, it

FIGURE 15.1

Benefits and Costs Relating to Fuel Leakage Associated
with the Static Rollover Test Portion of FMVSS 208

Benefits:	**Savings**	180 burn deaths, 180 serious injuries, 2100 burned vehicles.
	Unit Cost	$200,000 per death, $67,000 per injury, $700 per vehicle.
	Total Benefit	180 × ($200,000) + 180 × ($67,000)+ 2100 × ($700) = $49.5 million.
Costs:	**Sales**	11 million cars, 1.5 million light trucks.
	Unit Cost	$11 per car, $11 per truck.
	Total Cost	11,000,000 × ($11) + 1,500,000 × ($11) = $137 million.

Source: Table 3 on Page 6 of the Grush/Saunby Report, as reproduced by Dowie (1977:24).

did not estimate that Ford's lawsuit cost would be $200,000 per death. This figure was NHTSA's (not Ford's) highest estimate of societal (not corporate) cost per death, mostly for "lost future wages" (Grush and Saunby 1973:7; see also U.S. Government Accounting Office 1976:34).

Like other work group members who helped prepare Ford's cost-benefit analyses, the report's authors, Ernest Grush and Carol Saunby, were "eggheads," not engineers (Camps 1997; contra Schwartz 1991:1020). Frank Camps (1997), an engineer closely involved in designing the Pinto, said their job was to project possible future scenarios. Years after engineers in Ford's technical core had made technical design decisions, these boundary spanning eggheads elsewhere in the company were immersed in the details of a loosely coordinated anti-regulation campaign that auto-industry elites hoped would at least stall what they viewed as overly restrictive and wasteful regulations. A close examination of the document, combined with an understanding of how auto-safety standards are debated and passed, lends support to Ford executive Herbert Misch's assertion that Grush/Saunby was part of the "normal [traffic safety] rule-making process" and nothing more (quoted in Wallace 1978:7). Law professor Gary Schwartz (1991:1025) accurately describes it as "within the range of expected and acceptable advocacy."

NHTSA's discussion of the Grush/Saunby report in the *Federal Register* (U.S. Department of Transportation 1974:10587) supports this characterization. NHTSA disputed "Ford's narrow analysis" and the figures used in the Grush/Saunby report, but acknowledged that NHTSA also "uses cost-benefit analyses as a decision-making tool." NHTSA disagreed with the number of deaths upon which Ford's analysis was based (a figure Ford took from a National Safety Council report), and defended the proposed safety standard "on the basis of its own analysis . . . [as] appropriate, reasonable, and necessary." Nothing in the *Register* indicates that Ford's use of cost-benefit analysis was inappropriate. NHTSA simply pointed out that "reasonable persons may differ on their cost-benefit projections. . . ."

Although cost-benefit analyses like Grush/Saunby were widely used in public debates about proposed safety standards, both auto makers and federal regulators realized that they represented one (imperfect) tool among many and could not form the basis for specific design decisions. In its public discussion of Grush/Saunby, for example, NHTSA directed attention to the "extremely imprecise assumptions concerning benefits" (U.S. Department of Transportation 1974:10587) inherent in cost-benefit analyses. Ford's eggheads also recognized this in a 1972 cost-benefit analysis, apparently one of their earliest. They discussed the "limitations and inadequacies" of the "assumptions" (Automotive Safety Affairs Office 1972:1) on which such analyses are based. The report's authors were explicit about the uses and misuses of cost-benefit analyses, noting that:

> . . . the attached figures should be used with caution. . . . We learned from this study that it is difficult to assess the probable effectiveness of a standard without making some fairly specific assumptions. . . . This kind of study *cannot provide any detailed direction on the design steps which might be taken in order to maximize overall real-world safety for a fixed total of product expense, nor alternatively, to minimize product cost for a fixed target level of safety.* (1–2, emphasis added)

A year later, the Grush/Saunby report included a similar caveat, "While the benefit analysis is not meant to be definitive and beyond criticism, it is based on assumptions and derivations believed to be quite representative of the *upper bound* on the possible benefits accruing from compliance with the requirement" (Grush and Saunby 1973:4).

"Institutional Logic" and Action at Ford

When viewed in appropriate temporal, organizational, and network contexts, we believe that the data show that participants at Ford in both time periods (design and marketing), and in both functions (technical and boundary spanning) acted according to an "institutional logic" (Jackall 1988) rather than a "coldblooded calculus." Accepted conventions (e.g., the use of cost-benefit analysis in debates with outsiders over safety standards) and beliefs (e.g., that small cars are inevitably less safe than large cars) figure prominently in the social production of this logic. Although we use it to explain action at Ford, institutional logic clearly guided the actions of other network members.

Generic organizational processes were embedded in this institutional logic. For example, self-censorship (Halberstam 1986:498)— the process by which organizational sub-units learn to stop making requests that are routinely rejected—effectively constrained participants. Gioia's (1996) work group was reluctant to pass its concerns up the hierarchy because they did not meet the established recall criteria. Likewise, engineers Frank Camps (1997) and Gene Bordinat (Lacey 1986) reported that those who initially had reservations about the Pinto believed themselves powerless to challenge prevailing "acceptable risk" definitions. This self-censorship insulated higher-level officials from the various and de-centralized safety concerns (e.g., safety glass, windshield retention, fuel tank integrity) of people who were working on the Pinto. Lee Iacocca's perceived unapproachability (Camps 1997; Dowie 1977; Lacey 1986) also discouraged communication, so he heard mostly from employees like Tom Feaheny (1997) who believed the car was safe.

Self-censorship illustrates that, at the organizational level, outcomes were emergent. What appeared from a distance as decisions made by rational, coordinated, profit-driven actors with fairly complete knowledge acting on an essentially economic pleasure/pain calculus, are better understood as non-rational outcomes of distinct subunit acts based on doubtful information. They were outputs of "a flow of intertwined processes, rather than a sum of juxtaposed decisions" (Laroche 1995:66; see also Allison 1971; Kagan and Scholz 1984; Kriesberg 1976). What outsiders and participants later called "decisions" are better understood as "the emerging part of an iceberg of unreflective action" (Laroche 1995:65). Both Feaheny (1997) and Camps (1997) point to the taken-for-granted lack of time allotted for developing and testing Pinto safety; even less time was available for reflective thought.

In fact, most changes in Pinto fuel tank integrity were inadvertent. In the design stage, for example, the decision to offer a hatchback eliminated the option of the over-the-axle tank placement. Similarly, although the earliest Pintos lacked "rear subframe members" (Lacey 1986:611), which would have better protected the gas tank, 1972–1973 design modifications during the marketing stage to meet a new federal bumper standard (adopted largely to reduce cosmetic damage to vehicles in low speed collisions [Crandall et al. 1986]) necessitated that the rear end be strengthened. The unintended consequence was better protection for the fuel tank.

So, although individual employees did not act as amoral calculators in the Pinto case, prevailing institutional logic organized auto-industry employees' activities in ways that deemphasized safety.[4]

NHTSA's Role in the Landmark Narrative

We now consider NHTSA's often contradictory contribution to the Pinto landmark narrative. Two issues are of primary importance: the selection of the Pinto for recall and NHTSA's use of cost-benefit analysis. NHTSA ultimately recalled the Pinto, but this outcome was far from predictable given the agency's record on the issue of fuel tank integrity. NHTSA's top administrator even testified *on behalf of Ford* in the Pinto's criminal trial (Strobel 1980). While NHTSA's actions appear "rational" from a distance, like Ford's they were the product of compromise, conflicting organizational interests and routines, and environmental pressures and constraints.

Before we examine NHTSA's actions concerning the Pinto, some background is necessary. Most accidents involve multiple factors contributing to the crash itself or the resulting death and injury. In detailed studies of specific accidents (see NHTSA C7-38), NHTSA

---

4. Institutional logic propelled the industry's elite boundary spanners to influence its regulatory environment. For example, in a conversation recorded in 1971, Henry Ford II and Lee Iaccoca tried to convince President Richard Nixon that regulations were going to bankrupt the American auto industry. During the conversation, Henry Ford II remarked that safety and emissions regulations threatened to increase the price of the Pinto "something like fifty percent" (Quoted in Cullen, Maakessad and Cavender 1987:157). These elites contributed to an organizational culture that viewed with contempt any interference in car design by the government or consumer groups (Lacey 1986).

employees made numerous recommendations for tougher standards regarding driver behavior (e.g., drunk driving laws), road safety (e.g., guardrails), and vehicle design (e.g., airbag standards). Outside parties (e.g., consumer groups, insurance companies, state government agencies) lobbied NHTSA to take action on particular problems. Therefore, deciding which problems to address was far from clear, given the blizzard of information and cross-pressures (Mashaw and Harfst 1990). Following two fuel tank burn deaths when a large truck rear-ended a Pinto in 1976, for instance, Pennsylvania's Bureau of Traffic Engineering pleaded with NHTSA for tougher truck braking standards, not auto fuel tank integrity standards.

As early as 1968, the year of its creation, NHTSA had attempted to adopt a fuel tank integrity standard. The specifics of the standard were subject to much disagreement. In addition to dealing with industry claims that NHTSA'S fuel tank integrity proposals would prove ineffective, NHTSA had to sort through a fog of ambiguous data on vehicle fires. An Insurance Institute for Highway Safety study (NHTSA C7-38), for instance, reported that only 72 (out of a sample of 1,923) fires in 1973 resulted from collisions. Of these 72 fires, only 24 originated in the fuel tank—most began in the engine compartment and were caused by electrical shorts. Additionally, a number of factors affected the likelihood of vehicle fires, including make and age of the vehicle.

The Pinto landmark narrative describes unique design features that purportedly made the Pinto less crashworthy than other cars: for example, bolts on the differential housing and a fuel filler pipe that easily pulled out in collisions. Yet these same issues had been identified much earlier with other cars. For example, a 1970 NHTSA report (C7-38), along with a 1968 Society of Automotive Engineers report, found that pre-1967 Ford sedans exhibited "gross fuel spillage [in crash tests] arising out of the detachment of the filler spout" and tank punctures caused by a "poorly located track-bar bolt." NHTSA did not recall these cars to fix this acceptable risk.

Forcing a "Voluntary" Recall

In September, 1974, NHTSA crash-tested a number of vehicles, including the Pinto, "to verify the [Department of Transportation's] rear-end moving barrier procedure . . ." (NHTSA C7-38). Several cars, including the Pinto, exhibited significant fuel loss in 30 mile-per-hour tests. A 1969 Plymouth station wagon exhibited a "steady flow of fuel." Like the Ford crash-test reports discussed above, NHTSA's report expressed neither shock nor concern, concluding only that "The tests indicated that the procedure would produce repeatable test results." None of the cars were subjected to follow-up studies or recall proceedings.[5] Also in 1974, Ralph Nader's Center for Auto Safety asked NHTSA to investigate Pinto fuel tank integrity. NHTSA beliefs and procedures were similar to Ford's: not enough evidence existed to warrant a full defect investigation (Graham 1991). The Pinto had no "recallable" problem, even though people were dying in Pinto fires.

By 1977, the social context had changed. Dowie's (1977:18) article had labeled the Pinto a "firetrap" and accused the agency of buckling to auto-industry pressure. Public interest generated by the article forced a second Pinto investigation and guaranteed that NHTSA would be under a microscope for its duration.

NHTSA engineer Lee Strickland was assigned to determine if Pinto (and Chevrolet Vega) tank problems warranted a mandatory recall. Strickland's work group held the Pinto and Vega to a higher standard than other cars (Strickland 1996). It dispensed with the usual moving barrier. Instead, it intentionally selected a large and particularly rigid "bullet car" to hit the Pinto's rear end. It weighed down the bullet car's nose to slide under the Pinto and maximize gas tank contact. It also turned on the bullet car's headlights to provide a ready source of ignition. And it completely filled gas tanks in both cars with gasoline rather than the non-flammable Stoddard fluid normally used. Strickland justified these actions as approximating real-world worst-case circumstances (Davidson 1983; NHTSA C7-38; Strickland 1996).

For NHTSA, the tests seemed an unqualified success: two 1972 Pintos burst into flame upon impact. In the summer of 1978 NHTSA announced that the Pinto gas tank represented a safety defect, leading to the largest recall campaign in automobile history at that time

5. NHTSA's files (C7-38) also contained a study conducted in 1973 by the Insurance Institute for Highway Safety on rear-end fuel tank integrity. This report found that all cars tested, including a Pinto, exhibited fuel leakage in car-to-car crash tests at less than 40 miles-per-hour, and that both a 1973 Toyota Corona and a 1964 Mercury Comet burst into flames. NHTSA did not initiate defect investigations for any of these cars.

(NHTSA C7-38; Strickland 1996). Ford agreed to "voluntarily" recall 1971–1976 Pintos. Other small cars sold during the 1970s were not recalled, even though most were comparable, or in the case of the AMC Gremlin probably less safe (Schwartz 1991; NHTSA C7-38; Swigert and Farrell 1980–81:180). Their manufacturers successfully defended them as acceptable risks (see Wallace 1978). When we asked why NHTSA forced a Pinto recall for failing the 35 mile-per-hour test, although most small cars could not withstand such a test, Strickland (1996) analogized that, "Just because your friends get away with shoplifting, doesn't mean you should get away with it too."

Selection of the Pinto

Beginning in the late 1970s, claims consistent with "Pinto Madness" readily gained public acceptance, but credible contradictory claims did not (e.g.. Davidson 1983; Epstein 1980). For instance, Dowie's "conservative" estimate of 500 deaths (1977:18) was accepted, while NHTSA's report that it could document only 27 Pinto fire-related deaths (NHTSA C7-38; Frank 1985) was ignored. A transmission problem that also caused 27 Pinto deaths (and 180 on other Ford products [Clarke 1988]) never became a social problem. Similarly, publics accepted claims of safety errors leveled by Harley Copp, a Ford engineer who was apparently overseas when early crucial decisions were made (Camps 1997; Strobel 1980), but ignored other safety-conscious Pinto engineers who believed windshield retention was a more important safety problem (Camps 1997), and lack of safety glass caused more deaths (Feaheny 1997).

Ford's cost-benefit analysis, a normal product of an interorganizational network, also facilitated the selection of the Pinto for inordinate attention. The year Ford sent the Grush/Saunby document to NHTSA (thus making it available to outside audiences), General Motors conducted a similar cost-benefit analysis (Nader and Smith 1996). Like Grush/Saunby, this analysis used the government's $200,000 figure as the value of a human life. Unlike Grush/Saunby, which addressed static rollover for all cars and light trucks, the GM analysis looked specifically at rear-end collisions on its own cars. These facts suggest that GM would have made a better target for Dowie's analysis, but the GM document did not enter the public

298 REACTIONS

record until 1988. Contingencies led to the identification of Ford as deviant, while other auto makers escaped scrutiny.

By the time of its Pinto investigation, NHTSA had essentially abandoned its original mission of forcing industry-wide safety improvements, in favor of investigating and recalling specific cars (Mashaw and Harfst 1990). NHTSA had two primary incentives in reinforcing the extant "focal organization" imagery of the Pinto narrative. First, NHTSA was pressured by specific organizations in its network (e.g., the Center for Auto Safety) and members of the public (see NHTSA C7-38) to take action on the Pinto's gas tank. Second, other network actors (e.g., courts, the Nixon administration, the auto industry) had increasingly limited NHTSA's ability to address systemic auto safety issues.

Cost-benefit Analyses as a Network Outcome

Cost-benefit analysis was common currency in government debates by the 1970s. Legislative, judicial, and executive branches of the federal government all increasingly encouraged explicitly weighing expected costs of safety standards against expected benefits. Both Ford and NHTSA responded to these network developments by producing their own cost-benefit analyses.

The legislative branch had focused on driver behavior and road design until Ralph Nader (1965) and others convinced Congress that many of the 50,000 annual auto deaths resulted from unsafe car designs. The National Traffic and Motor Vehicle Safety Act in 1966, one year before Ford began designing the Pinto, produced America's first significant federal auto regulation. It asserted that an absence of federal auto-safety standards was producing "senseless bloodshed" (see U.S. Department of Transportation 1985:102–103). Its goal was not to reduce traffic deaths to zero, but to achieve a new balance between safety and cost—in effect to attain a more "sensible" level of bloodshed.

Judicial branch use of cost-benefit analysis has a longer history. In 1898, the Supreme Court's "rule of reasonableness" mandated that regulatory impact on affected businesses be weighed against expected benefits (*Smyth v. Ames*; see Cullen, Maakestad and Cavender 1987:125). Two federal decisions written shortly before the Grush/Saunby Report extended the 1898 constraints to auto regulation.

A 1968 court ruling forced NHTSA to evaluate and respond to every industry objection before issuing a standard (*Auto Parts v. Boyd* 1968). A 1972 decision required that safety standards be "practicable" and provide an "objective" safety benefit (*Chrysler v. DOT* 1972:661).

Similarly, in the executive branch of the early 1970s, NHTSA was being told to justify the cost-effectiveness of its standards (U.S. General Accounting Office 1976; Mashaw and Harfst 1990) because critics of all stripes worried that over-regulation was strangling the American economy. The trend among agencies to *quantify* the costs and benefits of their rules became a requirement in 1974 when President Gerald Ford issued Executive Order 11,821.

Cost-benefit analyses were so widely accepted at NHTSA that cost-benefit arguments were written into the preamble of NHTSA's fuel tank integrity standard (U.S. Department of Transportation 1988). One section reads, "The proposal that there be zero fuel spillage was almost universally opposed for cost-benefit reasons" (1). The Recreational Vehicle Institute pressed claims that the entire standard was "not cost-beneficial" (7). NHTSA reviewed the claims, and concluded that "the need for such increased fuel system integrity is sufficient to justify costs" (7).

Conclusion

Our interpretation of the Ford Pinto case builds on the work of scholars who have begun to question the customary use of the "focal organization" perspective in landmark narratives about organizational deviance, and organizational action in general (Hannan and Freeman 1989). For example, Vaughan's (1996) compelling reassessment of the *Challenger* space shuttle disaster rejects the conventional amoral calculator imagery, acknowledges the larger networks in which the actions of NASA (and its contractors, engineers and managers) were embedded, and shows how routine processes can generate an unintended tragedy. Similarly, the Bank of Boston was singled out as a deviant organization for activities that became labeled as "money laundering," yet these practices had been widespread and routine within the banking industry for years (Nichols

1977). Analyses of other cases, like the Tuskegee Syphilis study (Jones 1993), workplace exposure to asbestos (Calhoun and Hiller 1988), deviance among tobacco companies (Rabe and Ermann 1995), environmental pollution (Stone 1977; Szasz 1986; Yeager 1991), and radiation experiments on humans (Lee 1998), have also demonstrated the importance of networks in the production of deviance and deviance labels.

Attention to the network level of analysis can help explain social problems that derive from the routine workings of social institutions. The taken-for-granted nature of much "sensible" bloodshed (e.g., 40,000 annual traffic fatalities), combined with the propensity of governments, media, and others to blame individual people or organizations for network outcomes can cause us to ignore social problems that flow from the interconnectedness of organizations. The Pinto case demonstrates that network conventions (e.g., cost-benefit analyses) that promote necessary interorganizational connections and stability, can lead to gaps between network participants and the larger society in the determinations of acceptable risk. More research on the social construction of deviance is needed before we can explain the question of why some gaps are exploited by moral entrepreneurs at particular historical points, while others are not.

However, it is clear that institutionalized norms among scholars play a role in the kinds of explanations offered (and published) to explain cases like the Pinto. As one anonymous reviewer pointed out, it is more than coincidental that the Pinto narrative, constructed in the immediate post-Watergate period by journalists and scholars engaged in a "social movement against white collar crime" (Katz 1980), emphasized conspiracy and amoral calculation. Later, some scholars simply added a concern with organizational level factors to the conspiratorial account (e.g., Kramer 1982). We speculate that the Pinto landmark narrative has been so widely promulgated because of its usefulness to journalists, business ethicists, sociologists, lawmakers, etc. Why it has resonated so deeply with the public should be explored further.

Finally, even our study probably imputes a greater degree of rationality to Pinto-related outcomes than existed. By focusing attention on one issue (e.g.. Pinto safety), studies of organizational processes and institutional contexts like ours tend to imply the existence of "decisions" (Laroche 1995). Despite our argument that a consciously cynical decision did not produce an unsafe fuel tank design, our description of the Pinto case probably implies an inflated level of rationality to what is better understood as institutionally embedded unreflective action. In fact, the Pinto design emerged from social forces both internal and external to Ford. There was no "decision" to market an unsafe product, and there was no "decision" to market a safe one.

The More Things Change . . .

Inflation has driven up the government's estimated value of a human life (NHTSA used $1.5 million in 1990), but the underlying calculation is unchanged from Pinto days: "medical costs, lost earnings, property damage" etc. (U.S. Department of Transportation 1990:27). Today's federal rear-end crash standard requires passing the same 30 mile-per-hour moving-barrier test that the 1977 Pinto successfully passed (U.S. Department of Transportation 1988). NHTSA has not tried to tighten the fuel tank standard, essentially because cost-benefit analyses still indicate that other less-costly changes would produce greater safety benefits (Solomon, Perkins and Resetar 1985; Wald 1997).

References

Adams, Scott, 1996. The Dilbert Principle: A Cubicle's-Eye View of Bosses. Meetings, and Management Fads and Other Workplace Afflictions. New York: HarperBusiness.

Allison, Graham, 1971. Essence of Decision: Explaining the Cuban Missile Crisis. Boston: Little, Brown, and Company.

Anderson, Jerry W., Jr., 1989. Corporate Social Responsibility: Guidelines for Top Management. New York: Quorum Books.

Automotive Safety Affairs Office, 1972. NAAO Working Safety Committee: FMVSS Effectiveness Study. Copy on file with the author.

Birsch, Douglas, and John H. Fielder, (eds.), 1994. The Ford Pinto Case: A Study in Applied Ethics, Business, and Technology. Albany, N.Y.: SUNY Press.

Calhoun, Craig, and Henryk Hiller, 1988. "Coping with insidious injuries: The case of Johns-Manville Corporation and asbestos exposure." Social Problems 35:162–181.

Camps, Frank, 1981. "Warning an auto company about an unsafe design." In Whistleblowing: Loyalty and Dissent in the Corporation, ed. Alan F. Westin, 119–129. New York: McGraw Hill.

———. 1997. Personal interviews conducted on February 27 and 28.

Clarke, Lee, 1988. "Explaining choices among technological risks." Social Problems 35:292–305.

Coleman. James W., 1985. The Criminal Elite: The Sociology of White Collar Crime. New York: St. Martins Press.

Crandall, Robert W., Howard K. Gruenspecht, Theodore E. Keeler, and Lester B. Lave, 1986. Regulating the Automobile. Washington, D.C.: Brookings Institution.

Cullen, Francis T., William J. Maakestad, and Gray Cavender, 1984. "The Ford Pinto Case and beyond: Corporate crime, moral boundaries, and the criminal sanction." In Corporations as Criminals, ed. Ellen Hochstedler, 107–130. Newbury Park: Sage.

———. 1987. Corporate Crime Under Attack: The Ford Pinto Case and Beyond. Cincinnati. Ohio: Anderson.

Davidson, Dekkers L., 1983. "Managing product safety: The Ford Pinto." Harvard Business School Case 383129.

Devine, Foy, 1996. Telephone interview conducted on May 29.

Doob, Christopher Bates, 1995. Social Problems. Fort Worth: Harcourt Brace.

Dowie, Mark, 1977. "Pinto madness." Mother Jones (2):18–32.

Eastman, Joel W., 1984. Styling vs. Safety: The American Automobile Industry and the Development of Automobile Safety. 1900–1966. New York: University Press of America.

Epstein. Richard A., 1980. "Is Pinto a criminal" Regulation 4:15–21.

Feaheny, Tom, 1997. Personal interview conducted on January 22.

Frank, Nancy, 1985. Crimes Against Health and Safety. New York: Harrow and Heston.

Friedland, Roger, and Robert K. Afford, 1991. "Bringing society back in: Symbols, practices, and institutional contradictions." In The New Institutionalism in Organizational Analysis, eds. Walter W. Powell and Paul J. DiMaggio, 232–263. Chicago: University of Chicago Press.

Gioia, Dennis, 1992. "Pinto fires and personal ethics: A script analysis of missed opportunities." Journal of Business Ethics 11:379–389.

———. 1996. Personal interview conducted on October 3.

Graham, John, 1991. "Does liability promote the safety of motor vehicles?" In The Liability Maze: The Impact of Liability Rules on Innovation and Safety, eds. Peter W. Huber and Robert B. Litan, 128–137. Washington, D.C.: Brookings Institution.

Greenberg, David F., (ed.), 1993. Crime and Capitalism. Philadelphia: Temple University Press.

Grush, Ernest S., and Carol A. Saunby, 1973. The Grush/Saunby Report. Copy on file with the author.

Gusfield. Joseph R., 1980. The Culture of Public Problems: Drinking-Driving and the Symbolic Order. Chicago: University of Chicago Press.

Hagan, Frank E., 1994. Introduction to Criminology. Chicago: Nelson-Hall.

Halberstam, David, 1986. The Reckoning. New York: William Morrow and Company.

Hannan. Michael T., and John Freeman, 1989. Organizational Ecology. Cambridge. Mass.: Harvard University Press.

Jackall, Robert, 1988. Moral Mazes: The World of Corporate Managers. New York: Oxford University Press.

Kagan, Robert A., and John T. Scholz, 1984. "The 'criminology of the corporation' and regulatory enforcement strategies." In Enforcing Regulation, eds. Keith Hawkins and John M. Thomas, 67–95. Boston: Kluwer-Nijhoff.

Katz, Jack, 1980. "The social movement against white collar crime." In Criminology Review Yearbook, eds. Egon Bittner and Sheldon L. Messinger, 161–184. Beverly Hills. Calif.: Sage.

Kelman, Herbert C., and V. Lee Hamilton, 1989. Crimes of Obedience: Toward a Social Psychology of Authority and Responsibility. New Haven: Yale University Press.

Kramer, Ronald C., 1982. "Corporate crime: An organizational perspective." In White-Collar and Economic Crime: Multidisciplinary and Crossnational Perspectives, eds. Peter Wickman and Timothy Dailey, 75–94. Greenwich. Conn.: JAI Press.

Kriesberg, Simeon M., 1976. "Decisionmaking models and the control of corporate crime." The Yale Law Journal 85:1091–1129.

Kunen, James S., 1994. Reckless Disregard: Corporate Greed, Government Indifference, and the Kentucky School Bus Crash. New York: Simon and Schuster.

Lacey, Robert, 1986. Ford: The Men and the Machine. New York: Ballantine Books.

Laroche, Herve, 1995. "From decision to action in organizations: Decision-making as a social representation." Organization Science 6:62–75.

Lee, Matthew T., 1998. "Explaining 'what a bad bureaucracy did to Joe Sixpack': Competing constructions of the human radiation experiments as a social problem." Paper presented at the Eastern Sociological Society Meeting. (March 20)

Lowrance, William, 1976. Of Acceptable Risk: Science and the Determination of Safety. Los Altos, Calif.: Kaufman.

Mashaw, Jerry L., and David L. Harfst, 1990. The Struggle for Auto Safety. Cambridge: Harvard University Press.

Mokhiber, Russell, 1989. Corporate Crime and Violence. San Francisco: Sierra Club Books.

Nader, Ralph, 1965. Unsafe at Any Speed: The Designed-In Dangers of the American Automobile. New York: Pocket Books.

Nader, Ralph, and Wesley J. Smith, 1996. No Contest: Corporate Lawyers and the Perversion of Justice in America. New York: Random House.

NHTSA Office of Defects Investigation, 1977. Internal Investigation Report: C7-38. Copies of cited material on file with the author.

Powell, Walter W., and Paul J. DiMaggio, (eds.), 1991. The New Institutionalism in Organizational Analysis. Chicago: University of Chicago Press.

Rabe, Gary, and M. David Ermann, 1995. "Corporate concealment of tobacco hazards: Changing motives and historical contexts." Deviant Behavior 16:223–244.

Schwartz. Gary T., 1991. "The myth of the Ford Pinto case." Rutgers Law Review 43:1013–1068.

Scott, W. Richard, 1998. Organizations: Rational, Natural, and Open Systems. Upper Saddle River, N.J.: Prentice-Hall.

Simon, David R., 1999. Elite Deviance (6th ed.). Boston: Allyn and Bacon.

Simon, David R., and D. Stanley Eitzen, 1990. Elite Deviance. Boston: Allyn and Bacon.

Skolnick, Jerome H., and Elliot Currie (eds.), 1979. Crisis in American Institutions. Boston: Little and Brown.

Solomon, Kenneth A., Penny E. Perkins, and Susan Resetar, 1985. Improving Auto Safety: The Role of Industry, the Government, and the Driver. Santa Monica, Calif.: Rand Corporation.

Stone, Christopher D., 1977. "A slap on the wrist for the Kepone mob." Business and Society Review 22:4–11.

Strickland, Lee, 1996. Personal interview conducted on September 4.

Strobel, Lee Patrick, 1980. Reckless Homicide?: Ford's Pinto Trial. South Bend, Ind.: And Books.

———. 1994. "The Pinto documents." In The Ford Pinto Case: A Study in Applied Ethics, Business, and Technology, eds. Douglas Birsch and John H. Fielder, 41–53. Albany, N.Y.: SUNY Press.

Swigert, Victoria Lynn, and Ronald A. Farrell, 1980–1981. "Corporate homicide: Definitional processes in the creation of deviance." Law and Society Review 15:161–182.

Szasz. Andrew, 1986. "Corporations, organized crime, and the disposal of hazardous waste: An examination of the making of a criminogenic regulatory structure." Criminology 24: 1–27.

U.S. Department of Transportation, 1974. "Part 571—Federal motor vehicle safety standards: Fuel system integrity." Federal Register 39:10586–10590.

———. 1985. National Traffic and Motor Vehicle Safety Act of 1966: Legislative History (Vol. I). Washington D.C.: GPO.

———. 1988. Motor Vehicle Safety Standard No. 301: Fuel System Integrity. Internal document. Copy on file with the author.

———. 1990. Motor Vehicle Safety 1990. Washington: DOT.

U.S. General Accounting Office, 1976. Effectiveness, Benefits, and Costs of Federal Safety Standards for Protection of Passenger Car Occupants. Washington: GPO.

Vaughan, Diane, 1996. The Challenger Launch Decision: Risky Technology, Culture, and Deviance at NASA. Chicago: University of Chicago Press.

———. 1998. "Rational choice, situated action, and the social control of organizations." Law and Society Review 32:23–61.

Wald, Matthew L., 1997. "Auto safety: Accident data review to focus on rollovers." New York Times, Internet document (March 14).

Wallace, Mike, 1978. "Is your car safe?" Segment appearing on the television show 60 Minutes (June 7). Produced by David Lowe, Jr. Transcript on file with the author.

———. 1996. Speech given at National Press Club Luncheon (March 14). Transcript on file with the author.

Weick, Karl E., 1995. Sensemaking in Organizations. Thousand Oaks, Calif.: Sage.

Yeager. Peter C., 1991. The Limits of Law: The Public Regulation of Private Pollution. New York: Cambridge University Press.

Legal Citations

Automotive Parts and Accessories Association v. Boyd, 407 F.2d 330 (1968).

Chrysler Corporation v. Department of Transportation, 472 F.2d 659 (1972).

Evans v. General Motors Corporation, 359 F.2d 822 (1966).

Grimshaw v. Ford Motor Company, 119 Cal. App. 3d 757. 174 Cal. Rptr. 348 (1981).

16

The *Challenger* Space Shuttle Disaster
Conventional Wisdom and a Revisionist Account[1]
Diane Vaughan

Scholars who study corporate and other forms of organizational
misconduct usually lack direct access to violating organizations.
When a particular case receives a lot of public attention, we benefit from data gathered and produced by others: official investigations and commissions, journalists, or whistle-blowers. While these
data can be abundant and allow us to study phenomena otherwise
unavailable to us, they are secondary sources. Unable to witness the
incidents as they are occurring, we rely upon the accounts of others.
As secondary sources, they sometimes contain biases and distortions that confound our analyses, and thus, the causal theories that
result from our research. Our reliance on secondary sources affect
theorizing for quantitative and qualitative data alike. However, I
will focus here on qualitative data, drawing upon my research
experience with a much-publicized, sensational case.[2] Based on a
nine-year study of NASA's fatal decision to launch the Space Shuttle
Challenger in 1986, I 1) show how going deep into primary sources
contradicted the historically accepted explanation of the disaster
by contrasting the Conventional Wisdom about what happened with
a Revisionist Account, 2) identify the socially-organized sources of
distortion and misunderstanding that outside investigators of a

From "Sensational Cases, Flawed Theories," pp. 45–66 in *Contemporary Issues in
Criminal Justice: Essays in Honor of Gilbert Geis,* edited by Henry N. Pontell and
David Sichor. Copyright © 2001 by Prentice Hall, Inc. Reprinted by permission

1. An earlier version of this paper was presented at the Annual Meetings of the American
Society of Criminology, Boston MA, November 16–19, 1995.

2. Diane Vaughan. *The Challenger Launch Decision: Risky Technology, Culture, and Deviance at
NASA.* Chicago: University of Chicago Press, 1996.

sensational case confront, and 3) conclude with some thoughts about the implications for future research on sensational cases.

The Research: Starting Assumptions, Contradictions, and Surprise

When the *Challenger* disaster occurred on January 28, 1986, then-President Reagan appointed a Presidential Commission to investigate the cause of the tragedy. At that time, I was looking for a case of organizational misconduct that involved a large organization (but not a corporation) for a three-case project I had begun.[3] The public hearings of the Presidential Commission appointed to investigate the accident and the media began revealing to the public NASA history and what had transpired during the launch decision. The case appeared to meet all qualifications for organizational misconduct, as I was defining it:

> Violations of laws, rules, or administrative regulations by an individual or group of individuals in an organization who, in their organizational role, act or fail to act in ways that further the attainment of organization goals.

The accident seemed to me to be an example of organizational misconduct because of the presence of the three factors most commonly associated with organizational misconduct: competitive pressures and resource scarcity; organizational characteristics—structure, processes, and transactions—that create opportunities for misconduct; and regulatory failure. These three structural factors, in combination, affect individual choice, encouraging individual

---

3. The project was about analogical theorizing: building general theory across case studies of similar events, phenomena, or activities that occur in different social settings. In my first case, I had developed a theory of organizational misconduct, and was planning a book that compared three examples of misconduct in organizational forms of varying size and complexity. I had chosen and was working on two cases: police misconduct and violence and abuse in the family, and wanted a third that was a complex organization. For detail, see Diane Vaughan, "Theory Elaboration: The Heuristics of Case Analysis," in Charles Ragin and Howard S. Becker, *What is a Case? Explorations into the Foundations of Social Inquiry*. New York: Cambridge University Press, 1992; Diane Vaughan, "The Macro/Micro Connection in White Collar Crime Theory," in Kip Schlegel and David Weisburd (eds.), *White Collar Crime Reconsidered*. Boston: Northeastern University Press, 1992; Diane Vaughan, *Theorizing: Analogy, Cases, and Comparative Social Organization* (in preparation).

decisions to violate rules and engage in harmful, violative acts in the interest of organization goals.[4]

From the Commission's televised hearings and media accounts, I learned that on the eve of the disastrous launch, NASA managers were warned against launching by engineers at Morton Thiokol, Inc., the manufacturer of the Solid Rocket Booster (SRB), the technical cause of the accident, yet NASA went against this recommendation, proceeding with launch. I also learned that on that night NASA managers at Marshall Space Flight Center had violated rules about passing information about the engineers' complaints about the booster problem up the hierarchy to their superiors. Moreover, the Commission discovered a history of decision making from 1977–1985 in which NASA continued to fly the shuttle with known flaws in the joint of the Solid Rocket Booster. During these early years, other rules were violated: industry rules about the design and requirements for use of the O-rings. In addition to these rule violations, televised and published accounts verified that the space agency was under extraordinary economic strain, which resulted in production pressure to launch shuttles in keeping with an extremely tight launch schedule. The capstone was regulatory failure. So inadequate was safety regulation at NASA that the Commission called it "The Silent Safety System."

I began collecting published media accounts and tracking the revelations of the Presidential Commission investigation as news was breaking. In June of 1986, Volume I of the Presidential Commission Report was published. The Commission concluded that the technical cause of the accident was the failure of a rubber-like O-ring that lay in a joint of the left Solid Rocket Booster. But they also implicated NASA management, and indicated that "decision making was flawed" at the space agency. The extensive documentation of flawed decision making, rule violations, and production pressures at NASA created what became the historically accepted explanation of the tragedy: NASA managers, experiencing production pressure in a year when many important launches were planned that were essential to the future of the space program, ignored the advice of contractor

4. These three factors act in combination to produce organizational misconduct. Their ability to do so is discussed in detail in Chapters 3, 4, and 5 of Diane Vaughan, *Controlling Unlawful Organizational Behavior*. Chicago: University of Chicago Press, 1983.

engineers and went forward with the launch, violating rules about reporting problems up the hierarchy in the process. The historically accepted explanation was a form of rational choice theory, wherein managers weighed the costs and benefits of their actions. Thus, the incident conformed to traditional explanations of elite and white-collar deviance in sociology: the amorally calculating manager model.[5]

This model is a consequentialist model that locates the cause of organizational misconduct in the utilitarian calculations of individuals, precluding any other influences upon individual choice. In contrast, my interest was in examining the social context: how organization, environment, and regulatory failure might have impinged on the decisions of these managers. Volume I contained over 230 pages of analysis, documents, reproductions of memoranda and letters, and quotes from the Commission's hearings testimony, along with extensive detail about how both the organization and the technology operated. This volume, I decided, would be the basis for my analysis, along with the now extensive files I had created from newspapers, journals, and magazines. But as I began analyzing Volume I, I learned that some of my most basic assumptions about the technology were wrong: for example, according to engineers, the shuttle did not explode. There was a structural break-up and a fireball, but no explosion. More serious were challenges to my hypothesis about what went on in the organization, discovered when I went beyond Volume I into the other four volumes of the Commission report, published months later in the summer of 1986.[6] For this to be an example of misconduct, I needed to verify the connection between production pressures, organization goals, and the rule violations by Marshall managers: the macro-micro connection. I chose to examine what appeared to be the most egregious of the reported violations the Commission uncovered: 1) Marshall Solid Rocket Booster Project Manager Lawrence B. Mulloy's sequence of six waivers of the booster joints' Criticality 1 status, which allowed six flights to proceed without altering the design after that Criticality 1 status was

5. Robert A. Kagan and John T. Scholz, "The Criminology of the Corporation and Regulatory Enforcement Strategies." In *Enforcing Regulation*, ed. Keith Hawkins and John M. Thomas. Boston: Kluwer-Nijhoff, 1984.

6. Presidential Commission on the Space Shuttle *Challenger* Accident, *Report to the President by the Presidential Commission on the Space Shuttle Challenger Accident*. 5 volumes. Washington D.C.: Government Printing Office, 1986.

imposed, and 2) this same manager's waiver of a launch constraint, which allowed the vehicle to continue flight after the launch constraint was imposed. These waivers appeared to be the surreptitious acts of a manager under extreme launch pressure.

In order to examine these rule violations closely and consider them within the social context of decision making, I concentrated on Volumes IV and V of the Commission Report. These volumes contained the full transcription of testimony at the Commission's hearings and appendices containing copies of rules about launch decision making. Now 13 months into the project, I discovered that the Commission had made a mistake. Mulloy's waivers were absolutely *in keeping with NASA rules, not violations of them.* The Commission had misunderstood NASA procedures. Both in the televised hearings (and so also in the hearing transcripts) and in Volume I, the Commission used the word waiver as a verb: e.g., Mulloy waived the Criticality 1 status. But I discovered that in NASA language, "waiver" is a noun. A waiver is a mechanism for giving Criticality 1 items an extra review. Hundreds of items on the shuttle were Criticality 1 (the Orbiter wings, for example, which had no back-up in case of failure, and thus were Criticality 1—if a wing failed, crew, mission, and vehicle were lost). When the contractor engineering analysis determines, through tests, calculations, and adjustments to the technical component that it is safe to fly, an item with Criticality 1 status can fly. So a Project Manager then must issue a waiver so that launch can proceed. Each of Mulloy's waivers were the consequence of the extra reviews by Thiokol engineers, who recommended proceeding with launch for every mission prior to the *Challenger* mission. Moreover, these waivers were always recorded; not the secretive surreptitious acts I believed, based on the Commission's hearings and Report. Waivers were routine at NASA—a safety procedure, a precautionary measure, not a rule violation.

This discovery altered the course of my project. Obviously, the Presidential Commission had not fully understood aspects of NASA culture, and therefore had mistakenly interpreted waivers as rule violations when they were not. Now, I questioned other reported rule violations, and so shifted my attention from the eve of the launch to the history of decision making. Were these other "alleged" rule violations true rule violations? And how had the competitive environment, organization characteristics, and regulatory failure

affected NASA decisions on the eve of the launch *and* in the past?
Thus, the research became an historical ethnography. I turned from
my original focus on the eve of the launch to include a reconstructed
a chronology of the past from archival data and interviews. I turned
to original archival data collected by the Presidential Commission,
stored at the National Archives. These data had not been examined
by other investigators. They included over 200,000 pages of original documents and 9,000 pages of interview transcripts. A team of
government investigators working for the Commission conducted
interviews with 160 NASA and contractor employees. They interviewed them on two topics: the eve of the launch teleconference
and the history of the Solid Rocket Booster problems at NASA. For
most of the 160 people, the National Archive files contain two
lengthy transcripts. Of the 160, only 40% testified before the Presidential Commission, so these transcripts were a very important
source of information. In addition, I relied extensively on the three-
volume Report of the House Committee on Science and Technology, published in October 1986. Contradicting many of the findings of the Commission, this Report was published later, by which
time the media had gone on to other sensational stories, so the
historically accepted explanation of the *Challenger* disaster remained
intact. Finally, I also conducted lengthy personal interviews.

These primary sources of data showed how the official investigation and media accounts had distorted history. I discovered many
more contradictions to the historically accepted explanation of the
launch decision produced by the Presidential Commission hearings,
Volume I, and the media accounts in the year the disaster occurred.
Here are some (but by no means all) of the contradictions that I
found. First, I list the Commission-generated, media-mediated conventional interpretation (the Conventional Wisdom) of events at
NASA, then my discoveries (the Revisionist Account).

**The Conventional Wisdom (CW) Versus
the Revisionist Account (RA)**

* CW: Commissioner Feynman's famous TV demonstration of
O-ring response to cold when a piece of a ring was dipped in ice

water revealed to NASA managers and engineers and the Presidential Commission the technical cause of the accident.

RA: All engineers and managers knew that when rubber gets cold, it gets hard. The eve of launch teleconference had centered on this issue, so when the disaster occurred, the people doing the hands-on engineering immediately assumed that the cold had affected the O-rings. Feynman enlightened the Commission, but not the teleconference participants, and not people at NASA associated with the Solid Rocket Booster Project. Also, his demonstration missed the complexity of the engineering problem on the eve of the launch. It involved not only O-ring resiliency in cold temperatures, but joint dynamics under enormous ignition pressures and timing, in milliseconds.

* CW: Thiokol engineers had convincing engineering analysis on the eve of launch and strong argument against launching

RA: All teleconference participants, including Thiokol engineers, agreed that the engineering argument was weak and not convincing. They posed a correlation between O-ring damage and cold temperature, but had data in their presentation that contradicted their no-launch position. Only one Thiokol engineer (Arnie Thompson) believed they had a good engineering analysis.

* CW: Marshall managers suppressed information about problems, violating NASA reporting rules. Thus, individual secrecy contributed to the disaster.

RA: Marshall managers followed all rules about reporting problems. Structural secrecy, not individual secrecy, contributed to the disaster: Hierarchy, division of labor, specialization, and segmentation that typify complex organizations divided information and knowledge, blocking understanding about the technology for people not directly working on the boosters.

* CW: NASA had to get *Challenger* off the pad that morning because of production pressure, the Teacher in Space mission, and Reagan's State of the Union message, scheduled for that night.

RA: For every launch date, NASA establishes two launch windows. Temperature in the afternoon was going to be in 40s or 50s; if Marshall managers truly believed it was risky, they could have delayed till afternoon without jeopardizing the goals of the space agency.

* CW: Cold O-rings, eroded by hot gases, didn't do their job. Erosion caused the disaster.

RA: The O-rings were the cause of the technical failure, but contingency also had an effect. If the O-rings had failed, they would have failed in first 600 milliseconds after ignition, resulting in a launch pad disaster. The O-rings were eroded by hot ignition gases, as Thiokol engineers had predicted, but the joint held. Fifty-three seconds into the launch, however, an unpredicted and unprecedented wind shear shook the shuttle violently, dislodging the charred material that was sealing the booster joint, allowing hot gases to penetrate first, the booster, and then, the external tank. If there had been no wind, the astronauts might have lived.

* CW: Marshall managers violated safety rules on eve of launch, failing to report information about the telecon up the hierarchy to superiors.

RA: Marshall managers followed every reporting rule, doing exactly as they and other shuttle project managers were required to do and had done in the past.

* CW: Marshall managers were risk-takers, acting amorally, throughout the history of shuttle program, putting production pressures and deadlines ahead of safety.

RA: Marshall Space Flight Center had a reputation with Thiokol and among the other NASA space centers as extremely conservative—in fact, they were criticized as *too* conservative; Marshall personnel had the nickname of "dinosaurs." Ironically, in the history of decision making, the positions of Thiokol and Marshall were often the reverse of what they were on the eve of the launch: the Marshall managers involved in the *Challenger* teleconference often argued against Thiokol engineers recommendations to launch, delaying launch for safety reasons.

* CW: The eve-of-launch teleconference was initiated by Thiokol engineers, concerned about cold.

RA: Marshall manager Larry Wear called Thiokol in Utah to see if Thiokol engineers had any concerns about the cold. If he had not called, the teleconference would not have happened because Thiokol engineers in Utah were unaware of temperature at the launch site at the Cape and Thiokol officials who were at the Cape (including Thiokol Project Manager Al McDonald), when asked, told the Launch Director that they did not see any problems with cold and booster.

* CW: Thiokol engineers were unanimously opposed to launching *Challenger*.

RA: Thiokol engineers were divided: some were in favor of launch, some were opposed.

* CW: Memos written by engineers at both Marshall and Thiokol were objecting to the Solid Rocket Booster design as early as 1978, but managers didn't listen, overriding engineering opinion.

RA: Every management decision to fly prior to 1986 was based on Thiokol engineers' analysis about risk acceptability and recommendations to launch. The same engineers that objected on the eve of the launch believed it was safe to fly, based on engineering analysis, during those years, and so recommended to their management. Memos surfacing after the disaster, authored by unhappy engineers, became part of the collective memory. But memos were taken out of the stream of actions in which they were created. What was omitted from the public record was that as problems occurred, the same engineers fixed them, finding the design acceptable.

* CW: On the eve of the launch, Thiokol engineers believed there would be a catastrophe.

RA: One engineer, Thiokol's Robert Ebeling, said afterward he thought there would be a catastrophe, but he said nothing during teleconference. None of the other engineers, including Roger Boisjoly, the engineer who most vigorously protested against the launch, foresaw catastrophe. They were very concerned. They foresaw problems and expected more erosion, but none believed a disaster would occur. Boisjoly, exiting the teleconference and angry about the outcome, stopped by a colleague's office, telling him that when the boosters were disassembled after the mission returned he should document the damage well because they would have a new data point enabling them to gain more insight about cold-temperature effects on O-rings.

* CW: After the disaster, Head of Astronaut Office John W. Young criticized NASA to the media, stating that the shuttle contained so many risky parts that astronauts on previous missions were lucky to be alive.

RA: Young, as Head of Astronaut Office, was part of NASA's launch decision chain, participating at the top of Flight Readiness Review, the formal pre-launch decision making procedure. He heard all the engineering analyses for all technical components of the shuttle prior to each launch. He, along with the rest of top NASA administrators, had consistently given the final okay for all launches.

The Conventional Wisdom provided the basis for amoral calculation as the historically accepted explanation of this event. The Commission's televised hearings and Volume I of the Commission's final report were the basis for many, if not most, public definitions of the situation. Receiving near-universal praise for what was the most extensive and expensive public investigation to date, the Commission successfully identified many problems at NASA that contributed to the tragic loss of the *Challenger* crew. In Volume I, however, we repeatedly read that "NASA" did this or "NASA" did that—a language that simultaneously blames everyone and no one, obscuring who in the huge bureaucracy was actually doing what. Top administrators making policy, middle managers, and the engineers at the bottom of the launch decision chain who were doing the risk assessments were indistinguishable. The Commission's report did not officially blame any specific individuals. But their questioning of NASA managers in the televised hearings, the erroneous finding that NASA middle managers violated rules in both the history of decision making and on the eve of the launch, and the Commission report conclusion that the "decision making was flawed" focused public attention in one place. The public drama created the impression that NASA middle managers alone were responsible for the tragedy. This impression was reflected in a comment one FBI agent jokingly uttered to Marshall SRB Project Manager Lawrence Mulloy as he left the hearings following testimony one day, "After they get you for this, Mulloy, they're going to get you for Jimmy Hoffa.[7]

Other aspects of the Commission investigation added to the public imagery of managerial wrong-doing. For example, the Commission's inability to fully grasp NASA reporting rules resulted in many post-tragedy accounts that had Marshall SRB Project Manager Mulloy suppressing information when he presented the engineering assessments to top NASA administrators. But a late-breaking video recording of Mulloy briefing top administrators prior to STS 51-E (the flight following the January 1985 cold weather launch) showed a full oral review of the O-ring problem that was consistent, both in form and content, with guidelines for NASA Level I reporting requirements.[8] The existence of this video

7. Lawrence B. Mulloy, telephone interview by author, 19 March 1993.

8. Lawrence B. Mulloy. Level I Flight Readiness Review, 51-E, 21 February 1985, Reel .098, Motion Picture and Video Library, National Archives, Washington, D.C.

was not known to the NASA or Commission investigations at the time of the hearings.[9] Therefore, neither Mulloy's full briefing nor the video of it were acknowledged in Volume I of the Presidential Commission's report. Because the video was discovered after Volume I had gone to press (it was published months before the other volumes), it was mentioned and transcribed only in Volume II, which contains nine appendices of technical reports of densely-packed detail in small print.[10] Had this video surfaced during the Commission hearings and its existence and transcription been reported in Volume I—or a press conference been called when it turned up—the historic record about managerial wrong-doing and "who knew what when" at NASA might have been different.

Another important distortion resulted from the selection of witnesses to testify. For the televised hearings, nearly eighty witnesses were called. Working engineers were underrepresented. Seven were asked, all of whom were opposed to the launch. But fifteen working engineers participated in the teleconference. The National Archives interview transcripts show that not all engineers who participated in the teleconference agreed with the position that Boisjoly and Thompson represented so vigorously. The engineers who differed did not testify, so these diverse views never became part of post-tragedy accounts. Furthermore, since the emphasis of the questioning was on the launch decision, the fact that the same working engineers who opposed the *Challenger* launch were responsible for the official risk assessments and recommendations for all booster launch decisions in the preceding years also got lost.

NASA managers were certainly implicated and responsible for their actions. But for the average citizen, the focus on managerial wrongdoing deflected attention from these other significant aspects of this historic incident. The Commission's Report, and the other post-tragedy accounts that were based upon it misled the public about the causes of the accident. It prevented them from understanding that the conditions that caused the disaster were not eliminated, so another disaster could happen. The causes of the acci-

9. For explanation, see House Committee, *Investigation: Hearings*, Vol. I, 410–412.

10. For acknowledgment of the video and a transcript, see Presidential Commission, *Report*, Vol. II, H2, H42.

dent went beyond the actions of individuals to the environment, the NASA organization, and the developmental nature of the shuttle technology.

1. **The Environment.** By focusing on amorally calculating managers, public attention was diverted from elite networks: top NASA administrators, Congress, and the Administration who made decisions that politicized the space program, created economic strain and production pressures, and put the teacher, Christa McAuliffe, on the shuttle. Their responsibility for the disaster and its consequences never became the center of public attention. Today, the agency remains politicized, economically dependent upon Congress, and underfunded. It continues to try to relieve economic strain by managing impressions in order to curry favor with the public and Congress, as the recent John Glenn mission attests.

2. **The Risky Technology.** Although both the Presidential Commission and the House Committee on Science and Technology stressed that shuttle technology was still developmental and therefore, extremely risky, the emphasis on amoral calculating managers left the public unaware of the unprecedented character of the technology, its developmental character, and the sheer difficulty that engineers encounter in assessing risk for this ambiguous, uncertain technology. The public assumes high risk technology is based on science, and therefore exact diagnosis is possible. But the shuttle is a large scale technical system that cannot be fully tested on the ground. Engineers do calculations, ground tests, and lab tests, but they cannot predict or test for the forces of the environment the vehicle will experience in space.

3. **The NASA/Contractor Organization.** Traditionally, when things go wrong in organizations, individuals are blamed: operator error, amorally calculating managers, incompetence, failure to abide by rules, etc. However, organizations, while a great asset that allows us many modern efficiencies, have their dark side.[11] They are comprised of structures, processes, transaction systems, and institutional logics that affect the cognition, meaning, and action of individual employees. These characteristics are common to all

11. Diane Vaughan, "The Dark Side of Organizations: Mistake, Misconduct, and Disaster." *Annual Review of Sociology* 25 (1999): 271–305.

organizations, producing harmful outcomes, even when personnel are well trained, well-intentioned, have adequate resources, and do all the correct things.

Scholars are only too familiar what Scott Sagan calls "the politics of blame."[12] In the historically accepted explanation of the tragedy, a failed booster technology, a flawed decision making structure, and amorally calculating managers were the culprits. Leaving managers twisting in the wind was the best of all possible outcomes for NASA because the cure was easy: fire and retire responsible managers, fix the decision making structure and the technology, and go on. The program could not survive public awareness that the technology was as risky as it really was/is because that awareness would have jeopardized the myth of routine and economical space flight that secured the space agency's future. And it definitely was not in the interest of the space agency or the White House to have top administrators implicated. The focus on managers effectively kept the public from wondering who put Christa McAuliffe on the shuttle in the first place.

The Socially Organized Sources of Distortion and Outsider Misunderstanding

Public understanding of this historic event developed, not from immediate experience, but from accounts created by the official investigations, media, and other post-tragedy analysts. The *Challenger* disaster generated an enormous amount of archival information as well as much conflicting public discourse, making possible analysis of a complex technical case not possible otherwise. But this advantage had an accompanying disadvantage. Dorothy Smith reminds us:

> Our knowledge of contemporary society is to a large extent mediated to us by documents of various kinds. Very little of our knowledge of people, events, social relations and powers arises directly from our own experience. Factual elements in documentary form, whether as news, data, information or the like, stand in for an actu-

---

12. Scott Sagan, *The Limits of Safety*. Princeton: Princeton University Press, 1993.

ality which is not directly accessible. Socially organized practices of reporting and recording work upon what actually happens or has happened to create a reality in documentary form, and though they are decisive to its character, their practices are not visible in it.[13]

The historically-accepted explanation of the *Challenger* disaster developed from the documentary accounts produced by many. The account of the Presidential Commission was definitively influential in the production of all others. The Commission findings were extensive and complex, covering every possible point of inquiry. But as the major initial source of public information, it was also the major initial source of public misunderstanding. The Commission's findings were distorted by three factors: Retrospection and hindsight, autonomy and interdependence between the Commission and the NASA/contractor system, and documentary accounts and the reduction of information. These three factors are common sources of outsider misunderstanding when organizations do bad things. Although this discussion focuses on the Commission, it logically extends to the media. And to us, as scholars who tend to use media and official investigation sources as starting points for research.

Retrospection and Hindsight

Starbuck and Milliken point out that when observers who know the results of organizational actions try to make sense of them, they tend to see two kinds of analytic sequences.[14] Starting from the bad result and seeking to explain it, observers seek the incorrect actions, the flawed analyses, and the inaccurate perceptions that led to the result. Nearly all explanations of crisis, disaster, or organization failure single out how managers "failed to spot major environmental threats or opportunities, failed to heed well-founded warnings, assessed risks improperly, or adhered to outdated goals and beliefs."[15] In contrast, analyses of success celebrate accurate managerial vision,

13. Dorothy E. Smith. "The Social Construction of Documentary Reality," *Sociological Inquiry* 44 (1974): 257–267.

14. William H. Starbuck and Frances J. Milliken, "Executives' Perceptual Filters: What They Notice and How They Make Sense," in *The Executive Effect*, ed. Donald Hambrick (Greenwich CT: JAI Press, 1988).

15. Ibid., 38.

wise risk-taking, well-conceived goals, and diligent, intelligent persistence, despite scarce resources and other obstacles. These two analytic sequences lead to a selective focus that oversimplifies what happened. First, they focus attention on individual decision makers, putting managerial perceptions as the cause of all organizational outcomes. Second, they neglect the importance and complexity of organizations as a locus of individual decision making. Third, they obliterate the complexity and ambiguity of the task environments that people once faced. Paying attention to all these factors, Turner, in *Man-made Disasters,* notes the tendency for a problem that was ill-structured in an organization to become a well-structured problem after a disaster, as people look back and reinterpret information pre-existing the disaster, ignored or minimized at the time, that afterward takes on new significance as signals of danger.[16]

The Commission followed the pattern of which Starbuck, Milliken, and Turner warned: Starting from the bad result and seeking to explain it, the Commission and its investigators sought out the incorrect actions, the flawed analyses, and the inaccurate perceptions that led to the result. Selective attention to information that seemed to explain the harmful outcome led the Commission to ignore the fact that NASA had frequently exercised caution, delaying many launches for safety reasons. In hindsight, the SRB joint problem became a well-structured problem for the Commission, as the tragedy made salient and selectively focused attention on the NASA decisions that seemed to lead inexorably to it. The Commission saw damage to the O-rings as a coherent trajectory of strong signals of potential danger, but for managers and engineers working on the problem, signals were mixed, weak, and routine as the problem unfolded chronologically. Retrospection led the Commission to call teleconference engineers who protested the launch to testify, omitting the testimony of those who were in favor of it. Furthermore, retrospection led the Commission to extract actions from their

---

16. Barry Turner, *Man-Made Disasters* (London: Wykeham, 1978); Barry Turner, "The Organizational and Interorganizational Development of Disasters," *Administrative Science Quarterly* 21(1976): 383, 392–93. Perrow found that in the accident at the nuclear power plant at Three Mile Island, warning signals before the accident were seen as "background noise;" only in retrospect did they become signals of danger to insiders. Charles Perrow, "The President's Commission and the Normal Accident," in *The Accident at Three Mile Island: The Human Dimensions,* eds. David Sills, Charles Wolf, and Vivian Shelanski (Boulder: Westview Press, 1981).

historical and organizational context in a stream of actions, the sequence of events and structures of which they were a part. Engineering memos complaining about the boosters became central to the documentary account, whereas the correction of booster design inadequacies and participation in launch recommendations by those same engineers never became part of the documentary record. Robbed of social and cultural context that gave them meaning, many NASA actions became hard to understand, controversial, and, in some cases, incriminating. The result was a systematic distortion of history that obscured the meaning of the events and actions as it existed and changed for the participants in the situation at the time they occurred.

Interorganizational Regulatory Relations:
Autonomy and Interdependence

Outside investigators have a structural relationship with the organizations they investigate that can be a source of distortion and outsider misunderstanding. Elsewhere, I have written about how autonomy and interdependence affect regulatory relationships.[17] The Commission was acting in its capacity as a Presidentially-appointed regulatory body mandated to investigate and identify the cause of the disaster. Autonomy and interdependence affect all regulatory relationships, and are consequences of interorganizational relations between the regulator and the regulated organization. The problem of autonomy grows out of the physical separateness of regulated and regulator. When situated external to the regulated organization, regulators have trouble penetrating organizational boundaries, which creates difficulty for the monitoring, discovery, and investigative stages of regulation. External regulators are restricted to information gathered after the fact and have trouble understanding the culture, language, and technology of regulated organizations. Interdependence refers to the fact that, despite being separate, autonomous bodies, regulator and regulated

17. Vaughan, *Controlling Unlawful Organizational Behavior* Chapter 6; "Autonomy, Interdependence, and Social Control: NASA and the Space Shuttle *Challenger*," 35 *Administrative Science Quarterly* (June 1990): 225–257; *The Challenger Launch Decision: Risky Technology, Culture, and Deviance at NASA.* University of Chicago, 1996, Chapter 8.

can be bound together by resource exchange or common interests, so that their past, present, and future are linked: they rise
and fall together. Interdependence affects the blame-placing and
sanctioning part of the process, frequently resulting in compromised sanctions. The work of regulatory bodies is always affected
(to greater or lesser extent) by both autonomy and interdependence, despite the intensity and resources devoted to a particular regulatory effort.

As a regulator situated external to NASA, the Commission's investigation clearly was affected by both autonomy and interdependence. With a mandate to publish a report within 180 days, the
Commission was faced with an enormous task. Although many
Commission members were affiliated with the aerospace community,
and two, Sally Ride and Neil Armstrong, were astronauts, none were
familiar with Solid Rocket Booster technology, nor were they familiar with NASA rules and procedures for hazard assessments or launch
decisions. Also, NASA engineering culture and the language were
tremendous obstacles for the investigators. In many sections of the
hearings testimony, NASA and Thiokol managers and engineers
clearly were working very hard to explain both the technology and
the decision making procedures to stymied Commission members.
This problem was exacerbated because the Commission was faced
with a deadline and an overwhelming amount of original documents,
so relied on two strategies that selectively reduced and sorted the
information on which they based their analysis.

First, they created a small organization, with an Executive Director and large staff to help them gather information. Their organization was hierarchical, and included a team of government investigators for interviewing plus special Task Forces, led by Commission
members, to investigate the technical aspects of the accident. This
team divided up the work, reporting to the Commission members.
In striking parallel with what happened at NASA about the Solid
Rocket Boosters, the investigation was affected by structural secrecy
and the successive reduction of information. Because of the division of labor, no one person had all the information. The team
members collectively discussed (but selectively) what each member
had found, then forwarded information they believed was important to the Commission. They omitted much, reducing the complexity of the event in the process (e.g., It was the team of govern-

ment investigators who recommended which engineers were to be called to testify). Second, all documents, interviews, and testimony were computerized, so Commission members could scan the data base to look for, say, a specific engineering memo or action. While this gave them speedy access to information, it also was selective, extracting actions from the chronological context.

The problem of interdependence is obvious in the selection of people to be on the Commission. Having Commission members who were outsiders qualified to conduct an accident investigation involving aerospace technology was essential to having a thorough investigation that would be publicly credible *and* provide the skills necessary to diagnose what happened. However, these same decision criteria meant that Commission members also all had a vested interest in NASA's continued well-being. The appointment of William Rogers was propitious in the same doubled-edged sort of way. As a lawyer and in his former capacity as Attorney General of the United States, Rogers had been involved in the Warren Commission investigation and others. In terms of carrying out a rigorous investigation, his experience was an advantage. For example, it was Rogers who decided that the hearings should be televised and that all information collected by the Commission should be made accessible to the public at the National Archives. This decision was made out of his concern about the conspiracy theories that continued to circulate about the Kennedy assassination, which he believed was due to the fact that the government investigation was closed and all documents were sealed.

However, in view of the fact that he was a Republican appointed by the White House and what we know about interdependence and the effect of common interests on regulation, we necessarily must conclude that his willingness to get to the bottom of things at NASA may have been jeopardized by a political agenda. It is clear, however, that Commission members were not of one mind, nor did they share a common worldview that was affected by links to the White House. Sally Ride, for one, was outraged by what happened; the astronauts who died were part of her NASA family. And Richard Feynman went his own way throughout the investigation, paying little attention to Rogers.[18] Regardless of the idiosyncratic positions

---

18. Richard P. Feynman, *What Do You Care What Other People Think? Further Adventures of a Curious Character.* New York: Norton, 1988.

and views of the individuals, autonomy and interdependence are structural characteristics that have systematic effects on social control, and they were factors here.

Documentary Accounts and the Reduction of Information

The third and final socially organized source of distortion and outsider misunderstanding was how the Commission's findings were disseminated and used by others. At the same time that documentary accounts were proliferating, expanding what was known about certain aspects of the accident, a successive and systematic reduction of information was in progress. The televised hearings and the summary Volume I represented only a small portion of the findings contained in Volumes II through V. And those volumes were further reduced from the several hundred thousand pages of data the Commission gathered. The media, working from the televised hearings and Volume I, seized on some of the discoveries, covering them extensively, while ignoring others. Not that this was intentional. Each post-tragedy account reconstructed the *Challenger* accident or some aspect of it for other audiences. Each analyst was faced with the same problems the Commission faced: overwhelming detail about technical issues, NASA organization structure and procedures, and organizational and human history. Each published account had to be abbreviated because, first and obviously, the full account could never be known. Second, limits on the time available to gather, understand and absorb information, on the time and space available in which to tell the story, and on the audience's ability to wade through the details made it imperative that each analyst shorten and simplify.

So facts were presented, individual actions were described, but of necessity excised from the stream of actions that gave them their essential meaning. This shrinking of information from the original documentary sources and the excising of action from historic context also was true of the Presidential Commission's report, which was a systematic, thorough, detailed attempt to construct an historic chronology that took into account both the organization and its context. The House Committee on Science and Technology investigation report was not published until October 1986. Advantaged by the data collected by the Commission and beginning with a review of the Commission report, the House Committee went on to write a report that contradicted some of the Commission's main conclusions, among them the finding of rule violations by middle managers. But the House Committee report, coming later, never received the same media attention. From the published and televised accounts, the public—overwhelmed with information—reduced it even more. Unable to retain all the information, they latched on to something that explained for them the unexplainable and went on. The image of amorally calculating managers, production pressures, and a controversial eve-of-launch teleconference at NASA was a consistent imagery that dominated the documentary accounts. Consequently, many people, at the time vicariously witnessing the event through the televised hearings and the media, believed wrong-doing by middle management was behind the launch decision.

Sensational Cases: Cautionary Tales for Scholarly Inquiry

The *Challenger* disaster qualifies as a sensational case, not simply because the media made it one, but because it was experienced as one by the millions who witnessed it. It was an historic event and national tragedy that became embedded in the collective memory. But my research-based explanation of it was far from sensational. The cause of the *Challenger* disaster was not amorally calculating managers. Neither was it organizational misconduct (as traditionally defined) because no rules were violated. No evil individuals were behind what happened at the space agency. It was, as Merton has so famously written, "the unintended consequences of purposive social action."[19] The causes of the tragedy lay in the generic structures and processes of organizations and their institutional environments. This finding does not deny the importance of individual actions (or individual responsibility, for people always must be held accountable for their acts), but shifts attention to the situated character of individual choice.[20] Nor does it deny that something bad

19. Robert K. Merton, "The Unanticipated Consequences of Social Action." *American Sociological Review* 1(1936): 894–904.

20. Diane Vaughan, "Rational Choice, Situated Action, and the Social Control of Organizations." *Law & Society Review* 32 (1998): 23–61.

happened with serious implications for other cases of organizational misconduct—even those where amoral calculation is a factor.

At NASA, the environment of the organization, organization structures, processes, transaction systems, and institutional logics normalized signals of danger, thus blinding people to the harmful consequences of their acts. The result was that Marshall and Thiokol managers and engineers alike repeatedly made official decisions in which incidents of technical deviation from performance expectations for the boosters were redefined as normal and acceptable for space flight. Moreover, as missions accumulated, they accepted more and more technical deviation—including the new condition of cold temperature that officially became an acceptable risk on the eve of the *Challenger* launch. It is important to note that the normalization of deviance is not a cognitive construct. It is an institutional and organizational construct, for these factors can neutralize actions, directing behavior toward organization goals even when individuals themselves object to a particular line of action. Neither the harmful outcome nor the normalization of deviance that led to it are banal, but it can truly be said that the organizational environment, institutional logics, organization structures, processes, and transaction systems that were the origins of the disaster were banal.

The *Challenger* disaster is not an isolated example of the discrepancy between an historically-accepted explanation of a sensational case and what research based on primary sources produces. Lee and Ermann's recent re-analysis of the Ford Pinto case reveals the complexity behind the amoral calculator explanation that has stood as the historically accepted explanation of that incident.[21] One by one, Lee and Ermann dismantle the blocks of the Conventional Wisdom and replace them with their Revisionist Account, based on interviews with former Ford employees and their analysis of trial transcripts and original documents, classified for years after the case was officially settled. They, too, undertook an organizational analysis, finding that the explanation of this sensational case was not sensational: No amoral calculators were found. They conclude, "... a consciously cynical decision did not produce an unsafe fuel tank design . . . There was no 'decision' to market an unsafe prod-

---

21. Matthew T. Lee and M. David Ermann, "Pinto 'Madness' as a Flawed Landmark Narrative: An Organizational and Network Analysis." *Social Problems* 46 (1999): 30–47.

uct, and there was no 'decision' to market a safe one."[22] Like the *Challenger* case, generic organization structures and processes, not amoral calculation, intersected to produce an unintended consequence. The decision(s) to launch and continue launching a flawed Pinto on the market, they conclude, was the outcome of "institutionally embedded unreflective action" produced by organizational subunits embedded in a larger network of organizational relations.[23]

These two cases may not be representative: Scholars who dig deep into primary sources to research other cases publicly identified as examples of amoral calculation may verify the historically accepted explanation. The affirmation or refutation of amoral calculation as a causal explanation notwithstanding, these cases are cautionary tales with implications for future research. We, too, are vulnerable to the sources of distortions and outside misunderstanding: Retrospection and hindsight, autonomy and interdependence, and documentary accounts and the reduction of information. But for scholars, sensational cases raise additional concerns.

1. We must maintain a critical stance about the media and official inquiries. In research on corporate and organizational misconduct, we sometimes tend to see the media as our colleagues because, in keeping with our critical stance toward the power elite, journalists tantalize us with exposees that attack the powerful. Scholars educated in the wake of Watergate and the heyday of Ralph Nader may also rejoice when Commissions produce findings that take the side of the less powerful, as when the Presidential Commission blamed NASA managers and supported working engineers. In our enthusiasm for the bounty of information sensational cases produce, we must remind ourselves of what sociological research tells us about the social construction of news[24] and how official inquir-

22. Ibid., 43.

23. Ibid., 43.

24. Malcomb Spector and John Kitsuse, *Constructing Social Problems*. Menlo Park, CA: Cummings, 1977; Gaye Tuchman, *Making News*. New York: The Free Press, 1978; Herbert Gans, *Deciding What's News*. New York: Pantheon, 1979; Victoria Swiggert and Ron Farrell, "Corporate Homicide: Definitional Processes in the Creation of Deviance," *Law & Society Review* 15 (1980): 161–182; Michael Schudson, "Why the News is the Way it Is," *Raritan* 2 (Winter 1983): 109–125; Noam Chamsky and Edward Herman, *Manufacturing Consent: The Political Economy of the Mass Media*. New York: Pantheon, 1988; James Curran and Michael Gurevitch, eds., *Mass Media and Society*. London: Edward Arnold, 1992. William A. Gamson, *Talking Politics*. New York: Cambridge University Press, 1992.

ies produce knowledge for public consumption.[25] Nichols has written extensively on both these topics.[26] Acknowledging the substantial literature examining how moral entrepreneurs construct social problems and media participation in these transformations, he notes the comparative neglect of official inquiries by scholars:

> Interpretive work on public issues is often accomplished through official inquiries that combine documentary researches and interrogation of witnesses. Such investigations generate texts (especially transcripts, interim and final reports) in which inquisitors claim both to articulate authoritative versions of events, and to provide authoritative guidance on policy options. Within official inquiries, public hearings with live witnesses are routinely held, sometimes in an open-ended series that facilitates continual redefinition of central problems. When controversial issues are probed, the products of hearing are often disseminated in mass media, thereby affecting how large external audiences define situations. Although these processes are of interest to symbolic interactionists, official inquiries have so far received relatively little attention.[27]

Maintaining a critical stance toward the media and official investigations also extends to avoiding a rush to judgement in the opposite extreme: In explaining why their inquiries produce the kind of accounts that they do, we should hesitate before assuming cause. How they construct accounts is an empirical question. Official investigations and media are themselves organizations with goals and

25. See, e.g., Anthony Platt, ed., *The Politics of Riot Commissions*. New York: Macmillan. 1971; Michael Lipsky, "Social Scientists and the Riot Commission," *Annals of the American Academy of Political and Social Sciences* 394 (1971): 72–83; Mirra Komarovsky, ed., *Sociology and Public Policy: The Case of Presidential Commissions*. New York: Elsevier, 1975; William L. F. Felstiner, Richard L. Abel, and Austin Sarat, "The Emergence and Transformation of Disputes: Naming, Blaming, Claiming . . . ," *Law & Society Review* 15 (1980-81):631–654; Charles Perrow, "The President's Commission and the Normal Accident." In David Sills, V. B. Shelanski, and C. P. Wolf, eds., *Accident at Three Mile Island*. Boulder CO: Westview, 1982: 173–184. Jacqueline Choiniere, "The Grange Commission: Why Nurses are Scapegoats." *Resources for Feminist Research* 14 (1985–86): 11–23.

26. Lawrence Nichols, "Reconceptualizing Social Accounts: An Agenda for Theory Building and Empirical Research." In *Current Perspectives in Social Theory*. Greenwich CT: JAI Press, 10 (1990): 113–144; Lawrence T. Nichols, "Discovering Hutton: Expression Gaming and Congressional Definitions of Deviance." In *Studies in Symbolic Interaction*. Greenwich CT: JAI Press, 11 (1990): 309–337; Lawrence T. Nichols, "'Whistleblower' or 'Renegade': Definitional Contests in an Official Inquiry." Unpublished manuscript, 1991; Lawrence T. Nichols, "Social Problems as Landmark Narratives: Bank of Boston, Media, and Money Laundering," *Social Problems* 44 (1997): 327–341.

27. Lawrence T. Nichols, "'Whistleblower' or 'Renegade': Definitional Contests in an Official Inquiry." Unpublished manuscript, 1991: 1.

interests. Rather than attributing their accounts to amoral calculation or conspiracy, we might find that the realities they construct
are explained by a complex mix of factors: a) both the media and
official investigations possess generic organizational structures and
processes that often produce unanticipated consequences—recall
that the autonomy and interdependence that affected the Presidential Commission investigating the *Challenger* tragedy are generic
problems of social control;[28] b) both may be influenced by the near-
universal American cultural belief in individualism, which creates
a general societal tendency toward reductionistic explanations when
bad things happen, thus neglecting the social forces that affect individual action,[29] c) they may lack sensitivity to and skill at identifying aspects of organizations as they might bear on the actions of
employees and participants; d) both the media and official inquiries are political actors, comprised of individual participants with a
variety of interests and dependencies that each tries to preserve.
These produce internal conflicts that may be played out in different ways, depending on the investigation; e) both operate on deadlines, which circumscribes the time available for the investigative
task, and thus the thoroughness of their analysis.

2. Available data give a distinctive shape to any causal analysis.
Although sensational cases present us with abundant data, it is important to remain sensitive to the limitations of that data.
Often, research on sensational cases of corporate and organizational misconduct is retrospective and dependent upon secondary sources. Both retrospection and secondary sources have effects on the theories of cause produced in our own accounts. This
caveat may seem prosaic and even unnecessary, but sometimes
we operate on taken-for-granted assumptions without question-

---

28. For insights about structures and processes relevant to Commissions, see Paul F. Lazarsfeld
and Martin Jaeckel, "The Uses of Sociology by Presidential Commissions." In Mirra Komarovsky,
ed., *Sociology and Public Policy: The Case of Presidential Commissions*. New York: Elsevier, 1975:
117–143, and Robert K. Merton, "Social Knowledge and Public Policy: Sociological Perspectives on Four Presidential Commissions." In Mirra Komarovsky, ibid.: 153–178.
29. In the disaster literature, this cultural belief is demonstrated when official inquiries consistently define cause as "operator error." See, e. g., Charles Perrow's account of the President's
Commission that investigated the accident at Three Mile Island. Charles Perrow, "The
President's Commission and the Normal Accident." In *Accident at Three Mile Island*, eds. David
Sills, V. B. Shelanski, and C. P. Wolf. Boulder CO: Westview, 1982: 173–184; Lee Clarke and
James F. Short, Jr., eds., *Organizations, Uncertainties, and Risk*. Boulder CO: Westview, 1992;
Scott Sagan, *The Limits of Safety*. Princeton: Princeton University Press, 1993; Diane Vaughan,
The Challenger Launch Decision, op. cit.

ing them. Since much of sociological research is retrospective, we tend to take that for granted, perhaps losing sight of it as a possible problem; also, what is a primary source and what is a secondary source can become confused, or at least in my experience it did. I spent quite a long time with Volume I of the Presidential Commission, treating it as a primary source—and compared to the hearings and the information pouring from the media in the first six months after the tragedy, it was. However, I spent several months analyzing it before I realized it was a secondary source: a summary volume of a 5-volume Commission report. As a summary, it distilled a much broader, deeper data base consisted of voices not heard and documents not presented that told a more complex story.

Both my *Challenger* research and Lee and Ermann's analysis of the Ford Pinto case benefitted from available data. We had access to primary sources: personal interviews, transcripts of interviews conducted by official investigators, and extensive original documents produced by the respective organizations in years before the incidents. Our analyses of these two sensational cases was different from those of scholars who had published research on these same cases before us because we not only had structural data, but had micro-level data on decision making. The extensiveness and quality of the decision making data in these two case studies showed more complex explanations for three reasons. First, the data to which we had access circumvented the problem of retrospection: In both case studies, it permitted a reconstruction of events as they were occurring within the organization at the time those events were taking place. Second, the available data allowed us to focus on the organization as a key unit of analysis, examining internal structures and processes as they intersected with external networks and the institutional domain. Third, in both cases available data allowed making macro-micro connections, joining social structural conditions with individual actions and choices.

3. One advantage of a sensational case is that it is sensational. Consequently, it produces huge amounts of information, otherwise unavailable to us. Passas' work on the BCCI scandal, Zey's on Michael Milken, and Calavita et al. on the savings and loan crisis are three recent others that immediately come to mind.[30] At the

30. Nicos Passas, "I Cheat, Therefore I Exist: The BCCI Scandal in Context," in *Emerging Global Business Ethics*, W. Hoffman, S. Kamm, R. E. Frederick, and E. Petry (eds.). New York:

same time that we are inundated with information from the media and official inquiries that engage in the production of knowledge about these incidents, the sensational case also can give us access to original data, created at the time. In fact, we may have more access to original documents with the sensational case than with one that does not receive so much attention, leading to a more complete analysis because the modern organization, unlike the "street criminal," produces a documentary record that allows us to reconstruct the past. The benefits are great. However, these advantages—the sensational aspect of the case and the extensive data available—combine to produce very particular problems for research.

The first problem is that many sensational cases may develop what Nichols calls a "landmark narrative": an historically accepted explanation that, despite variations on the theme, is a shared overarching definition of the situation that is commonly held.[31] Gamson, in *Talking Politics*, shows how media frames become cultural understandings that shape the beliefs and actions of individuals.[32] These landmark narratives influence our decision to investigate a particular case. We read the secondary sources and develop an understanding that shapes the theoretical perspective and assumptions that we bring to our analysis. Our data—and data sources—are always biased. Typically, in research, we control for these biases by conservative methods, like analytic induction and primary data sources, that force us to consider alternative possibilities and hypotheses, intentionally seeking out information and sources that will challenge our assumptions. The second problem with the sensational case—and one that compounds the problem of the landmark narrative—is that the data from documents are often vast and unwieldy. Not only does this require new methods of data management and analysis, but these data will produce information that both supports and contradicts the historically accepted explanation. A landmark narrative develops from information that *surfaces* and becomes publicly acknowledged as part of the historically accepted explanation. That supporting information surfaces because it is more readily acces-

Quorum Books; Mary Zey, *Banking on Fraud*. New York: Aldine, 1993; Kitty Calavita, Henry Pontell, and Robert Tiliman, *Big Money Crime*. Berkeley: University of California Press, 1997.

31. Lawrence T. Nichols, "Social Problems as Landmark Narratives," op. cit.

32. William A. Gamson, *Talking Politics*. New York: Cambridge University Press, 1992.

sible and understood. Initially, we tend to support our starting hypotheses because we begin with the information that is readily accessible and understood. But as we dig deeper and deeper into what begins to feel like a bottomless pit of data, we may begin to discover information that contradicts the assumptions based on the historically accepted explanation.

In the *Challenger* case, I experienced these discoveries as mistakes in my own understanding, based on common sense assumptions about the case I initially developed as the media and the Presidential investigation repeatedly affirmed circumstances surrounding the event that seemed to typify it as an example of organizational misconduct.[33] My discovery of facts that contradicted my starting assumptions went on throughout the research project. The research took nine years both because the sensational case produced data that were abundant and because it had an historically accepted explanation: I continued to discover mistaken assumptions that forced me to continually reconceptualize the analysis and keep on digging. Committed to the principles of analogical theorizing and analytic induction, I persisted, pursuing discrepant bits of information for many years. But nine years devoted to one project is not an option for many, without tenure and under pressure to publish. The person who takes on a sensational case needs to be aware of and weigh the costs and benefits.

4. Finally, the sensational case is, of course, a case study. This quality brings up yet one final cautionary tale. Shapiro once wrote, "Trying to develop general theory from a sensational case is like trying to teach Introductory Sociology from readings in the *National Inquirer*."[34] That she was pointing out was the tendency to generalize from a case study, without paying attention to what is different about it. Sensational cases are indeed different, which is why they become publicly identified as sensational in the first place. Many are unique because of the amount of harm done, the drama inherent in the harmful act, the duration of the pattern of offensive behavior, the size, public character, or success of the organization,

---

33. See Vaughan, *The Challenger Launch Decision*, Chapter 2.

34. Susan Shapiro, "The New Moral Entrepreneurs: Corporate Crime Crusaders." *Contemporary Sociology* 12 (1983): 304–5.

or the distinctive position, public reputation, or number of the individuals who commit the harmful act. Scholarly inquiry into sensational cases of organizational misconduct must not only pay attention to how and why they are different, but also be balanced by inquiry into the non-sensational: the small organization, the routine and undramatic offense with extensive harm, the outcome with limited harm, the offenses of marginal or failing organizations—all those that the media and official investigations ignore.[35]

---

35. See, e.g., Hugh Barlow, "From Fiddle Factors to Networks of Collusion," *Criminology, Law, and Social Change* 29 (1993): 319–337; Sections of Chapters 2, 8, and 9 in Stephen M. Rosoff, Henry N. Pontell, and Robert Tiliman, *Profit Without Honor: White-Collar Crime and the Looting of American.* Upper Saddle River NJ: Prentice-Hall, 1998; Sections of Chapters 4, 5, and 6 of Gary S. Green, *Occupational Crime.* 2nd. ed. Chicago: Nelson Hall, 1997.

About the Editors

M. David Ermann, professor of sociology at the University of Delaware, received his B.S. from the University of Pennsylvania in 1963 and his Ph.D. from the University of Michigan in 1973. In addition to organizational deviance, his teaching and research interests include complex organizations, especially those in business and health care, and the social impact of computers. He has written and cowritten several chapters for books as well as articles in these areas, cowritten *Social Research Methods* (Random House, 1977) and *Corporate Deviance* (Holt, Rinehart and Winston, 1982), and co-edited *Computers, Ethics, and Society* (Oxford University Press, 2002). Professor Ermann continues to study why some usually nondeviant organizations and their people intentionally hide hazards and thereby knowingly cause human injury and death.

Richard J. Lundman, professor of sociology at The Ohio State University, received his B.A. from Beloit College in 1966 and his Ph.D. from the University of Minnesota in 1973. Before his affiliation with Ohio State, he taught at the University of Delaware. His teaching and research interests include organizational deviance, police and policing, and juvenile delinquency. He has written and cowritten papers and books in these areas, including *Prevention and Control of Juvenile Delinquency* (Oxford University Press, 2002) and *In the Company of Cops* (Oxford University Press, 2002, forthcoming). Professor Lundman is currently examining the factors that shape homicide clearances by police and selection bias in newspaper coverage of homicide.